3 9351 004876506

D1370913

w/D

What others are saying about this book :

<> Superbly illustrated !
        --*Harry Burke*

<> *The first* HAMILTON ART CATALOGUE !

<> At last, a PRICE GUIDE for Hamilton's artwork.

<> Fascinating portrayal of Philadelphia's most successful
      Impressionist Painter.

<> *The definitive book* on Hamilton's career.

<> A monumental contribution to art history.

<> A case study in the sociology of a Transitional Age
      expatriate artist.

<> A goldmine of bibliographic sources on Nineteenth
      Century artists.

<> Richard Alperin is the expert on art by Hamilton.
        --*Robert D. Schwarz*

<> Detailed and meticulous research provides a wealth of
      information...on Hamilton's work...and unique
      experiences...
        --*Mark Sullivan Associates*

<> Dr. Alperin *is* the biographer of JOHN McLURE HAMILTON
      --*Brandon Fortune; William I. Homer;
      S. Morton Vose, II*

JOHN McLURE HAMILTON's self-portrait, 1918 at age 55,
oil 75" x 38 1/2." Formerly in collection of Harry
Burke. All picture legends are for Hamilton's works
unless otherwise noted

ART'S ANGLO—AMERICAN PAPER LION: JOHN McLURE HAMILTON'S UNTOLD STORY

[Lavishly Illustrated]

by

RICHARD J. ALPERIN,   Ph.D.
FIICS, LFIBA, DDG, IOM

<c> 1993

JUNIUS,INC.

842 Lombard Street

Philadelphia, PA 19147-1317

ISBN 0-9603932-6-9

Library of Congress Number 93-91581

Card Catalog Description

Printing 10 9 8 7 6 5 4 3 2 1

CONTENTS

ADVISORY PANEL

Harry Burke, *HARRY BURKE OF PHILADELPHIA* (deceased)

Carl David, *David David,* Philadelphia

Jeff van Gool, *Nationaal Hoger Instituut en Koninklijke Academie voor Schone Kunsten,* Antwerp, Belgium

G. Gray, Kilmarnock, Scotland

William I. Homer, Ph.D., *University of Delaware,* Newark,DE

Cheryl Leibold, *Pennsylvania Academy of Fine Arts,* Philadelphia

Sue Levy, *CIGNA Museum & Art Collection,* Philadelphia

Jenny Martin, Ph.D., Brussels, Belgium

W. Andrews Newman, Jr., *Newman Galleries,* Philadelphia

Michael Reedy, *McClees Gallery,* Ardmore, Pennsylvania

Erda Ryan, *Mitchell Library,* Glasgow, Scotland

Robert D. Schwarz, *Schwarz* Gallery, Philadelphia

Linda Simmons, *Corcoran Gallery of Art,* Washington, D. C.

FOREWORD

This monograph, only the second book published about John McLure Hamilton, aims to fill one of the missing links in the growing history of Anglo-American painting of the *Transitional Age* (i.e., late Nineteenth and early Twentieth Century).<1> Current research clearly places Hamilton in a professional category distinct from the many starving *Impressionist* and *Realist painter*s, whose work has gradually become a part of art history.

Perhaps Hamilton's first job in his native city was as an artist in a fashionable photographic studio. Later, he chose to go to *Antwerp* for graduate training under de Keyser. After briefly returning home for the Centennial, he migrated to *London* to seek fame and fortune in 1878. He became a well-known "plein air" painter, pastelist, caricaturist, and cartoonist for a newspaper. Also, he became a high-society portrait painter for the British, French, and German courts.

Although his painting career began in Philadelphia and ended in Jamaica, B.W.I. approximately seventy years later, Hamilton spent his best fifty years in London where he exhibited regularly at the *Royal Academy* and simultaneously at the *Pennsylvania Academy of the Fine Arts (P.A.F.A.)*. He became acquainted with famous artists like Abbey, de Keyser, Eakins, Gerome, Pennell, Sargent, van Lerius, and Whistler, who became his early important professional contacts. His painting experiences in various cities in the United States,

1

A survey of all Hamilton's documented works done in 1992 revealed how significantly each class contributed to the artist's reputation. Information from 1,050 pieces was gathered for the analysis. The numbers/class appear in Table B. Refer to the legend at the left of the pie graph for a listing of the twenty-four classes Hamilton used. For ease in display only twelve pie wedges were allowed to create the graph. Some were constructed by pooling unrelated smaller classes.

Legend :

A	Animals
BI	Book Illustrations
Ca	Charcoals
C	Greeting Cards
Ch	Children
Ct	Cartoons
DA	Graphic Journalism
E	Etchings
G	Genre
I	Interiors
IS	Inks/Sepia
L	Landscapes
Lit	Lithographs
Ma	Marines
Mo	Monochromes
O	Oils
PA	Pastels
Pe	Graphites
Re	Religious Themes
SC	Sculpture
sc	Souvenior Cards
SL	Still Life
Te	Theater Curtain
W	Watercolors

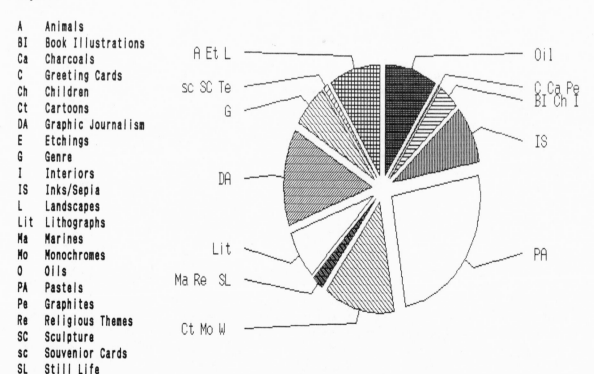

HAMILTON'S REPUTATION.
Frequency vs Class (Content/Technique)

2

Canada, Scotland, Ireland, England, France, Spain, Germany, and Belgium are reflected in different size portraits, including half size canvases. All of the people who sat for him are prominent, historically-important characters of the Transitional Age, *King George V, Prince Otto von Bismarck, Prime Ministers Asquith, Balfour, Gladstone, Lloyd-George, Chamberlain, and Churchill* are among them. Others were clergy, jurists, members of renowned families, publishers, theater personalities, and great scientists. A major portion of these paintings is still in private ownership, but the artist is well-represented in museum collections. Some of his previously unrecorded portraits are still being found today after a four-year worldwide survey.

Recently discovered personal letters and gallery records have been utilized to help reconstruct the career of John McLure Hamilton. Until the present, his work and biography have been unrecorded. An important unpublished oral history and manuscripts have been consulted, revealing valuable information documenting his family life and career.

Table **A** provides the names of more than thirty index categories searched in a survey of the periodical literature of art history and indicies of relevant books published in the last half century where Hamilton's contributions should have been cited but were omitted.

The one hundred thirty illustrations and a catalog of art by Hamilton listing more than 1,050 works presented in this volume convey a range of the artist's versatility from traditional styles of oil painting to those unique to Hamilton. He was influenced heavily by the Old Masters and modestly by the Orient. He was mildly sentimental, but not to the degree of *Alfred Stevens,* the modern Flemish painter. Hamilton dabbled in ballet paintings, but never produced a racing picture.

A study of Hamilton's art done in 1993 revealed in the numbers how each of fifty-two classes (content or technique) contributed to the artist's reputation. All reported works by Hamilton were sorted in the analysis. The numbers/class that resulted appear as Table **B**. Refer to the Table's legend for a list of the twenty-four significant classes where his activity was documented. For ease in display as a pie graph, only twelve percentage groupings were allowed. Thus, some pie "wedges" were constructed artificially by "clumping" several smaller, unrelated classes.[pie graph]

The illustrations include genre pieces other than portraits and many surprises like his editorial cartoons, engravings, lithographs, nudes, and art satire (Tab. C: Hamilton Study Collection). This book will be welcomed by artists, auction houses, collectors, dealers, historians of art, librarians, museums, and others interested in Anglo-American portraiture recorded in more than 1,050 paintings and drawings.

During his fifty years of international fame, Hamilton created many of the Century's most indelible images. Unfortunately, he lived the last five years of his life as a virtual recluse. Hamilton was certainly not wealthy. According to common critical consent, he was one of the great portrait artists of the English-speaking world, surpasing Eakins in awards and honors. Except for his *Glasgow period*, he was never wildly popular with the mass audience. Nevertheless, he was dubbed, "Art's Anglo-American Lion" by C. H. Bronte.<2>

There are several reasons to write a monograph about John McLure Hamilton : art historians have thought him worthy of a biography, there is need for a *catalogue raisonne* of his work in several media, a living person should see more than thirty of the artist's paintings assembled in one place, there should be a single commentary on Hamilton's many stylistic periods, innovative techniques and methods, his work should be cataloged in America, Europe, and South America, a memoir to his career should be written, and the artist's life story should be told. The latter point is important because there are many forgotten firsts in his career. Also, from the standpoint of accuracy in historical reporting, there should be correct attributions of his work and his achievements credited.

The goal of this book is to present Hamiltoniana (i.e., his art, artefacts of his career, and memorabilia) with an interpretation of his life and art, based on recently collected documents and testimony. Hopefully, it will correct the numerous errors and put to rest the myths that have crept into the literature concerning this painter and illustrator. These have included his place of birth, citizenship, exhibition record, and authorship of specific works. Not only has there been a paucity of printed information about Hamilton's work, there is also evidence that this luminary's personal papers were largely uncollected in dozens of locations. Consequently, his tale could not be told until now.

This Hamilton Art Catalog is the first ever published, which presents the facts for more than fifty of Hamilton's one thousand fifty surviving works. Also, it presents Hamilton's products in twelve media.

The artist's *documented biography* is the first one published in seventy years, and the chronology of his travels is based upon six hundred references. This biography was organized to display *his development as a professional* and was set against a background of his times, including four wars that impacted upon Imperial England and the United States of America.

Hamilton's only enemy was the well-known colorful personality and artist, *Whistler,* who may have hated him for any of the following reasons Hamilton exhibited more talent in more diverse media and had greater industry, or because Hamilton was generally a better-quality human being.

Listed are some setbacks experienced while researching Hamilton : few first-person anecdotes have survived about him, there was no definitive biography written in his lifetime available to draw upon, and none of his personal papers, notebooks, etc. seemed to have survived the hurricanes of Jamaica since 1940. However, exhibition catalogs, some back issues of a few relevant magazines that list his work, and two hundred twenty-eight of his letters have been discovered and collected.

The principal aim of this book is to report, in one volume, the results of extensive travel and skillful research by Dr. R. J. Alperin, informing the reader about Hamilton-the-artist and Hamilton-the-man. Eventually, discovering his personal recipe for success and to place his art in the context of his time and friendships. Implicit in this activity is a call for additional information to settle unsolved mysteries and to relate the previously untold story of Hamilton a great among Impressionist painters.

December 16, 1993   The Publisher
Philadelphia

HELEN WESTON HENDERSON, c. 1911, pastel on kraft paper
28" x 22." Formerly in collection of W. Andrews Newman.

SCOPE AND PURPOSE

JOSEPH PENNELL, c. 1913, oil 30" x 43 1/2." Philadelphia Museum of Art : given by Gustav Wynne Cook.

I : INTRODUCTION

When archivists, museum curators, restorers, print sellers, artists, and antique dealers learned that a study of the life and works of the artist John McLure Hamilton (1853--1936) was in progress, the most frequent response was, "never heard of him, was he from around here ?" In reply, I gave a brief synopsis of his achievements which included the creation of the first satire on an exhibition of art in America (1878), a Coronation portrait of England's King George V (1911), portraits of the popular former Prime Minister W. E. Gladstone (1892), and the marketing of about one hundred ten lithographic subjects. His art was highly prized by Andrew Carnegie, Mrs. Mary Harriman, William W. Corcoran, John G. Johnson, David Croal Thomson, William Trost Richards, and institutions like the Luxembourg Palace. He corresponded with well-known Philadelphians, including Albert Rosenthal, Honorable Simon Gratz, Dr. A. S. W. Rosenbach, and Thornton Oakley. In England, he wrote to Mrs. Mary Gladstone Drew, Joseph Pennell, and numerous others.

Hamilton's status in the art world during his life can be judged from his quadruple gold medal status. All of his medals were awarded at juried exhibitions held in the United States in *Chicago*, 1893; *Buffalo,* 1901; *St. Louis,* 1904; and *Philadelphia,* 1918; while he resided in London.

Hamilton began his sixty-six year association with the *Pennsylvania Academy of the Fine Arts (P.A.F.A.)* as a student in 1870, when art was a wasteland in Philadelphia

9

before its Broad & Cherry Street Building was erected. Hamilton eventually became the president of its *Fellowship* in the period 1919--1922, after being its London-based exhibitor from 1878.

Although he studied with Professors van Lerius, Beaufaux, de Keyser, and Gerome, he was primarily a self-taught, independent artisan. He expressed creativity in many diverse media, such as bronze, charcoal, clay, crayon, graphite (=pencil), ink, lithography, oil, pastel, water-color, and woodcut engraving. His surviving products include book illustrations, caricatures, cartoons, graphic journalism, documentary art for news stories, genre pictures, human figures, lithographs, portraits, still lives, and even a theater curtain mock up. His unique perception of the world was portrayed in more than one thousand fifty cataloged works often signed *"Hamilton."*

The art critics of his day noted his work and boldly expressed their approval in print.[1] Quoting Devree of the *NEW YORK TIMES*, "Hamilton's best pastels, done between 1910--1920, are equal to those of Degas and Renoir," and such pieces commanded $ 500.00 or more in the 1930s art market. Most of his oil portraits are pastel-like, exhibiting sitters with pearly skin, like the paintings of Rubens or van Eyck. Hamilton's paintings were sold to Mrs. Catharine Gladstone, and the Luxembourg Palace at $ 5,000.00 in the 1890s. Thus, a conservative estimate of his lifetime income from art sales exceeded $ 350,000.00 between 1876 and 1936, while other Impressionist painters literally sold nothing in their life. Since their deaths, their works have become high finance instruments. In contrast, one of those artist's paintings auctioned for $ 82,500,000.00 in today's art market, while Hamilton's sold under $ 50,000.00.[2]

Because of his great status in art circles, Hamilton served on international juries with Edwin A. Abbey, Halsey C. Ives, Joseph Pennell, John Singer Sargent, and James Abbott McNeill Whistler.[3]

Hamilton was generous and befriended his former teacher, the outcast-genius Thomas Cowperwaite Eakins, and the enterprising journalist, Sheridan Ford.[4,5] The latter even dedicated his book, titled the "GENTLE ART OF MAKING ENEMIES," to Hamilton. It contained the collected spicy letters to the editor written by Whistler, and had

attracted public attention in many European newspapers.
Ford's trickery earned for Hamilton Whistler's undying
displeasure.

STRONG FAMILY TIES TO PHILADELPHIA, DELAWARE, CANADA,
AND JAMAICA

John McLure Hamilton, born in 1853, was the grandson of
an Irish immigrant merchant / prince turned real estate
speculator, John Hamilton, Senior. He was also the son of
George Hamilton, a Civil War era physician from
Philadelphia, a sophisticated medical metropolis, and the
nephew of John Hamilton, Junior, a lawyer/gentleman farmer,
and of John C. Mercer, a millionaire.

Artist McLure Hamilton was the second of four children
and sole surviving son of Dr. George Hamilton
(1808--1885).<6>   (The artist's elder brother had died in
infancy.) The artist's mother, Caroline Delaplaine Hamilton
(182[7]--1915), was the subject of several portraits done in
life, as well as the subject of portraits done from memory
in a pose reminiscent of the painting, "Whistler's
mother."<7> She was the daughter of a famous French-
speaking lawyer whose family came to America before 1663.<8>
Her father, James Delaplaine, was elected to the Delaware
legislature and served as Treasurer for New Castle county,
where he resided before serving as a Wilmington bank
director with E. I. du Pont. <9>

John Hamilton, Senior (178[0]--1858), the artist's
paternal grandfather, arrived in 1795 from Ireland. John
McLure Hamilton was his grandfather's namesake.<10> His
grandfather first earned his living as a grocer with three
partners, Hood, Newell, and Mercer. Their surnames are
recorded as the middle names of several of the artist's
relatives.<11> Hamilton's grandfather was the neighbor of
William Pennell (1814<12>) and he also had a business
interest in a real estate transaction with L. M. Sargent
(1821), formerly of Boston. His grandfather also made an
investment in the *University of Pennsylvania* (1825) shortly
before George Hamilton, the artist's father, earned his
M. D. degree there (1831).<13>

In a more recent generation, Hamilton painted a

portrait of his maternal cousin, Governor Robert Pyle Robinson (1925--1929 of Delaware) in 1928.<14> Through marriage the artist was related to Charles A. Yeager, Jr., father of Mrs. Ethel Hamilton Lucas, and probably to the deceased Joseph Yeager, one of Philadelphia's successful engravers from an earlier generation.<15> A paternal cousin, Alexander Hall Hall, was an American artist in Rome in an earlier generation.<16> Hamilton's wife and grandfather both had relatives in Canada.<17> The artist painted several Canadian V.I.Ps on his trips north.<18> John McLure Hamilton was proud of his son, George Hall Hamilton (1884--1935), a published astronomer and expert studying the planets Mars and Jupiter. He also studied Jupiter's satellites through three telescopes he had built while in Mandeville, Jamaica.

EUROPEAN CAREER

McLure Hamilton studied in Antwerp, Belgium and then in Paris, before he settled permanently in London in 1878. Except for nearly a dozen visits to the U. S. for portrait commissions, and exhibitions or vacations in France, Holland, and Spain, he resided in England until 1932. His values, professional experience, and career developed more in Europe than in the sterility of America. As an American expatriate, he lived in two worlds. The European press thought he was forever an American visitor working there. Before World War I, however, the American press regarded him as an Anglophile journalist and expert on continental politics and art in Europe.

During his career, Hamilton exhibited his work in more than twenty-nine cities.<19> Though it was said that he painted only for pleasure and seldom exhibited, an analysis of exhibition catalogs proved otherwise. Many would envy his prodigious exhibition *vitae*. He exhibited more often in Philadelphia than anywhere else and he earned the distinction of being Philadelphia's most recognized Impressionist painter/illustrator. An historian, George Morgan (1926) listed him with other "outstanding men in the large and varied gallery of Philadelphia's artists."<20> Most of Hamilton's art sold in the United States.

Hamilton liked the out of doors. In 1902, he and his wife, Clara, bought land in Frederick township, Montgomery county, Pennsylvania, where they could pursue their hobbies of shooting, farming, and fishing. While in Europe, he also enjoyed golfing.

Hamilton's father collected books, engravings, lithographs, and plants. His collection of art and books numbered in the tens of thousands.[21] Thus, it is not surprising that the artist became a collector, too. The artist bought paintings by *del Sarto, Lawrence, Rembrandt Peale, Raffaelli,* and *Guido Reni.* He also bought old Persian rugs and rare furniture, dating from the Middle Ages, which soon filled his home on the *Thames.*[22]

John McLure Hamilton and Sherlock Holmes were contemporaries during the 1890s, a golden interval in British history. Although Sir Arthur Conan Doyle's detective was fictional, Hamilton was recording honest impressions of Imperial England. This was a time of Great Britain's glory, ten years before the Boer War, the death of Queen Victoria, the Coal Strike, and World War I.

WILLIAM COSMO MONKHOUSE, 1896, oil. National Portrait
Gallery, London : given by the artist.

II : AS CRITICS SAW HIS PRODUCTS

To understand the achievements of the artist and how he built his international reputation, one needs only to read the words of contemporary authorities who had seen his performance.

From a survey of news stories published in Europe and America during a fifty-nine year period, there exists a dramatic chain of observations about his work starting in 1877 in *New York City*. News reports continue from his native city (1878, 1911, 1916, 1918, 1926, 1931), from *London* (1896 et seq), from *Chicago* (1896, 1917), from *SCHRIBNER'S* (nationally circulated) *MAGAZINE* (1900), and ending in London and New York City in the 1930s. In the Foreword, about Hamilton's book (1921), a friendly English observer, Mary Drew, spoke for the public reporting about his masterful portrayal of people in oil portraits, and other techniques. While the *NEW YORK TIMES*' art critc, Howard Devree, placed Hamilton's pastels beside Renoir's or Degas' and found his equal to their best.

Perhaps the finest tribute that could be paid to Hamilton was when other artists would pay his fee ($ 1,000.00) to commission their portraits. The list of twenty-nine names clearly constitutes a WHO'S WHO OF WORLD-CLASS ARTISTS including fellow architects, professors of art, sculptors, and art critics.[1]

CRITICS' COMMENTARY

Abstracts from the published commentary of critics is arranged chronologically starting in 1877 and ending in 1936.

"The figure and face [in 'Le Rire'] are foreshortened in a way not easy to handle, but treated with firmness and spirit. The picture possesses that power which very few painters possess,-- the power of telling much more than they say." <2>

"It is a clever performance, this, and the satire is of so kindly a tone that the artists who are parodied can but join in the laugh against themselves. The drawings are full of spirit, and for the most part are true caricature in that they really represent the essential characteristics of the original, carried to an extreme...The title of the work is L'Academie pour Rire." <3>

"Though he is a profound admirer of the 'Old Masters,' there is not a tinge of convention in Mr. McLure Hamilton's work; and though he belongs to no party in art, his methods, and also his way of seeing things, are distinctly modern. He is a painter, above all things, of light; his art is done for 'art's sake;' he delights especially to catch the fleeting vision; he is as accidental and impromtu as an artist can be. Moreover, he is a painter of the plein air, he is an impressionist and a pastelist; and, though he can be called an imitator of no man, it is plain that he belongs to the same period as Whistler and Claude Monet. Indeed, it is his opinion that the latter painter has had more influence upon his art than any other."

..."Whatever he has a desire to paint, most persons will like to see, and his faculty of selection is regulated by a delicate taste. His color is fine and pearly, his illumination subtle and refined. Though his arrangements are apparently casual, they are nearly always happy and decorative. In the suggestion of texture and substance his success is often wonderful, as in the velvet in 'Embroidery,' the porcelin in 'Breakfast;' but still more to be praised is the quality of his flesh, of which this exhibition affords many instances, from rosy youth to sallow age."...

"Mr. McLure Hamilton's art is a perpetual spring, as spontaneous and unspoiled as new-born nature. He loves the green shoot, he loves the bud, but rarely gives us the full-blown flower. There may be richer and riper work, but surely there is little that is so fragrant and so fresh." <4>

"There is a subtle charm, a spontaneous touch and an engaging personal note in all of the works of John McLure Hamilton..."

"At first glance the oils seem dry, but on close inspection it is found that the artist intended his pigment to tell his story frankly, without the use of varnish. His technic is individual, powerful; his color delicate, his settings and lighting all that can be desired. He is a realist, a lover of human character. He presents his subjects surrounded by their individual environments. He cares little for the usual accessories of furniture and drapery, except as they bespeak the bent of his sitter's mind... It is, as it were, a leaf taken from the diary of the (sitter's) life. "

"Mr. Hamilton has a keen sense of beauty, but he is always honest and subordinates all other motives of his pictures to the salient characteristic of the subject. He sets forth his *dramatis personae* as they live their average daily life. It would be difficult to find a simpler and more honest portrait...There is as well...an undercurrent of sentiment, a glimpse into the...sitter's...heart. Few of Mr. Hamilton's portraits are carried beyond a sketch, which accounts largely for their sparkling spontaneity."

"His paintings of children are intimate, caressing...(For the rest) the study...is most suggestive and it is as well an excellent example of the artist's technic casual, but happy...Portions of (his) work suggest *Monet*."

(His Landscape) "evinces a fine feeling for out-of-doors painting, and it is full of sensuous color and soft shadows..."

"One of the attractive features of Mr. Hamilton's portraits is that they are, generally speaking, considerably less than life size. They do not require a gallery; they can be enjoyed intimately even in a small home." <5>

"It has been Mr. Hamilton's habit to seek his sitters amid their natural surroundings--the statesman in his home or at his desk, the lawyer amid his books and correspondence, the doctor in his consulting-chamber, the artist in his studio-- and hence we have in these remarkable portraits not only the man but his accessories, his shell, so to speak, the expression of his being as it lies about him embodied in intimate objects..."

"McLure Hamilton gives expression to contemporary motives...the analytic qualities (that) he has displayed with such penetrating force, the frankness and definiteness of his observation, the novelty of his presentation, and his preservative style combine to give his best portraits the enduring characteristics which have made precious the portraits of...an age after their personal interest has vanished."<6>

"...typical of Hamilton's methods, there is a remarkable fidelity and ability for placing the whole character and characteristic environment of the subject in front of the beholder. You see Gladstone just as he was, as he lived, thought, acted, but portrayed always with subtlety of insight which reveals to your eye infinitely more than you would have perceived in an acquaintance of years."<7>

"One of the most distinguished artist's in the English-speaking or any other world."<8>

"This [*John H. Converse gold medal* from the *P.A.F.A.*] is one of the highest honors that can be bestowed on an American artist in this country. It is given at the discretion of the Academy's Board of Directors to American painters, and sculptors who may be exhibitors at the Academy or represented in the collection in recognition of high achievement in their profession or to those who for eminent services in the cause of art or to the Academy have merited the distinction."<9>

"Regards...'A game of Chess' and 'Paul Bartlett,' this is the way to handle pastel."<10>

"Subtle characterization and masterly craftmanship won general admiration...All Mr. McLure Hamilton's portraits are distinguished by unanimous technical accomplishment, and the rarer attributes of psychological insight and reverence. The peculiar mentality of each sitter is unmistakably differentiated."<11>

"Of delight to the artists and students are Hamilton's pastel sketches of the human figure. Sketchily done with color marking to heighten some characteristic phase, those works were a looked for feature of the Academy's annual watercolor exhibition many years ago."<12>

"Hamilton's art is in many respects, symbolic of a fading grandeur when a cultured man of the brush passed from studio to King's court. Eloquent, also of Anglophile tendencies, he stems from the influence of Whistler rather than from Eakins. Many of his admirable pastels lead from the boudoir to reception room. They are particularly handsome in the modeling of semi-nude backs, and in the delicate handling of female furbelows."<13>

Hamilton painted for pleasure and made a fortune from sales of his rapidly-produced portraits. They are of excellent quality and have become enduring fine art of investment scale. From 1864 through 1933, he produced works in every medium except bonds, calendars, cigarette cards, currency, diplomas, fans, monotypes, murals, postage, and stock certificates. (Refer to Tab. B for numerical details of his productivity in the various techniques.) He painted to the delight of critics, his family, famous sitters, museum goers, and millions of newspaper readers.

Now we turn to chapters that constitute a memoir of his family and an analysis of the roots for the artist's personality planted in Philadelphia. Refer to Tables D (Education), E (Hamilton's pedigree), and F (Clara's pedigree).

THE

HAMILTON

FAMILY

OF

PHILADELPHIA

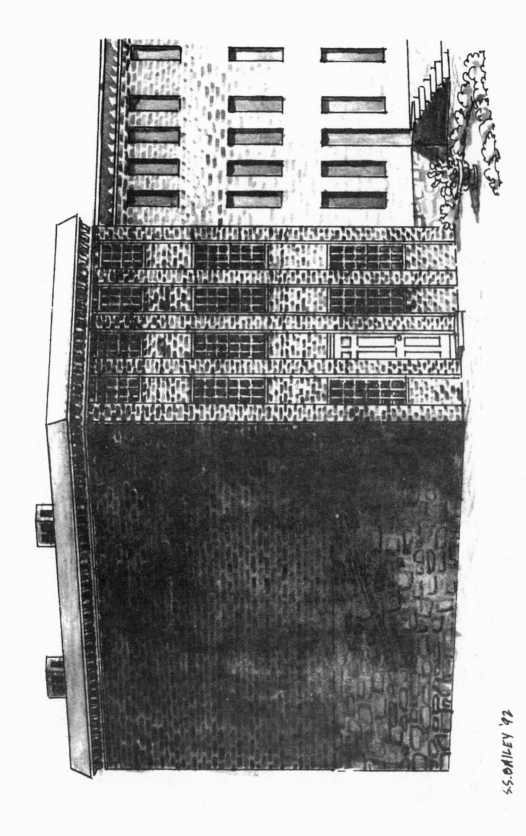

S.S. BAILEY '92

(S. S. Bailey's, 1992 reconstruction) Philadelphia's
HAMILTON HOUSE, c. 1886. Ink with sepia on board
8" x 10."

III : GRANDFATHER

The Revolutionary War was over, the Constitution was written, and Philadelphia was a bustling business center in the U. S. when young John Hamilton arrived in 1795. He was born in Ramelton, Ballymena, county Antrim, Northern Ireland about eighteen years earlier.<1> (Refer to Tab. E for his family line.) In 1799, he lived at 17 Lombard Street and earned his living as a *baker*. In the same year, he married Elizabeth Hall, from his home town. She was about five years younger than her husband when the ceremony was performed by Rev. William Erwin at the Second Presbyterian Church. <2> The following year, the Census record shows that the family lived in the western sector of the city's Northern Liberties suburb, where their daughter Catherine was born. Sequentially, David (1803--1864), Elizabeth (1805), twin daughters Jannette and Euphenia (1807), Dr. George (1808--1885), Margaret(1812--alive 1909), Sarah McClellan (1813), Ann Jane (1817--1886), and Mary Frances (1818) were born.

By 1819, John Hamilton became the guardian of three minor children surnamed Baird, who were all under fourteen years old. They were related to his recently-deceased partner in the grocery business, John Mercer. He was to use money from the estate of his late partner to purchase a bake house on Lombard Street in trust for his wards.

Hamilton's youngest son, John, Jr., was born in 1820 and became a famous lawyer, practicing until 1909. In 1821,

John Hamilton was a *grocer* with only two business partners,
John McClellan Hood and John Newell. In the same year, a
Bostonian named L. M. Sargent sold the parcel of land at
High St. (now Market) and Schuylkill Fifth St. (now 18th
St.) to Hamilton. Next, Jane (1824) and Lydia Isabella
(182[5]) were born into the family. In 1825, *Hamilton &
Leghorn* became partners in a dry goods store at 20 South
Second St.<3> The baptisms of Sarah McClellan, William
Newell, Ann Jane, and John, Jr. were held at the *First
Presbyterian Church.*<4> The Census of 1830 placed the
family in the city's South Ward between Chestnut and Walnut
Sts., north of Seventh. In this year, the *Tenth Presbyterian
Church* (13th & Walnut Sts.) welcomed John Hamilton, his
wife, Elizabeth, and their twins Jannette & Euphenia,
following their examination on religious material. The
family took the public profession of faith on September 30,
1830. Similarly, their daughter Elizabeth professed her
faith on December 19, 1830 and two years later, Lydia
Isabella and Mary Frances did likewise, on March 18, 1832.

(A chronology of the Hamilton family's activity may be
consulted in the Appendix. It begins in the year 1831 and
places events in their lives against a backdrop of politics
and scientific advancements.)

Religion was at the core of Hamilton family activity.
Abruptly, the family moved to *Hopewell, PA* before July 10,
1832 to follow their minister, Dr. Robert Cathcart. After a
few years sojourn, the Hamiltons returned to Philadelphia
probably for commercial pursuits. In 1837, *The City
Directory* places the family at 24 South Second Street near
John's business. In 1846, the Hamiltons moved to the corner
of Summer St. and Schuylkill Seventh a new mansion.<6>[M002]
When the Census of 1850 was taken on August 1st, the
grandfather of the artist was seventy years old, and a
retired resident at 1600 Summer St. (Hamilton House). It did
not reveal that he was the largest wholesale grocer and wine
merchant in the city.<7> He was also a leading reformer
pushing for standard weights and measures especially for
tare (packaging allowance) in bulk sales of commodities.
The grandfather died in 1858.<8>

John, Jr. was admitted to legal practice before the
Philadelphia Bar in 1845. By 1852, he bought a house at
Delaware Seventh St. and Catherine St. in Moyamensing
township, a Southern suburb within walking distance of his

OLD WELSH WOMAN, 1899, pastel on canvas 60" x 30."
Courtesy of the Pennsylvania Academy of the Fine Arts,
Philadelphia. Archives (catalogue illustration from the
17th Annual Exhibition of the P.A.F.A., 1901.

23

father's new house.<9>

   Betty, widow of John, Sr., and mother of the Hamiltons
introduced above, was seventy years old and the owner of
$ 45,000.00 in real estate with taxable personal property
of $ 2,500.00 by 1860. Her eldest son, David, was retired
and lived at the same address. Either of Betty's daughters
was probably running the family household on Summer St. It
consisted of thirteen people and the daughter was assisted
by two servants. The artist, little John McLure, was seven
years old and attending (public ?) school nearby. His
youthful mother, Caroline, was 21 and his mature father, Dr.
George, was 45. The artist's sister, Jennie Mercer, was just
one and her elder sister, Lillie Hall, was five.<10> This
vignette shows that the artist grew up in a highly stable,
affluent, northern family unit just prior to the American
Civil War.

   By 1870, one of Dr. George's two maiden sisters,
Catherine or Margaret, probably ran the household for their
aged mother with the aid of two servants. Dr. George
practiced medicine there while his resident relative, James
Biddle, was an agent for the railway. One of Dr. George's
married sisters, Lydia Isabella Biddle, had a son, John C.
Mercer Biddle, who was four years younger than the
artist.<11> The Hamiltons survived the War materially
unscathed. They participated in the new prosperity of the
city where the arts blossomed at a modest level compared to
European cities.

   It took three generations to create a climate for an
artist to grow in the Hamilton family. But for the industry
of John Hamilton, Sr., the immigrant who fled the Irish
rebellion, his son, George Hamilton, would not have become a
physician, life-long student, and patron of the fine arts.
As a result, an indulged son of his old age, John McLure
Hamilton, became a world-class artist.

IV : FATHER

During the first thirty-two years of John McLure's life, George Hamilton, M. D., had the greatest positive influence over his intellectual development. George, who was raised as a traditional Presbyterian, loved languages and had a reading and speaking knowledge of English, French, German, and Italian.<1> (Refer to Tab. E for information about his parents and progeny.) He loved to read and enjoyed discussing books. Above all he loved art. Dr. George's broad taste included the works of artists like *Boldini, Corot, Daubigny, Diaz, Jean Francois Millet*, and *Alfred Stevens*. He collected engravings by *Audran, Drevet, Edelinck*, and *Wille*.<2>

George Hamilton has an impressive profile as a physician, medical scholar, and influential father. He was the son of Betty Hall and John Hamilton, Senior, who were Scotch-Irish, former British subjects who immigrated from Northern Ireland. George's parents probably arrived in Philadelphia during 1795, escaping the trouble associated with the rebellion a few years later. The balance of the chapter is set in Philadelphia. They married in the Old City and George was born in 1808.<3> Dr. George was the fourth of nine children. He was educated privately by *Dr. Banks* and others and matriculated at the *Medical School* of the University of Pennsylvania as a teenager for a year and a half.<4,5> His clinical training began under *Pennsylvania Hospital*'s Dr. Hewson in 1828. George was elected to the *College of Physicians & Surgeons* about this time and

ROBERT PYLE ROBINSON, Delaware's Governor, 1928 and
Hamilton's cousin. Oil 44" x 35." Delaware State
Archives.

received his only degree from Pennsylvania in 1831. Since he never had the opportunity for a liberal arts education he craved, he directed his education for the next fifty-four years by reading thousands of books in four languages.<6>

George left Philadelphia two years after finishing medical training. He went to Delaware's Christiana Hundred (township) in New Castle county to practice in a small, remote, post office community of farmers. He served as the hospital-on-horseback for eleven years, while residing at Centreville in the northern part of the state.<7>

After returning to Philadelphia in 1844, George Hamilton drew on his broad clinical experience in family practice and built a solid reputation. He became a prominent member of the local medical profession for the next forty-one years. He was first elected a member of the *County Medical Society* in 1859, and then its president for several terms starting in 1868. By 1872, he was a member of the *American Medical Association.*<8> Being a socializer, he visited functions of the *St. Andrews Society.*<9>

He practiced daily out of the family's home at the South West corner of Schuylkill Seventh and Summer Streets. [M002], which had been his father's unfinished house from 1846. Previously, he occupied a house at Thirteenth and Wallace Sts. Now he and his wife resided with his parents, two of his brothers (David and John, Junior, by then an attorney), and two maiden sisters.

The aging physician married in October, 1849. His wife, Caroline Delaplaine, was the daughter of a successful lawyer, James Delaplaine. He was known to the du Pont's and served as an elected official in several capacities in Delaware. The Delaplaines had been residing in America since the Seventeenth Century.<10>

George and his bride, Caroline, moved to the now completed house of grandfather, John Hamilton, Sr. located north of the City limits in a fashionable suburb within walking distance of Broad and Market Streets. It measured thirty feet wide by sixty feet deep, three stories tall, and made of brick and stone.<11>

In 1860, George, Caroline, and John McLure represented twenty-five percent of the twelve-member, three generational family living at Hamilton House. According to the Census report, what was now Aunt Margaret's house was worth $ 2,500.00 and Dr. George had additional assets of $ 2,000.00. This was a comfortable level in those days but clearly not wealthy.<12>

By 1870, the value of the family's real estate portfolio had increased to $ 36,000.00 and Dr. George's additional assets reached $ 7,000.00.<13> There was now money for investing in stocks and bonds, surplus funds could be used for book and art buying. George had some leisure to study art and to direct John McLure's education as an artist.

In the interim, George had a heavy patient load. He became involved in professional organizations and wrote several scholarly papers.<14> He bought many books at auctions and soon his library grew to 14,000 volumes. He also collected engravings and etchings and owned approximately 7,000. He "botanized" traveling great distances from his home to collect specimens as well. George was a horseman and often raced south down Broad Street.

He spoke out forcefully against experimental surgery involving animals and as a result of his words, the artist painted *"Vivisection,"* an editorial (genre) picture. (While unlocated, the content of this oil was described in Morris' first article. It presented a white pigeon, blood-spotted, lying on an experimenter's bench. An appealing Scotish terrier, also doomed, sat beside it. Tomkins produced a copper engraving and mezzotint after the original painting in 1883.)

As the scholarly president of the *County Medical Society*, George was asked to memorialize three famous colleagues, two Philadelphians (Gebhard, Meigs) and one from New York (Beck).<15>

John McLure was thirty-one years old when a fire destroyed Hamilton House killing Dr. George's younger, single daughter, *Jennie Mercer Hamilton, John Alsop King,* the elder daughter's husband, the grandson, *Charles Ray King,* and the maid.<16> Also, half of Dr. George's book and art collections were lost along with a sketch of the Doctor by John McLure.<17> Hamilton House, protected by insurance, was rebuilt about 1886.

The tough, stoic physician who had cared for and comforted so many sick and bereaved patients was emotionally shaken by this experience. George died eight months later at seventy-seven. He was buried at *All Saints* (Protestant Episcopal) *Cemetery* in the Torresdale section of Philadelphia and John McLure was the executer of his father's estate. The doctor's bronze bust, by Edward Onslow Ford, *R. A.* had a place of honor in John's home for many years but was then presented to the *County Medical Society.*<18>[M003]   A drawing of his father made from memory was sent by John McLure at the request of the Society' secretary, since Dr. George had been its president immediately following the American Civil War. A daguerreotype photograph, made in 1876, of the doctor was presented to the *College of Physicians'* library by Dr. John Madison Taylor, a long-time family acquaintance. Some of George's rarest books were presented to the *Ridgeway Library,* the *Library Company of Philadelphia,* and to the *Historical Society of Pennsylvania.*

It is interesting to note at this point that the early art of John McLure (1864--1884) was likened to that of *Alfred Stevens* by Breslau Professor Richard Muther (1907). Hamilton's oil portraits have been likened to that of *Giovanni Boldini* by Corcoran Gallery of Art's Curator, Mrs. Linda Simmons (1981).<19>

We recall now that it was Dr. George who placed John McLure under the tuteledge of drawing teacher, George W. Holmes. At that time, John McLure met Henry Joseph Thouron, perhaps Clara Raiguel, and entered the serious world of art training and professional career development.

(Photographer unknown) JOHN McLURE HAMILTON sans beard,
1881. 4 1/8" x 2 1/2" original. Charles Roberts
Collection. Haverford College Library, PA.

V : EARLY YEARS, 1853--1877

John McLure was born on January 31, 1853. (Tab. E) Many people were starving and homeless in Philadelphia that year, much crime was on the streets in this predominantly Protestant industrial city, and the immigrants were poor, rural, Irish Catholics.<1>   Cholera and Typhoid Fever were serious public health problems in many neighborhoods. (See : the Chronology in Appendix for a timeline of the artist's life.) <2>

The artist's father continued to practice medicine in the Northern Liberties suburb not far from Broad and Market Sts. He walked to the homes of his patients, or used public transportation. George may have delivered his son at home, since *Pennsylvania Hospital*, where he had trained, was over a mile away and the weather was harsh at that time of year.<3>   John McLure's household included ten other family members and an Irish servant girl. The home was presided over by his grandparents. His grandmother may have served as the model for *"Old Welsh Woman,"* pastel on canvas.<4>[A150]

John McLure was one of four children in the home. The artist's elder brother was born in August, 1851, but died in infancy; a frequent occurrence in that day. His younger sister, Lillie Hall, the future Mrs. John Alsop King, was born three years after the artist. Their youngest sister, Jennie Mercer, was born in 1859.

During fifty-five years in the grocery business and

Detail, memoranda of colors for theatre curtain, 1864.
Oil 41" x 25." Formerly in collection of Harry Burke.

speculation in real estate the grandfather, John, Sr. had
prospered. By local standards the Hamiltons were affluent.
Though most people were affected by the financial
depression, the early years at 1600 Summer St. (in the
city's Tenth Ward) were relatively free from want for the
Hamiltons.<5> Discipline and hard work had made the first
native American generation of Hamiltons into lawyers,
physicians, and merchants. The climate was right for an
artist in the second generation.

Little is known about John McLure's primary education.
He was probably tutored at home and then sent to nearby
public schools. By age ten, while the American Civil War
raged, he was already a student at the after-hours private
drawing school of *George W. Holmes*. This school was located
at 134 North Eleventh Street (near Filbert) within walking
distance of John McLure's home. He learned to draw by
copying from engravings of Roman casts. Also, he painted and
socialized with other art-conscious students. The school was
a gathering place for young people from all over town,
including Henry Joseph Thouron, with whom the artist formed
a lifetime friendship.<6>

One of Hamilton's kinsmen, from his father's side
(Gemmill), was later involved with the City's theater
industry, specifically, with the *New Concert Hall* (or Third
Chestnut St. Theater) located at 1211--1215 Chestnut, an
important business street.<7> At eleven, John McLure,
prepared a "*memoranda of colors,*" which was a landscape
proposed to be painted on a stage curtain for his uncle's
theatre. The scene was executed five times on one mock up.
In each successive effort, additional colors were added with
a penciled label, specifying the oil pigments to be used.
The memoranda' scenes portray a site on the Schuylkill River
near the *Fairmount Water Works* on a 43" x 26" canvas. A
legend appears on the reverse. It reports that the mock up
hung in a damp basement for nine years. These five views on
the memoranda represent the earliest surviving art and
(handwriting ?) of McLure yet discovered. The mock up
survives though the finished product and theater are gone.

The actress Sarah Bernhardt played her first engagement
at the New Concert Hall in 1881, perhaps under our artist's
curtain.<8>[A226]

Philadelphians were to play a major role in Hamilton's

career. Former artist *Francis M. Drexel* was a successful broker in town. Later, his banking firm would represent the artist's business interests while abroad. The Honorable *Richard Vaux* was the city's successful *Democratic* (party) Mayor. Later, the artist would paint his portrait.[A128] In the small town atmosphere of Philadelphia, the Biddles, Pennells, and Sargents were known to the Hamiltons on a first name basis in the 1850s.

John McLure entered high school in 1866, joining the 63rd class at *Central High School*. Members of his class included Henry Martin Chance, Solomon Solis-Cohen, Emanuel Furth, William W. Perrine, Eli Kirk Price,Jr., William T. Tilden, Charles William Woddrop, and J. William White. Also, 150 other boys in this class became V.I.Ps of medicine and the law by the turn-of-the-century. The artist graduated in February, 1870 from the Juniper St. and Penn Square campus.<9>

McLure had apparently done many things in his seventeen years, and church attendance did not appear to be a priority of his youth. He was finally baptized in 1870, probably under the influence of his devout grandmother, Betty, and her equally observant daughter, Mrs. Ann Jane Mercer.<10> The latter wrote a poem which became a hymn.<11>

By October of that year, McLure resided at 1123 Chestnut St., apart from his family. Perhaps he moved to be closer to the rented facilities of the P.A.F.A., where he attended classes in the "Antique," taught by Professor Christain Schuessele (1824--1879).<12>   He drew casts of arms, legs, and various body parts during the six weeks of instruction in the Academy's temporary home.

McLure went to Europe alone to study at the Antwerp Academy under the guidance of Professor van Lerius. Although McLure was only twenty, he spoke and read French fluently by contemporary American standards and demonstrated considerable promise as a draughtsman. Recall that he had painted in oils since he was eleven.

As a student, Hamilton acquired great skills and valuable experience in oils. Canvases done by Hamilton in the reflected light style revealed a warm glow on the face of each subject. [whether from an open book A025, A028 or from papers on the desk before the sitter A027, A092]

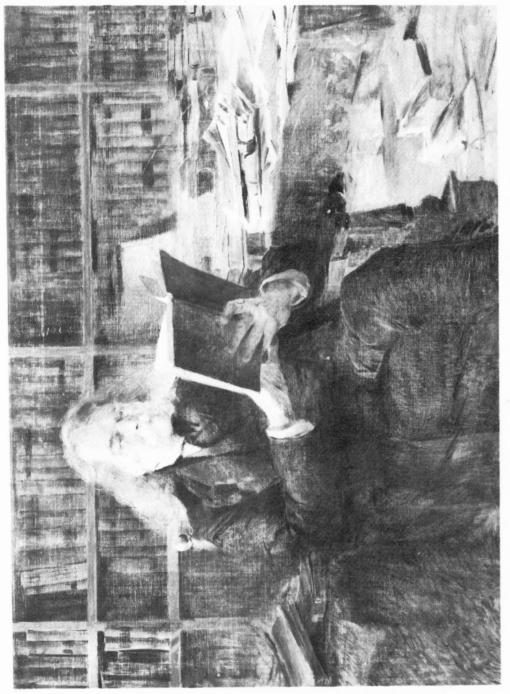

Honorable RICHARD VAUX, 1895. Oil 28" x 36." Courtesy of the Pennsylvania Academy of the Fine Arts, Philadelphia. Gift of Alexander Biddle, John Cadwalder, Anthony J. Antelo, George C. Thomas, William L. Elkins, Charles Harrison, George H. McFadden, John H. Converse and Edward H. Coates.

In Antwerp, Hamilton compulsively studied the paintings of the Old Masters displayed in museums, including Hals, Rembrandt, and Velasquez. As an apprentice to his great teachers de Keyser, van Lerius, and Beaufaux, Hamilton learned to prepare glazes, paint thinly, and gain mastery in the techniques that would help him metamorphose into a Flemish master in the grand tradition that he so admired. He became an important painter for the next fifty years. Unfortunately, no letters document this period of his career.

Hamilton exhibited two paintings at the P.A.F.A. in October, 1877.<13> They were hung alongside those of Biard, David, Jacob Eichholtz, Fussel, Moran, Rothmel, Strother, Thomas Sully, Vanderlyn, and Williams. This was Hamilton's first known cataloged public exhibition in his native city. A third painting was exhibited at the *National Academy of Design* (NYC), which received a rave notice in the NEW YORK TIMES, *"Le Rire"* (April 8, 1877). It became his best known work for the next ten years (original unlocated). He exhibited in NYC on three other occassions (1878,1890, and 1920).<14>

When he was twenty-five, Hamilton drew a unique piece of American literature about art titled,"*49me Exposition des Beaux Arts. Philadelphie, 1878. L'Academie pour Rire."* It is an eight-page collection of forty-six satirical cartoons lampooning the student show at P.A.F.A. Below the cartoons, a French comment gently spoofed each work shown. This represented a first in America. It was commented upon in the PHILADELPHIA JOURNAL (April, 1878). Hamilton was credited with its authorship.<15> At the time, two additional Hamilton paintings were exhibited (*"Afternoon Repose"* and *"Le Rire"*) and he also exhibited in Paris that year. <16>

A study of the writings of a Quaker preacher, Edward Hicks (died 1849), the folk artist of the early Nineteenth Century, provided reasons why Hamilton left Philadelphia in 1873 for training in Antwerp. For the same reasons, Hamilton chose to immigrate in 1878 and to reconfirm that decision to live abroad in 1893. Rev. Hicks, speaking for many residents in the Quaker city, believed that painting, like dancing, music, and fiddle playing were the Devil's work. Hicks felt guilty about his own desire to paint and believed that such work was worthless in the larger sphere of life. Rev. Hicks elected, instead, to paint signs for a living, as it was a more pious vocation than fine art. He had, however, cravings, revealed in his letters, to paint on canvas and produced hundreds of oils, including his famous *"Peaceable Kingdom."*<17> Where fine art was concerned, Philadelphia was a wasteland so its native sons, like Hamilton, had to leave to further their careers or die as professionals.

Richard Vaux, a Quaker, former Mayor of the city, served as the president of the P.A.F.A. in the Nineteenth Century. He reported that even in the 1890s, no one ever came to art shows in town.<18>

Philadelphia produced the artist but could not feed his insatiable curiosity about the rest of the world, especially fine art. As a result, he began an almost sixty-year-long Odyssey pursuing beauty, culture, truth, and values unavailable locally in the milieu that existed following the Civil War. Hamilton, like so many other expatriate artists, made Great Britain his residence far from his American home.

Diagram for stained glass window, SAINT ALBAN, a 5 3/4"
x 2 1/2" woodengraving frontis to T. B. Hennell's 1901
poem, THE LAY OF ST. ALBAN, published by A. N. Wallace
of Kilmarnock. Courtesy of the Poetry Collection, the
Mitchell Library, Glasgow.

VI : FLEMISH EXPERIENCE

In 1873, Antwerp was the only place in Europe for advanced study by wealthy American art students. In Hamilton's words, "the finest painters in the world are the Belgians."<1>

This phase of Hamilton's career was like a pilgrimage to Mecca for an observant Moslem. He attended the *Antwerp Academy*.<2> For about three years, Hamilton studied with the giants of two-dimensional Flemish art, de Keyser, van Lerius, and Beaufaux.

Nicaise de Keyser (1813--1887), a Belgian native, was a former pupil of Joseph Jacops and Martin J. van Bree. He was famous for his Romantic history and genre paintings presently in prominent collections. He made a reputation by portraying biblical subjects, giant-scale battle scenes, and as the painter of historical genre. He was versatile. He produced illustrations for books, cartoons, murals, and portraits of Royalty. Between 1836 and 1862, de Keyser received every major medal and honor to which a European painter might aspire. They were conferred from Antwerp, Bavaria, Brussels, Paris, Sweden, and Wurtemberg. In 1855, he was appointed *Director* of the Antwerp Academy, serving there for more than twenty years. His funeral was a semi-state affair in Belgium. This was a rare tribute to this unique, world class, painter among painters in the highly competitive Nineteenth Century world of art.<3>

Hamilton's second Flemish master/teacher was *Joseph Henry Francois van Lerius* (1823--1876). He was a native of a small town near Antwerp and had been a pupil of Baron Egide Charles Gustave Wappers (1803--1875). By 1854, van Lerius became the Professor of Painting in Antwerp, a city renowned for painters and the training of painters. The professor had built his reputation on his expertise in costume history, genre painting, lithography, and portraiture. One of his paintings done in 1870, "*Lady Godiva*," sold seven years later, at the record price of 18,000 francs.<4>

Hamilton's third mentor was *Polydore-Constantin Beaufaux* (1829--1904), who was born at the Court of St. Etienne and studied at the Antwerp Academy. Beaufaux had mastered the painting of religious subjects and costume history before being appointed to the faculty at the same Academy. Another of Beaufaux's famous students was L. van Aken.<5>

Hamilton left Antwerp before *James Sidney Ensor* (1860--1949), a Modern Flemish painter matriculated at the Academy. *Francis Davis Millet* (1846--1912), from Boston, had been an older contemporary, as had been Emile Claus (1849--1924), a Modern Flemish painter. *Walter Tyndale* (1855--1943) of Brugges was a fellow student and one of Hamilton's life-long friends in the profession. Tyndale's reputation as a British watercolorist is well-known.<6>

Hamilton received all this education between his twentieth and twenty-third birthdays. He probably acquired a heavy dose of Roman Catholicism directly and indirectly while in Belgium, along with knowledge of the Old Masters' technology of concoting pigments, preparing canvas, and capturing light or shadows. Also, he passively received schooling in historical and religious themes by visiting museums and reading.

Even sixty years later, evidence of Hamilton's admiration for works on a religious theme can be seen from an analysis of Howe's Inventory of *Hamiltoniana*. They were works which the artist had preserved for his proposed museum even in the face of his cash flow problems in Jamaica. That collection, prized by Hamilton, contained no less than five pictures clearly religiously iconographic. Some were done by other artists. These included : a six foot tall etching of the "*Crucifixion*," perhaps after de Keyser's oil of 1834; a

Christus portrait; a Madonna and Child portrait; "*Ecce Homo Dei*" (the Holy Child and St. John kissing) by Andrea del Sarto (1487--1531); and finally, "*Sampson and Delilah*" by Guido Reni (1575--1642).<7>

Available evidence suggests that Hamilton arrived in Antwerp before April 3, 1873, eleven years before the age of postage stamp art began in Belgium. Hamilton registered officially for only four night courses at the Antwerp Academy, which had an interesting history. After the French invasion of Belgium, Napoleon presented it to the citizens of Belgium for use as an art school. These traditional courses included the "Antique," in which students drew casts of human anatomy in order to upgrade their skills in observation, composition, speed and precision, and the "Nature," in which drawing a nude figure from life was the principle objective. For insight into the schooling practices, we may view Dermond O'Brien's (1845--1945) oil (1890), showing a model flanked by students at work in the oil painting class at the Academy after Hamilton's tenure. For more information, we may read Charles Boom's comments on his days at the Academy when he was de Keyser's student.<8> Hamilton took the former course three times, growing with each experience. Some students studied a specialty for seventeen years. On average, six Americans were at the academy each year and represented a minority of far less than one percent in the Antwerp Academy.<9>

The names of other students from America appear in dictionaries of artists and Who Was Who publications today.<10> [Robert Arthur (1850--1914) of Baltimore, Dewey Bates (1851--1899), also from Philadelphia, Daniel Jerome Elwell (1847--1912) of Boston, George Albert Frost (1843--??) of Boston, Robert Hinckley (1853--1941) of Boston, and Millett of Boston.]

Hamilton was trilingual and could associate with artists and art students from English-, French-, and German-speaking lands during this period. Some of the better known individuals included Samuel Putnam Avery, the engraver and publisher (1822--1904), Charles Boom (1858--??), Auguste Rodin (1840--1917), and Sir Laurenz Alma-Tadema (1836--1912). Although one might have expected to find criminal activity by art students no listing of any of Hamilton's contemporaries could be found in the police records of the city, because as a group, Hamilton and his acquaintances

LEWIS CAMPBELL, M.A., LL.D., Hon. D. Litt., Professor
of Greek, St. Andrews, 1885. Oil. Courtesy of the
University of St. Andrews Art Collection.

were quiet and law-abiding in the 1870s. <11>

For a time, Hamilton lived at 77 Morteus Street, adjacent to the *Grote Markt*, probably subletting from Dewey Bates. This property still stands 120 years later. A store occupies the ground floor and four floors of rooms extend to the roof. Later, Hamilton lived at 4 Kaasrui (1874), a house where Walter Tyndale also resided.<12>   Because there had been a stock market crash in the United States in September, 1873, the availability of cash from home may have been briefly reduced for Hamilton. This might explain the reason for his sublet tenancy.<13>

A night student of art may have used his daylight hours working for a newspaper to earn money for living expenses and art supplies. Abraham Verhoeven produced the world's first newspaper (1605) in Antwerp. By the 1870s, even the academy had a weekly paper the *"Vlaemsche School,"* to chronicle activities of its more than one thosand five hundred students. An equal number of donors to the school took an active interest in the transmission of culture and artistic skills to young people.<14>   It may have been convenient for Hamilton to work at one of the numerous newspaper offices or printing houses, since one was located close to Professor Beaufaux's residence. Hamilton may have also sought work as an apprentice painter, because Director de Keyser was creating a giant-scale, panorama, the *"Battle of Waterloo,"* which required many hands. Additionally, he may have worked as a copyist for the many portraits being used by the firm of *Stalins en Janssens Antwerpen*, which was restoring a giant, early 16th Century stained glass window located in Belgium's largest *Kathedraal*. The church area being rehabilitated was the 1502 *King Henry VII* window in the Chapel of St. Anthony. It was completed in 1879 and is extant today.<15>   Still another work opportunity existed for Hamilton, it was preparing material for the *Belgian Pavilion*. The material was fabricated for the *American Centennial Exposition* scheduled for Philadelphia in 1876. Robert Arthur did this work.<16> He may have gotten some practical experience as an apprentice to a master sculptor or worked for a painter by mixing pigment, priming canvas, and other technical support work. He may have flirted with the idea of an apprenticeship in the diamond trade, since Antwerp was the place to do so. Such training took just under three years.<17>

However the problem of finance was solved by Hamilton, it can be assumed that he sketched and painted in solitude much of the time. He was formerly an avid scholar at Central High School in Philadelphia and Antwerp was a city of scholars. For certain, he associated with the other American students at the *Koninklijk Musea voor Schone Kunsten Antwerpen.* It is assumed that he also enjoyed the larger museum in Brussels, the cafes for Belgian beer, the Saturday Vogel Market, and probably he explored the multitude of art in the dozens of churches within walking distance of his residence.

Any visitor to Antwerp could not fail to notice a finely-executed sculpture of the Madonna and Child at every intersection in the downtown area. Each piece of art was the masterwork of an aspiring sculptor. With so many examples of art outside of the buildings, surely the germ of Hamilton's own Madonna and Child must have been taking shape in his mind. His portrait in oils, which won his first gold medal (Chicago's 1893 *World's Columbian Exposition*), portrayed Mrs. Myles Kennedy holding her infant son in her arms.[18] It had earlier been exhibited in Paris and Vienna.

The work of Alfred Stevens (1828--1900) was known to Hamilton through his father's collection. The young artist probably saw Stevens' original oils exhibited in Antwerp.

Hamilton walked and bicycled into the fabulous countryside, especially in the spring and summer weather to sketch and paint watercolors having been influenced by Charles Francois Daubigny (1817--1878).

The COMMERCIAL DIRECTORY of 1874 reveals that Antwerp boasted no less than three hundred fifty-four professional artists. Each artist earned a living, paid taxes, and was valued as an established resident. They usually lived along side of the bakers, beer brewers, butchers, chocolatiers, and bankers. The categories of artists included lithographers (17), wood engravers (4), copper and metal engravers (7), gem and stone engravers (7), painters in oil (120), architectural, decorative, and furniture painters (118), carriage painters (5), stained glass artists (2), photographers (16), manufacturers of plaster figurines and small statuary (5), sculptors, and fabricators of large statues (38).[19]

The citizens of Antwerp were internationally-minded, because being so was good for business in French, Dutch, Flemish, and other languages. There were no less than eighty-four professors of the language arts listed in 1874. *Edoard Riegle* served as Secretary to the Director of the Academy, de Keyser. His surname may be a variation of Hamilton's wife's maiden name, Clara Raiguel.

Contacts existed between people and institutions in the U. S. and the Antwerp Academy in Hamilton's day. Philadelphian *Morris Patterson* (1809--1878), merchant and philanthropist, had written (August 30, 1873) to the *Royal Society for the Encouragement of the Fine Arts* in Belgium. The letter was regarding the purchase and shipment of three pictures from the contemporary *Antwerp Expostion* (1871--1873) to Philadelphia.[20] *Robert Curren* (Clerk, Cooper Institute, NY) acknowledged, on behalf of *Francis A. Stout,* two gifts sent to their American art school (Sept. 10, 1873). The gifts were catalogs of the various scientific and artistic disciplines represented at "*L'Exposition.*"[21]

The final step for American art students, who had completed their two-year sojourn in Antwerp was a minicourse in oil painting at Paris. It was directed by another member of the Antwerp Academy, Professor Gerome, of the *Ecole des Beaux Arts, Paris.* Hamilton adhered to this pattern and probably left Belgium during the summer of 1875.[22]

Hamilton studied in Paris with the French-born Professor, *Jean Leon Gerome* (1824--alive 1884), at the Paris school. Earlier, Prof. Gerome had taught Eakins about charcoal sketching and had initiated him into the fraternity of oil painters.[23] Hamilton may have become Gerome's student at an early phase in his career development and remained under Gerome's influence for about thirty days. The reasons Hamilton left Gerome's guidance are unknown. Letters or independent records have not surfaced on this brief experience. Hamilton returned to his native city in the fall of 1875. He did, however, exhibit an oil painting at the *Paris Exposition* of 1878 called "*Le Rire,*" mentioned earlier.

Joseph Pennell reported that he met Hamilton after his training in Belgium. Their long professional and social association followed in England, Europe and in the U. S. until 1926.[24]

Lord FREDERICK LEIGHTON, P.R.A., 1880. Oil 29 1/10" x
24." Courtesy of Leighton House Museum. The Royal
Borough of Kensington and Chelsea.

(George Frederick Watts) Lord FREDERICK LEIGHTON, 1880.
Ink on board 9" x 14." Later etched by P. Rajon.
Formerly at Christie's, London in a large autograph
collection.

One can discern the Antwerp influence in Hamilton's work. There are three splendid examples. An obvious case is found in "*Lord Frederick Leighton, P.R.A.*" (1830--1896) an oil portrait [A079] done about 1890. The backlighting treatment of the hat and face can be likened favorably with the 162(7) P. P. Rubens (1577--1640) self-portrait hanging in the Rubenshuis [M005].

A second case of the Antwerp influence is found in Hamilton's 136 member Prominent Profiles series. Those images were recorded in his Glasgow residency period between 1902 and 1905 and include the oil portrait of "*Professor Campbell*" [A015]. In these images, Hamilton was influenced by Franz Hals (1580--1603), one of his favorite artists. From study of the composition and lighting recorded in Hals' "*portret van Stephanus Geeraedts, Schepen te Haarlem,*" it can be discerned that a distinguished local sitter and his coat-of-arms were presented exuding reverence and majesty.

The third case is in Hamilton's life-sized self-portrait [A067] in a cape and a high, top hat. The artist's face is transfixed by light *Caravaggio*-fashion, illuminated from a single point source. Whether this was achieved by cellar painting or by painting in gas light illumination is not known, but the model was portrayed in darkness with only a single beam of light.<25>

Significant original career data has not surfaced from Hamilton's intriguing Antwerp period (1873--1875). Nevertheless, there is room for speculation about his observations, experiences, associates, teachers, and the value of this period in his overall career development. Earlier, some of the Antwerp artists known to Hamilton were listed who worked in two-and three-dimensional art. Weinberg's research on *Millet*, Simpson's on *Abbey* in England, D'Haese's work-in-progress on *Claus*, and the extensive series of notices and reviews published weekly as the "*Vlaemsche School*" record student-related experiences in the 1870s.

If additional information should become available about Hamilton that suggests he was nothing more than a part of the wallpaper and drapery design of Antwerp for these critical years in his career, the value of the experiences he had and the skills he acquired are still of as pivotal importance to his artistic development as the legendary beers, chocolates, cookies, mussels, and *Vogel* market are to the town. If this was a time in his life when he was just a shy, workaholic watching, listening, and learning but not producing works then it was a profoundly important incubation period where he grew far beyond his Philadelphia training and rapidly.

It is reasonable to assume that he acquired and developed his omnivorous intellectual dietary preference for the works of Beaufaux, Caravaggio, de Keyser, Hals, van Lerius, Reni, Rubens, and Alfred Stevens in Antwerp. (see Tab.V)<26> However, it is not so easy to probe inside his mind to unravel his process of creating art in the absence of letters and contemporary reports about his specific activities. An 1870 catalog exists for the *Antwerp Museum* and the *Register of students' names* at the academy also exists. Though Hamilton's name was absent from the exhibition lists and prize lists at the academy during his tenure, he probably attended the exhibitions held in February of each year. He viewed the 1873 triennial exposition, but missed the 1876 event because he had returned to the U.S. The Philadelphia-based *Centennial Exposition* may have drawn him home, but surely other reasons existed for drawing him home.

An unnamed reviewer in the (London) *TIMES* said of John McLure Hamilton, that "he is a faithful impressionist, presenting the personality in (the sitter's) general conditions as produced by fall and quality of light; but that his preference for grey schemes and subdued colours conduces to a hushed mood in the spectator. What distinguishes Mr. Hamilton as a portrait painter is his power of suggesting character, in the psychological sense, without departing from a purely pictorial statement, with special reference to relations and gradations of tone." <27>

In reply to the reviewer, I conclude this chapter with the opinion that Hamilton assimilated his knowledge from Antwerp into his style and his techniques.

TEARS, 1879. Oil on wood 7 3/4" x 4 15/16." Courtesy
of the Pennsylvania Academy of the Fine Arts,
Philadelphia, gift of Mr. and Mrs. John McLure
Hamilton.

VII : WIFE

Hamilton's wife Clara appeared in more of McLure's portraits than any other model. Born in Philadelphia in 1854, early members of her extended French Hugenot family settled there one hundred years earlier.<1> She was baptised at *St. Michael's & Zion Church* in May, 1855.<2> Clara's childhood was spent in a home of only five. *Mrs. Sarah C. Ellis Raiguel* was the artist's mother-in-law but Joseph W. Raiguel her late husband never met McLure. *Joseph Lloyd Raiguel* and *Valerie Raiguel*, the future Mrs. Milton L. Leffler of Washington, D. C., were her siblings and the artist's contemporaries.<3> (Tab. F)

At the time of Clara's marriage, her age was recorded as twenty and the groom's was twenty-seven.<4> Later sources prove that she was only months younger than McLure. Their good friends, *Elizabeth Robins* and *Joseph Pennell*, were married in 1880 at City Hall. Clara was raised in an atmosphere where the women in her family adjusted their ages by subtraction.<5> The Hamiltons were married in the *Second Presbyterian Church* at 16th St., north of Race St. by *Rev. John A. Dales, D.D.*<6>

After moving to London, Mr. Hamilton painted his wife in *"Tears."* She was portrayed from the side view, as a comely brunette. She was seated at a dressing table before a wall mirror, homesick and crying.<7>[A189] In style, it resembles a *Sir Joshua Reynolds* painting. Clara reported (1936) that this small genre piece was the first done following her arrival and sold for the equivalent of just

$ 5.00. Many years later, McLure repurchased it for sentimental reasons at $ 50.00. This was reported in its 1936 deed of gift to the P.A.F.A from the pair. In their second year in London, the magnitude of the artist's reputation improved when he was commissioned to paint a pair of portraits for a gentleman and his wife for the equivalent of $ 1,500.00. He had just painted a portrait of a grand-daughter of a peer with the prospect for a further commission to paint four of her siblings for the tribe *Rowley*, whom I believe to be grandchildren of the *Earl of Ravensworth* based on an 1881 letter to Hamilton's father.<8>

In 1884, the future astronomer, *George Hall Hamilton,* Clara's son and only child, saw his first stars at *Grey House*, located on the Hornton Street in Islington.<9>

Hamilton would portray his wife and favorite model literally hundreds of times during the next forty-seven years. She was the exclusive subject of his well-received pastels portraying a woman's back. Those pastels prompted the *NEW YORK TIMES*' art critic to observe that they were of equal quality to those of Degas or Renoir. Six oil paintings of her have also been located.<10> The artist said (1921), "much of the merit they possess and certainly their charm is due to the lady they represent."<11>

The father of McLure's mother-in-law, Mrs. Sarah Raiguel, was born in Wales and worked as a shoemaker. Her mother was born in Pennsylvania.<12> Mrs. Raiguel's was one of eight children and one of her brothers was a manufacturer of silver jewelry cases.<13> The Raiguels, like the Hamiltons, were a successful middle-class family that spoke French like the Delaplaines.

As late as the 1930s, Clara Hamilton retained her maiden name on legal documents in England and Pennsylvania. Thus, she maintained a separate legal and financial identity from her successful conservative artist husband. Her grandfather, *William Magee Raiguel*, was a prosperous dry goods merchant and land owner. She may have been an heiress in her own right.<14>

Mrs. Hamilton was the central figure in McLure's life from 1879 to 1936.<15> Clara provided the quiet power behind her man. She was his love, best friend, and primary art critic after the artist, himself. She exhibited two of

QUI VIVE!, c. 1914. Pastel & stump 22" x 29 7/8" in collection of Corcoran Gallery of Art, gift of Mrs. E. H. Harriman.

(her ?) paintings in the *Paris Salon* of 1890.<16> Thirty-two
of the Hamilton letters collected for this biography
revealed some information about her activity in her
husband's career. She provided him with a warm, intimate and
harmonious home-life in their long succession of apartments
and houses. (see : ABODES chapter for more details about
their living conditions.)

     Clara grew up and grew apace with her husband during
his changing taste and style periods as their joint career
blossomed in successive seasons. (Tab. **I** introduces the
names of forty-two of their most influential friends of
which we have details displayed as petals of a rose.)

     There are many anecdotes about Clara, the good
socializer, helping in the career effort, with the wives of
other professionals like *Elizabeth R. Pennell* and with the
family of various sitters like the Gladstones. Clara was a
friend of and comforter to *Dorothy ("Dossie") Drew,*
granddaughter of Prime Minister Gladstone, in instances
where Clara's friendship mattered a lot, just prior to
Dossie's marriage to *Colonel Parish,* birth of their children
and immediately after the early, war-injury related death of
her husband.<17,18,19> Clara may have been the matron of
honor at Dossie's wedding, while McLure was the person for
whom one of Dossie's sons, John, was named. Clara was a
gracious hostess even at their most elegant home, THE
HERMITAGE. She welcomed journalists writing about McLure,
and routine guests which included the wives of several Prime
Ministers and their husbands. Even (friends ?) like Mr. and
Mrs. *Sheridan Ford* of GENTLE ART fame were permitted the use
of the Hamilton's earlier home and pickings from the
Hamilton's food garden in their absence as they were in
need.<20,21,22> Clara often read aloud to soothe the people
sitting for her husband during a portrait session, as
well.<23> Clara loved travel as much as her husband did.
They generally traveled as a team. Their adventures included
Canada, California, Jamaica, Maine, Scotland, etc., and
easily totaled more than fifty long-distance expeditions.
Rarely did McLure go alone.<24>

     Clara shared her husband's passion for outdoor life and
could *fish* and *shoot* with the men in the Poconos, Wales, and
Zieglerville. She gardened, too. Clara was a patriot, and
during the *World War* I, she volunteered with the *Red Cross*

in England.<25>

In their series of homes, Clara shared her journalist husband's passion for literature, news of the day, and the issues currently occupying philosophers. It was her habit to read aloud to him at breakfast very early in the morning, a practice that has gone out of fashion in our age as radios and televisions can be found in every home.<26>

Analysis of the inventory of household goods placed in storage in anticipation of their third trip to Jamaica in 1931, suggested additional things about Clara.<27> For example, the items listed, which ran to more than twenty pages, revealed the quiet but essential crafts a wife performed to aid her family. She may have *sewed* at home---either out of need at times or for pleasure. Clara did own a dress maker's manikin and probably did millinery work at home with a niece.[A061, A078] She may have also enjoyed embroidery producing table linen and wall hangings.

There are numerous examples of Clara's and McLure's frugality as when they bought *used* frames and inquired about others.<28> They sought justification from gallery owners even for small fees by postal inquiry, from thousands of miles away and questioned their fees charged for shipping or the costs quoted for restoring paintings.<29,30,31> Clara was above all else McLure's business partner in numerous matters.

AUNT JANE'S COMPLEX LEGACY

McLure's beloved paternal grand aunt, *Mrs. Ann Jane Mercer*, died in April, 1886. Since she had no children of her own, she had attempted to influence her nephew's upbringing in many ways, including the encouragement of his religious education. In McLure's youth, she had supported his art school training in 1878 by purchasing an early work of his.[A144] Mrs. Mercer survived her husband, John C. Mercer, by three years. He had been a highly successful merchant and may have been the son of John Hamilton, Sr.'s partner in the grocery business. John C. Mercer had apparently become heir to his father-in-law's interest at *Hamilton & Hood* and vastly improved its assets during his stewardship.<32>

Since Mrs. Mercer had no heirs, her will included substantial cash bequests to the artist's mother, *Mrs. Caroline D. Hamilton,* to the artist's sole surviving sister, *Mrs. Lillie Hall King,* and to McLure and Clara.<33> However, after the will's probate, Mrs. Mercer's estate of nearly $ 700,000.00 lacked sufficient ready cash to provide funds for the numerous bequests. The four bequests to the Hamiltons, which totaled $ 100,000.00, were not paid in cash. Instead, the four received only an award of real estate. Specifically, they were the new owners of the former Mercer mansion, a farm house, a barn, some out-buildings, and nearly seventy-four acres of farm land containing the mentioned items situated in *Whitpain township,* Montgomery county, PA. The property was known collectively as the *Mansion on the Mount.* The Hamiltons deeded it to the *John C. Mercer Home for Disabled Clergymen of the Presbyterian Faith* for the sum of one dollar, while all but his sister, Lillie, lived in London.<34> This gift was a substantial act of religious charity by a sister-in-law, niece, nephew, and his wife.

Although Mrs. Mercer's will had stipulated that an additional $ 100,000.00 portion of her estate (later known as the *Mercer Fund*) be used for an endowment to maintain selected ministers of the Presbyterian Faith who did *not chew or smoke tobacco if retired and disabled,* history would not follow her intention. In 1909, the Hamiltons were living in England. Mrs. Mercer's heirs included *John Hamilton, Jr.* (her brother, the attorney, and author of her will, age 89), *Margaret Hamilton* (her sister, a free, life tenant in McLure's *Philadelphia Summer St.* mansion, age 92), the *estate of Mrs. Lydia I. Biddle,* her deceased sister, their respective heirs, McLure, Clara, Caroline Hamilton, a niece, *Mrs. Ethel Hamilton Lucas* (nee Yeager), and their respective children. The heirs filed a law suit in Common Pleas Court. In the brief, Uncle John, spokesman for the heirs, alleged that the Managers of the *Mercer Fund* and *Home* had not complied with the terms of Mrs. Mercer's bequest. The listed heirs further petitioned to have the *Mercer Fund* divided with its assets returned to Mrs. Mercer's heirs, citing that it was then the intention of the Managers to liquidate the real property and other assets (the Fund) after having clearly failed to live up to its purpose. The Managers wished to consume the assets for the benefit of all four hundred fifty clergymen without regard to their habits. This proposal, in the heirs' view, was a violation of Mrs.

Mercer's expressed intentions, the stated conditions of the bequest, and the terms of the gift given by McLure, Clara, Mrs. King and Mrs. Caroline Hamilton. Recall that these heirs of Mrs. Mercer were to have been beneficiaries of a $ 100,000.00 cash bequest *and* the *Mansion on the Mount* (property), which instead became the *Mercer Home* and *Fund* in 1886.<35> The disposition of the suit is clouded in mystery as only three in four court records survive in City Hall.<36>

In summary, from the modest documentation available, efforts to reconstruct the role of Clara in her husband's career reveal a portrait of her as an equal partner in the Odyssey that was McLure's seventy-two-year-long career journey. (Tab. **H, J**) She was on board for at least sixty-seven of those years. A few of her roles included wife, mother, daughter-in-law, aunt and cousin, model, McLure's personal art critic, confidante, traveling companion, hostess, and family nurse. In short, *Clara Hamilton*, was a woman of valor who sacrificed her modest career in art to be a major player in her husband's career. It proved to be a successful joint venture paying many dividends from its beginnings in Philadelphia prior to 1879 to the last stockholder's meeting in Jamaica in 1936. Later, Clara's paternal cousin, *Dr. George Earle Raiguel,* an opthamologist and author on many topics outside medicine, presented McLure's oil portrait of her to the *Philadelphia Museum of Art* in 1938, two years after her death.[A061] In 1992, a friend from her days in Mandeville reported that Clara's face was not that of a cosmetically pretty woman, nevertheless, we see in McLure's rendering of her only beauty. A second neighbor reported that Clara guarded her husband's estate in the Jamaican wilderness with her shot gun. Those two eyewitness reports about Clara are positive recommendations of her inner beauty and great strength of character, even in those final days in the tropics. To paraphrase what John McLure Hamilton said about his favorite model, the merit and charm of his most famous pastels for which Clara modeled were due to the qualities of the lady herself. These thoughts probably represent Clara's finest tribute by the one person who knew her best.

Artist's niece, MRS. NORA KING BUCKLEY [=Young woman trimming hat], c. 1893. Oil 35 1/2" x 47 1/2" formerly in collection of Harry Burke. Courtesy of Schwarz Gallery, Philadelphia.

VIII : SON AND DAUGHTER-IN-LAW

George Hall Hamilton was born on January 31, 1884, nine months after his parents' trip to Seville in Spain. The date corresponded to the artist's thirty-first birthday and George was named for his grandfather, *George Hamilton*, the Philadelphia physician and *Hall* after the maiden name of his grandmother Betty's family. George's birth registration took place in the Kensington subdistrict of Middlesex county where London is located. John McLure & Clara Augusta lived at Grey House. George Hall became one of McLure's models at an early age. He appears in more than twelve works. He was brought to the U. S. as an infant (1884).<1> Perhaps he was placed in the care of his grandparents for a time at Hamilton House on Summer St. while McLure sought commissions for new work. First, George was portrayed in a white bonnet and frock in the fenced yard with several striped chickens at the family home.[A202] Second, he was portrayed crawling on the living room floor with a large spotted dog, while a cat meowed from the adjoining kitchen doorway as seen in its facial expression.[M018] Third, he appeared seated on a bed in *"Green Robe"* at about age two.[A204] A life-size portrait of George was painted on his third birthday in *"Boy in Long Pants."* As the central long-haired figure of a fourth portrait, he was perched on a fringed plush pillow atop a wooden stool wearing a cap, muffler, and green winter overcoat. A fuzzy muff, was in his grasp. George was standing, pulling an unseen toy with both hands in *"Child playing."*<2> He was wearing a velvet suit with a belt sash and a lace collar.[A028] The artist's niece, Nora King, and

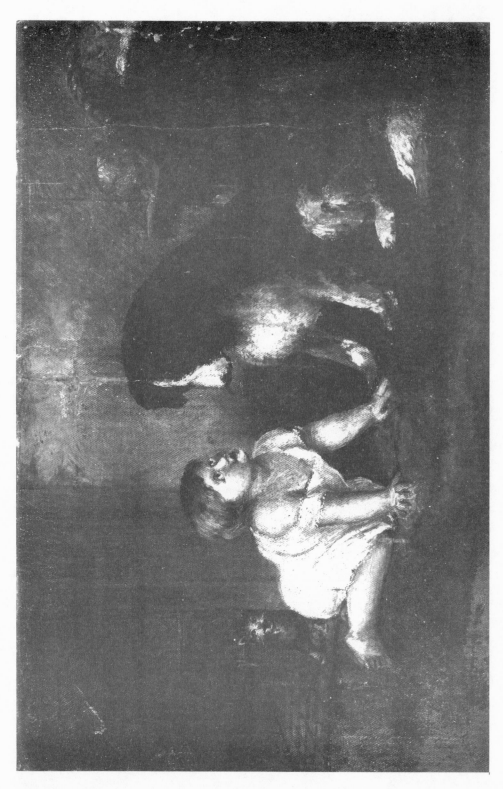

GEORGE HALL HAMILTON, artist's baby son at home with pets, c. 1884. Oil 12" x 18" formerly in collection of a New York state physician.

YOUNG BRITONS COURSING, autumn, 1890. A lithograph
13.2" x 16.5" based on oil, The HUNTERS. Courtesy of
National Museums & Galleries on Merseyside, Walker
Art Gallery, Liverpool.

George appear in *"Children in White # 2."*[M019] Nora was the daughter of McLure's sister, Mrs. King.<3>   The children appear again in *"Four Children on the Beach."*[A209]   In another portrait, *"Grandmother & Child,"* George's grandmother, Mrs. Caroline D. Hamilton, was portrayed with little George squirming on her lap.[A059]

George Hall is not portrayed again until he is a half-grown boy, about seven years old, in *"The Hunters,"* an oil, which became the lithograph, *"Young Britons Coursing."* [A210]   In this group portrait, three almost-naked boys appear with a dog, a slain rabbit, and butchering a large game animal on the ground. At this age, George was already an excellent Chess player, according to William H. Pickering (Professor of Astronomy at HARVARD COLLEGE) and a skilled mathematician.<4>

About two years later, George and his grandmother appear side by side, on a couch in a portrait called *"Knitting Lesson."* Mrs. Anna Lea Merritt, who was a painter, a friend of McLure since his teens, and a P.A.F.A. contact in the 1890s said that this portrait was the best child's portrait ever done. It was reproduced and commented upon in the magazine story in which Mrs. Merritt was interviewed as a prominent artist.<5>   Earlier, it was exhibited at the *World's Columbian Exposition* in Chicago (1893) and Hamilton won his first gold medal for it. Harrison S. Morris, President of the P.A.F.A. and an authority on Hamilton's art from 1896 through 1936, thought it was an outstanding work comparing youth and age. <6,7>

The portrait, the *"Young Navigator,"* except for its date, could easily represent George as a young teenager because he was small for his age.<8> [A211]

George briefly attended the Pennsylvania Military Academy in the year McLure painted *"Dr. Riche"* for Central High School's alumni class.<9>

George obtained his Bachelor of Arts degree from Cambridge University.<10> He volunteered as a workman at the Oxford Observatory under Professor Turner, perhaps for two years. Professor Pickering reported that George became an expert machinist and optical bench technician during those years. The previous year, George had obtained his Master of Arts degree from Trinity College.<11> He was then

employed as professor of astronomy, French, and physics at
Bellevue College for the next four years.<12> The College
was located near the village of Fort Collins, a U. S.
military reservation. He expected to go to England, but
McLure worked behind the scenes to defeat George's plan to
work on a project there. The artist felt that the proposed
project was at that moment in the World War's history, "insane
for a civilian."<13>

    As World War I was ending, McLure and Clara gave George
the house and three tracts of farm land in Zieglerville,
PA.<14>

    Prof. Pickering met George when was appointed as staff
astronomer at the Lowell Observatory of Harvard College, at
Flagstaff, AZ. McLure thought this was where his son should
be and where his fatherly ambitions for him might be
satisfied.<15,16>

    McLure reported, "an era of perpetual sunshine has fallen on that part of the
world, where peace and plenty might keep George far from the strife of noise in the air at
Washington, D. C. and of guns at the front... If George were 'fit,' he would be preparing with
the rest of the young men to go over to fight." <17>

    A while later (1920), George read several papers
presenting his research at a scientific association meeting
in El Paso, TX.<18>   McLure, the proud father, sent copies
of these papers to his pen pal, Mrs. Drew. George was
elected to the *Royal Astronomical Society* shortly
thereafter.

    In 1922, George met and married a fellow mathematician
and astronomer, Elizabeth Langdon Williams, who preferred to
be called Langdon.<19> They honeymooned at a Prescott, AZ
mining property where George had a financial interest. His
wife was a serious, scolarly person five years his senior.
She was then forty-three and he was thirty-eight.<20,21>

    Twenty-three years earlier, Langdon matriculated at
Boston's MASSACHUSETTS INSTITUTE OF TECHNOLOGY (M.I.T.) and
graduated validictorian of her class. As a result, a local
newspaper published her photograph and story.<22> She led
the class in math and at commencement, she read her
scientific paper on physics titled, *"An Analytical Study of
the Fresnel Wave Surface."* Her abstract which she read

YOUNG NAVIGATOR, 1884. Oil 58" x 38 1/2." Courtesy of Sotheby's, Inc., New York.

astounded mathematicians in the audience to a surprising degree. Langdon was the first woman invited to speak at M.I.T's commencement. Along with ten young men, she participated in the program at the graduation exercises in the *Rogers Auditorium* on June 9, 1903. She was awarded a Bachelor of Science degree from M.I.T.

Langdon was preeminently a mathematician, and had planned the teaching of math as her life's work. In sexist language, Langdon was described by the BOSTON GLOBE's journalist as " a girl student, slender, tall, thoughtful and intelligent." Langdon " had won her distinguished honors by her perseverence of industry and her application to the work that she had in hand. Her grandmother reported that she did not participate in any evening entertainment. She would retire to her room with her mind all absorbed in her school studies to a late hour. If her mind had been absorbed in the whist table, the ball game, the dance hall, and kindred matters, she would not have attained this honorable achievement." <23>

Langdon was a computer and mathematician who had been assistant to Dr. Percival Lowell (Harvard College) for fifteen years following her graduation.

Until this time, George's parents had a very close relationship with him. His parents felt that their exclusive relationship was shattered by what they viewed as his impetuous decision to marry Langdon, an older woman. Since George was born, his father had looked upon him as an extension of himself. The hasty termination of that relationship emotionally devasted the parents and changed their plans to join him for a reunion that summer.<24,25>

At that time, McLure wrote, "the confusion of our lives becomes more exasperating and more unnerving every day! I find my energy is exhausted in the effort to control my emotions and there is little to be saved to meet the practical needs of life...The news (of George's marriage) was received quietly enough, (but) the after contemplation of this event has raked up emotions heretofore unknown." <26>

Children were part of George's thoughts while in America. For example, he presented an opinion that wheeling an infant with his head backward would have a deleterious effect on the future mental outlook of the child, because his first view of life would be backward and retrospective. "If this practice is not checked," he asserted, "the coming generation of Americans will be entirely deficient in forward-looking and forward-reaching ambition and we shall have a race of meditative, ruminative, chewing-the-cud people --- one may almost say a bovine race." <27>

Within a month after the newlyweds returned to their apartment on *Observatory Hill* (Flagstaff), George's parents arrived from London to meet their daughter-in-law, of whom George wrote, "I am delighted." <28>

Between 1923 and 1935, George and Langdon resided near Mandeville, the most English town in Jamaica, B.W.I. He worked at the Harvard Observatory with Prof. Pickering and later on his own with the able collaboration of Langdon.<29> The press in Jamaica regarded her as a renowned scientist. The geography of their site in the mountains of Manchester parish and the lack of air pollution made for excellent observations of the night sky, since no artificial lighting impeded planetary observations. In this period, George published several popular articles and a book.<30,31> He became the acknowledged expert on these topics. George understood the manufacture of reflecting telescopes for observations of heavenly bodies and built three while in Jamaica. Through their use he became an expert in planetary astronomy, developing a world-wide reputation. He pioneered in the modern study of Mars. He never quite gave up his belief in Schiaparelli's double "canals" (on Mars), which he felt were evidence for intelligent life there since he thought they were real constructions on the planet's surface.

George and Langdon went to Mandeville in 1923 to start work under Professor Pickering's supervision (with Harvard's equipment and support) for a few years. His studies were mainly focused on Mars. He also was an authority on Jupiter and its satellites and did some excellent work about the Moon.

During his third and subsequent years in Jamaica, George constructed telescopes for the HAMILTON OBSERVATORY that were of twenty-one inch aperature, because Harvard ceased to provide equipment and support for the colony of astronomers there.<32> These larger new telescopes clearly showed what George perceived to be the canals on Mars. George's research observations were greatly aided by his talent as an excellent machinist.<33> He steadfastly held that there was life on Mars in debates with Professor Pickering, but was quite modern in all his other views as judged in the standards of 1935. Prior to George's work in Jamaica, McLure painted a series of portraits of the famous French astronomer, *Camille Flammarion* (1842--1925, portraits

unlocated), and had done a profile of the Scotish
astronomer, *Prof. William Jack* (1834--1924), while in
Glasgow.[A590] George was elected to the *French Society of
Astronomy* for his scholarly work about 1925.[A028]

Following a surface reconciliation with George, his
parents supported their children's research in Jamaica but
the idyllic relations between the elder Hamiltons and their
only son may never have been the same.

George derived his mathematical proficiency from his
father and was described by Professor Pickering as a tiny,
neat, and positive man, shorter than his father.
Unfortunately, unlike his father, he was a chain (cigarette)
smoker, a habit his Presbyterian relatives would have
strongly criticized, and from which he probably developed
lung cancer at age fifty-one. McLure's legal and financial
problems during George's final illness probably tore the too
hastily-mended relationship between the generations. It may
have contributed to Langdon's departure to New Hampshire
after George's death the following year but during her
in-laws time of greatest need.<34>

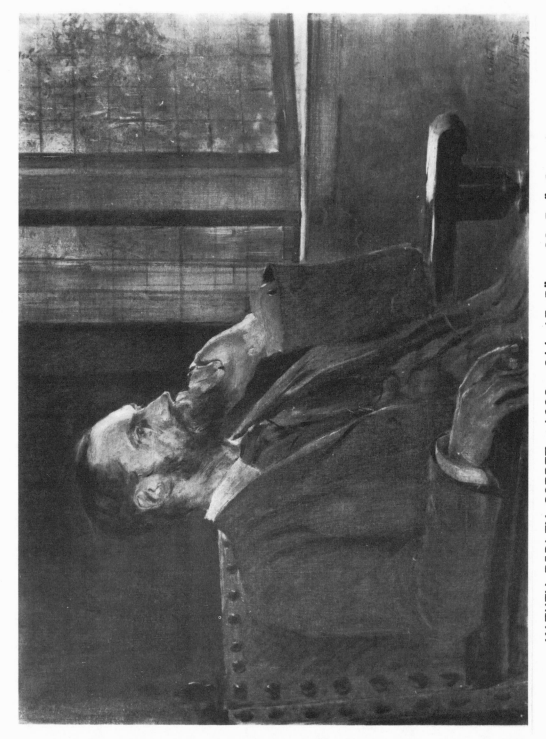

MATHEW RIDLEY CORBET, 1893. Oil 17.5" x 23.5." Courtesy of the National Portrait Gallery, London. Gift of the artist.

(Waverly, Photographer to the Queen. 164 Regent St.,
London) EDWARD ONSLOW FORD, c. 1892. Sepia photograph
8" x 10." Formerly at Christie's, London with a large
autograph collection.

REVERIE IN A BROWN CHAIR, c. 1870 showing Eakins influence. Oil 9 3/4" x 6.5" formerly at R. W. Skinner, Inc.

IX : ABODES, 1853--1936

Hamilton knew *Charles Darwin* and *Sanford Robinson Gifford* (1823--1880) and may have caught the explorer's bug to travel from them. Hamilton traveled to meet the demands of his profession and to further his career. Clearly, he was never a homeless, wandering Bohemian painter. He was, instead, probably the most purposeful and peripatetic artist of the period 1878 through 1931. From their residence in London, it is documented that McLure and Clara made more than forty trips to France, eleven to Glasgow, twelve between England and New York, one each to Austria, Belgium, Germany, and the Netherlands. While in America, they made two trips to Delaware, many to New York, several to Maine and eastern Canada (Ottawa and Montreal), five journeys to California, at least one each in the direction of Mexico and Oregon, three to Washington, D. C., one to Virginia, and four voyages to Jamaica. This Hamilton travel summary is unquestionably incomplete because of lost records and missing letters.

Though McLure's mental reference for home was always in Philadelphia, his focus was on his career and as a Nineteenth Century painter he had to travel to further his career or he would stagnate as a professional. To reconstruct McLure's birthplace, one must rely on the eyewitness accounts of various trained observers, since the building was demolished a generation ago.<1>[M006] First, a report in the words of a local watercolorist, *David J. Kennedy,* 'in the year 1844, I lived on the S. E. corner of

[Castle on mountain] Wood engraving 1 7/8" x 1.5" from T.B. Hennell's 1901 work (op. cit). Courtesy of Poetry Collection, Mitchell Library, Glasgow.

Schuylkill Eighth St. and Rittenhouse (now 16th & Summer Sts.). The walls of *Lloyd's Row* (houses) were put up, and the floor joists laid, no roofs or cornices, the cellars full of water, no curbing, paving, or pavements laid, all was soft deep mud; opposite on the N. side were the brick yards extending out to *Schuylkill Fifth St.*, brick kilns and large deep holes full of water where the brick clay has been dug out. No railings around *Logan Square*, only two, three-story brick houses (now Nos. 1617 and 1619) there now, occupied the N. side of *Race St.* from 16th to 17th St., with three cellars dug E. of them, which remained so for several years."<2>

Another report was from eyewitness, *Mr. Joseph Sorger,* a knowledgeable antiquarian furniture dealer who lived on Lloyd's Row (1624 Summer St.) for thirteen years starting in the 1960s.<3> He remembered that (HAMILTON HOUSE) No. 1600 was a *Greek Revival Building*, architecturally comparable to *Strickland's Portico Row* (S. side of Spruce St. between 9th & 10th Sts.) Some significant differences recorded in the watercolor sketch (Kennedy, 1845 now at the H.S.P., Mss. Room) suggest that relocation of the entrance of No. 1600 must have occurred many years after the building was erected, perhaps after the fire of 1885. At the date of Kennedy's sketch, the marble steps were not installed. He reported that various construction problems caused delays of about five years before Lloyd's Row houses, including Hamilton's house, could be occupied. The architect for the houses was *Thomas Ustick Walter* (1804--1887) and the house eventually occupied by John Hamilton, Sr. and family was situated on the S. W. corner of 16th & Summer Sts. (directly opposite Kennedy's observation point). The houses were three stories tall with level grade roofs. Hamilton's house was the mirror image of the property at S. E. corner of 17th St.; a photograph of which appeared in 1973.<4> From these three sources, enough details can be obtained to describe the facade (on Summer St.), containing five pilasters measuring 24" wide by 4" deep, extending down from cornice level past the above ground level basement to the pavement. The house had oversized windows and the building's exterior was painted grey in Mr. Sorger's day. Further, he reported that he inspected the interior of the *Hamilton House*. It contained fireplaces, located in the front room and back room on each floor. Some rooms still had elegant black marble mantles intact and the wooden trim throughout the house was of Egyptian motif, narrow above and broadening

(David J. Kennedy) 1845. Watercolor on paper drawing 5 1/4" x 9 1/4." South side 16th and Summer Street, Philadelphia during construction of HAMILTON HOUSE at S.W. corner of 16th. The Historical Society of Pennsylvania.

WILLIAM TROST RICHARDS, 1906. Oil 46 1/4" x 36 1/8."
Courtesy of the Pennsylvania Academy of the Fine Arts,
Philadelphia. Pennsylvania Academy purchase.

[Figure study : two women reading], c. 1893. Pastel on laid paper 24 5/8" x 19." Courtesy of the Pennsylvania Academy of the Fine Arts, Philadelphia. Gift of the Fellowship, P.A.F.A.

toward the floors. The main entry doorway of Hamilton's house had been relocated to Summer St. by Mr. Sorger's day; however, the probable reason and time of the changes were suggested earlier. The house was set back on the lot and measured 36 feet deep. In front, a brick pathway framed a mini-garden area around a centrally located oval potted planting. Also, behind the house, there was a garden.

In the late 1970s, Hamilton's house, together with all of Lloyd's Row, was razed despite a valiant effort to save these architecturally significant buildings from the wrecker's ball. This struggle, led by Mr. Sorger, went to the U. S. Capitol's historical commission on architecture. The Commission felt that Lloyd's Row was an important example of the period and that the unique houses were worthy of preservation. Today the *Wyndham Franklin Plaza Hotel* (2 Franklin Plaza) covers the site of Hamilton's house.

At age seventeen, McLure moved out of Hamilton House in 1870 recently after being baptized. This was a precaution to protect the new Central High School alumnus from the potential evils of art school, where he would soon matriculate. McLure's new address was closer to the P.A.F.A. on Chestnut St. and the school was located in temporary, rented quarters between 10th & 11th St.<5>

While in high school, he had received the required one to three lessons per week of drawing instruction and training in penmanship mandated of all students for each term of the four years.<6>

Other distinguished artist/alumni of *Central* included William Sartain,* Dewey Bates,* James B. Sword,* William Trost Richards,* Thomas C. Eakins,* Albert Rosenthal,* William Bispham, the brothers Louis and William Glackens, John W. Louderbach, Frank M. Howarth, and Augustus Koopman. There is evidence that Hamilton knew the first six. All were important enough for Edmonds to mention in his book about successful alumni of *Central High School*, while Hamilton was omitted perhaps because he was living in London according to its POST OFFICE DIRECTORY. Hamilton's painting of Dr. Riche was reproduced in Edmonds' volume. Hamilton later painted Edmonds' portrait.<7>[unlocated]

At age twenty-five, McLure became recognized exhibiting his *"L'Academie pour Rire"* and the oil,*"Cerise"* aka *"Le*

Rire" in Philadelphia and New York.<8,9> In January, 1878,
he relocated to London permanently, having visited as an art
student earlier.<10> His first documented addresses there
(in 1881) were 41A Cathcart Road, S. W. *Kensington*, and
later at 6 William Street, *Albert Gate*.<11,12> They were
probably rented apartments. By this time, he was accompanied
by his favorite model, his wife, Clara. (Refer to Tab. **G**
for a display of McLure's abodes arranged chronologically
during his seventy-two year career.) Clara was portrayed in
oils on a small, wooden panel titled, "*Tears*," which is
signed and dated 1879. It was donated to P.A.F.A. in late
1936, accompanied by a note recognizing that it was the
first oil done in London by McLure and sold for the
equivalent of $ 5.00 at the time it was painted.<13>

     The Hamiltons lived in a number of houses in London,
all more or less interesting, and some unusually attractive
and individual.<14> Was the artist always seeking new
backdrops and props for his paintings? Their next residence
was *Grey House*, at 102 Hornton St. situated near the corner
of Abbey Mews in the district of Kensington, where George
was born in January, 1884.<15>

     Starting in 1889, McLure's fourth residence was *Alpha
House* in *Regent Park,* N. W. London. Its garden was designed
by one of the gardeners of the grounds of the *Crystal
Palace,* and it contained a weeping ash (tree) supposed to be
the largest in England. While living there, Hamilton painted
the series of Gladstone portraits, the portraits of
Professor Tyndall, and *Cardinal Manning.*   The household was
served by a butler, cook, and housemaid.<16>   In
anticipation of McLure's trip to Austria for an invited
sitting by *Price Otto von Bismarck*, McLure sublet Alpha
House to the actress, sculptress, and writer, *Sarah
Bernhardt* (c.1892).<17>

     Several years later, the Hamiltons moved (c.1898) to
Murestead at 6 Grove End Road, N. W., *St. John's Woods*.<18>
The house's name was derived from "a fine mulberry tree which bore each
year the most delicious fruit. The house cointained a great deal of old oak (paneling), Dutch
tile (fireplaces, etc), and the garden abutted *Lords Cricket Grounds* where the great people of
the U. K. assembled yearly to see their sons and heirs from Eton, Harrow, and the universities
play cricket. Here Hamilton painted the portraits of William Trost Richards, Edward Onslow Ford,
Sir Alfred Gilbert, Edward Honor Coates,' and many others.<19> In 1903, the
Hamiltons moved to No. 12, remaining there until 1910.
<20>[A103]

McLure developed serious ties with the largest newspaper in the U. K., *THE GLASGOW EVENING TIMES.* McLure and Clara may have lived at a studio in town initially, since at least ten short expeditions north to Scotland have been documented. The longest expedition lasted about eight months. McLure's name appeared in the *Postal Directory* at a six-story building now occupied by offices in the center of the old city. It is not far from the *Gladstone statue*, a sketch of which McLure published on the occasion of the dedication of the new city park where it was installed.<21>

Perhaps Hamilton's many successes in Scotland led to a better offer in London. The family, including McLure, Clara, Mrs. Caroline D. Hamilton, and Clara's niece, moved to their most elegant residence, *The Hermitage.*[A152] It was located on the Portsmouth Road at *Kingston-on-Thames.*<22> At this time, George was earning his master's degree. This house would be the Hamiltons base in England until 1931.<23> It overlooked *Hampton Court Meadows* and the *River Thames.* The house was "a small old-fashioned, ivy-clad brick house with a loggia, and contained many large lofts and rooms used as studios." In this house, Hamilton finished the series of pastel drawings in October 1915 that were begun in Italy in 1911. It was in this residence that several portraits of McLure's mother were painted from earlier studies, which according to Howe, may have disturbed Whistler, who had already popularized the theme.[A060] Hamilton also painted portraits of *Prime Minister Balfour, Lord Armistead, Baron Henry N. Gladstone,* and *Sir Archibald Geike* while in this house.

Since 1898, interwoven among the memories of all the houses mentioned, there is the Hamiltons' vacation house, *Stone Hall* at Wolfscastle, Pembrokshire.[A569] Frequently, McLure and Clara fished and shot birds for sport there in one of the prettiest valleys in that picturesque county of Wales.<24>

While the Hamiltons were away between 1919 and 1920, their *Hermitage* property was sublet to Emma Bye and Martha Cheeseman.<25> The Hamiltons' dog, *Belle,* and the caged canary were part of the deal.[A220] In 1929, tenants Arthur and Mary Smith, occupied the house while the Hamiltons were abroad.<26,27> From 1932 through 1933, it appears that the house was unoccupied; however, in 1934 William Sherrin bought it and renamed it *The Hermitage Club.*<28> From 1940 through 1946, no occupancy data was available, implying perhaps that it was empty. In 1970, the property was razed and a six-story apartment complex was built, called simply *The Hermitage*.

(For comments about *HAMILTON HALL*, the Jamaican abode for the family, refer to the chapter "Decline & Adieu" where its selection, relative size, cost, and functions are discussed.)

In summary, the Hamiltons lived in numerous apartments, hotels, and houses many of which are documented through their fifty-seven years of marriage and business partnership.(Tab. H)   Vignettes of their many locations appear in documented oil paintings and pastels, showing their gardens, pets, kitchens, porches, living rooms, other family members, and guests of high-born and average social status. An anonymous art critic and an anonymous journalist allocated several pages to descriptions of the Hamilton abodes using words like *"beautiful"* and *"warm"* to convey the physical appearance and domestic tranquility of the homes documented following inspection. It seems, however, that as both McLure and Clara were born in Philadelphia and remained loyal, they were American expatriates to the end of their days. Philadelphia remained McLure and Clara's favorite abode. They continued to own property in Pennsylvania until their respective estates were settled in 1940.

CHARLES E. DANA, JOHN McLURE HAMILTON, HENRY J. THOURON, & HERBERT WELSH, c. 1895. Oil 33 7/8" x 49 1/8." Courtesy of the Pennsylvania Academy of the Fine Arts, Philadelphia. Gift of Charles Morris Young.

ARTIST'S CAREER

KING GEORGE V, March 25, 1911, Buckingham Palace for London's DAILY CHRONICLE feature called Historical Portrait Scenes of the Coronation printed separately by T. R. Way. Courtesy of the Victoria & Albert Museum, Print Room.

X : LONDON PERIOD,1878--1902

Hamilton was encouraged to settle in London by a friend, *Joseph Rowley,* who was one of seven cricket-playing brothers.<1> An artist's opportunity of a lifetime can develop as the result of personal recommendations, serendipity, or random luck. Such was the case in the early 1890s when three charming young daughters of Joseph Rowley made an appointment to visit the Alpha House residence of Hamilton. While they were there, they suggested that he seek an opportunity to paint "the most famous man of the 19th Century : William Ewart Gladstone." The lead spokesperson for this idea was *Maud Rowley,* (later Mrs. Strickland), whose family had lived in the parish of *Hawarden* near the Gladstones and the *Glynnes.*<2>

Mrs. W. E. Gladstone was born Catherine Glynne. Her daughter, *Mrs. Mary Gladstone Drew* (1847--1927), became a thirty-five-year long pen pal, confidante, and friend of McLure and Clara Hamilton. The artist accepted an invitation to paint W. E. Gladstone and twenty-three known portraits were executed in watercolors, pastels, oils, and sculpture during a five year period. In this series of portraits, Hamilton captured the *Prime Minister*, his wife, and other family members in their daily routines. One oil portrait of the Prime Minister was even exhibited in the *Paris Salon* of May, 1892, where it received an *honorable mention.*<3> This was a rare distinction for an outsider's work, especially for an American. Subsequently, that portrait was purchased for $ 5,000.00 by the Government for the National Museum

[Mr. Gladstone at Hawarden Castle], 1899. Color lithograph on tan paper 8.5" x 10." Courtesy of the Pennsylvania Academy of the Fine Arts, Philadelphia.

Prime Minister WILLIAM EWART GLADSTONE, Hawarden, Sept., 1890 reading a history of Parliament. Oil 18" x 24." Courtesy of Luxembourg Palace, Musee D'Orsay, <c> Photo R. M. N., Paris.

being created at the LUXEMBOURG PALACE in Paris.<4>[A044]
The collection was a unique grouping of *Modern Art* and at
the time, only two other American painters had been so
honored. These were *John Singer Sargent* ("Carmencita") and
James Abbott Mc Neill Whistler ("Mother"). When Whistler
heard of Hamilton's selection for this world-class
distinction, he was mightily vexed. He exclaimed, "why drag
in Hamilton ?"<5> Hamilton was far younger than Whistler,
never as flamboyant, and always a gentleman. Hamilton was a
devoted admirer of Whistler's etchings and paintings, never
missing an exhibition of the works of a man whose talent he
worshiped.<6> Hamilton thought Whistler was a better etcher
than *Rembrandt*. Some say that the measure of a man is the
enemies that he made in his profession. In 1890, Hamilton,
age 37, became the mortal enemy of his fellow artist, Jimmy
Whistler. It appears that Hamilton had entered the big time
arena for world-class painters.<7> Whistler was also an
American expatriate artist. Definitely, Whistler was a
person bent on making history in 1862. From then on he
influenced the prevailing values and attitudes in art in
that period. Although Hamilton did not make his acquaintance
until very late in Whistler's life, the elder became and
remained his enemy. Whistler had accused, tried, and
convicted Hamilton for high crimes and misdemeanors. The
crimes existed only in the elder artist's perception of
events surrounding publication of THE GENTLE ART OF MAKING
ENEMIES. The misperceptions were incited by the viperous
Sheridan Ford.<8> An objective presentation of the facts of
this affair was published in Hamilton's own words and
attested to by *Joseph Pennell,* Sheridan Ford, and
subsequently by others. Whistler was so self-righteous that
he even refused an invitation to Hamilton's home on March
28, 1890, presumably because of views Whistler had of
Hamilton's activity. This activity was falsely reported by
Sheridan Ford and subjectively perceived by Whistler.<9>
Whistler strenuously objected to Hamilton's *"Gladstone"*
being hung at the Luxembourg, even though he had personally
selected one of Hamilton's paintings for the *International
Exposition* of 1898.<10> Later, Whistler refused to speak to
Hamilton at Pennell's home when both were present.<11,12>

(Refer to Tab. **I** which displays the names of about
forty other influential friends of the Hamiltons on the
petals of a rose with Clara & McLure at the center.)

Hamilton had been accorded three opportunities to paint

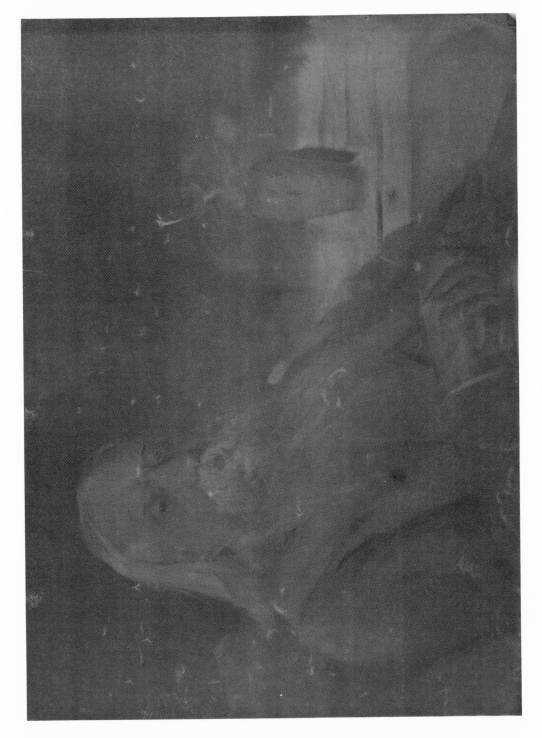

ALEXANDER ANTON von WERNER, Professor of Painting at Berlin and Prince Bismarck's portraitist, 1892. Oil 18" x 24." Formerly in the collection of Harry Burke.

a portrait of Mr. Gladstone. The first was during a thirty day expedition to *Hawarden Castle,* the Prime Minister's private residence located in Flintshire, N. Wales. During this visit, Hamilton stayed at the nearby *INN AT QUEEN'S FERRY.* The second opportunity was at Number 10, Downing Street, and the third opportunity was back at the *Castle,* near the *Dee River* bank. (Years later, the artist was again commissioned to paint *"Paul Wayland Bartlett"* for the *Luxembourg Collection.*<13>[A006]

In mid June, 1892, Mr. Gladstone, a member of Parliament, wrote on Hamilton's behalf to the former Austrian *Chancellor,* Prince Otto von Bismarck. Mr. Gladstone suggested that a portrait sitting be granted to Hamilton at the artist's instigation.<14>   As a calling card introducing Hamilton to the Chancellor, the artist painted *"Professor of Art: Anton Alexander von Werner,"* the official Court Painter at Berlin.[A133]   After passing the test, Hamilton was granted a sitting and invited to dine with the great man and his family.<15>   Hamilton painted four works of Prince Bismarck, one in oil.<16>[A008]

During 1893, Edward Onslow Ford sculpted a bronze bust of McLure's father, *"George Hamilton, M. D.,"* from memory and he also sculpted the artist from life (*"John McLure Hamilton").*<17>[A007]   Hamilton painted *"Master Wolfram Ford"* and *"Edward Onslow Ford"* about this time.[A029, A030, M008]   That same year, Hamilton exhibited three works at Chicago's *Columbian Exposition* and served on its *Advisory Committee for England.* One Hamilton oil, *"Madonna & Infant Christ,"* disappeared. Earlier, it had been exhibited in Paris and Vienna. *Mrs. Myles Kennedy* posed for the painting with her son in her arms.<18> Professor Thomas C. Eakins, one of the artist's teachers, mentors, and friends, portrayed Hamilton in oils in 1895.<19>

The next year, Hamilton had a major one-man-show at the internationally famous GOUPIL & Company, which received considerable acclaim in the press in London, Paris and New York.<20> Another former teacher of Hamilton and of Eakins, *Gerome,* was related to the Gallery's owner by marriage. In November of the same year, McLure and Clara, fat and sassy, vacationed in *St. Moritz* at the *Hotel Kulm.*<21>

Hamilton had a good year in 1897. He sent several works for the *Annual Exhibition* at his *alma mater* (P.A.F.A.). The

"*Nunnery Garden*" had a price tag of $ 3,000.00 and one of the "*W. E. Gladstone*" series of oils was advertised at $ 5,000.00, with the stipulation that it was going to be exhibited in the *Paris Salon* in 1897. By the end of December, McLure and Clara returned to Paris for four months. While in Paris, George bought old books from street vendors reminiscent of his Philadelphia grandfather's activity.<22>

By mid May, 1898 Hamilton had lost a major benefactor, the former Prime Minister, Mr. Gladstone. Hamilton wrote a condolence letter to the *Prime Minister's* daughter, Mrs. Drew and to her mother expressing his sympathy, admiration, and respect for his former patron.<23,24>

The Pennell and Hamilton families had a close relationship for nearly twenty years. Hamilton was Joe's surrogate older brother and Pennell was McLure's voice of critical analysis and business agent with the Art Establishment. Both families often wrote, socialized, and dined together. Professional and technical advice was given and received kindly between the men. Pennell worked for the *London* DAILY CHRONICLE and was a professor at the *Slade School*.<25> At this time, Hamilton created a lithograph of "Gladstone" and liked the reproduction so well that he made several different color editions of it.<26> He also created a lithograph, "*Machiavelli*" on a stone. He continued the series of what would become more than one hundred varieties of lithographic subjects. Hamilton became famous in that medium, as well. Soon, the artist was elected to the *Senefelder Club* (London) and Joseph Pennell was its first President.<27> The following year, McLure and Clara went to Italy (Venice and Rome) on business.<28> In 1900, Hamilton's *alma mater* bought his marvelous pastel of "*Edward Cardinal Manning*" for $ 300.<29,30>

The next year (1901) was another gold medal year, the second year of four for Hamilton. McLure exhibited the portrait of "*Professor Henry Thouron*," a friend since 1878, at Buffalo, New York's competition.<31> He also exhibited "*Gladstone at Downing Street.*"[A042] This work was eventually purchased and donated to the P.A.F.A by Edward Honor Coates and a group of other friends of the artist. During this year, Hamilton was still residing in Glasgow and his time was mostly occupied with newspaper, documentary art, or graphic journalism and exhibiting abroad. From late

August, 1902 through April of 1903, his PROMINENT PROFILES series of caricatures, portraying distinguished Scots like the *Very Reverend Principal* John Story of *Glasgow University*, appeared weekly.[A588]

ANNA LEA MERRITT, painter, 1906. Oil 24" x 18."
Courtesy of the Pennsylvania Academy of the Fine Arts, Philadelphia. Gift of Arthur H. Lea.

XI : GLASGOW PERIOD, 1903--1909

John McLure Hamilton exhibited at the *Royal Glasgow Institute of Fine Arts* first during the 1881 season. He submitted pastels, oils, and lithographs for *Glowigeans* to admire and to buy.<1> Although Hamilton had won two gold medals already, for the next ten years he still worked as a documentary artist for newspapers.<2> His period of greatest productivity is measured by the frequency of his publications.<3> He contributed caricatures of real people, allegorical cartoon characters, and impressions of major news events.<4> Hamilton recorded what he saw on his drawing pad. His earliest material appeared in THE BAILIE newspaper, which was issued once a week.<5> Since the paper sold for one penny, its high price probably limited its circulation to a middle and upper class cultured, prosperous readership in Scotland and elsewhere in the U. K.<6,7>

At the same time, Hamilton was employed by another publication under the same ownership, THE EVENING TIMES. It was the third Glasgow paper published in *Edinburgh,* and it was owned by *George Outram & Co.* The paper's format was nine columns per page and exactly eight pages were issued daily. It circulated to 250,000 readers each day and boasted proudly that it was the largest afternoon paper in the U. K. This newspaper sold for only half a penny. Hamilton's work frequently appeared there from September 2nd, 1902 through April 12th, 1905. His best known specialty was a feature on Wednesdays that he pioneered called PROMINENT PROFILES. It was located in a dedicated space at the top of page four. It

Very Rev. Principal, Glasgow University, JOHN STORY,
D.D., LL.D., 1902 IX 15. Ink & sepia drawing 9" x 6"
for PROMINENT PROFILES engraving, "Senatus Academicus,"
1903 IV 22.   Courtesy Glasgow Art Gallery,
Kelvingrove Street.

from the
New York Herald.

SIR THOMAS LIPTON AND THE CUP.

Sir THOMAS LIPTON from THE BAILIE 1903 VIII 19
engraving. 8.5" x 5.5." Courtesy Mitchell Library,
Glasgow Collection.

occupied two column widths and more than two columns in the length. In all it appeared 136 times without interruption. [A259, A461, A588, A593] A typical *Prominent Profiles*, within a bold bordering box, exhibited a Hamilton-conceived coat-of-arms in the upper left corner. It provided a clue to the subject's occupation or avocation. All but one of the subjects were men. The profile of the famous Scot being honored was at its center. At the bottom, a legend or citation proclaimed the reason in a word or two. Strangely, the sketch was never accompanied by a paragraph of explanation providing the person's identity, biography, career activity, and the like. One wonders if *Prominent Profiles* was intended as a guessing game thought of by the artist and agreed to by the editor.

When Hamilton emmigrated from Scotland, presumably for greener pastures in London, *Tom Maxwell* took over his now well-known feature, *Prominent Profiles*. However, now it lacked the bordering box and the familiar Hamilton-designed coat-of-arms. During Hamilton's tenure as the artist to the EVENING TIMES, he published cartoons, editorial cartoons, news (feature) documentary drawings, portrait sketches, *Prominent Profiles*, etc. at a rate of about one per day.<8> His documented work is signed variously : "H," "JMH," "J. McLure Hamilton," "J. M. Hamilton," boxed "J. M. Hamilton," or with his holographic signature as though he were searching for the correct identification for posterity to label his art. Referring to Hamilton, the phrase "our artist" is mentioned respectfully and proudly many times in the pages of the EVENING TIMES.<9> Prior to Hamilton's employment by the paper, the EVENING TIMES did not print illustrations of any kind for any purpose. By the height of Hamilton's Glasgow Period, there were five regular contributors of art in the newspaper besides Hamilton.<10>

The paper's layout was changed specifically to accomodate art by Hamilton when he was hired. The layout changed from a six column page done in monotonous black ink and a tiny type on white paper, to a two-color-ink illustrated format with considerable eye appeal.<11> Prior to Hamilton's tenure, it was rare to find a photograph on its pages and infrequently an ad with accompanying line drawings. However, under Hamilton's influence, graphics were introduced to break up the paper's earlier line-on-line of type. His drawings informed, entertained and educated the reader to the changing fashions of the day and to subjects like alcohol abuse.<12> The paper was issued six days per week and never on Sundays. Examples of his reports include news about the Glasgow visit of King Edward VII and Queen Alexandra with portrait studies. Similarly, he drew Mr. Neville Chamberlain and young Mr. Winston S. Churchill. He also recorded the visit of the Italian King, Victor Emanuel III and Queen, Helena.<13>

Hamilton's success can be explained in part by his willingness to travel to every small village and town. He recorded unusual events, whether of secular or religious character.<14> His official travels brought him to London and Edinburgh. Thus, his *news beat* was all of the U. K., including Wales and Ireland, where he exhibited his art as early as 1880.<15>

When there was a major news event happening anywhere in the U. K., the EVENING TIMES dispatched Hamilton to document it producing a diaryist record. Perhaps he traveled tens of thousands of miles by bicycle, as his long-time friend *Joseph Pennell* did, or in part by train or even by barge. Although he was the fine artist to the paper, he frequently provided quick sketches of the worthies, the superstars, and the near greats of the late 19th and early 20th Century for his readers. Hamilton wasn't the exclusive artist for the paper, but he always had been its expert art director with specialties such as new buildings, genre pieces, and portraits.<16>

It was during his Glasgow years that Hamilton exhibited at five U. S. cities, London, and Paris.<17> He was elected to *honorary membership* in Philadelphia's unique Sketch Club because all of his portraits were recognized by local experts as brilliant.<18>

In Buffalo's *Pan-American Exposition*, he was awarded a second gold medal for his oils and at St. Louis' *Louisana Purchase Exposition,* Hamilton's work was recognized with a third gold medal. Nevertheless, Hamilton's career view was panoramic and his turf became most of the English-speaking world. He would never be regarded merely as one of the *Glasgow Boys*.<19>

It seemed Hamilton was a thrifty man of many skills, many media for expression of his ideas, and considerable creative industry. He was blessed with Clara, his supportive

Lord JOHN KELVIN, 1903. Color lithograph from the
luxury edition, PROMINENT PROFILES. 9.5" x 6.5."
Courtesy Mitchell Library, Glasgow Collection.

[Highlander proposing the toast to Queen Victoria],
1898. Engraving from THE BAILIE. 9" x 6." Courtesy
Mitchell Library, Glasgow Collection.

wife, and generous family. It is not surprising that he was
listed under several designations in the POST OFFICE
DIRECTORY, a hybrid publication produced when an old-
fashioned city directory was crossed with a yellow pages
phone book minus the phone numbers.<20> When most
practioners of photography were content with *contact
printing*, Hamilton made enlargements. He advertised his
skills in the POST OFFICE DIRECTORY to the trade as an
enlarger of photographs. He continued to own a camera
through 1936 for photo-documentation.<21> His studio was
situated at 93 Hope Street, Glasgow.[M030]

XII : SUCCESS AFTER GLASGOW, 1910--1919

King George V chose Hamilton to draw his regal portrait
(sans coat-of-arms) after seeing the *Prominent Profiles*.<1>
The resultant Coronation piece presents a fresh, youthful,
full face image of the King in uniform.[A035] By this
time, Hamilton had painted many portraits of the most prized
subjects possible for an artist of the Transitional Age.<2>
Because of all his earlier commissions, the artist had high
name recognition. And "Hamilton" clearly belonged on such
important state documentary art as a Coronation drawing.<3>

Hamilton had painted more celebrities than any other
artist of the day. Many discriminating critics contended
that *Hamilton had invariably painted them best*.<4> After
all, how many other artists had portrayed *seven Prime*
Ministers, three Kings and three Queens before they were
fifty-eight years old? <5>

Emery Walker presented a photogravure print (1910) of
the small *"Gladstone"* portrait, when Baron Henry Neville
Gladstone became Governor General of a United South Africa.
Meanwhile, Hamilton was exhibiting his other works in Italy,
France, and later in Berlin, Dusseldorf, and Munich. The
French government bought his little "Gladstone" for
$ 5,000.00 in 1892.<6>

The artist served on the jury of selection for the
Panana-Pacific Exposition.<7> McLure and Clara made another
trans-atlantic voyage to the port of New York, traveling to

I. INFLUENTIAL FRIENDS OF HAMILTON'S CAREER
IN EUROPE & AMERICA, 1879--1936 (N=46)

100

PROMINENT PROFILES.

"LIBRARIES."

LIBRARIES [= ANDREW CARNEGIE], 1903. Engraving from the
EVENING TIMES. Courtesy Mitchell Library, Glasgow
Collection.

Wilmington, DE to visit with his relatives.<8> Finally, they headed west to San Francisco, CA for the *Exposition*.

During 1915, Hamilton lost his beloved mother, Caroline, at age eighty-nine.<9> She had been a member of his entourage since 1886, during the artist's Glasgow and London periods.<10>

After his mother's death, Hamilton took Clara to *Montreal* where her relative through marriage, Kenneth G. Rea, F.R.I.B.A., practiced (architecture) and resided with his children.<11> While in Canada, McLure was commissioned to paint a portrait of Jack Ross, who had just endowed a building for the school at Lennox[ville].<12> Mr. Ross was an engineer and capitalist who built part of Canada's railway.

As befits a veteran newspaper man, Hamilton remained a keen observer of the world's political events and trends. He commented upon current events for the press in many places, including China and France.<13> He had done the same work in the 1890s for *THE BAILIE* and *THE EVENING TIMES*.<14>

Next, McLure and Clara visited Pasadena, CA for a caucus of Lithographers in 1915.<16> The *Print Makers of Los Angeles* (later the *Print Makers Society of California*) had been organized in 1915 near *Arryo Seco*, west of Pasadena.<17> Five years later, McLure was exhibiting in this medium in Europe and America.<18> The shows were first staged at the *Museum of History, Science and Art* and subsequently at the *Los Angeles Museum' Exposition Park*, where his prints of *"Sarah* (Bernhardt)" were exhibited.

In 1917, Hamilton's mail was being directed to *Drexel & Company* (at Philadelphia) while the team traveled to *Hot Springs, VA* then *Bar Harbor, ME*, where the Dr. John Madison Taylors had a vacation home.<19> The team then returned to New York City by December 27th for Christmas with the *Pennells*.

In a reversal of roles, *Wayman Adams* was commissioned to paint a portrait of John McLure Hamilton (before January, 1918 when Hamilton was awarded the P.A.F.A's lifetime achievement gold medal). In Hamilton's opinion, it was a remarkable painting. Hamilton stood tall in the foreground, caped, hatted, gloved, and fringed by Thomas Sully-esque clouds before a blue sky field.<20>[M009]

  Charles Carroll Glover (President, Riggs National Bank, Washington, D. C. and a power at the *Corcoran Gallery of Art)* was a loyal supporter and friend of the Hamiltons for many years. McLure painted three oil portraits of Mr. Glover. The earliest portrays Charles Carroll Glover as a robust-standing, Sargent-esque, executive (1900) and the latest (1917) portrays him as a seated lion in the winter of his days.[A052,A053] In numerous letters to *Mr. C. Powell Minnigerode*, Corcoran Gallery's Director, Hamilton never failed to ask about his good friends, the Glovers. Mrs. Glover was the daughter of Admiral Pool.<21>

  The next year, 1918, was the pinnacle of Hamilton's career. He received his *fourth gold medal* at age sixty-five.<22> It was awarded by his beloved P.A.F.A. in recognition of high achievement in his profession, his 42 years as an exhibitor, *and* for being represented in the P.A.F.A's permanent collection 60 times.<23> Hamilton, always quick to volunteer for community service, was elected to serve as president of the Pennsylvania Academy of the Fine Art's *Fellowship,* a fraternal and beneficial organization for art students in Philadelphia.<24> This opportunity represented a fourth situation for which he could have been cited to receive the academy's medal, namely for eminent services in the cause of art and for service to the academy itself. Founded by his friend, J. H. Converse, the *Gold Medal of Honor,* had been awarded twenty-one times earlier, mostly to artists.<25>

  When in Philadelphia, McLure and Clara always stayed at the same famous *Ritz Carlton Hotel.*<26> In 1919, Hamilton set up a studio in his native city then vacationed during August in England.<27>

  A full-page spread, illustrating Hamilton's pastels, appeared in VANITY FAIR for August, 1919. The article, with minimum text, was titled, *"An American Master of Pastel."* It presented four portraits of Clara, including a rare one of her face. At the time, the pastels were exhibited at the *M. Knoedler Galleries* in New York City. The author of the magazine article revealed that French artists had always excelled in this medium, but that the American and the English artists had not until Hamilton. McLure's work was then likened to that of the 18th Century French master

George and Nora [=Children in white #2], c. 1890. Oil
with Goupil & Company London & New York canvas
markings 29" x 25."

MAUD & MUFFIN AT THE PIANO [=Mrs. Strickland & Mrs. Edwards, daughters of Joseph Rowley], c. 1893. Oil 18" x 24." Courtesy of Schwarz Gallery, Philadelphia.

Maurice Quentin de La Tour. A seeming paradox of Hamilton's career comes into focus. When he had immigrated permanently to England to seek his fortune (in 1878), he took only the shirt on his back.<28> Even though he was there for fifty-three years, he actually earned the majority of his income through exporting his English paintings to the United States.<29> The exact number of Hamilton trans-atlantic missions, sales trips, and expeditions is unknown. However, at least twenty were documented between 1872 and 1930. Much evidence suggests that McLure sent unaccompanied freight for exhibition and sales on dozens of additional occasions. Though he would pass for a fully-assimilated Englishman, in his heart, he called Philadelphia home.<30> He was in exile for more than sixty years and was ransomed by supportive Americans. The clearest evidence for his affinity to Philadelphia is the fact that he never sold the family home, *Hamilton House,* at 1600 Summer St.<31,32> Instead, it was always rented and his Zieglerville, PA farm probably was, too. Presumably, those funds were deposited to his account at *Drexel & Company.*<33> Hamilton never lost contact with his high school peers, academy friends, neighbors, fellow club members, and his extended family. Thus, the artist was a member in good standing of an old boy's network and remained an ardent member of that club to the end of his days. The social support system that he believed in functioned. Even in his eighties, in decaying health, and before social security in America, he paid his dues for more than sixty years by playing the club circuit simultaneously in England, Jamaica, and Philadelphia. He could fully expect the club system to support him, Clara, and their desire for a memorial museum in the relatively primitive wilderness of Mandeville in the 1930s.

XIII : THE APEX, 1920--1929

The year 1920 provided public recognition of the artist's excellence after a long audition and a productive exhibition career as a painter in Europe and America. (*See*: Tables **H, I, J, & K** for a display of the objective evidence which supports this statement.) In January, Hamilton had exhibited at the *Corcoran Gallery* and his works included "*Cyrus. H. K. Curtis*," "*Lord Halifax*," Churchill's competitor for Prime Minister, "*Margot Asquith*," the Prime Minister's wife, and one of the *"Gladstone"* series.[1] In February of the previous year, Hamilton had gone to France for about two days during the *Paris Peace Conference*, where he sketched *"Colonel E. M. House"* (U.S. President Woodrow Wilson's *Ambassador*) and met Mrs. House, also. The conference concluded World War I.[2] The work was commissioned by the *Christoffer Hannevig Foundation* to be one of the original twenty-five portraits for the newly-created *Smithsonian/National Portrait Gallery (Washington,D.C.)*.[3]

About this time, Clara and McLure had entertained British *Prime Minister* and Mrs. Asquith, and former *P. M.* Arthur J. Balfour and Mrs. Balfour as dinner guests at the *Hermitage*. Later, their guests reciprocated, and the Hamiltons lived at *the Wharf* (home) of Prime Minister Asquith for seven days.[4,5]

McLure had corresponded with members of the Gladstone family continuously since 1892, a span of thirty years at this point in Hamilton's career.[6] By late April, Hamilton was elected president of the *Fellowship* (of Philadelphia's P.A.F.A.) *in absentia*. Afterwards, the team took an extended holiday in Warwickshire through mid July.

McLure's coffeetable book manuscript, MEN I HAVE PAINTED, occupied much of the painter's time during 1920.<7> It presents a series of brief anecdotal reports of forty-eight, portrait-painting episodes with famous sitters. Most of his subjects were males, one a woman, and two were horses. (Their names appear in the HAMILTON ART CATALOG.) By this time, he had already recorded over eight hundred eighty impressions of his famous subjects. Thus, the only other book ever published about his career treats less than five percent of his documented works.

His book was finally published by a friend, Thomas Fisher Unwin.<8> He was the same man who had produced "LITHOGRAPHY," which contained Hamilton's red auto-lithograph, *"Gladstone reading."*<9> Hamilton painted Unwin and portrayed him at his office desk. Since it was difficult to find a publisher in America this could have been a *quid pro quo*.[A126]

Immediately after the *Panama-Pacific Exposition* in 1915 Hamilton's sizable number of pastels was purchased by Mrs. Edward Henry Harriman. Mary was the widow of the "little giant of Wall Street," described as the most powerful man in the U. S. because of his personal control over 60,000 miles of U. S. railways. She had bought more than thirty pastels by Hamilton. They were then sent on a traveling exhibition to numerous U. S. cities including Philadelphia. This helped to popularize Hamilton's work in his native country. Before February of 1921, Mrs. Harriman donated her collection of Hamilton pastels to the *Corcoran Gallery* for their permanent collection and to be used for study by students.<10,11>

Britain's reigning monarch, KING GEORGE V, sat for a second portrait by Hamilton. No doubt it was arranged through Mrs. Drew.<12>

Next, Clara and McLure vacationed at a hotel at *Alassio* on the *Italian Riviera* in April, 1921 and later he painted *"Henry Neville Gladstone,"* the future Baron. Though the artist's residence remained the Hermitage in England, the Hamiltons stayed at *Camp Elsinore* located in the *Adirondak Mountains* (New York) while traveling in America towards the end of May.<13,14>

Since the Hamiltons planned to be in America for an extended time, "The Hermitage" was rented to *Dr. Edmund Edward Fournier d'Albe* who wrote a biography of Sir William Crookes while there. Dr. Crookes had discovered the new chemical element, thallium, edited the *Chemical News*, and was a famous physicist and chemist.<15,16>

Hamilton delivered a formal lecture on the "State of Artists" at *St. Martin's Lane Theatre* when he returned from the U. S. He was then half past his seventieth birthday and concluding fifty years in London.<17> His ever-supportive pen pal, Mrs. Drew, wrote a cheering card to buoy up the painter's sagging spirits regarding the unexpected marriage of George to a woman unknown to the parents. After mid July, Clara and McLure crossed the ocean to New York for the tenth time in fifty years. They used the ocean as we might employ the New Jersey turnpike to New York today. It was on this passage that Hamilton met the legendary book dealer of Philadelphia, *Dr. A. S. W. Rosenbach*.<18> They were all traveling on the Hamiltons' favorite liner, *S. S. Majestic*, of the *White Star Line*.

By August, Clara and McLure would again be in California to visit the sights in *San Diego* and *Los Angeles*.

Both generations of the Hamiltons were in *Jamaica* until March, 1923, for about six months, during which the parents became acquainted with their daughter-in-law.<19> Some paintings date from this first tour in the Caribbean. Even though Hamilton was born in Philadelphia, he practiced his craft in Jamaica, recording *"Port Royal"* and *"Street Scene"* there. After Clara and McLure returned to the U. S., they traveled to *Tobyhanna* (near Mount Pocono, PA) towards the close of September to honor a commission to paint *"Newton S. Brittain, Esq.,"* a former Auditor General of Jamaica. During the weeks spent there, the Hamiltons enjoyed shooting pheasants among the rhodendron and relaxed.<20>

The Hamiltons went to New York then to *Halifax, Nova Scotia*.<21> The team then went south to Delaware to visit with McLure's family and then to Washington, D. C. to visit friends including the Glovers. While they were there, they viewed an exhibition of Hamilton's art at the *Corcoran*, where *"Judge Alexander Carson Simpson, Jr.,"* "Corn Husker,"

"Grandmother and Child," "Children and Roses," and "Mr. Brittain" could be admired.<22>

By the first week in December, the Hamiltons went north again to a farm in *Washington county, N. Y.* and then to *Boston, MA* where the E. A. Abbey collection is kept in the *Public Library.* The Abbeys and the Hamiltons were great friends. Afterwards, the team returned to Philadelphia's posh *Ritz Carlton Hotel* at its original location by mid month.<23>

Hamilton's book was not a best seller when it was first released. Life in America had a different tone than that to which Clara and McLure had grown accustomed. Hamilton was an after dinner speaker at the *Art Alliance of Philadelphia.* His topic was civic beautification through creating the *Benjamin Franklin Parkway,* a project that needed all the support it could get in the 1920s.<24>

During this period, Hamilton's mailing address remained *Drexel & Company* even though the artist had been the owner of the family mansion since 1895. It was located within a two block walk of the proposed site for the Parkway project at 1600 Summer Street. All of those years, the building was rented to a succession of tenants. They were mostly physicians who maintained professional offices there as Hamilton's father had done so long ago. A complication was *Mayor Kendrick's* evolving plan to redevelop *Logan Square* by adding the adjoining *Parkway* to it.<25>

Hamilton exhibited at the *Philadelphia Sketch Club,* the *Philadelphia Watercolor Club,* and the *P.A.F.A* in 1924. The works included "*A Game of Chess,*" "*Paul W. Bartlett,*" which was commissioned for the *Luxembourg Palace Collection,* "*Girl reading,*" "*A Bit of Color,*" and "*The Listener.*" Hamilton did business with *McClees Gallery, Philip Rosenbach* and another friend, *Louis Grieumard,* storaging or transporting art around the U. S. for various exhibitions.<26,27>

Hamilton was listed as a resident exhibitor at London's *Pastel Society,* where his work generated much critical praise.<28> By April,1927, the team was on the ocean again while "*Lords of Appeal,*" "*U.S. Senator, William Morris Stewart,*" "*Peace on Earth,*" "*Children and Roses,*" and "*Grandmother & Child*" were on display at the *Corcoran.*<29>

One of McLure's maternal aunts, *Frances Delaplaine*, was residing in Delaware. She married *Robert L. Robinson*, a financial leader. They soon had a son, *Robert Pyle Robinson*, who was elected *Governor of Delaware* (1925--1929). Hamilton painted his cousin's official portrait while on a three week vist to Wilmington, (Nov. 6, 1927) without his $ 1,000.00 fee.<30,31> [A105]

By September, 1928, the team returned to England from its second voyage to Jamaica, ostensibly to see the younger Hamiltons since they were now on friendly terms. From the time of this visit, the parents began to underwrite the costs of George's scientific research and publishing. (Thus, the senior Hamiltons set in motion unwittingly their financial downward spiral which would create major problems from 1931 *et seq.*) During this year, three portraits were exhibited at the P.A.F.A., including *"Mr. Gladstone at Hawarden," "General William Booth,"* and *"Joseph Pennell,"* all of whom were now deceased.<32>[A055]

The lofty reputation of Hamilton's pastels (by Feb., 1929) affected their prices at exhibitions on both sides of the Atlantic. They sold well at $ 500.00 each in Canada and in the U. S.<33> Hamilton, the American outsider, had achieved stardom and a unique niche in the inner circle of money, power, and influence in the English-speaking art world. His tenacity, street smarts, fifty-plus years of painting, and plodding one step in front of the other had made him a leader in British art circles. His reputation was based on skill, education, merit, and labor from before sunrise to long after sunset. He learned to mix imperceptibly with the supporters of the correct causes, to understand the correct people, and as a result, their club system rewarded him well. By now Hamilton was Art's Anglo-American Lion in the words of C. H. Bronte with a substantial treasure.<34> Perhaps Hamilton had a portfolio of stocks and bonds equal to that of his financially-comfortable sister, Mrs. King, (or like that his father had possessed). Thus, a conservative estimate of his *net worth* at the conclusion of this period would be in the neighborhood of $100,000.00, exclusive of personal property. Hamilton had accumulated the professional status, public name recognition, and assets of a highly successful painter.

MAN'S AMBITION, 1898 III 2. From THE BAILIE engraving
8.5" x 6." Courtesy Mitchell Library, Glasgow
Collection.

XIV : FINANCE

The economics of the 19th Century American expatriate artists has been a neglected topic in the literature of art history and the sociology of artists. Thus, little is known about basics like their costs of living and their lifetime incomes. Business ledgers are rarely available from art galleries, though occasionally the name of a specific painting, sold by a dealer, is known. When a career chronology is assembled, it often raises more questions about cost of an individual's *travel* than it answered. In stark contrast, the analysis of available details revealed much about the economics of one such artist, John McLure Hamilton, who was active as a painter from 1864 through 1933, inclusive. This corresponds to a period in American History counted from the third year of the administration of U. S. President Abraham Lincoln through the first year of President Franklin D. Roosevelt's tenure.<1> The data implied much about the sociology of artist's of the period as well.

Table **M** presents a conservative estimate of Hamilton's lifetime income from all known sources. A critical analysis of the table's details fleshes out the bare bones of the lifestyle the Hamiltons could afford to lead. The categories of income included items like *portrait commissions, sales* of original art in diverse media, and sales of *reproductions* prepared for collectors of modest means. Unfortunately, the *salary* data was not available from his days as a documentary artist for the newspaper in Glasgow. A reasonable estimate for total income appears to be under $ 400,000.00.

Table N lists legacies to the artist from the estates of seven family members. They were an uncle, grandfather, three aunts, and both parents. A moderate estimate of his inheritance seems to be at least $ 100,000.00.

Table O lists the prices realized on original art sold during Hamilton's life, whether by private treaty or through intermediates like a dealer or gallery. Such transactions may have netted the artist only 68% of the retail price on transactions, which ranged from $ 10.00 to $ 5,000.00 per painting sold through the year 1900.

Table P presents donations made to the Hamilton Relief Committee and total sales figures of secondary works at auction in Philadelphia to 1938. Details were abstracted from various sources including the *Thornton Oakley papers*.

Table Q presents an estimate of his net worth under a best case scenario.

Table R presents recent prices realized on specific Hamilton oils and pastels from published sources, supplemented with unpublished data from 1939 through 1993.

This chapter presents a perspective on the personal finances of Hamilton. He was a commercially successful painter of the period. (This study is an oasis in the desert as no other biography or monograph offers like data.) Hamilton's profile clearly does not fit the stereotype about most artists of the period. The inaccurate view of artists' lives included the following twenty-one assumptions, none of which apply to Hamilton. These are : 1) artists were difficult to track down because of frequent address changes in one community; 2) artists lacked credentials, whether academic or technical; 3) artists were frequently unemployed and at leisure; 4) artists were hidden occupationally in the U. S. or English Census records; 5) when employed, artists worked more often in jobs unrelated to their art; 6) artists painted, or sculpted, during spare time on weekends; 7) artists always lived on the fringe of society; 8) artists' landlords were their unwilling bankers; 9) artists were generally alcohol-dependent; 10) artists were generally drug-involved; 11) artists were agnostics; 12) artists were amoral; 13) artists were counter-culture types; 14) artists

were rarely participants in a "nuclear" family; 15) artists
do *not* attain a living wage during their careers; 16) living
artists sold their paintings for the price of materials
alone; 17) artists were always tenants but never landlords;
18) artists lacked practical business savvy; 19) artists
were illiterate, illogical, primary school alumni; 20)
artists practiced only one technique, career-long; and 21)
artists failed to avail themselves of continuing trade
educational opportunities.<2>

Contrary to this rather hostile job description and
sociological profile of a hypothetical 19th Century
composite artist, it is known, from Hamilton, that a day
laborer earned about $ 250.00 a year. A successful parson
with a family of twelve children would earn about $ 750.00 a
year, while most clerics earned $ 400.00 a year.<3> A person
could survive well on $ 10,000.00 yearly or live comfortably
on $ 25,000.00, whereas one of the super rich might earn
$ 5,000,000.00 yearly.<4> An art gallery might exact a fee
of 32% from the sale of a living artist's work.<5>

TRAVEL AND THE HAMILTONS

We live in the age of bonus mileage programs for repeat
business travelers using airplanes. There were neither
airplanes nor incentive programs sixty to one hundred years
ago during the Hamiltons heyday of global journeying. It is
interesting to estimate just what their total mileage may
have been, what their aggregate costs were, and how much
time of the team's career was taken up by land and sea
travel. A quick accounting from letters and news stories
suggests that the Hamiltons logged in the neighborhood of
four million miles during fifty years. The largest blocks of
travel calculated for McLure and Clara were the twenty round
trips to England, five round trips to Jamaica, forty trips
to France, and the host of journeys chasing news-worthy
stories while on the newspaper in Scotland. We recall that
these trips were often to satisfy sales or commissions for
paintings. Sometimes, the trips had a vacation sandwiched in
here and there.<6>

At ten cents a mile, including the costs of travel,
meals, lodging, and a clothing allowance, the aggregate cost
approached $ 400,000.00.

If five percent of the year was allotted to travel, then the team traveled about two and one half years out of fifty. Thus, with only a little arithmetic and the few actual busines records available, the investigator estimated the Hamiltons may have spent for travel as much as Hamilton earned from commissions and sales, exclusive of income from bequests. In arriving at the estimate, local, state, and federal taxes were ignored as they were then considerably lower or non-existant! Medical expenses were also not included.

A reading of the *Torah* reminds us that a baby enters this world with no possessions or money and that an old man ought to leave it with none, as well.<7> Thus, Hamilton may have performed according to traditional Jewish values, having done business to the fullest in Europe and America while he paid taxes in five jurisdictions.<8>

Armstrong, the second U. S. Consul stationed in Jamaica during the Hamiltons' years, perceived Hamilton in 1936 as a poor old, artist. Armstrong was probably deceived by Hamilton through lack of information and his own in action concerning the size of Hamilton's estate located there at that time, which included real estate, pastels, and oils in great number. Mr. Armstrong's report would have been more accurate if he had said that the Hamiltons were cash-poor but asset-rich.<9> Since social security benefits did not exist, their financial portfolio was tied up in the probate of George's estate, and McLure and Clara had expenses on a daily basis. It seems that the Hamiltons had a high net worth in the absence of cash flow.

The fair market value of Hamilton's art works in Jamaica in 1936 all-tolled plus the real estate, known as Hamilton Hall, was rather high and may have been worth an additional $ 100,000.00.<10>

To contrast, using *recent price* data for Hamilton's art listed in Table R, one of his oil paintings sold at $ 40,000.00 and one pastel sold for $ 4,000.00.

Hamilton could have used the proceeds from the sale of just one pastel at today's prices but available in 1936 to build his *proposed* Art Museum in Mandeville! The value of just one Hamilton oil painting calculated at today's market value could have paid for the project and endowed an art school there, as well.

ADIEU

XV : DECLINE AND ADIEU, 1930--1936

Hamilton wrote to Dr. Rosenbach, a Philadelphia gallery owner, from England. Hamilton planned to relocate shortly to Jamaica and he had some interesting family heirlooms for sale.<2> The articles were old Persian carpets, antique English furniture, rare books from his father's collection, and several letters with family provenance for upwards of one hundred years. These letters included one from *George Washington,* one from *(Robert) Morris* to *John Hancock,* and a 1779 letter from *Lord (Charles) Cornwallis,* whom *General* Washington had defeated at the Battle of Yorktown.<3>

Clara and McLure settled in Jamaica. After making their third voyage to the Island, Hamilton wrote that he intended to remain there permanently.<4> Much of his artwork was still abroad for an exhibition one year later at Barbizon House on Henrietta St., London, and additional work appeared at the Burlington Gallery thereafter. London critics raved, and praised his pastels. Hamilton reported that he had painted a portrait in April, 1931 and then hung up his palette for the last time.<5>

Hamilton's earliest surviving oil (a landscape), dated 1864, was painted when he was eleven years old. His retirement from that medium meant that he had used oils to express his talents for more than sixty-seven years. Now he was seventy-eight. Present at that time, nine oils in England were reserved for purchase by the National Gallery's Permanent Collection as soon as funds became available.<6>

ADIEU, 1901. From T.B. Hennell's book (op.cit). Engraving 2 1/4" x 2." Courtesy Mitchell Library, Poetry Collection.

Ultimately, five were to become a gift from the artist.<7>
Five more oils were owned by the Gladstones at Hawarden
Castle and an additional four were at the prestigious Tate
Gallery for a time.<8> It was in April, 1931, that the
hometown newspaper published a farewell interview based on a
visit to the Hermitage.<9> It summarized the Hamilton's
English experience in this order : he visited in 1872,
settled in 1878, married Clara who joined him a year or so
later, and then was elected to the *Royal Academy of Portrait
Painters* in 1884 (the year George was born). Thereafter,
John McLure Hamilton sketched, painted, and ascended to the
pinnacle of British art, and into the hearts of millions of
readers. His work found its way on to the walls of forty-six
of the world's leading museums.<10>

     The Hamiltons retired to Mandeville permanently
following their third trip and a search of the *Island
Records Office* revealed that Hamilton Hall, their Jamaican
estate, was purchased in 1931.<11> That parcel was situated
in the mountainous parish of *Manchester*, about seventy miles
from Montego Bay. The site was probably chosen for its
proximity to George and Langdon's *Observatory.* The
Observatory had been in the same community since 1924. The
artist's parcel included two choice pastures from a part of
a far larger site, known locally as "*Woodlawn.*" The retired
painter obtained by mortgage the title to "*Quashiba*" and
"*Round Hill,*" containing together about fifty-four acres for
L 1,000 (equal to about $ 5,000.00).<12> The mortgage money
was obtained from a Jamaican widow, *Mrs. Maud Eleanor
Halliday*, who lived in England.<13>

     The year 1932 was a time of adjustment to this great
move, a time of settling into the new homestead, and a time
during which cataracts and arthritis made everything a bit
more difficult and more expensive than the Hamiltons had
anticipated.<14>

     From evidence in an old auction catalog, the surprise
discovery of a Hamilton signed, watercolor dated 1933,
revealed that the artist was again at work in that
challenging medium. A letter revealed that Hamilton had
created a series of paintings of flower arrangements.<15>
In a letter to Thornton Oakley of Philadelphia about his
latest paintings, Hamilton expressed his intention to
reproduce the flowers he had painted in Jamaica for
commercial purposes perhaps in the form of prints, his
earliest appeared in 1883.<16>

Meanwhile, the Rosenbach Company arranged a New York City exhibition in their gallery of Hamilton's pastels, including ninety items.<17> At that time, Howard Devree, a critic for the NEW YORK TIMES, proclaimed, "Hamilton's best pastels equaled those of Degas or Renoir."<18>[A171,A181] Subsequently, *McClees Gallery* held a comprehensive retrospective exhibition of Hamilton's paintings in the artist's native city.<19> An Eakins-like minature in oils, *"Reverie in a Brown Chair,"* was one of the pieces that the gallery sold.[A190]

Now that the Hamiltons had passed through their Jamaican homestead phase successfully, they showed obvious pride in George and Langdon's professional accomplishments. George was determined to help build a museum to complement the Hamilton *Observatory*, now in place. To this end, the artist granted an unusual mortgage to Mr. Henry James Jackson in the amount of L 350.00. The artist's son, George, witnessed this contract.<20>

The contract was valid for a three year period. With seven pounds (percent interest) payable annually plus costs.<21> For this sum of money, Mr. Jackson agreed to go to England and act as the artist's agent. Mr. Jackson was to pay the *London Army & Navy Stores* their fees for storage and arrange for the packing and shipping of Hamilton's precious furnishings and paintings to *Mandeville* for the fourth trip. The inventory supposedly had a declared value of no less than L 800.00. Since the team had lived in Glasgow for ten years, it can be assumed that the Hamiltons tended to Scot frugality where anticipated costs were concerned. So the declared value is probably low. As an agent, Mr. Jackson had to agree to personally guarantee the safety and delivery of each article to Mr. Hamilton, who would issue a written receipt on delivery upon satisfaction. Additionally, the contract stipulated that during shipment the articles shall be insured above L 350.00. The fees for the insurance policy were to be prepaid by Mr. Jackson, who was responsible for security, repair, or replacement of each missing item. In the event of missing articles, a search was to be permitted to locate the missing ones. The articles were scheduled on twenty sheets of paper.<22>

Approximately two weeks later, the artist sold seven acres of the land parcel to Mr. Jackson, making him a neighbor. Until that time, Mr. Jackson had been a pen keeper (tenant farmer), and now he was a landowner with a parcel valued at L 142.00.<23>

A financial squeeze may have driven Hamilton, the consumate manager of public relations, to make the first tactical error of his career. In Philadelphia, he attempted to collect an old debt due from a portrait commissioned thirty-two years earlier. The sitter was Dr. George Inman Riche, fourth president of Central High School, whose tenure included the artist's school days there. Hamilton was a member of the class of January, 1870. The surviving alumni of the class were, in the artist's view, delinquent in payment to him. Hamilton, the indefatigable letter writer and journalist, wrote letters to the *Auditor General of Pennsylvania*, the School Board, etc. to demand payment of half his standard fee (or $ 500.00) from them. He had pledged the other half as his personal contribution to the anniversary celebration of the School in 1902. The story appeared in the Philadelphia newspapers and the resultant publicity was unfriendly to Hamilton's business reputation in that town.<24> The story made him seem too commercial, money-orientated, and a tad eccentric for the first time in his career. He never got paid.

The artist had sent a telegram from his remote home in the mountains to the U. S. Consul in Jamaica, William W. Corcoran, stating that he wanted to palaver with him about a matter of great urgency. Mr. Corcoran evidently knew of Hamilton's golden reputation as a painter and he respected him. The now famous newspaper article, *"the last wish of a great American artist,"* was the result of that conference with Mr. Corcoran held at Hamilton Hall. It was then published simultaneously in Jamaica and in the United States.<25>

In summary, the news story conveyed Hamilton's last request to his loyal supporters world-wide. He suggested that one of his *"Gladstone"* portrait series be purchased for donation to London's *National Portrait Gallery*. Publicity about this point appeared in Philadelphia's newspapers, as well.

The year 1935 was a silent year because Hamilton's letters have not surfaced relating to events such as the death of Professor George Hall Hamilton, the artist's son, nor to the departure of George's widow, Langdon, who was traced to Enfield, New Hampshire (1937).<26>

During the last week in February, 1936, there was a report of the Philadelphia retrospective exhibition of Hamilton minatures at *McClees Gallery.* It had been arranged by some of Hamilton's long-time friends. They formed a committee to market a portion of his collection to benefit the Hamiltons' medical expenses with their legal consent. Three members of the *Hamilton Relief Committee*, named in the order of their financial importance to the cause, were Mr. Harrison S. Morris, Mrs. Emily Drayton Taylor, and Thornton Oakley. In Morris' newspaper column, a human interest piece, the public was informed that 'Hamilton was now ill and in need.' As a result, their Jamaican enterprise was in need of fluid cash. There was a glut of first-rate paintings located there and still Hamilton owned real estate elsewhere. In Philadelphia, however, the art market was saturated and prices were depressed.

The artist's facile mind and strong hands were slowed now. In the words of a new U. S. Consul at Kingston,'it is hard work to do anything for this poor old artist who has ideas of finance no further advanced than those of the students and children in La Boheme.'<27>

Miss Helen W. Henderson, whom Hamilton had portrayed in a vibrant and colorful pastel, wrote a revealing and supportive column, *"About McLure Hamilton"*.[A071] She wrote the History of the Pennsylvania Academy of The Fine Arts in 1911.

During this period of his career, Hamilton and his devoted wife experienced the biological dwindlinding of his health. He had lost vigor, strength, endurance, eyesight, hearing, recent memory, and physical mobility.

Although Hamilton had hidden his treasured paintings in England and the U. S., he was still a relatively wealthy man by the standards of the 1930s, when he retired. His goal was to move to a warmer, more healthy climate in the Caribbean to be near the remainder of his family. While there, Hamilton planned to leisurely sell a few pieces from his vast collection of furniture, rugs, letters, Old Masters' paintings, and extensive inventory of Hamilton original art. Instead, in two years, the artist's health decayed, and his son pre-deceased him at age 51. The cause of death was lung cancer. George's chain-smoking while at work in the mountain Observatory may have triggered the problem which led to his premature death.<28> The elder Hamiltons' assets had been depleted by the cost of George's research expenses and their home's construction. Hamilton's plan had been to transfer many of his assets to his wife and to his son during his declining years in exchange for continuing health care, which was a common practice of estate planning. No one had anticipated the consequences of George's death or that this set of events would include serious cash flow problems, nor had anyone anticipated the early migration of George's young widow.<29>

Thus, Hamilton family members became cash-poor for the first time since their 1795 landing in America. Recall that the artist had been a man who had earned by one estimate in excess of $ 350,000.00 in his creative lifetime from manufacturing marketable goods. He had also been successful at selling them at high prices and dealing with the Royals. Prime Ministers had wined and dined him less than eight years earlier. Although the Hamiltons had always been frugal, now they were all but destitute because George's estate was in probate for years. Meanwhile, the artist was deaf, blind, chair-ridden, then bed-ridden, needing the services of a butler, secretary, and nurse since his wife of fifty-six years was then in equally fragile health.

XVI : REMNANTS, 1936--1993

George's funeral service was held in Mandeville and it was conducted by the Rev. *E. B. Baker*, M. A., L. L. B.<1,2> Many friends of the family and local dignitaries were present with his widow at his burial at the *Public Cemetery*.<3> Quoting the zoologist *Fabricius* (1555), "death comes to all, but great achievements raise a monument which shall endure until the sun grows cold."

Impressionist painter, *John McLure Hamilton*, died one year, one month, and six days after his son.<4> When Committee member and friend, Mrs. Taylor received the news early the next day, she alerted the wire services.<5> The late artist's obituary was published in America, England, and Jamaica. Notices appeared in more than fifteen news-papers.<6> *Mrs. Clara Hamilton*, through her neighbor, *Mrs. Hyacinth Rebhan*, wrote a note conveying the news to Thornton Oakley, another Committee member. She informed Oakley of the artist's opinion about him, "I liked the man."<7> When Clara died thirty-two days later, she was buried beside him at the Cemetery.<8> The graves of George's parents adjoin his on the same row in the Anglican section, according to a published report.<9>

After the investigator's visit to the city clerk in charge of cemetery business to find the artist's tombstone, which should have been situated parallel to the old truck road (*now* Grove Road), a visit revealed that the entrance region of the cemetery had been recently modified to provide

space for public works. The improvements included under-
ground cable, and road widening and paving. In the course of
the project, the row of graves containing the Hamiltons,
perhaps forty in all, had been discovered by a worker's
digging tool. According to an eyewitness, skeletons
and skulls were partially disinterred. The graves were then
hidden in the paving phase of the project. Armed with this
unsettling news, a complaint was filed with a very
sympathetic official in charge. It was revealed that
Jamaican law is very clear in this situation and that the
contractor(s) were obligated to exhume, reinter, and mark
appropriately the new grave for Hamilton and the others
whose sites were desecrated. Two years have passed since the
1991 complaint was filed. Time will reveal whether the
appropriate action will be taken by those in charge. Future
tourists interested in art history could then be able to
make a pilgrimage to the cemetery to pay their respects at
the grave of Jamaica's most famous artist, a Jamaican by
choice, John McLure Hamilton in Mandeville's Public
Cemetery.<10,11>

Hamilton had a great sense of humor and he lampooned
many situations with his cartoons published in THE BAILIE.
<12> A reaction to the scene encountered there during the
138th anniversary of his birth would be summarized by a
cartoon postal card (reproduced here), which was the work of
an unidentified artist. It represents a black-humored
response to the situation just described, something Hamilton
never did. It describes one observer's reaction there that
day.<13>

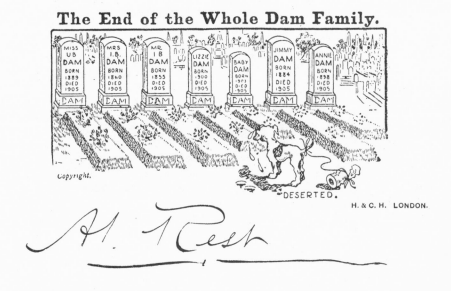

The End of the Whole Dam Family.

"DESERTED."

H. & C. H. LONDON.

(H. & C. H., London <c>) AT REST / THE END OF THE WHOLE
D... FAMILY. Engraved postal card cartoon used 1906
VIII 7 in London. 3.5" x 5.5."

The details of the settlement of the Hamiltons' estates are somewhat complex because of the accidental confluence of their three deaths within 433 days of each other.<14> Their unfinished business and legal affairs in America, England, and Jamaica, and in the communities of Phila-delphia, Zieglerville, Kingston-on-Thames, Wolfscastle, and Mandeville formed a tangled, interwoven network for estate lawyers to unravel. Considering the value of their modest estates at the time, the lawyers' fees could have been substantial if invoiced on an hourly rate. Further complications were revealed, as the artist died leaving no will. Clara's American will was ruled invalid, as her designated heir, the CARNEGIE TRUST, did not exist in the eyes of the Montgomery county, PA court.<15> The Jamaican and American portions of their only son (and descendant) George's estate was apparently absorbed into those of his parents for probate purposes.

Although Mr. Oakley had sent letters to Hamilton in Jamaica and to U. S. Consul Armstrong discouraging future shipments of Hamilton's art property, as of March, 1936 at least one additional parcel had been sent to Phila-delphia. <16,17,18> Unfortunately, Mr. Oakley was in Europe at the time of the proposed delivery and the notice of the attempt-ed delivery went unanswered. Consequently, the duty and express fees were not paid and the parcel was then seized by the *U.S. Customs Service*. The parcel contained oil paintings by Hamilton labeled *"unfinished"* (to reduce duty obligations). Then at the port of Philadelphia they were auctioned at the OLD CUSTOM HOUSE. Mrs. Emily Drayton Taylor, who knew Hamilton's unsigned work by sight, said "the paintings are worth a small fortune."<19>

A veteran Philadelphia antique dealer reported that in the Spring of 1937, he went to the auction held at *Second & Chestnut Streets,* where he bid on Hamilton's canvases seized for non-payment of $ 4.06 duty and 56 cents in express charges. He found a few of them hung on a clothes line for inspection. The rest were being walked on, face down, floor-mat fashion, with shoe-prints on their reverse. None had stretchers, as they were shipped wound on a wooden roller from Jamaica. That was the first time the dealer had handled oil paintings of the famous artist, and he remembered that Thornton Oakley, an Impressionist painter, was present that day. The dealer bought the lot as high bidder at $ 56.50. The lot had an appraisal value of $ 500.00, a bargain price for *thirteen* Hamilton oils.<20>

On October 27th, 1937, the artist's estate in
Philadelphia county, included additional watercolors, oils,
pastels, crayon sketches, chalk sketches, lithographs,
furniture, and the mortgaged *Hamilton House* at 1600 Summer
Sreet.   *Ancillary Letters of Administration* were issued to
William Hobart Porter, partner in *Drexel & Company* and
attorney for the next-of-kin.<21>   Hamilton's heirs
designated by the Court were Mathew Brooke Buckley, a minor,
and the grandson of the artist's now deceased sister, Mrs.
King. Also, former Governor, R. P. Robinson, a maternal
cousin of the artist, and lastly, the heirs to Clara's
estate. These heirs shared equal thirds of the artist's
estate. (Tab. S)   In April, 1938, *Samuel T. Freeman &
Company,* the Philadelphia auctioneers, sold over four
hundred lots of Hamilton's work and memorabilia at "dirt
cheap prices." (Tab. O, R) A local reporter (D. G.)
thought he saw a warning for other artists in the relatively
poor results of the auction of items from Hamilton's studio.
The studio may have included items that should have been
culled by the artist earlier on.<22>   Derek Clifford, a
scholar once said that incompletely executed drawings are
often filled with life, feeling, and nearly always are
illuminating and have a few fine things which shed light on
their neighboring pieces.<23> Among the *Baron Henry N.
Gladstone Collection* of letters [A038], the following
appropriate comment was discovered, not in Hamilton's
handwriting, 'there is no such thing as 'finished' and 'unfinished;' Whistler said
(that) a work of art is complete from the beginning. You know that fools talk when Angel's fear
to whisper.'<24>

By June, 1938, the Philadelphia portion of the artist's
estate had been probated for a total of $ 2,082.00.<24> This
amount was applied to the claim by the mortgagor of 1600
Summer Street, Judge Alexander Carson Simpson,Jr., also a
benefactor of other artists. He was portrayed by Hamilton in
several oils.[A018]

By November, the portion of the artist's estate in
Jamaica equaled L 44 and there was no comment in the probate
records about title to *Hamilton Hall.* Tax records indicate
all obligations were paid, however. Also, omitted from
mention was the hoard of additional paintings, and
furnishings known from the *Howe Inventory* of over 200
lots.<25> No additional information is available about the
mortgage contract with Mr. Jackson, which was in effect at

the date of Hamilton's death.

The thirty-four acres of farm land at Zieglerville, PA had been acquired in 1902 for use in recreational hunting by the Hamiltons. It was transferred to George in about 1917 and then it reverted to Clara's estate. It was subsequently awarded to her cousins, the three children of the Canadian architect, *Kenneth G. Rea*.<26>

Although Clara wrote wills, one was ruled invalid in PA and another was lost (hidden) in her Jamaican residence and recovered ten years following her death. It would be interesting to have more information about these circumstances. From the Court's point of view she died intestate, too.

By the summer of 1940, a surprising set of events began to unfold. Letters reached several museums and dealers in the United States from the *Justice of the Peace* at Mandeville, Mr. Sydenham J. Howe, U.E.L. He had purchased original art by Hamilton and some paintings owned by Hamilton but done by other hands. All were to be the nucleus for Hamilton's last project. Now, Howe wished to use them as the basis for the proposed John McLure Hamilton Memorial Art Museum of Jamaica. Mr. Howe revealed that he was leading a Committee whose goal it was to raise funds (L 1,000.00) for that noble project by canvasing various North American dealers, museums, and individuals.<27>

Meanwhile, in August of that same year, the guardian for the *Rea* children of Canada sold their farm in Zieglerville, PA to *John K. Williams* for $ 1,200.00.<28>

Eight years later, when Lady Margot Asquith visited Mandeville, a news report appeared locally that a few pastels by Hamilton were for sale in Jamaica.<29>[A002]

About twelve years thereafter, on the occasion of the first Soviet Space mission, Sputnick, a Jamaican news reporter recalled the memory *Professor* George H. Hamilton and repeated his opinion that life existed on Mars.<30>

George's widow, Mrs. Elizabeth Langdon Hamilton, died at age 101 (in 1981) in New Hampshire.<31>

In the fifty-five years since John McLure Hamilton's death, all direct contacts, such as neighbors and most friends, have vanished. After several years of placing newspaper advertising in Jamaica and America, no evidence for the whereabouts of his diary, journal, ledger, or sketchbook was forthcoming to the investigator.<32> Nevertheless, hundreds of previously unpublished letters to and from the artist (dating from 1881 to 1936) have been assembled. They have provided a previously untold outline of Hamilton's daily activity and some of his thoughts, ideas, feelings, plans, and views of his achievements. They, however, were originally only intended for close associates, friends, and family members. (see: HAMILTON LETTER COLLECTION, LOOO, in Appendix) Hundreds of exhibition catalogs have also been assembled. (see: EOOO, in Appendix) Study of their content has helped to chart the movement of Hamilton's paintings across the U. S. through twenty-two cities. An extensive news story file retrieved from Europe and America helped to "flesh out" some of the otherwise obscure phases of Hamilton's career development. (see: NOOO, in Appendix)

HAMILTON MEMORIAL APPEAL

A letter from the artist's former neighbor, Sydenham J. Howe, U.E.L, J.P., dated July 11, 1940, provides more information on Hamilton's treasured paintings at that time and the activity of loyal friends and admirers from Mandeville just prior to World War II. It is reproduced here unedited except for factual errors, and for clarity.<33>

"Re: *proposed HAMILTON MEMORIAL*

JOHN McLURE HAMILTON, whom you will, I think, have known intimately, came from England with Mrs. Hamilton, to settle near their only son, GEORGE, who was an ASTRONOMER, having formerly been connected with HARVARD OBSERVATORY, but later had his own 21 inch Glass, and was studying MARS in particular, and publishing his views in scientific journals, and in his own publication, "MARS (at its Nearest)."

GEORGE, dying quite unexpectedly left Mr. and Mrs. Hamilton in very unfortunate circumstances, but they continued building the very large House and observatory, intending it NOW to be a MEMORIAL.

Mr. Hamilton had become blind and bedridden and died in Nov. (actually Sept.), 1936, and his wife a few weeks later.

My connection with their affairs began with my offer to stay at night during that period, and I learned much about them and the PICTURES, Furniture, and BOOKS, but especially the Pictures which were to a large extent the work of Mr. HAMILTON.

Later, I was in charge for 6 months, for the Admninistrator General. The Property, and furniture were sold, The PICTURES were packed under my supervision as if to go to America, but have been stored in KINGSTON.

Knowing well the wish of the Hamiltons, I have kept in touch with the Admr. and the pictures, and recently when the opportunity occurred, I BOUGHT ALL THE PICTURES FROM THE HOUSE, in one lot. The price at which I obtained them is quite a nominal one considering the real value in ordinary times and conditions, but even so, they are of course FAR above my personal means. I HAVE BOUGHT THEM FOR A MEMORIAL (to the artist). I have paid part of the price, and have arranged for a period of TIME, during which I believe I shall receive sufficient support from FRIENDS, and admirers of the pictures, to arrange (for payment of) the balance.

Suggestions have been made by me re: Board of TRUSTEES, but in the meantime I carry on.

MY PRESENT SUGGESTIONS

We have in MANDEVILLE, a young but active FREE LIBRARY, in which I take an active part, and over a year ago suggested to their BOARD that they work actively with me, and combine a proposed Memorial and the Library. After a hearing they passed a resolution that they would CONSIDER THE SUBJECT SYMPATHETICALLY if I could obtain the pictures.

I appeared before the PAROCHIAL BOARD, and THE CITIZEN's ASSN. and after a hearing, they passed a similar resolution, I am of the opinion that some of the MEMBERS have quietly used their influence in favor of the proposal.

THE PAROCHIAL BOARD loaned the present Library building, which is of cut stone. The BOARD wants the SITE so as to increase the MARKET, but they would take down the library building.

The proposal now is, for ALL to join forces The TRUSTEES for the MEMORIAL to collect enough money to pay for the pictures, and START a new building, in the centre of the Town, on a site which the Parish would give. WHEN THIS HAS BEEN ACCOMPLISHED, I AM PRACTICALLY ASSURED of L 500. from a different source for the Building Fund, I am not permitted to give particulars of this at present, but am quite confident that the amount will be forthcoming AT THAT STAGE.

When the NEW BUILDING can protect the BOOKS they will be transferred, and the Parochial Board will use the CUT STONES from the Library to increase the NEW BUILDING. The PICTURES would then be hung in suitable order, the bookcases to run down long room or, in the middle, and be low enough to allow of a view of pictures from all points. THERE WOULD BE TOP LIGHTING, with electric lights as might be found suitable.

The expenses of running the joint memorial and library would be less than a MEMORIAL alone, and not much heavier than the LIBRARY alone. At present about 25 Ladies and Gentlemen give their services at the Library free, except for cleaning. They have free telephone, postage, and lighting at half price. These would be continued.

Insurance, some caretaking, repairs, and sundries would not be very heavy items, and the people of Mandeville who are now interested would, I am quite sure, be prepared to carry on the joint undertaking.

THIS would be the FIRST ART COLLECTION IN JAMAICA. though the INSTITUTE of JAMAICA has some fine Pictures mostly of former GOVERNORS (Sir HENRY MORGAN being among them) and prominent Public Men.

The INSTITUTE gets a grant from the Govmt. but this subject can not be mentioned for the present.

Writing PERSONALLY for a moment--I am exceedingly fond of good Pictures, but do not paint. I was a BANKER a few years ago.

I know to a certain extent the Galleries of Washington, New York, Boston, Philadelphia, Chicago, San Francisco, some in Canada, many in England, Scotland, Ireland, France, Italy, Japan, and the ART of Ceylon, Burma, and Siam, which is mostly connected with their Beautiful TEMPLES. The Dutch Indies, Phillipines, and Hawaii have also interesting Art, I found.

I have a few good things of my own, and friends in Jamaica would also add to the Memorial, IN TIME, as they now do to the Library.

All the BOOKS being GIFTS.

NOW I FIND MYSELF UP AGAINST WAR CONDITIONS. and being of the old ENGLISH stock that went to Massachusetts in 1637, their descendants later going to NOVA SCOTIA, I find it practically impossible to advise the people here to give anything but WAR FUNDS, and I ALSO have my duty to perform in that respect. Against that, it must be remembered that ONLY IN WARTIME would the PICTURES be available to us at a possible price.

I, NOW, acting for the TRUSTEES in making, HAVE TO FIND THAT FIRST FIVE HUNDRED POUNDS, required to pay for the pictures, AND START THE NEW BUILDING. THEN--the other L 500 comes in, and the PAROCHIAL BOARD, adds the CUT STONE from the present Library, which will complete the necessary space for the present ACTUAL NEEDS.

DO YOU THINK, (I believe) THE FRIENDS OF THE HAMILTONS, and THE ADMIRERS OF HIS PICTURES, and the Art Assns., Galleries, etc. in the UNITED STATES will assist materially, in this, or some other plan, to perpetuate the memory of A GREAT AMERICAN ARTIST AND GENTLEMAN, the "SMILING SAGE," of whom the plaque (no.52) overlooks my desk?

A FEW AMOUNTS FROM DIFFERENT SOURCES WOULD BE SO HELPFUL, AND ENCOURAGING at this time.

I much regret that it is not possible to discuss matters with you direct, and get the benefit of your advice direct. Possibly you may be able to pay a visit to this beautiful Island and help in solving the problems before me. We need a good PLAN such as YOU have no doubt in your city, but of course on a smaller scale. Your BOSTON LIBRARY for instance, with its beautiful ABBEYs, is too ambitious for us.

(The ABBEYs and The HAMILTONs were great friends, and exchanged visits, and appreciated the others work, though so entirely different.)

Have you a copy of Mr. HAMILTON's book "MEN I HAVE PAINTED"?

For the present, Mr. and Mrs. Bell, of the MANDEVILLE HOTEL, have put their BALLROOM at our disposal, Three cases are still unopened, but so far the damage is less than expected.

His EXCELLENCY, THE GOVERNOR, Sir ARTHUR RICHARDS, and LADY RICHARDS are expected here on the 20th and I may be able to have them visit the PICTURES, Lady Richards does good work with her brush. They were in Malaya when I lived there a few years ago. At present one has to be very diplomatic, BUT CAN ONE PERHAPS LAY THE FOUNDATION FOR SOMETHING IN THE FUTURE ?

WILL YOU DO ANYTHING YOU CAN TO HELP ME ?

I shall be so very much obliged to you.
    Believe me to be,
        Very sincerely yours,
           (signed) Sydenham J. Howe

    (A catalog of almost 200 items followed, see chapter XVII note 23)

PRIMROSE DAY, 1898 IV 20. From THE BAILIE engraving
8.5" x 6.25." Courtesy Mitchell Library, Glasgow
Collection.

(detail) Prime Minister DAVID LLOYD-GEORGE, 1919.
From pastel of three men at the Paris Peace Conference
concluding World War I, 22" x 27." Formerly in
collection of Harry Burke.

THE TALE OF AN EMPTY POCKET AND AN UMBRELLA

THE TALE OF AN EMPTY POCKET & AN UMBRELLA, 1895. THE BAILIE engraving about Hamilton. Courtesy Mitchell Library, Glasgow Collection.

XVII : HUNTING HAMILTONIANA

Thirty years after Jamaican independence from Britain, an expedition was made to the mountain town of Mandeville, to search for evidence of the career of the artist, John McLure Hamilton. Presently, eighty thousand inhabitants live in the town's relatively cool serenity and tropical beauty compared to Kingston's heat and crowding. Mandeville's impression is created by the trees, agricultural crops, domestic animals, and ornamental foliage. Downtown there are small shops, minor shopping malls, vendors, and many churches dot the countryside. Small donkeys provide traditional transport, but cars are now found everywhere. The sound of mooing cattle is often heard. Insects, fish, and lizards are present in profusion. New highways are being carved out of the red earth to help the owners of new homes commute to work. In recent years, there has been a major home construction boom. Some of the more ecologically-minded lot owners have planted cash crops.<1> On a three acre plot, a minature but self-sufficient plantation can exist. The community has two excellent hotels, guest houses, and many tourist attractions, including mineral springs, a golf course, tennis courts, riding horses, swimming pools, art galleries, craft fairs, and plant nurseries.<2> Relatively inexpensive beef, chicken, fish, goat, lobster, and shrimp are always on the menu. The food is spicy. Fresh vegetable salads are not so plentiful as one might have expected.

The last Hamilton family member left Jamaica more than fifty-six years before the expedition to retire in New

Hampshire. Nevertheless, the expedition began a search for the artist's foot-prints in the iron-rich, red soil of Mandeville and environs in 1992. This was actually the second expedition. The first had been only a brief seven-day survey of Kingston, Spanish Town, and Mandeville in December, 1990. This time, the *Archives* and records of the *Land Office* in Spanish Town were combed for traces of the Hamilton deeds, and those of their nearest neighbors and friends of the 1930s. Several hurricanes had since redesigned parts of the Island and some records were lost after much property damage from the hurricanes. Next, Kingston's title office was surveyed for transfers from the 1990s back to the 1950s, when the Island nation was still British. In a relatively short time, a puzzle emerged, since the chain of title to Hamilton Hall could be traced only to a mining company, the earliest owner since independence.<3> It was not possible under the extant legal system to obtain the application proving how that firm had acquired title from the Hamilton estate though lawyers were consulted and residents were interviewed. Presently, that giant corporation owned by its successor, *Alcan Aluminium of Canada*, is responsible for fifty percent of the island's total annual revenues. In 1992, the Hamilton land was largely occupied by modern homes, valued for tax purposes in excess of three million dollars which was less than fair market value.<4> (Value quoted in U. S. dollar equivalents.)

The artist's land was clearly the most valuable real estate in all of Jamaica in 1992 according to official records.<5> It was by far the most beautiful as well.

A visit to the *Tax Evaluation Office* confirmed earlier suspicions of the investigator and deepened the mystery concerning the heirs' interests at the time of Hamilton's probate in the 1930s. An interview with a neighbor and close friend of Mrs. Clara Hamilton, Mrs. Rebhan, shed some light on the enigma regarding the early gap in the chain of title.<6> She reported that under the prevailing *British Intestate Law* of the 1930s, all such property went to the government.<7> Her daughter, Mrs. Moss, was a small child in those years, but she had a clear recall of Mr. Hamilton's convalescence, as the daughter provided some of the limited, necessary nursing care.<8>

Some details of the probate on the artist's estate in Jamaica were handled by his attorney, *John Malcolm*

MacGregor of Mandeville.<9> He also arranged for the burial
of three members of the artist's family who died between
August, 1935 and November, 1936. A conversation with his
daughter-in-law, Lady MacGregor, and his grandson did not
reveal the estate documents sought. This is not an unusual
circumstance after more than fifty years in the tropics,
where severe rainstorms occur regularly and hurricanes can
destroy the average home. Total house replacement once every
five years is not unusual for the average resident.

An interview with the widow of a former tea planter
documented the missing link in the chain of title. *Hamilton
Hall*, including the house and grounds, was purchased from
the government on April 20, 1937. The tea planter changed
the name of the property to *Dickwella*.<10>   His widow
reported that in her earliest recollection, the house was in
shambles for lack of maintainence by the Hamiltons. Cash
flow problems were responsible for the condition. She
remembered that the house had been built on two levels. It
was unfinished, measuring about forty feet square and about
the same distance from the road. A sizeable vegetable garden
had provided the Hamiltons with their daily foodstuffs.
Further, she recalled that Mrs. Clara Hamilton guarded her
front door with a shotgun. Security achieved with window
bars, door grills, and the ever-present patrol dogs is still
a consideration for all Jamaican residents. Miraculously,
the house still exists and is occupied.<11>

The tea planter's widow sold Dickwella to the mining
corporation in 1953. Subsequently, the company carved up
much of the remaining forty-seven acres into building lots
and provided free housing for its senior employees. However,
since 1960, when the island gained independence, that
practice was abandoned. The homes and available land were
sold gradually to individual owners. A current survey of the
land's tax records revealed that the average house sold for
the equivalent of $ 50,000.00, while the best house sold for
about $ 200,000.00.<12>   Real estate formerly belonging to
the artist but seized by the British government has by now
been developed with houses and has a value in excess of
three million dollars, compared with Hamilton's initial
investment of $ 5,000.00 in 1931.

In a third interview conducted with persons to be
mentioned shortly, some surprising additional information
surfaced about the artist's post-retirement career activity

in the tropics. This information caused the investigator to reconsider the artist's absolute statement in one earlier letter that he had painted his last portrait in 1931. The testimonies of a local farmer, *Brother* Martin Luther Campbell, and the Hamiltons' butler's sister, *Miss* Sarah Allen, strongly suggested that Hamilton had a remission of symptoms for a few months, enabling him to paint again, while retired in Jamaica for health reasons.<13,14> During this interval, 1932--193(3), Hamilton created a series of watercolors and at least one oil portrait. The sitter was Mr. John Allen, a former butler in the service of *Prime Minister* Ramsay MacDonald. In Jamaica, Mr. Allen became the Hamiltons' butler. According to Miss Allen, the artist painted her brother's portrait with a large pineapple-like plant on his head, to convey that the work was done in the tropics.

The farmer in 1992, interviewed at 98, reported that he had been an employee of the astronomer, George H. Hamilton. The farmer had planted the Hamilton's garden, did scientific work with the telescopes, and was taught carpentry and house painting by McLure Hamilton. Subsequent to George's death, the astronomical instruments were sold to the *West Indian Training School*.<15> All of the scientist's papers and other belongings went with his widow to New Hampshire during the Hamiltons' lifetime. Surprisingly, she maintained contact with the farmer for forty years after her departure. She sent him seeds for his Jamaican gardening annually until she died in 1981, at 101.

A phone call to the youngest partner of the law firm, *Mac Gregor, Williams, and Swaby*, which administered the artist's estate in Jamaica, resulted in the first tangible lead to Hamilton's original art still in Jamaica.<16> As a child, Mr. Swaby remembered seeing several pastels by Hamilton hung in the famous MANDEVILLE HOTEL. The former manager of the Hotel recalled the sale of the two pieces of art to a real estate developer in 1986.<17> That individual and his brother graciously made two pastels available for study, but declined permission for photodocumentation. One of the pastels looks much like the published photograph of "*Stressing Her Tresses*."<18> They present a dorsal view of Clara in a ballet costume adjusting her hair. They are executed in bold colors on brown paper and both are signed and dated.

In the earlier interview with the tea planter's widow, then 91, she told about a small oil "*beach scene*," now located in England with her son.

An interview with a Canadian citizen revealed the location of two additional pastels, one in Toronto and the other in Britain with her sister.<19>

The most productive contact was with a retired attorney who had control of three signed paintings by Hamilton. One was a large pastel ("*Two Women*," 1920), another was an oil on panel ("*Coquette of Seville*"), and the third a small landscape ("*The Thames*").<20>

So far unrecovered is the "valuable private collection of John McLure Hamilton," described as an English historian, which was donated to the *Manchester Parish Free Library* in the 1930s and then lost. This could be some of the rare books of the artist's father or even the letters, diaries, and sketch books of the artist. <21>

The investigator's extensive advertising in Jamaica, the United States, and Europe has not yielded the location of Hamilton's treasured art collection and memorabilia.<22> The search for it could productively occupy scholars and dealers for the next Century.

[The Sulker] = BONDEUSE, 1915. Pastel on paper 27" x
19." Courtesy Schwarz Gallery, Philadelphia.

INGREDIENTS FOR SUCCESS

The Right Honorable WILLIAM EWART GLADSTONE at Downing Street, 1893. Oil 31 1/4" x 35 1/8." Courtesy of the Pennsylvania Academy of the Fine Arts, Philadelphia. Henry D. Gilpin Fund.

XVIII : IMAGE, PERSONALITY, AND BEHAVIOR

IMAGE

Hamilton was born one year after the publication of
Stowe's UNCLE TOM'S CABIN. His physician father was
forty-five when the artist was born. W. T. Richards was
twenty. Jimmy Whistler was nineteen. T. C. Eakins was nine.
H. J. Thouron only two. E. A. Abbey was born one year later.
J. S. Sargent was born three years later and Joseph Pennell
was born seven years later than Hamilton.

If you had been standing on a *London* street corner in
1881 as John McLure Hamilton walked by on a summer day, you
would have seen a short, bald young man about twenty-eight.
<1,2> Hamilton was about five feet, five inches tall with a
thin, almost delicate frame and a large, long-haired brown
moustache. The rest of his face was clean shaven, and he
wore a double-breasted suit jacket open at the neck,
revealing a ribbed knit tie.[M011] He was slightly older
than the average art student.

Another hypothetical encounter at *Glasgow*
approximately fourteen years later would have revealed
Hamilton with a thin face, pointy nose, and wearing a
flat-topped summer straw hat with a broad brim.<3>[A559] In
THE BAILIE cartoon series, his scalp hair and bang showed
from under the brim.<4> He wore a dapper bow tie, a vest,

HERBERT SPENCER, c. 1890. Oil. National Portrait Gallery London. Gift of the artist.

and a two-piece suit while carrying an umbrella, because it usually rained in Scotland. You might have noticed his rapid gait and that he was oblivious to everything but his work, giving the false impression of absent-mindedness.

Perhaps if you had encountered Hamilton in *Philadelphia* a few years later as Thomas C. Eakins, the brutally honest painter had in 1895 [M012], you would have noticed that a beard had been grown and this added to his "*precise*" but "*dainty*" masculine appearance.<5> Hamilton dressed invariably in a three-piece sports ensemble with a single breasted greyish brown sports coat with wide lapels. He wore baggy, dark grey trousers with black shoes.

In 1912, Hamilton would have appeared to be a maturing French man of forty years, even though he was sixty.<6> Perhaps he seemed French as the result of his frequent trips to the annual Paris Salon, which may have numbered forty from 1875 onward. He had decided to cultivate his Parisian image through clothing as well as speech. He *sported* a pointed beard that extended just past the line of his lower jaw and past his ears to the scalp hair, which only fringed his bald cranium. He wore a flowing silk tie, peg top trousers, and low, squared-toe, fashionable shoes.<7>

Working as a full-time artist was a solitary activity which kept Hamilton apart from the crowd of humanity, the intimacy of family, and the emotional support of friends during his long working hours. As an artist, Hamilton only articulated through membership activity in clubs, fine arts societies, and museums. He also "socialized" through exhibiting his works in galleries and attending receptions and parties.<8> Occasionally, word-of-mouth gained Hamilton a commission for a portrait. Hamilton's hard-won reputation was built at exhibitions of his work based on the quality of his paintings. More often than not, even the most accomplished artist *traded upon the reputations* of his sitters to gain customers for his services. In Hamilton's day, it often meant traveling great distances to fulfill a commission. *Book illustrating* led to adventures in mezzotint and lithography, where hundreds could afford ownership of one portrait at a fraction of the price an original oil commanded.<9> For example, by 1890 a framed lithograph might sell at three pounds while the latter might command fifty to two hundred, depending on the size. The same held true for engravings published in the newspaper, where

(Thomas C. Eakins) 1895. JOHN McLURE HAMILTON. Oil 80"
x 50.25." Wadsworth Atheneum, Hartford. The Ella
Gallup Sumner and Mary Catlin Sumner Collection Fund.

MR. McLURE HAMILTON, 1895. Woodcut engraving 3.25" x
2." British Museum, Print Room.

250,000 readers could own the artist's work for the day at half a penny each or some might choose to clip and save one for a lifetime.<10>

Hamilton did not distribute *business cards* or publish *artist-for-hire advertisements* in the newspapers, as it would have changed the image of exclusiveness to a commercial one. However, after the turn of the Century in Glasgow, several POST OFFICE DIRECTORY listings were found for the painter under headings "*artist*" and "*photoartist*". <11> Instead of advertisements, Hamilton made contact with prospective clients by *working the correct crowd* at parties, smiling to the "right" people at receptions, appearing appropriately at openings of great buildings, recording at sporting events, attending political rallies and church functions, and most important, through the press. The quiet, influential words of distinguished patrons, friends, and admirers of Hamilton's portraits should never be under-estimated in this regard.<12> His readers included many *Royals*, the *landed*, the powerful, as well as the masses.<13>

PERSONALITY

Hamilton's individuality was defined in part by genetics and by his experiences in the business of art. Hamilton was educated to have a disciplined mind and the habit of life-long reading. These skills were added to the reportial skills of a diarist - a well-practiced listener, with a problem-solving approach to new challenges presented in graphic communication in a dozen media. Hamilton was a *good social mixer* with persons at all levels of English society, including the *Royals*, the peers of the Realm, politicians, clerics, scientists, physicians, men of commerce or industry, artists, musicians, writers, actors, and women. Yet, Hamilton had an explorer's eye and a sympathetic heart for people out of step with the establishment with which Hamilton dealt so well in his illustrations done in the Glasgow period. He understood *Socialists,* the *Worker's Party* members, and those who favored *Home Rule for Ireland* in the 1920s.<14> To Hamilton they were individuals who perceived that changes in that solid society of Hamilton's day were overdue.

As a painter, Hamilton could dissect and psychoanalyze a sitter in two hours with only pastel, chalks or watercolors at his hand. By then he recorded the essence of the sitter's personality on a paper before him for others to see through his own eyes. To paint an oil portrait, Hamilton only required three weeks to honestly portray the individual on canvas better than if most had known that sitter for a generation.<15>

In 1878, Hamilton exhibited cartoons that were the products of his honed skills as a *feature extractor*. Using the modern terminology of a computer scientist, he had done *pattern recognition* in order to portray just the right *bits* in his ink and sepia caricatures captioned PROMINENT PROFILES. He used this skill for book illustrations and even for newspaper cartoons during his Glasgow Period. His goal was to extract from a person's situation only that small set of details, clues, or relevant facts needed to present the essence of their personality. Hamilton created an almost Orient-inspired, impressionistic image of people for any observer to savor. It is this attribute of Hamilton's art that is cherished for its simplicity, drama, and impact. Hamilton was a human computer (scanner) one hundred years before the technology was invented.

Three news story quotations provide the opinions of critics about the artist's image. The quotations are based on direct knowledge of him by contemporary witnesses.

"John McLure Hamilton, who was accorded a special sitting to secure a portrait study of KING GEORGE V at a time when Americans were supposed to be distinctly below par in popularity at the British court, has been, probably the most interesting American personality among artists living in England since Whistler's picturesque figure disappeared."<16>

"Certainly one of the most picturesque characters in the art life of Philadelphia is John McLure Hamilton, the portrait painter, who now heads the *Fellowship* (P.A.F.A.).
Some men simply paint, some painters when they talk, indulge in verbal pyrotechnics as lurid as the most flagrant of *Cubist* masterpieces, but there is a quiet charm about Hamilton, the master of the portrait art, that few men dare to have."<17>

"Oh, I'm an old duffer and an old fogey,"Hamilton said in discussing Modern Art. "I much prefer the Old Masters."<18>

Hamilton inherited the *accounting skills* of both of his grandfathers and used the *business savvy* worthy

149

of his millionaire uncle.<19,20> He used the *panoramic vision* inspired by his physician/art collector father and employed the *legal writing skills* reminiscent of his Philadelphia-lawyer uncle. Hamilton negotiated contract law when nearly blind designating an *agent*, Mr. Jackson, to act on his behalf. Mr. Jackson acted as his agent half-way around the world, in London, involving the bulk of his estate, while Hamilton remained in the Jamaican mountains.<21>

The modest painter always had great presence of mind, now of feeble constitution (crippled, deaf and blind), drew an agreement of more than twenty pages specifying : required receipts, service performance standards, mechanisms for possible damage claims, details of inventory sufficient for retrieval of his *treasure,* the insurance requirements for its transatlantic shipment and trans-mountain shipment of household goods, his library, and the museum-quality art, he harvested during fifty years of discriminating collecting in London.<22> After Hamilton accomplished those requirements, Masta Harry Jackson, his agent, performed the task and the treasure arrived in Mandeville at *Hamilton Hall* without a problem.

Even though Hamilton was frequently in the midst of social drinkers and alcoholics, he drank rarely. However, he enjoyed red wine, rye whiskey, and Bavarian beer.<23> He frequently lampooned alcoholism in print during his Glasgow days.<24>

During stressful occasions, Hamilton called upon his reservoir of inner strength derived from his religious convictions. He refers to them in numerous letters written to Mrs. Drew. He had observant religious values inculcated by Mrs. Betty Hamilton, his Ulster born grandmother, and his aunt, Mrs. Ann Jane Mercer, and her daughter.

The painter, John McLure Hamilton, was a *family-orientated man* born into a thirteen-member household at *1600 Summer St.* in Philadelphia. He remained so until he was buried next to his son's plot in the Cemetery at Mandeville 83 years later. From 1885 through 1915, the artist's London household consisted of three generations including his recently widowed mother from America and various nieces of Clara's. Hamilton was a devoted husband who never *womanized* even though he painted beautiful women like Dorothy, Helen, and Marion for at least fifty-two years.

As a father, Hamilton did not smother George's independence. Instead, unlike Franklin, he nurtured and supported his son's education and career development, though it cost Hamilton every available dollar to do so.

Cancer killed his son, George, and the experience apparently estranged his widowed daughter-in-law, who emmigrated 1,200 miles north to New Hampshire. Clara and McLure faced their impending mortality after fifty-six years of marriage. The Hamiltons sent a flurry of letters and gave gifts of his art to friends in the United States who had been supportive in happier times. Hamilton had a high sense of purpose, self-direction, and community focus.

Hamilton had spent time painting men's portraits as memorials for when they were gone. Hamilton was an intense collector for almost eighty years and longed to establish a museum as a memorial to the scholars of his family in his last hometown, *Mandeville*. He also wanted to house his father's collection of rare books and his own papers and books. The cost of this last public service project, the *Hamilton Art Museum*, was estimated at $ 3,000.00, a sum greater than the team had in cash by 1936. He attempted to provide leadership for the project, from the bed where he was confined and sought angels (donors) from the United States to back it. The letters were dictated to his butler-turned-secretary, John Allen. Now, *our artist*/sculptor was keen to place the bronzes of his father and of the artist in Philadelphia, their native city. Letters to Thornton Oakley, his younger friend, indicate that these two goals were achieved.<25> We observe in Hamilton, the same industry and frenetic activity that had made him one of a pair of American Lions in British Art Circles during the first third of the Twentieth Century. The other was Joseph Pennell, Hamilton's friend since 1875.

Table U lists Hamilton's attributes and personality traits based on documents gathered during a fifty-eight year interval of his career, 1878--1936.

GIRL YAWNING, 1914. Pastel 22" x 17 3/8." In the
collection of Corcoran Gallery of Art. Gift of Mrs.
E. H. Harriman.

[Seated beauty, woman of the Rowley family], c. 1900.
Chalk oval. Mentioned in W. W. Corcoran article and
letter.

It was in his native city, Philadelphia, that Hamilton attended his first club meeting at the *Sketch Club*, which was a fraternal and professional organization. He paid a $ 5.00 entrance fee to that Club on January 3rd, 1876.<26> Howard Roberts was the President and the meeting took place at *10 North Merrick St.*, located west of *Penn Square*. We learn from *Sidney Lomas'* in his CLUB HISTORY 'the new, magnificent stone and brick building for the *P.A.F.A.*, a masterpiece of the Furness period, was completed ...for the celebration of the *Centennial of the U.S.* The Academy... opened officially with a large... Club exhibition that contained work by ...John McLure Hamilton"... and others.<27> Hamilton was present at subsequent *Club* meetings held on December 28, 1876, January 4, 1877, and December 27, 1877, while he was believed to be a *photographic artist*.<28>

After an absence of forty years, Hamilton was nominated for reinstatement to the *Club* on March 9, 1918 by Charles S. Frishmuth and seconded by John J. Dull (1859--1949). Both men were prominent members and officers of the organization. A program was printed for the formal dinner held at the *Sketch Club* and it was the custom for all guests to sign it.<29> The first and largest signature was Hamilton's signature. By December 14, 1918, Hamilton was elected to the *Board of Directors* of the Sketch Club for a term of one year.

The *Watercolor Club*, another organization in town, was directed by Charles Edmund Dana from 1900 through 1914. It met initially at the *P.A.F.A.*(building). Hamilton was elected to be a member of this *Club* in 1901 and was elevated to *honorary membership* in 1915.<30> Hamilton attended the *Annual Meeting* of 1918 where he was elected to the jury for the next annual exhibition (1919), and subsequently to its hanging committee with Joe Pennell, the only other participant.<31>

In 1924, Hamilton attended the annual meeting of the Watercolor Club while in Philadelphia. He was elected to the jury a second time for the next *Annual Exhibition and reelected to the* Hanging Committee (1925).<32>

At the 1930 annual meeting, a piece of art by Hamilton was added to its permanent collection.<33> It was the pastel sketch of *Charles M. Burns* (architect and club member).

The club paid $ 9.00 to frame it several years later.<34>
[A014] John Frederick Lewis donated a second Hamilton work
"The Corn Husker," to the club. It paid $ 7.00 for framing
the same year.<35,36>

Although it was customary of clubs to honor the memory
of famous departed members with a tribute of some kind, no
such honor was given to Hamilton during Oakley's protracted
term as Secretary and later President.<37>   Several people
who knew Oakley expressed a dislike for him and thought him
treacherous.

COMMENTARY ON HAMILTON'S BEHAVIOR DURING HEALTH AND ILLNESS

A collection exists of Hamilton's correspondence to
his family, friends, distinguished sitters, museum
directors, and gallery owners, spaning the period 1881
through 1936. It numbers 228 letters from several sources
(see: HAMILTON LETTER COLLECTION in Appendix). Obviously,
the collection does not include every letter he ever wrote
nor does it represent a continous record of daily events or
experiences in his personal and professional life. It is, at
best, a set of individual fossilized experiences expressed
in the artist's own words. Thus, each find was valuable,
informative, and enlightening but required interpretation.
Each letter reveals segments of his personality. The
collection is definitely incomplete and more letters were
lost than remain. It is a fragmentary collection, but an
intriguing source of *Hamiltoniana*. An analysis of the
content revealed information about Hamilton that was
unavailable from other sources. For example, his health was
generally vigorous enough to support a lifestyle that
included long hours of travel, sketching, and painting on a
daily basis for almost fifty years in London. Reading his
words aloud, one hears a positive attitude toward art as a
career, Hamilton's paintings, his family situation, sitters,
friends, museums, galleries, and shipping agents. Hamilton
was a happy man, comfortable with success. The artist's
words present an individual who was neither neurotic nor
ego-centric. Thus, Table T lists about twenty episodes of
sickness that caused him to miss work or a deadline for
various professional appointments, an infrequent and unusual
circumstance for Hamilton. Eight episodes involved the flu,
severe colds, or upper respiratory infections, perhaps a
side effect of breathing paint fumes. An intriguing report

GARDEN IN SEVILLE, Spain 1883. Oil 30" x 20." Formerly
in the collection of Harry Burke.

[Concentration], 1884. Oil on Broadbent & Taylor,
Philadelphia Photographer's studio board 10 7/16" x
13.75"

in 1890 mentioned an infection caused by fleas during the three week interval he was painting *"Herbert Spencer."*[A110] A possible *sequella* of the ectoparasites's presence is the triggering of a long term auto-immune disease, known as *arthritis.* He frequently mentioned this malady from 1930 to 1936 in his letters. I suspect that he suffered from milder symptoms much earlier, as he wrote a sympathetic observation about a contemporary artist, *Mrs. Lucy Graham-Smith,* similarly afflicted. She painted in watercolors with considerable merit in spite of her crippling disease and was the sister of Margot T. Asquith, the Prime Minister's second wife.<38>

An eyewitness, *Mrs. Peggy Simpson Johnson,* reported that she had met Hamilton as a child of about seven years of age. She recalled that Hamilton wore a fur coat in the Spring time. One is tempted to interpret this report, medically, as a behavior that palliated his symptoms of peripheral circulatory impairment and arthritic pain, when he kept his arms, hips, knees, and legs warm even in relatively mild weather.<39> In one letter to his confidante, Mrs. Drew, Hamilton referred to a brief exposure to morphine prescribed for relief of pain associated with his condition.<40> In this letter, he expressed concern whether its temporary use might alter his ability to communicate lucidly. He specifically requested the addressee to obtain an opinion from the eminent legal scholar, *Lord Charles Halifax,* regarding the artist's probity under the temporary influence of that pain-killing drug.

During the Fall of 1931 and for about eighteen months, Hamilton was in the health resort of Mandeville. He was physically ill and examination of his handwriting samples reveal a worsening condition in his hands.<41> The least legible sample was from March 20th of 1931, when his handwriting was practically illegible compared with the rest of the letter series. It was the custom of Mr. C. Powell Minnigerode, Director of the Corcoran Gallery of Art in Washington, D. C., to obtain typed translations of letters from Hamilton during this interval before acting upon their substance.<42> Hamilton resumed *still life painting* of island flowers in watercolors while in Jamaica, perhaps mimicking the inspiring example of the artist sister of Mrs. Margot Asquith during a remission of his symptoms. Baths in the mineral springs there are thought to be helpful with various medical problems.<43>

When the artist was 81 years old, the size of his
handwriting was exactly double that of the earlier standard,
implying progression of the cataract condition.<44> William
W. Corcoran reported that Hamilton was nearly blind at this
time (1934).

At that time, the artist said, 'all my work should be carefully
preserved as they are finding their way into museums and state capitols and form valuable assets
for my wife and son. I am in somewhat the same position as Thomas Eakins before he died. It took
some time for New York (City) to admire the merit of his work.'<45>

In Hamilton's 83rd year, Mr. John Allen, his butler was
scribbling messages that the artist dictated to various
addressees, including Thornton Oakley in Philadelphia. By
February, the artist's precise math acuity was diminished.
He then once wrote of himself as being 85 years old, when in
fact he was two years younger.<46>

ROLE IN PLANNING PHILA.'S CIVIL WAR SOLDIERS AND SAILORS' MEMORIAL, 1921

Hamilton's father had been President of the *Philadelphia County Medical Society* during the post-Civil War
era. Creating a Memorial to those veterans may have had a
special meaning for the artist, who was alive during that
period and very impressionable, since one of the artist's
paternal uncles had died in 1864.<47>

Hamilton wore many hats,[A067, A559] exhibited many
skills, and expertly performed many communal functions in
Europe and America based on a lifetime of practice and
success. An interesting situation occurred in 1919 while
Hamilton presided over a committee dinner. It was to be
held in Philadelphia and the purpose of the dinner was to
plan for a monument to honor fallen veterans of the World
War I.<48> Three prominent speakers were invited from New
York. They were Paul W. Bartlett, Thomas Hastings, and
Joseph Pennell, but none spoke on the announced theme.

Hamilton directed Bartlett to discuss the excellence
and deficiencies of French sculpture. Hastings was to review
the history of architecture in a condensed format and
Pennell was to be himself. Thus, Pennell told the audience
how much he had enjoyed that splendid feast, and pronounced,
'Philadelphia was a dirty, down-at-heel, snobbish town.' He further added that

'the people who think that they are 'it' in Philadelphia were the greatest fools in the world and they don't know anything except what they read in the PUBLIC LEDGER.'

One should hasten to explain to the reader that each of the speakers were long-time, close friends of Hamilton. Reading between the lines of the news report about that evening, one would speculate that the conspirators had agreed up front to speak about anything and everything but war memorials.

Three unofficial speakers were also asked by Hamilton to speak extemporaneously on the theme.<49> The speakers were Lt. Commander Henry Reuterdahl, Violet Oakley, and Albert Kelsey. Lt. Cmr. Reuterdahl chided Bartlett and Hastings for a few minutes. Next, Miss Oakley chided Bartlett, Pennell, and Hastings. Then she advised the audience to plan to wait until the monument planning committee in France had completed its work before Philadelphians should plan for one. Lastly, Mr. Kelsey advised the audience toward caution about any financial schemes whose purpose was to construct any buildings designated as war memorials.

Ultimately, the City of Philadelphia spent $ 88,000.00 on such a project honoring the AMERICAN CIVIL WAR VETERANS. In its finished form, two massive sculptured pylons were erected of granite and marble. They now stand at the entrance to the *Benjamin Franklin Parkway* at Twentieth St. They rise impressively about twenty feet above the backdrop of trees. The sculptor was Herman Atkins MacNeil.<50>

Under Hamilton's guidance, dinner conversation included anything but war memorials. But in committee, he probably organized the community interests, recruited *co-conspirators* from as far away as New York, and together they hatched the plan and carried the proposed project to completion by 1921. It is interesting to reflect upon a famous painting by Wayman Adams, a member of the Watercolor Club, titled "*The Conspiracy*" [MO13], which presents Hamilton, Pennell and C. M. Burns. It provides a clue to the identities of those who constructively redirected the purpose of the project. The monument honors all veterans, it specifically honors the memory of individuals their country had long neglected from the forgotten, local war which had torn the nation apart in the 1860s. The war was one in which Philadelphians played a major role. Surely, this incident is to the credit of Hamilton, our hero.

Prime Minister GLADSTONE EDITING BISHOP BUTLER'S WORKS, 1893. Watercolor on linen 24" x 18." Formerly in collection of Harry Burke.

THE BAILIE'S WELCOME [to KING EDWARD VII & QUEEN
ALEXANDRA], 1903 V 13. Engraving from THE BAILIE 8 3/4"
x 6 1/4." Courtesy Mitchell Library, Glasgow
Collection.

XIX : PUBLIC WORDS, 1878--1934

As a writer, a documentary artist for a newspaper, and the recorder of Glasgow's daily events, Hamilton developed and maintained a keen interest in chronicling politics, changes in society, and progress in public works projects. <1>[A237] It is hoped by collecting and presenting even a few of his published words that a view of not only *art history* but *world history* will be revealed. In his words, we find *everyday history* recorded together with that of the pillars of British society seen through the eyes of a respected insider of American birth. Hamilton comments about the important paintings of Old Masters and what he felt should be taught to future generations about great art of the past.

In *"L'Academie pour Rire,"* we encounter the French language humor and wit of a twenty-four-year-old Hamilton lampooning an American art exhibit for the first time in recorded history for the American audience. This occurred two years after the opening of the *Pennsylvania Academy of the Fine Arts's* new building.<2>

By 1901, Hamilton reported, "King Edward's [A395] choice of Edwin A. Abbey as the artist of the Coronation picture, is of course, a matter in which, we, all of us, may justly rejoice. Mr. Abbey is probably the best-known of American artists in England, and quite as prominent a figure as any in the art circles of the English capitol."

"America need fear no competition in art. Her art is going into Europe, just as her other and more commercial products. American art influence is something Europe is finding she has to

OUR PREMIER VENTRILOQUIST — VOICING THE ARMY & NAVY.

[Prime Minister A. J. Balfour] OUR PREMIER
VENTRILOQUIST, 1905 I 18. THE BAILIE engraving 9" x 6."
Courtesy Mitchell Library, Glasgow Collection.

GLASGOW'S CORPORATE OCTOPUS, 1903 VIII 12. THE BAILIE
engraving 9" x 5.5." Courtesy Mitchell Libary, Glasgow
Collection.

take into account. It began with West and Sully, and it is decidedly in evidence with Sargent and Whistler."<3>

In December of 1916, Hamilton told us, "Lloyd-George already under fire? Of course he is! All Premiers and their Cabinets come under the fire of critics. But I think Lloyd-George is apt to be as successful as any Premier since Lord Beaconsfield."

"As to Ellis J. Griffith, who is reported to be the new Home Secretary, it would be perfectly natural for Lloyd-George to appoint a Welshman to the office. And Carson? Why, I don't think the Home Rulers feel antipathy to Carson. They regard him as a strong, determined man who will risk his life for what he believes to be his patriotic duty."

"I know Balfour and Carson personally." [A311]

"The new Cabinet is the strongest combination of men that could have been found among the leading statesmen of Great Britain and it's entirely conservative in character. This is very remarkable but since the war, Lloyd-George has undoubtedly discovered the good qualities of the Conservatives."

"I believe Lloyd-George will prosecute the war with renewed vigor, but it doesn't make any difference what men are in the Cabinet. The men at the helm are the admirals and generals who command the forces by sea and by land."[A081]

"I never cared for Asquith."

"I often hear men say there is no opportunity in England for a man to rise from obscurity. Where can you find in history a more striking evidence of the falsity of this than in the case of Lloyd-George. It is a far cry from Criecieth, North Wales, to the Premiership of the British Empire."

"And then, he added, there was "Dick Whittington and his cat, who came to London and was chosen Lord Mayor."

"John Burns, earlier in his career once said that no man was worth a salary of more than $ 2,500.00, but he attained an office with a salary of $25,000.00."

"But to return to the war. It will be decided by the army, the navy and the people. Don't forget the people."

"And I have no doubt the Scots are quite prepared to continue the war--even if England should drop out," added Mr. Hamilton dryly.

"Austria and Germany were prepared to walk into Rumania and overcome a small army, while Russia, for a reason one can't understand, didn't come forward in time."

"But that will not affect the outcome. The war must be settled on German soil, by France and England on the one side and Russia on the other." <4>

In February, 1918, Hamilton reported, "France is not bled white! It is time to protest vigorously against this insidious, subtle and mendacious method of giving comfort to the enemy and discouragement to the people of America."

"There is sufficient evidence of an informed and authentic character to prove the falsity of these views."<5>

In August, 1919, Hamilton commented on an architectural plan for Philadelphia, "and why shouldn't we be concerned about our Parkway? For it is my feeling that our Parkway is unique in its promise."

"Just now we are at a stage in the building of the Parkway when we can make some serious mistakes, and at the same time we have opportunities that should be seized upon in order to remedy the neglect of opportunities in the past."

"The initial mistake was made when the authorities did not see the practicality of purchasing a considerable area on both sides of the (proposed) Parkway. Consequently, we see private owners now erecting edifices that will permanently disfigure the approach to this bouvelard. Contrast the unevenness of the Parkway skyline with the quiet and regular charm of the buildings along the boulevards of Paris."

"The Parkway should have been driven through *Logan Square* in order to create a vista straight through to (Fairmount) Park, instead it is broken by the circular (shape of the) square and interrupted by trees. Also, the square is broken up by overhanging wires of the street cars. I am sure that there is a very ancient law, still on our statute books, which says that private interests shall never interfere with these public squares of ours."

"The design of the Parkway, as conceived by Jacque Greber and Paul Cret, offers every indication of a very magnificent thoroughfare culminating in a beautiful Municipal Art Gallery (now The Philadelphia Art Museum) on the high mount at the Green Street entrance. There are, however, two important considerations in carrying out that plan."

"The first necessary step is to get away from too much dependence on the grove-like character of the surroundings of the Parkway, and it would seem to me better to devote more attention to the architectural lines and beauty of the buildings erected there. We have in the Park itself groves of trees that are quite sufficient."

"I would consider any diminution of the foundation of the reservoir a serious mistake, rather it should be increased in size. In this matter, we should take warning from experience of Washington, (D. C.). The *Lincoln Monument*, there, instead of being raised from the plain of the Park is now so low that it is only effective when (viewed) close at hand. The Monument loses its size when viewed from a distance, especially from Arlington on the other side of the Potomac."
<6>

On a different architectural topic, Hamilton said, "no matter where that (proposed Camden to Philadelphia) bridge is placed there is always going to be

MIXED BATHING, FRANCE, 1896 IX 2. THE BAILIE engraving
9" x 6.25." Courtesy Mitchell Library, Glasgow
Collection.

SENSIBLE SUNDAY, 1905 VI 14. THE BAILIE engraving 8.5"
x 6." Courtesy Mitchell Library, Glasgow Collection.

certain regrets, for you can not place a bridge anywhere without greatly changing the physical aspect of the district surrounding it."<7>

Concerning sculpture, Hamilton said, "the bronze equestrian statue of George Washington was done by some German artist. Washington looks for all the world like Frederick the Great, although I have heard other people say that it resembled a portrait of some keeper of the Zoo. Every artist abominates that statue, for there is so little character to it. There is a plan afoot to place it in all its hideousness in front of the steps going up to the Municipal Art Gallery. The approach to the Gallery should be open and not marked by another piece of German frightfulness. I intend to get out an injunction, as a taxpayer, if this statue is moved to the steps of the Art Gallery."<8>

In February, 1924, Hamilton revealed, "there is no plan for the development of the Parkway and no centre in any city ever has been constructed without a very fine plan."

"There should be a plan to build up the Parkway and use it as an entity." Philadelphia has the opportunity of making itself more beautiful than any other city in the U.S. The architects should get together."

"One building alone on the Parkway leads one to hope for great things. That building is the Public Library. I agree with Joseph Pennell that *City Hall* is a terrible pile of stones, and if we pass by the opportunity to make Philadelphia beautiful we will build nothing better."<9>

"The (Kendrick Plan) looks like a scheme to put up cheap edifices, save money and make the City('s appearance) worse than it already is."

"The perpetuation of the William Penn tower in no way would ease the traffic problem. If this tower is exposed, in all its monstrous ugliness, standing barefaced and ashamed in the centre of the City, it will more than fulfill Joseph Pennell's prophesy that Philadelphia is incapable of erecting anything better than the existing City Hall."<10>

In November, 1927, Hamilton commented, "I like Rubens and the other Old Masters. When I see the modern paintings by *Cubists* and *Futurists*, I sometimes wonder what Rubens would say if he were living and viewed some of their work."

"You want my opinion of Matisse? Well, what have I to say abou him? I have only bad language and surely you would not print my thoughts."

"No, I can not assume a liberal attitude toward these modernists. For you see, I haven't a liberal thought in my mind. What they paint are pretty productions and are not worth considering. Modernists are detestable to me anyway."

On Whistler, "I can say this : he was never a modernist, but was probably the best etcher, even sometimes, I believe, surpassing Rembrandt."

Of Pyle, 'more than an illustrator, a master and a painter, not a modernist.'<11>

In 1931, Hamilton commented on softness and beauty of his pastel drawings, 'you see, I don't like (to use) paint, and I hate varnish. At the (Royal London) Academy all you see is shining paint. There is no softness anywhere. Of course, technically, the modern paintings are extremely clever, but they lack beauty and have no satisfying qualities.'

On Futuristic sculptors, 'they ought to be drowned and one whom I know should have his sculpture tied around his neck and be thrown into the Thames.'

On Elgin marbles, 'they should be kept for the salvation of British art so that people can see what is real art and can compare its beauty with the atrocities which are being produced today. Why not print photographs of Futuristic pieces beside Elgin marbles? It would be a fit object lesson for the public.'

On portraiture, 'We (sitter and artist) each did our own work without interfering with the other and for me that is the only way of getting a true character portrait. Unless it is an extremely brilliant affair, I dislike a deliberately posed portrait.'<12>

In 1934, Hamilton asked, 'Oh why do we not all speak the same language?' On people, Hamilton said, 'the French are delightful.'<13>

John McLure Hamilton was more than the consumate artist being an entrepreneur of 1864 to 1936. In his view, a painter should have been merely ethological; however, he was also a land speculator, thrifty Scot, businessman, raconteur, humorist, political analyst, news commentator, and occasional editorial writer.

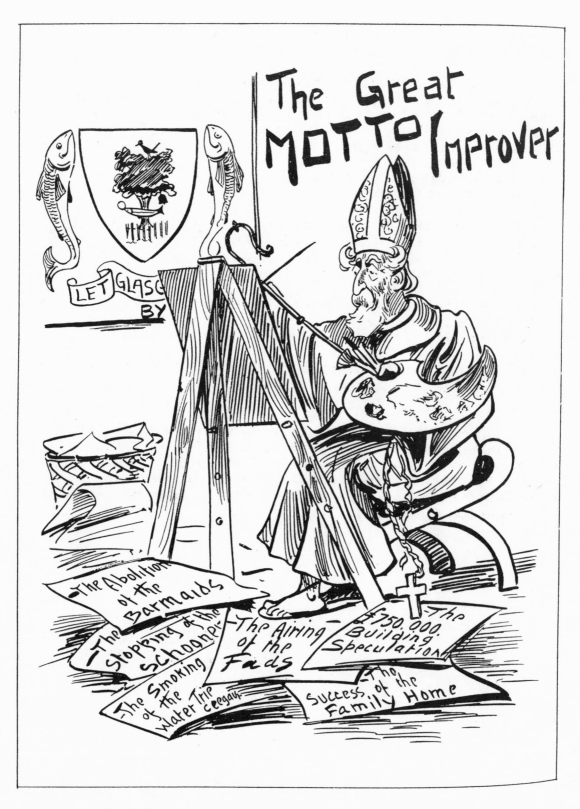

THE GREAT MOTTO IMPROVER, 1902 V 28. THE BAILIE
engraving 8.5" x 6.25." Courtesy Mitchell Library,
Glasgow Collection.

ST. MUNGO GETS INTO HARNESS AGAIN, 1899 VIII 2. THE
BAILIE engraving 8.5" x 6.25." Courtesy Mitchell
Library, Glasgow Collection.

A OUTRANCE.

A OUTRANCE (George Outram & Company was the publisher
of THE BAILIE & THE EVENING TIMES and Hamilton's
employer), 1903. EVENING TIMES engraving 3.75" x 3.25"

XX : PRIVATE THOUGHTS, 1881--1928

This chapter is a contrived interview held on John McLure Hamilton's 140th birthday at Philadelphia's *Wyndham Franklin Plaza Hotel*.<1> The hotel was chosen for the celebration because it occupies the site where *Hamilton House* stood and where members of the artist's family owned property from 1846 to 1937. The sources for the interview's content were the artist's personal letters numbering in the hundreds, including materials from his long career and complex personal life. Most of these were previously unpublished and obviously intended as private thoughts communicated in confidence only to family, friends, and trusted business associates. For the purpose of the interview, his thoughts are arranged chronologically. Only a paragraph or two was extracted and then his words mildly edited for economy. An analysis of their subject matter reveals his perceptions of career experiences, his insights to the great men and women of the day, the artist's political opinions, his devotion to golf, his insecurities as an aging professional, and his tolerance toward members of the Jewish minority, which was rare in the early part of the Twentieth Century.

Hamilton speaks in the first person for the balance of the chapter.

'I have just finished the portrait of the grand daughter of the *Earl of Ravensworth* which I commenced, finished, and received the money for within a week. And I now have the prospect of doing her four sisters. I also have a commission to paint a man and his wife for

MRS. [CLARA] HAMILTON, c. 1911. Oil 39" x 20." Philadelphia Museum of Art : given by George Earle Raiguel,
M.D., nephew of Mrs. Hamilton.

AMERICAN CATHOLIC BISHOP [Robert Seton], c. 1912.
Lithograph proof heightened with gold. British Museum,
Department of Prints & Drawings. Gift of artist.

$ 1,500.00--and perhaps others." <2>

"I met Mr. and Mrs. Sheridan Ford. (He) was writing notices for the N.Y.Herald('s London edition), and (she) had been interesting picture dealers in the work of such men as Swan, Clausen, Melville, and others. Ford had the idea of collecting and editing Whistler's published letters as a book, The GENTLE ART OF MAKING ENEMIES, with the cooperation of Whistler, their author. The latter changed his mind about Ford's involvement in the book project on the threshold of publication. In the meantime, Ford brought (to Hamilton) the advanced proofs to read, and the latter spent a great deal of time going over them, sometimes suggesting alterations and improvements. A note from Ford reached (Hamilton in the South of Wales) telling (the artist) that the book was finished and asking (his) permission to dedicate it to (him). Hamilton wrote back declining the privilege citing reasons. Nevertheless, Ford went forward with the (Hamilton) *book dedication*, in Antwerp, without permission. Whistler developed an instant irrational hatred of Hamilton from that time without having a prior meeting with him (or knowing the true events and actors). Whistler even wrote to Hamilton of his displeasure at being injured in a copyright and a personal sense.<3>

In a letter to the *Right Honorable* William Ewart Gladstone, *Esq., M. P.,* Hamilton wrote your 'small portrait had been selected from the exhibition at the *Paris Salon* (1892) by the French Government for the *National Museum of France* (Luxembourg Palace)." (Hamilton requested a letter of introduction to Prince Otto von Bismarck, and it was sent.)<4>

"The recent exhibition at *Goupil's Gallery* advertised my works at prices from $ 3,000.00 to $ 5,000.00" <5> [MO19]

In a letter *to P.A.F.A's Director Morris*, art critic and friend of the artist, Hamilton said, I "thank you and your colleagues at P.A.F.A. for their courtesy and appreciation of (Hamilton) and his work. My goods and chattels are scattered all over the world and I fear that it will be left to my executers to collect them." Hamilton wrote at age 45.<6>

"Some of the happiest hours of my life have been spent in the quiet and seclusion of the hallowed library at *Hawarden* (Castle) and no one who was privileged to silently commune with the great spirit (W. E. Gladstone) who occupied the temple can realize without emotion that its material presence is gone forever." <7>

(The artist was pleased with the quality of the color reproductions of *"Gladstone"* and *"Machivelli"* sent by Mr. Morris.)<8>

Hamilton tried to obtain permission and an appointment with *U. S. President* William McKinley to make a sketch of him as he worked in the Oval Office, but, he reported 'the President has been lately a simple hand shaking machine and until the hoardes of Western politicians have returned to their homes it will be impossible to get a sitting from him.'<9,10>

Most owners of valuable paintings would have lamented the financial loss and sought compensation but Hamilton commented after a glazed, framed six-foot tall pastel on canvas had been severely damaged in transatlantic shipment, 'these accidents must happen now and then and the painters should be willing to bear a share of the loss.'<11>

Where accuracy in the press was involved, Hamilton said, 'several (Philadelphia and N.Y) newspaper cuttings have reached me (in London) stating that I have been commissioned to paint a Coronation picture (of King George V). The King has recently given me a sitting for a portrait which I was commissioned to do for reproduction, that is all.'<12>

'I shall call and see Mr. (Andrew) Carnegie in N.Y.C. to tell him of the third completed portrait of Lord Armistead (his good friend) and give (Mary Drew) later an account of the interview.' Hamilton's wish to see Carnegie not realized at that time. <13>[A461]

'On my return, I hope to go to Hawarden to paint Mrs. (Catherine) Gladstone in her red dress which Clara (Hamilton) told me about--and paint Dossie (Mrs. Dorothy Parish, Mrs. Drew's daughter) with the two boys.'<14> [unlocated]

Hamilton said on his rare solitary ocean voyage to N.Y. in the midst of World War I, which had to be made even without Clara, 'I must be a very courageous person to be able to overcome the cowardice of my nature.'<15>

When the Hamiltons were in Virginia's Hot Springs for health reasons, they wrote to Mrs. Drew that he would shortly go to England, but that Clara would remain in Canada for lack of a passport. He declined to make even small contributions for needy children of England because 'expenses grow every day and my work hardly keeps pace with them. I can not uproot the Hermitage and living here (in the U. S.), in the way I must, is very costly. But if I prosper, I shall have something to spare for (Mary Drew's charity). We have both been ill for two months and are here for the waters... I want to see this War won by England on land as well as sea.'<16>

'The (Thomas) Eakins (Memorial) exhibition closed here yesterday. I hope (C. Powell) Minnigerode (Corcoran's Director) will be able to show a selected number of (Eakins') works, the two large pictures 'the Gross Clinic' and the 'Agnew Clinic' are the Masterpieces of American Art.'<17>

'Pennell and (Hamilton) are keping this Quaker town (Philadelphia) pretty busy as you may see from the (PUBLIC LEDGER) clipping. Pennell is to be given a degree by the University of Pennsylvania; on Thursday, (P.A.F.A.) gave (Hamilton) its Temple Gold Medal of Honor.'<18>

[Glasgow man in greenhouse], c. 1902. Oil 24" x 18."
Formerly in collection of Harry Burke.

[Glasgow man spading walled garden], c. 1902. Oil 30" x 20." Formerly in collection of Harry Burke.

Hamilton requested that his exhibition of pastels remain up until after the reception for the visiting *Archbishop of York* at the Corcoran in Washington, D. C. (Hamilton's request was denied.)<19>

On publication of Mrs. Drew's book about the career of her late mother, *Mrs. Catherine Gladstone*, Hamilton said, "I feel that it is a great privilege to be associated with this volume of loving memories of a mother, and one of the real and good women of the Empire." Hamilton's work, *"Mrs. Gladstone at home,"* done about 1893, was included unbeknownst to the artist.<20>[A037]

In a Hamilton letter to Corcoran's Director Minnigerode, he wrote, "a newspaper rumor reaches us (in London) that (*Herbert*) *Hoover* is to become the candidate for the Presidency. Let it be hoped that the *Republican Party* will not select him. *General* Leonard Wood would be a better man in the *White House* than any other unless it may be *Admiral* Sims. If you meet *Attorney General* Palmer, please compliment him for me on the policy he is taking of getting rid of Russians (anarchists) and socialists and tell him to exterminate them all, root and branch." <21>

"*Canon* Armour writes me this morning that things are pretty bad, (*Prime Minister*) Chamberlain has not made them better by preaching his reply to the memorialists in the monetary positions. What is needed is confidence and hope. The position is simple : increased production; increased exports; greatly diminished imports; economy of expenditure among workers and the great middle class in every thing but sheer necessities. Lavish expenditure by the rich on luxuries of British manufacture."<22>[A430]

"I feel just a little dazed after my (stay at) the home (known as the "*Wharf*") of P. M. Asquith. The feeling is not unknown to me when something very unusual happens but I always wonder at it, for I generally memorize and applaud, inwardly my presence of mind. But you will admit, that it does not fall to the lot of every man to live for a whole week with a *Prime Minister of England* whose wife is a literary star of the first magnitude."<23>

After the naming of one of Mrs. Drew's three grandsons, Hamilton observed, "Johns make good saints but bad kings. I feel that there is a great friend of saintliness in my makeup but I do not always draw upon it. The result is a good balance to my credit. A sort of negative capital that needs to be expended to be fruitful."<24>

"A brief announcement in the latest issue of *Federation of Arts* (alerted Hamilton, author of the pastels mentioned in the magazine) that the *Corcoran Gallery* has become the proud possessor of *Mrs.* (E. H.=Mary) Harriman's Collection of drawings by your humble (?) servant."

"I am very glad of this and very much elated because I will remember how they looked there at the time you were good enough to show them to the Public in Washington (D. C.)."

"In my mind's eye the drawings seem to fit your Gallery in tone and character. And of all other museums, it is the one I would have chosen for their home. There, they will be seen by a larger and wider public than could be brought to any other town. And their friends from the West, who know them, will I am sure be glad to see them again."

"I speak thus impersonally about the drawings because I feel that much of the merit they possess and certainly their charms, is due to the lady they represent." **Clara, his wife of forty-one years, had been the model.**<25>[A161,A171]

Hamilton wrote to Mrs. Drew in 1921,"I am so grateful for what you have done to persuade the King (George V) to sit for his (second) portrait. Thank you so much for the letter which I would like to keep but return in this."<26>

But eleven months later, Hamilton wrote again to Mrs. Drew, "as for coming to the Boltons (Manor), much as I desire to , this weather and the epidemic of *influenza* keep me safe at home, if one can be safe anywhere. People do not seem to mind passing on their diseases. You will recall I went to (artist's G. F.) *Watts'* with a "cold" and how he waved me away with out ceremony."<27>

"(Mrs. Drew), you have noticed how high I am about golf. The MORNING POST did not publish a letter I wrote them on the golf lesson at *Cannes*. What a complete justification of my theory of golf (it was)!"<28>

On visiting Jamaica for the first time, Hamilton wrote, "this journey wears a different character from all former journeys, it does not seem like a "trip abroad" but more of an adventure. Although, it is odd for people of our age to become adventurous."

"It is an epoch (change) in my life for I have ended, in my seventieth year, a half century's experience of London."

"The *Hermitage* is still ours so we feel that our Destiny is to be, in some sense, wrapped up in its walls, for good or ill, we go eagerly forward to meet George and greet his wife."<29>

"At my age to aspire to riches in this world would seem presumptous unless the wind, under the mountains and the sun in the desert are to renew my strength beyond all my expectations. And yet so strange seems to be the happenings of the last few months that I am, at some moments filled with a strange longing and a living hope that my days may be prolonged for a new, and perhaps useful, work to be given to my head or hand. In a fit of despair and almost fainting with weakness I picked up from the dressing table (aboard ship) a little book and mechanically opening it, I read at the top of the page, 'spare me a little that I may repair my strength before I go hence.' The prayer seemed to be prompted from the unknown and as I repeated it, strength seems to come to me."

"This great ship is plowing its way with majestic movement (*S. S. Majestic*, White Star

Line) through a calm sea to that mystery land of the west (Jamaica) where my son and his wife are, for the time, delving into the Earth for treasure, turning their gaze from the golden Heavens to the more sordid golden one whose fascinating glitter has tempted men from more worthy things of the mind. They expect us at their camp in this wilderness."

"We wonder what we shall find there? Now we are resting, soon we may be moving again within a circle of unrest and of new excitements."<30>

"Most of the company (on board) seems to be Jews, sometimes, after dinner, when dancing is going on everybody looks Jewish, save perhaps *Lord* Chan, who is a prominent Scot and his daughter who is characteristically English."
(A.S.W.)" Rosenbach : a great book buyer is on board who will handle my (father's rare) books."<31>

While Hamilton was in Mandeville in the Jamaican mountains, he wrote, "in spite of what *Lord* Burnham says, there is a feeling among some of the Jamaicans in favor of annexation to the U. S. And I do not wonder for the Island has been, and is still, neglected by England. Lord Burnham has to admit that American capitol has done more to improve the conditions here than British. But that capital is handled by the *United Fruit Company of Boston* whose activities are resented by many and praised by few. But, we have seen very little of the Island as yet and can not speak with knowledge. In contrast, with the settled districts of California and Florida its appearance betrays neglect."<32>

Fifteen months later, Hamilton in the U. S. wrote, "the world is going on in spite of all (*P. M. David*) Lloyd-George is saying. Everyone must eat and sleep. Most people are working for bed and breakfast so I can not see the awful conditions described by newspapers and politicians. Every one is moving fast over here. No one seems quite happy. Although all seem to be nourished and well clothed."

"The people have two passions, motors and movies. Plasterers and (house) painters earn L 5.00 a day. School teachers earn L 12.00 a month. All workmen keep cars, while the poor rich ride on the tramways or walk."<33>

Three years later, Hamilton commented, on a letter to the editor written by himself, "the commotion produced by my letter has filled me with dismay. The faith of my Ulster grandmother was not merely a hope, it was a conviction. She knew that her Redeemer liveth. She expected to change the sorrows and troubles of the Earth into the peace and joys of Heaven. That faith she instilled into me as a child and it was maintained as a living force by my father. It will not die! It rises above the mud in which I walk and mingles with the stars where I can see the immensity of God's purpose."

"I thought the idea of motion in space borne on the wings of an Angel (snowflake) a very pretty and satisfactory one."

"It was a suggestion of morphene[sic]."

"The letter was a record of an experience in which I expected you to sympathize. But my main impression was one of pain and in my own pain I could see pain everywhere."

"Below the shining surface of life where joy reigns, I could see an army of doctors and nurses (cuing up?) to deliver the pain of myriads of babies and children, of youth, and age. And it was this harrowing sight that madened my work hours."

"It was not the national killing of the three young men which moved me to ask, 'why bear the pain of the parents who were left behind?' And this simple incident is typical of what has been a primary one since parentage and the emotions pertaining to it first became the principle factor in perpetuating life. Faith is not recovered by knowledge. Have I become as a little child, I shall in no wise see the Kingdom of God."

"As for (John Aldous) Huxley, I think the thoughts expressed in his letter was contemptible and unworthy of a thinker."

"Men who never suffer pain do not understand."

"I am troubled; not about Eternity but about earthly matters."

"Much of this sort of trouble common to most of us-- could be removed by charitable thoughts, by greater kindness on the part of each of us. To be taught how to live well and be happy on Earth is more important than to be taught how to win importantly. A body saved now means a soul saved then."

"I would like to know *Lord* Halifax' opinion of this letter."<34>[A054]

Twenty-five months later, Hamilton wrote to C. Powell Minnigerode, "the result of the recent U. S. elections moved me strongly. The voting was for *Protection*, for *Prohibition* and for *Protestantism*. The majority of the women cast their votes for Prohibition because they do not want the saloon or the hotel bar restocked, and they are quite right! The respectable Christian vice soon dies out, and then there will be very little drinking."

"Never mind about the absence of my work from the exhibition (at the Corcoran). Another year will soon come around and then I may be able to send something, old not new. New art is like a newly dropped calf, ill formed, lazy on its legs, helpless and hopeless."<35>

In the absence of the artist's diaries, which were last seen in Jamaica fifty-three years ago, quotations from the letters revealed the details of the artist's relationships with and perceptions of others and his views on various issues. The people included Ravensworth's family members, Whistler, Sheridan Ford, *Prime Minister* William E.

Gladstone, H. S. Morris, Carnegie, Armistead. Eakins, Pennell, Mary Drew, *Canon* Armour, *Prime Minister* Neville Chamberlain, *Prime Minister* H. H. Asquith, Mrs. Harriman, Watts, Burnham, Rosenbach, *Prime Minister* Lloyd-George, and Huxley.

ST. HIBERNIAN AND THE DRAGON.

The Monster of the North Conquered at **Last.**

ST. HIBERNIAN & THE DRAGON, 1902 X 4. ENENING TIMES engraving 5.25" x 3.5." Courtesy Mitchell Library Glasgow Collection.

"ALL IN."

(artist unknown) c.1904. Lawrence Publishing Company, Dublin. NOW THEN PAT,...Woodengraving 5.5" x 3.5."

ALL IN, 1904 X 1. EVENING TIMES engraving. 5.5" x 3.5." Courtesy Mitchell Library, Glasgow Collection.

"Now then Pat, move on !!"

"Arrah lave me alone, sure its only playin' the Harp I am."

Lawrence, Publisher, Dublin

XXI : THE HAMILTON STYLE, A COMMENTARY

My Hamilton Study Collection currently includes more than 230 photographs. They are reproductions of publication-quality, in 8" x 10" format of Hamilton's artwork in all media.<1> (Tab. C)

Over 1,050 works of art by Hamilton have been discovered from a careful search of old exhibition catalogs, news stories, magazine articles, books, auction catalogs, the *Howe Inventory*, the *INVENTORY OF AMERICAN PAINTINGS TO 1914,* and the *CATALOG OF AMERICAN PAINTINGS.*<2,3,4> (see: *Notes & Sources* in Appendix and the bibliography for a complete list of the more than 650 references listing Hamilton's works.)

After analyzing the photographic images for content and listing the titles of all Hamilton's documented art work, a realization occurred to me that not one critic, art historian, family member, artist, possibly not even Hamilton, himself, had seen an overview of his masterpieces. An illustrated and comprehensive Hamilton Art Catalog had never before existed. This was no doubt due to a series of factors, such as the great length of his career, the many style periods through which his talents metamorphosed, the far flung path he followed, the early state of and historically high cost of photo-reproductions, and the broad range of techniques he had mastered. Information about Hamilton's materials, supports, and grounds have never before been reported. (Tab. Z).

HENRY JOSEPH THOURON painting goddess of Victory, 1900.
Oil 23 15/16" x 18 1/16." Courtesy of the Pennsylvania
Academy of the Fine arts, Philadelphia. Gift of the
artist.

It is possible that the scattered published descriptions and critical judgements of his works, available in the literature to date, are minimal, biased, and based upon the study of too few samples of his work to be truly representative. Reading Hamilton's thirteen critics revealed that they saw a total of about *twelve* oil paintings or *ninety* pastels exhibited at one place. Not one scholar had examined his drawings and or engravings. In contrast, presented here for the first time is an illustrated, comprehensive catalog of all Hamilton's work documented in all his styles and techniques. Images of sixty-one percent of them have been located. The reader can then select from over one hundred illustrations, his/her favorite Hamiltoniana, reassembled here from a world-wide, three year survey and numerous research expeditions.

An artist's style includes design, construction, and expression in many forms. Table V reports the names of more than fifty *artists* whose style *Hamilton admired* and commented upon in B012 and in press interviews. These artists obviously *influenced Hamilton's own expression* of ideas as traditional art or motivated him to purchase a sample of their work for his private collection (which was later to be for his proposed museum). Hamilton reinvented his style more than a dozen times during his career. Table W is a summary of the works and techniques of Hamilton, arranged as twenty-three theme categories. These categories include : animals, book illustrations, caricatures (*PROMINENT PROFILES*), cartoon characters, children, editorial cartoons, interiors, landscapes, portraits of famous men, religious subjects, portrait sculpture, still life, and portraits of women. [A235, A330, A505, A317, A245, A285, A306, A314, A140, A145, A055, A116, A214, A187]

In Table X, Hamilton's art is arranged according to the eleven diverse techniques that he practiced. They are collected only from sources with respectable provenance. These techniques include: chalks, charcoals, clays, crayons, engravings, graphites (pencils), lithographs, monochromes, oil paintings, pastels alone (or pastels heightened by chalk or charcoal or both), and watercolors.

The range of size for supports, used by Hamilton, are tabulated in Table Y which was compiled from measurements taken on a sample of 418 pieces of art arranged by frequency of occurrence *versus* greatest length (expressed in inches). About half of the sample was assembled from data taken from old exhibition catalogs, while the balance was measured directly.

Table Z reports the variety of supports for pastels and oils found. Lastly, a report on suppliers of materials, supports, grounds, and tools that Hamilton used is available.

HAMILTON'S TECHNIQUE : PASTELS

Pastel portraits were a saleable commodity in America when Frederick Gutekunst opened his Philadelphia studio at 706 Arch Street. (Hamilton's earliest pastels were realistic portraits too.) A handsome example [MO16] is one of the youthful, first president of *Haverford College*, the astronomer and mathematician, *Joseph Gibbon Harlan*, painted in 1857.<5>[MO16] In contrast, the "*Standing Woman*," a work of Hamilton's of 1910, demonstrated his academic training. "With a very minimal application of pastel, he gives us a graceful and unusual depiction of his model turned three quarter view with her back to the observer. Blocking in her dress with spontaneous pastel notations, he conveys its floating skirt and delicate off-the-shoulder sleeve; her back is rendered with a more finished technique. In her somewhat mannered pose, the model presents a challenge. Hamilton conveys her elegance and poise, rendering the work with lightness and ease." <6>

In the words of William W. Corcoran, " as I arose to leave...*Hamilton Hall*, the artist's last home in Jamaica... my eyes again rested on the exquisite picture of...Joseph Rowley's...daughter; there as in all of Hamilton's pastels, is the decidedly evanescent, will o' the wisp, elusive beauty, bespeaking the spiritual."<7>

Helen Weston Henderson, one of the beautiful women he portrayed in this medium, recognized that the beauty, color, and value seen in the sweeping folds of a voluminous silk dress had delighted the artist.<8>[A071, A187]

The artist reported that three pastel sketches of *Colonel* E. M. House took two hours and that one sketch of *General* William Booth required but twenty minutes.<9>[A074, A075, A011]

Sir Claude Phillips reported that *our artist* was..."far ahead of all draughtsman using this medium...as...an artist delightfully youthful in temperment, though he has long since reached maturity. He brings forward under the laconic title *"Backs,"* a

[I WON'T], 1914. Pastel on board. 28" x 22" Formerly
Mrs. E. H. Harriman collection.

[THE WIND = Elegant Lady], 1914. Pastel on board 28"
x 22." Formerly Mrs. E. H. Harriman collection;
Sotheby's, Inc. London; then Sloan's.

whole series of delicately-tinted chalk drawings of the backs of *danseuses* emerging from the very slightest of tulle garments. His touch is as vivacious as it is precise, his rendering of these bird-like creatures, resting as it were, between flights, has a charm that is in no wise sensuous."<10>[A182]

A 1980s student of art history, Karen E. Luik, attempted an analysis of some pastels by Hamilton done between 1911 and 1915. She actually reviewed twenty-two pastels and reported that they had "delicate outlines and tinting;" with a "crisp and energetic line" when the paper color was used as one of the primary tones. She observed further that the artist had emphasized with a white chalk relief from the background the highlights of the dress fabric.<11>

Some of his largest pastels measured 24" x 72" and were executed on canvas.[A150]

OILS

"In spite of the series of portraits of distinguished Englishmen, Gladstone, Manning, Tyndall, Watts, and the rest which constitute (Hamilton's) best-known work, he belongs rather to the American brand of the Cosmopolitan School. His little portraits (they are as a rule less than half-life size) give the sitter in the familiar surroundings of his books or papers, with more of the intimacy of actual life and less of the official pose than usual. The painting is thin, the background just covered by a warm glaze on which the lights are touched in cool gray tones, without much body but so surely that they give a solid modelling. It is not at all an English manner of work but has something of the French accuracy of drawing added to the warm shadows of Antwerp, which eclecticism of workmanship ought to constitute him an American."<12>[A042, A044, A086, A123]

In 1907, Richard Muther said of Hamilton that he based himself upon Alfred Stevens. "Afternoon Repose" is an example of this class of early Hamilton genre picture.<13> [A142]

Fourteen years after that, Mary Drew reported, Hamilton "must paint what lies before...him. And that these words might have been written about the artist by himself. He is intensely read. He is a true Impressionist. He paints what he sees, and as he sees it, and not as he imagines it. He paints the real, though the ideal may unwittingly be sometimes included. It is the same with his book (MEN I HAVE PAINTED)." She had studied his work for twenty-nine years when she wrote those words of explanation and introduction to his coffee-table book.<14>

Ten years later, a critic wrote, "techniques even in his oil paintings suggest pastel...one of the artist's best qualities is his careful treatment of the hands.'<15>

At the close of Hamilton's career, a NEW YORK TIMES'
critic said, 'Hamilton's brilliant, swift, nervous, half-finished stroke...was...used in
virtually all portraits shown. Exceptions are *Dr. Geike in his Library* and *Lord
Leighton.*'<16>[A031, A079]

Back in the 1870s, Hamilton had worked upon
cabinet-sized, wood panels measuring 5" x 8." *Reverie in a
Brown Chair* [A190] dates from his Eakins-influenced period.
Later, he favored the 18" x 24" (half life sized) canvas as
his "stock size" for expression. The artist reported,'I ground
the colors in petroleum (bitumen) for my paintings on evenly woven, French twill canvases. And
sprinkled water over the dried painted surface which had become glossy from overnight oxidation,
that was followed by a very gentle rubbing with a *cuttlefish bone* which had been trimmed to
remove its hard bony edge.' This procedure, first done on his
"*Gladstone*" series, removed the glossy finish which the
artist found undesirable (1890s).<17>

In one example of this period, the threads measure ca.
50 to the inch.["*The Hunters*"] Later in his career, Hamilton
used slick, more densely woven canvas as in 1916, "*Lady with
a Fan.*"[A135, A064] There, the threads measure ca. 72 to
the inch.

Hamilton's canvas on wood roller titled "*Memoranda of
Colors,*" dated 1864, included his earliest pallet and a
graphite instruction to use a strong glaze first before
starting the proposed theater curtain in oils. The border
for the curtain was to be white and the landscape was to be
executed in the following pigments: dutch pink, rose madder,
burnt umber, raw umber, chrome green, chrome yellow, red
ochre, ultramarine rose, scarlet lake, vermillion, and spown
brown.<18>[A227] He mentioned using bituminous colors in
B012, which restorers report never dry.

A reconstruction of Hamilton's process for painting a
portrait might reveal that he followed the same procedure
for the numerous commissions of famous men and women based
on his academic training. First, Hamilton prepared a
charcoal sketch, then a head study in oils, followed by an
18" x 24" canvas on which he sketched the entire body in
pastels or watercolors. He would record or create the
backdrop and foreground furnishings and props upon a
separate oil canvas, and lastly, the final portrait was
ready for a harmonious assembly from all previous
components. Each had been a carefully composed, recorded

[Mr. Jones = model's head] SKETCH # 4, c.1913.
Lithograph 12 1/8" x 10 5/16." The Carnegie Museum of
Art; Carnegie Institute Purchase 16.43.

[Miss E], 1877. Profile of portrait's sitter resembles
that of subject of MY MOTHER (a 1911 Hamilton lithograph). Graphite sketch with Whistler influence.

mosaic for reference use later. The final composition on canvas took shape rapidly in one day's labor, as if the result of one divinely inspired episode of creative energy drove the artist to execute the whole drama from the sum of its parts. For the skeptic, we can report finding, surviving from the "*Gladstone*" series, thirty-five such mosaic elements (canvases) in watercolors, pastels, and oils. The *Prime Minister* was the most famous subject that a portraitist could attempt in the Nineteenth Century and Hamilton's portraits of him are clearly his best known works of portraiture. For "*William Trost Richards*," the great marine painter, only three pastels were located for the two oils Hamilton created for his customary fee of $ 1,000.00. Thus, the pattern of professional, painterly activity suggested earlier is supported by the available evidence presented in the Hamilton Art Catalog and pictorial portions of this book. As a retrospective catalog, this was clearly based on far fewer pieces than were actually created by Hamilton.

Hamilton, in my judgement, the traveling artist *par excellence*, journeyed far to capture commisions (in oils) of more than one hundred V.I.Ps. Only two exceptions to his practice of portraying live subjects are the pictures based on historical figures that could not possibly have sat to him. They may have been Hamilton's interpretation from engravings by others.<19,20>

Hamilton, who described himself as a "painter of reflected light," always portrayed the sitter in shadow. Only the subject's face was illuminated by reflected light from a book or papers on his desk. It seemed as if it were done as part of a Spanish school bodegon (still life with people) from the age of Valesquez.

Hamilton could never be described as an isolated, destitute genius, oblivious to the rest of the artistic world. He was never unmindful of his fellow artists' activity. In contrast, the available evidence demonstrates that he actively studied works of others during his many annual pilgrimages to the Salon at Paris, where he inspected the best of his competitions' products, studied details of the current crop of paintings, followed the painterly trends, and Hamilton always turned what he had seen into a unique personal style statement. Thus, he never lacked for validation or cues for comparison to his work. He was constantly scrutinizing the products of the other leaders in the field for external standards of excellence. Hamilton searched out novelities and constantly made style innovations.

"*Cerise*" [or"*Le Rire*," A148] is a work documented from his Antwerp studies with Professors de Keyser, van Lerius, and Beaufaux. There are no documented works from his first brief Paris schooling under Professor Gerome, though many of his genre works have French titles. Not one forgery of his work has been discovered, though several important works have been copied; one by Charles John Tomkins, another by Frank Atkinson, and a third by Mabel B. Messer.<21,22> A lovely print of Hamilton's "*Dove and the Mouse*" was prepared by Atkinson from the original oil. It resembled a *bodegon*. <23> [A219] In 1883, Tomkins prepared a copper engraving and mezzotint of "*The Vivisection.*"

LITHOGRAPHY

Hamilton was elected to the newly formed (London) Senefelder Club, named for the father of lithography, when Joseph Pennell was its president.<24> When Whitman's PRINT COLLECTOR'S HANDBOOK was revised and enlarged by M. C. Salaman, Hamilton's work was valued like A. S. Hartrick's, T. R. Way's and other top performers.<25> Later, in HOW TO APPRECIATE PRINTS, F. Weitenkampf enumerates Hamilton on a par with G. F. Watts' in this medium of artistic communication.<26> Distributed in the widely read INTERNATIONAL STUDIO (a London magazine) was an "auto-lithograph" of "*W. E. Gladstone*" by Hamilton, which appeared in red.<27>[A047] Another portrait of the same subject was "*The Right Honorable W. E. Gladstone*," drawn after Hamilton's lithograph appeared in LITHOGRAPHERS & LITHOGRAPHY, authored by Joseph Pennell.<28>

At the exhibition of the South Kensington Museum, now called the VICTORIA AND ALBERT, *a Loan Collection* show included two lithographs of "*Gladstone;*" one in colors measured 7" x 9." <29>

ENGRAVING

Hamilton was described as an engraver during his

McLURE'S DOG, Belle. Pastel and charcoal 17.5" x 22 3/8." In the collection Corcoran Gallery of Art, gift of Mrs. Armistead Peter, III.

(print with F. Atkinson) THE DOVE & THE MOUSE, 1883.
British Museum, Print Room.

Glasgow Period.<30> His documented newspaper series of 136 PROMINENT PROFILES was published in the form of engravings to service his 250,000 loyal readers. They appeared in the EVENING TIMES, and then later as a bound volume including the first twenty-six reprinted under that title. Only six of these editions have been traced.<31> The originals for the engravings were ink and sepia wash drawings done in 1902 and later.[A588]

A magnificent *woodcut* titled *"Mr. McLure Hamilton"* was discovered at the *Department of Prints and Drawings* (BRITISH MUSEUM). It showed Hamilton facing to the right and it was made from a photograph, then printed on yellow paper. It was acquired June 17, 1895 as #628 in their Collection.<32> [M021] It bears an uncanny resemblance to the Thomas C. Eakins' full-length oil of Hamilton done in 1895. The photographic print of the painting must have been cropped to rib level for the woodcut. The photograph may have been an Eakins product, as well.

Wood cuts (xylographics) were obtained only from blocks of soft woods like apple, beech, pear, or sycamore. They were sawed with the grain, about an inch thick. They were used to illustrate finely-printed books.<33> Hamilton illustrated Hennell's THE LAY OF ST. ALBAN in 1901 with thirteen woodcuts.[A560, A569, A570] (see Catalog) This technique was at its height during recent history in March, 1885, when the *International Society of Wood Engravers* meeting was held at Stationer's Hall (London). *Prof. Sir* Hubert von Herkomer was the chairman for the second year.<34>

An engraving by P. Naumann, after Hamilton's *"William E. Gladstone,"* appeared in the CATALOGUE OF ENGRAVED BRITISH PORTRAITS IN THE BRITISH MUSEUM. Hamilton's *"Professor John Tyndall"* was listed, also.<35> The latter measured 7 1/2" x 9 3/4." Though no engraver is listed for the Tyndall piece, the source was PHOTOGRAPHISCHE GESELLSCHAFT IN BERLIN. (Messer's oil is based on this subject.)

A *revolution* in technology occurred by 1908 and the need for an engraver was eliminated by the availability of the improvements in transfer paper manufacture. Prior to this, Pennell said that the process of *artistic* lithography was made up of "mystery and expense." When the secrets and mysteries were exposed, its formula was revealed as "lemon juice, trade unionism, stale beer, and hide bound stupidity.'<36> Self-publishing

from copper plate presses cost eighteen pence for each
impression, while the professional charged five shillings
each. "Artists (including Hamilton) had studied in the schools, under (London) City Council
teacher, F. Ernest Jackson, (they) bought their own presses, (then) found new ways of working"
by 1913.<37>   Two of Hamilton's oils portray the master
lithographer, Pennell at his press.

WATERCOLORS, SCULPTURE, ETC.

Hamilton produced watercolors on small format
stretched linen (sample : two[A049, A072]) and on paper
(sample : seven). One hundred fifty watercolors were
described in the available exhibition catalogs collected.
The majority of them date from his Glasgow Period's
PROMINENT PROFILES, some from Spain, and a few from the
London Period. Nine examples in remarkable condition and
freshness have been examined. Hamilton was elected a member
of the *Royal Society for Painters in Watercolor* by 1901.<38>

While Hamilton also worked in bronze, charcoal, clay
and crayon, few representatives of these classes were found
for examination.

ON SUPPORT FOR PASTELS, c.1839

"A good and very cheap mode of making large diagrams, is to get a frame of the size
wished, and to stretch upon it strong, smooth, machine-made brown paper. (Furnished by paper
maker at four cents per yard, four feet broad, and of any length. In stretching, the sheet
should be dampened with a sponge, pasted on the frame, and then a hot smoothing iron passed
along the pasted part to dry it first.) Give this a strong coat of whitening and size (or glue),
and when dry, draw the figures with water-colours and size, of what ever shades are desired.
Then cut them off the stretching frame, and nail them, at the top, between pieces of tape and a
slip of wood to hang by, and between tape and a roller below. When smaller drawings are wished,
different coloured chalks and cartridge or drawing paper may be used, giving them afterwards a
coating of isinglass or skimmed milk. A good size for the larger sheets of diagrams (which are
in general preferable) is four feet by six; and a good colour, where particular parts are not
required to be distinguished, is Burnt umber, to be had from any house-painter."<39>

ON SUPPLIERS

While in London Hamilton bought his artist' supplies

PAUL WAYLAND BARTLETT in his Paris studio, 1927. Pastel on paper 31" x 41." Courtesy of Westmoreland Museum of Art, Greensburgh, PA. Gift of Mrs. Armistead Peter, III, 58.24.

GEORGE MEREDITH, c. 1911. Oil 29 1/8" x 38 1/8."
Courtesy of the Pennsylvania Academy of the Fine Arts,
Philadelphia. Henry D. Gilpin Fund.

from Goupil & Company in 1890s or L. Cornelissen & Sons, a company founded in 1873 with other branches located in Paris and Vienna.<40> He also patronized Reeves & Sons and George Rowney & Company. The suppliers were named in the descending frequency that their marks were documented on the reverse of Hamilton's canvases in the Study Collection.

While in the United States, Hamilton bought materials from Jno. C. Ripka including *Anco, Inc.* stretchers and *a Royal Crest Ilustrating Board* from *Harlock Brothers*, Philadelphia.<41> Many Hamilton canvases are unsigned and undated so manufacturers' marks, style of the work, and recognition of his thinly painted works aid the attribution process.

SUMMARY

In 1874, C. F. Adams, Jr. had cautioned Francis D. Millet against "versatility," and told him that it was professionally "dangerous."<42> However, it was Hamilton's multifaceted talent (with quality performances) in diverse media that provided the ingredients that made Hamilton's career commercially successful in the late Nineteenth Century and sustained him later in his career. His polydextrous approach to solving the challenges of professional growth provided Hamilton with the *guerilla tactics* required in the marketplace to remain successful in the art business for more than five decades.

The tables upon which this chapter rest help to summarize Hamilton's heroes of style, techniques he used, the size range of art he produced, and the materials he used. Although only positive opinions from his fellow artists and the contemporary critics are known about his work, the same independent judgement can be made following examination of the originals almost sixty years after Hamilton's death.

Hamilton's recipe for manufacturing his paintings is undeciphered to this day, but in a sentence often spoken by dealers, 'he was a fine artist!' 'And with four gold medals,' I might add.

Someone unfamiliar with Hamilton's oils could exhibit "*Lord Leighton*" and the viewer would infer that it was by the hand of P. P. Rubens. One could exhibit "*C. C.*

Glover"(as a young man) and it would be perceived as by the hand of J. S. Sargent. One could show "*Reverie in a Brown Chair*" and it would be received as T. C. Eakins' work. One might exhibit the "*Woodgatherer's Donkeys*" and it would pass for a Camille Corot painting. "*Afternoon Repose*" looks like one of Alfred Stevens' oils. "*Lady with a Fan*" resembles Boldini's work. And for one who has not seen a graphite sketch by Hamilton one could exhibit "*Edward O. Ford*" or "*Miss E*" and the viewer would infer that it was by J. A. McNeill Whistler.[A137, M024] The foregoing list *is* the best tribute one can make to the assimilitative talent of Philadelphia-born artist, John McLure Hamilton. He had a remarkable ability to transform his style and to reinvent his expression of it. The fact that he translated what he saw into his own *new language* represents his enduring legacy to Art History.

This chapter is an overview of the engravings, oils, pastels, and watercolors that issued from Hamilton's prolific mind and were executed with speed and grace. Also, some details emerge about his materials, many of his role models identified, and themes which interested him recognized. All this was revealed from an analysis of his art into classes, but attempts to probe inside Hamilton's mind during the process of creating art in his own style were not fruitful. That remains an enigma.

I set a large task as my goal. I provided a commentary on Hamilton's style, techniques, and materials. Had I succeeded in sharing all there was to be seen in these few pages, it would not have been sufficient to disclose the artist's recipe for his long streak of success. Hamilton choose to express his Impressionist view of the world and people about him in great diversity as he journeyed through life on two sides of the Atlantic for he was indeed, Art's Anglo-American Paper Lion!

HISTORIC GATHERING IN ST. ANDREW'S HALL, GLASGOW.

Mr. Chamberlain Opens His Propaganda in Favour of Reciprocity Within the British Empire.

"I DO NOT PROPOSE A TAX ON ANY RAW MATERIAL... WHAT ABOUT FOOD? ..... YOU MUST PUT A TAX ON FOOD."

The future Prime Minister NEVILLE CHAMBERLAIN, 1903 X 7. EVENING TIMES engraving 8.5" x 6.5." Courtesy Mitchell Library, Glasgow Collection.

WINSTON CHURCHILL IN ST. ANDREW'S HALL.

The future Prime Minister WINSTON SPENCER CHURCHILL,
1904 XI 11. EVENING TIMES engraving 5.25" x 4.25."
Courtesy Mitchell Library, Glasgow Collection.

(Edgar Degas) [OLD WOMAN with bonnet, cape, umbrella, and repaired teapot] 7 3/8" x 4 7/8" ink, sepia heightened with white. Formerly of collection in Scotland.

EPILOGUE

Mrs. Mary Drew (nee Gladstone) called for a biography of her pen pal, John McLure Hamilton, in 1921. She suggested that the most appropriate writer would be one of his forty-six famous fans described in the painter's coffee-table book. Her reasoning for suggesting the proposed biography was that Hamilton was such an interesting, real, sincere, and truthful person.<1>

Hamilton is to art what Mark Twain was to literature, but previous biographical notices about Hamilton were partially fictionalized. Recent research proves that they were riddled with erroneous information, myths, or bias in reporting because of failure to collect adequate evidence.

Some examples of the numerous small errors include (Teddy) Godwin's report of a March *birthday* for Hamilton instead of January. Another error is the artist's *birth year* given as 1858 but was really 1853.<2,3> A third is the artist's *middle name* listed variously as M'Turl, MacLure, McClure instead of *McLure* (or M'Lure), which he used.<4> Additional examples of minor errors provided him with a *new identity* as *James* M. Hamilton or *J. M. C.* Hamilton.<5>

Hamilton's *citizenship* should never have been in doubt, although he was falsely listed as a British national. He was a third generation Philadelphian merely living in England, Scotland, and Jamaica for sixty odd years. This myth

CHARLES CARROLL GLOVER, vigorous capitalist, 1900.
Sargent influenced oil 59" x 35.". National Portrait
Gallery, Smithsonian Institution.

CHARLES CARROLL GLOVER, mature & retired friend of
artist, 1917. Oil formerly of Harry Burke Collection.

persisted in various news stories and legal documents, but is not substantiated in official naturalization records in England.<6,7>

Lastly, his alleged impoverished condition was exaggerated in the news stories in the U. S. and Jamaica and was reported by journalists presumably to aid liquidation of his huge art inventory to fund the *proposed* Hamilton Museum in Mandeville.<8>

It was said that he seldom exhibited, but without much effort one hundred exhibitions were documented during a sixty year period of public exposure of Hamilton's treasures.<9>

Also, in 1989 there was a misattribution of his work to other hands by Falk in the case of his innovative art satire, "*L' Academie pour Rire.*"<10>

A major flaw in the previously published literature about him is a consequence of the critics' failures to research his works before they published their views. This is demonstrated repeatedly even though the reviews of his work were complimentary.<11> Recently, the sampling error problem has reappeared. This time resulting in a historically groundless criticism.<12> Thus, it was wrongly asserted that he was neither innovative nor influential and that his works lacked the 'technical brilliance of Sargent.' On the latter point, Miss Luik had only to view "*Charles Carroll Glover as a young man*" located nearby in Washington, D. C. to refute that faulty assertion.

Luik's second assertion that Hamilton's work lacked the 'subtlety of vision of Whistler's' is refuted by the contemporary critics including Morris and Whistler's almost insane responses to Hamilton's work and to the younger man in the social setting. Further, Pennell reported Hamilton's analyses and insights to the art of Whistler and others.

Luik's last petard, asserting that Hamilton's reputation rested on a little niche that he carved for himself, is refuted by his global sales and heavy income derived from sales of Hamilton's diverse works of art.

I plan to recapitulate Hamilton's documented but previously untold career story, which appeared in these pages for the first time. Although the accounts of his contributions were missing from the literature of art history in the period 1930--1993, the results of a class weighted analysis of his reputation in the various media he used prove that Hamilton's reputation was *not* based upon a 'little niche that he carved out for himself,' as Luik asserted. It was based upon twenty-three distinct themes and twenty-four classes of images, across all media.<13,14>.   Among his numerous innovations was the first satire of an exhibition of art in America, a Coronation portrait of England's King George V seen by millions of loyal readers, and paintings of the most famous but illusive man to capture on canvas of the Nineteenth Century, *Prime Minister* William Ewart Gladstone.

"Our artist," as he was known to his readers in Glasgow, was awarded four American gold medals during juried exhibitions between 1893 and 1918. This was official recognition of his global influence while he resided in London. Hamilton's unique perception of the world, depicted in his works, presented men and women simply and directly in a fashion that twenty-nine fellow artists admired enough to sit for him at $ 1,000.00 each.<15>

As an artist who painted for pleasure, Hamilton earned a fortune estimated to be in excess of $ 350,000.00 from sales of his rapidly-executed portraits. His work delighted his audience, which included Carnegie, Harriman, (Pierpont) Morgan, and Philadelphian, John Graver Johnson.<16>

Hamilton was a product of a devoted, intergenerational, religious, and supportive family. His grandfather's industry helped the artist's father to become a physician, life-long scholar, and art collector. Then, the artist's parents subsidized his years of art training in Europe after providing for a cultured and tranquil childhood in the midst of chaos in America. The seeds for his greatness were planted during two and one half years acculturation in Antwerp. His talent was pruned and shaped in Paris under Professor Gerome and during forty short trips to the Salon.

After Hamilton met Miss Clara Raiguel, fellow artist and love of his life, they were married in their native Philadelphia in 1880. Their son, George Hall Hamilton, was born in 1884 at their London home. But the artist's life was shaped by many tragedies. A fire in Philadelphia killed his youngest sister, Jennie Mercer Hamilton, and his

[Mrs. Caroline D. Hamilton & George Hall Hamilton=]
GRANDMOTHER AND CHILD, c. 1894. Oil 60" x 48.5"
Allentown Art Museum, PA, gift of Anna & J. I. Rodale.

[Mrs. Caroline D. Hamilton=] MY MOTHER, c. 1910. Oil
62.75" x 49.5." Formerly of Harry Burke Collection.

nephew in 1885 and hastened the artist's father's demise. With the several emotional losses, there were unexpected but useful bequests that provided for improved living conditions above the necessities of life for the expatriate American artist's household in London. His beloved aunts died shortly thereafter, each thinking of the future financial needs of the artist with his growing family.

Subsequently, Hamilton was employed by THE (Glasgow) EVENING TIMES, the largest afternoon news daily in the English-speaking world, as their principal artist (1902-
-1905). From their long hours and team work, the family of four *plus* three servants enjoyed a comfortable life in Europe. The artist and his entourage then migrated to London where Hamilton accepted commissions to create portraits of the cream of English Society. While residing there, he experimented with pastels, portraying his wife, Clara, more than four hundred times. Critics likened his pastels to the work of Renoir, Degas, and La Tour. Hamilton explored lithography, which gradually became a vehicle for populariz-ing his originals making them accessible to all people at prices they could afford. Most of his oil paintings (portraits and genre pieces) were sold to Americans.

Throughout his long career, Hamilton was a faithful club member and the relationships developed were pivotal to his further career enhancement. His career reached its zenith in the 1920s and extended to both sides of the Atlantic. A bonus included socializing with numerous Prime Ministers in England and the first cabin people of American art circles. Even a coffee-table book was published about his career during this period which is out-of-print. Gradually, he became the arbiter of what was right in urban planning and trends in art. His opinion was sought by critics, journalists, and others on many topics of the day, including global politics. Hamilton had risen from his modest artistic roots to become Art's Anglo-American Lion with a net worth conservatively estimated at $ 100,000.00. Hamilton's ultimate importance is that he createded the standard of excellence in portraits and pastels by transforming the craft of the Old Masters into the language of the Transitional Age for the American and British audiences.

Based on available evidence, Hamilton's travels and finance were tracked. From the analysis of his travels and finance, the sociology of Transitional Age artists can now be presented in a novel and unusual form illuminating trends that were previously obscure. These include a studio artist's income sources and their relative magnitude, and comparative costs of living, traveling and exhibiting on three continents.

He was a charitable, religiously-observant, public-spirited, communal worker. The role was reversed late in his career when Hamilton and Clara needed support from friends and admirers of his works for some of their immediate living expenses during the protracted probate following the death of their son. Their anticipated expenses included the *proposed* Memorial Art Museum of Mandeville, Jamaica. Since the project was not completed for lack of cash, the Hamilton treasure was auctioned and dispersed locally in Jamaica of the 1940s. Unfortunately, extensive advertising has not yielded the secret locations of much Hamiltoniana. The search for it could productively occupy scholars and dealers for the next Century. The artist's acquaintances included the great and near great in politics, banking, and art. Many of whose names are familiar sixty years after his death.<17>

During his lengthy career, he never used business cards or artist-for-hire newspaper advertising. Hamilton preferred to make contact with potential clients by working the crowd at parties, receptions, and on referals based on satisfaction with his paintings.

Hamilton, in the Twenty-First Century, will be recalled as a master of *feature extraction* and *pattern recognition* who could dissect the essence of a sitter's personality to record him/her for posterity. Hamilton was an Impressionist painter/illustrator of the Transitional Age (1881--1931) without equal according to the evidence. Though a famous son of a famous father, Hamilton did not smother his son's independence. Instead, Hamilton chose to nurture and support his education and influence his career, though it cost the artist all but his last available dollar.

Unfortunately, no one ever had access to an overview of Hamilton's masterpieces presented in an illustrated, comprehensive study collection of original art before this

[Figure study : Back], c. 1914. Pastel 28.5" x 21.5"
Philadelphia Museum of Art : given by Philadelphia
Watercolor Club.

FOUR CHILDREN ON THE BEACH, c. 1920. Pastel on brown paper 15" x 22." Westmoreland Museum of Art, gift of Mrs. Armistead Peter, III, 58.25.

time.<18> Thus, the previous literature is biased by the examination of small sample sizes (e.g., *twelve oils* or *ninety pastels*), their geographical dispersal world-wide, and remoteness of time since their last public exhibition. Here, over one hundred thirty illustrations of original Hamilton art appear for the first time, revealing trends in his numerous style periods and demonstrating his versatility in expression available in diverse techniques interpreted in the context of his biography.

H. L. Menken's words remind us that, "the great artists of the world are never Puritans and seldom even ordinarily respectable."<19> But as we pause to remember the exceptional career of John McLure Hamilton and his works, it should be said in the words of the prayer book, "Blessed art Thou, Lord our God, Ruler of the universe, who hast given Thy wisdom to men to portray such beauty in Thy world, who art the Creator of the universe, Thy power and Thy might fill the universe, and remembering Thy covenant Thou art true to it and faithful to Thy promise." <20,21>

SOURCES & NOTES

(Frederick Gutekunst, Philadelphia pastelist and photographer) JOHN GIBBON HARLAN, M.A.(hon., Harvard), 1857. Pastel formerly of Haverford College Art Collection.

GEORGE HITCHCOCK, c. 1893. Watercolor, gouche and graphite on linen 6 3/8" x 8 3/8." Courtesy of the Pennsylvania Academy of the Fine Arts, Philadelphia.

ACKNOWLEDGEMENTS

(Geographical/Alphabetical)

In the course of working on the biography, I was given help and scholarly courtesies by many persons in many places. I should like to thank those who answered querries and supplied information or further leads.

I wish to thank the following institutions and their staff members who aided my research in Europe and the Americas assembling the Hamilton Letter Collection and Art Catalog.

With a deep sense of gratitude, I wish to express my indebtedness to the owners of paintings by John McLure Hamilton, both in private and public collections for their repeated courtesies. Without their permissions to see portraits, to secure reproductions and without their providing historical and general details relating to many of the paintings, the Hamilton Art Catalog would have been sadly limited.

AZ, FLEISCHER MUSEUM, The Perimeter Center (Annabelle Markstein)
CT, YALE CENTER FOR BRITISH ART, New Haven
DE, ASSOCIATION OF HISTORIANS OF AMERICAN ART (William I. Homer, Ph.D.)
    Division of History & Cultural Affairs
    State Archives
    LIST OF AUTHORITIES & EXPERTS IN AMERICAN ART
    Library, WINTERTHUR (Eleanor McD. Thompson)
FL, Mr. Mendy Ullman
GA, GEORGIA MUSEUM OF ART, Athens
IL, Library, ART INSTITUTE, Chicago
MA, DICTIONARY OF AMERICAN PAINTERS, project in progress, Vose Archives, Inc. (S. Morton
        Vose,II)
    R. W. SKINNER, INC., Boston (Coleene Fesko)
    Brucia Witthoft, Ph.D., Framingham State College
MD, C. G. Sloan & Co., Bethesda
    WASHINGTON COUNTY MUSEUM, Hagerstown
MI, ART MUSEUM, Grand Rapids (Kathleen M. Ferres)
MN, INSTITUTE OF ART, Minneapolis (Brian J. Mulhern)
MO, HAMILTON NATIONAL GENEALOGICAL SOCIETY,Inc., Oak Grove
    George Hessler, St. Louis
NH, CURRIER GALLERY OF ART, Manchester
NY, MUSEUM, Brooklyn, Linda S. Ferber
    Diane P. Fischler, Pratt Institute, Brooklyn
    ALBRIGHT-KNOX ART GALLERY, Buffalo
    BUFFALO & ERIE HISTORICAL SOCIETY, Library, Buffalo
    CHRISTIE, MASON & WOOD INTERNATIONAL,INC., Books & Manuscripts (Nina Musinsky)
    FRICK ART REFERENCE LIBRARY, NYC
    HISTORICAL SOCIETY, NYC, Susan M. Sivard
    METROPOLITAN MUSEUM OF ART, NYC, T. J. Watson Library, Reader Services (Linda Seckelson)
                Curator of Prints
    PUBLIC LIBRARY, NYC, Artists Files, Art & Architecture Collection, Miriam & Ira D. Wallach
                Division of Art, Prints & Photographs, Astor, Lenox, & Tilden Foundations
                (Charlotte Dixon) [H54/B1-3 1940 letter from Howe, S.J.]

SOTHEBY'S, Inc. NYC, Holly Goetz
    Francine Tyler
PA, ART MUSEUM, Allentown
    AMERICAN BANK NOTE COMPANY, Horsham, Aurelia Chen (archivist)
    Library, Special Collections, BRYN MAWR COLLEGE
    CARNEGIE MUSEUM OF ART, Pittsburgh
    Library, Roberts Autograph Collection, HAVERFORD COLLEGE
    McCLEES GALLERY, Ardmore
    SWARTHMORE COLLEGE, Constance C. Hungerford, Ph.D.
    VALLEY FORGE MILITARY ACADEMY & JUNIOR COLLEGE
    WESTMORELAND MUSEUM OF ART, Greensburg (Paul A. Chew)
    Wolfgram Memorial Library, WIDENER UNIVERSITY
    PA MAGAZINE, Albert E. Holliday, editor
    Phila., Mrs. Elsie Levenson-Burke
          Mr. Harry Burke
          CIGNA MUSEUM & ART COLLECTION (Sue Levy)
          DAVID DAVID, Inc., Carl David
          FREE LIBRARY, Parkway, Art Department
          GENEALOGICAL SOCIETY OF PA
          Mr. Henry Gerlach
          HISTORICAL SOCIETY OF PA
          Mrs. Peggy Simpson Johnson
          JUNIUS, Inc., HAMILTON PICTORIAL IMAGE COLLECTION
          LIBRARY COMPANY
          GEORGE S. MacMANUS, CO. (Clarence Wolf)
          MUSEUM OF ART, Library
                  Prints, Drawings & Photographs Department (Beth Venn)
          NATIONAL ARCHIVES, branch
          NEWMAN GALLERIES (Walter A. Newman, Jr.)
          PA ACADEMY OF FINE ARTS, Archives (Mrs. Cheryl Leibold)
                  Fellowship (Bill Greenwood)
                  Library (Mrs. Marietta Bushnell)
                  Registrar (Ms. Judy Heywood Moore)
          SCHWARZ GALLERY (Robert D. Schwarz)
          Urban Archives Center, Special Collections, Library, TEMPLE UNIVERSITY
          UNIVERSITY OF PA (Jacqueline Jacovini)
                  Fisher Art Library
VA, Mr. F. Grice Whitely
WASHINGTON, D. C., CORCORAN GALLERY OF ART, Lisa Luedtke
                            Mrs. Linda Simmons, Curator
         NATIONAL ENDOWMENT FOR THE HUMANITIES, Reference Materials (Michael B.
                      Poliakoff)
         NATIONAL GALLERY OF ART, Photo Archives, R. Philbrick, Curator
                        Christopher With, Art Information
         NATIONAL MUSEUM OF AMERICAN ART, Smithsonian Institution
           George Gurney, Associate Curator
            ARCHIVES OF AMERICAN ART, Catherine Stover, Archivist
                          Peggy A. Feerick, Photos
                          Joan Stahl, Coordinator, IMAGE COLL.
                          Judy Throm

INVENTORY OF AMERICAN PAINTINGS EXECUTED BEFORE 1914, Christopher
Hennessey, Coordinator
JoAnne Triplett, Assistant Coord.
INVENTORY OF AMERICAN SCULPTURE
NATIONAL PORTRAIT GALLERY
CATALOG OF AMERICAN PAINTINGS, Linda Thrift, Keeper
Deborah L. Sisum, Deputy

SMITHSONIAN ART INDEX

BELGIUM, Antwerp. Herwig Todts, Ph.D., Koninklijk Museum voor Schone Kunsten
Brussels. Jenny Martin, Ph.D.
CANADA, Toronto. THOM FINE ART, Ltd.
ENGLAND, Cambridge. A. & C. BLACK, LTD.
Eastbrooke. TOWNER ART GALLERY & LOCAL HISTORY MUSEUM
Kew. ROYAL BOTANICAL GARDENS (M. J. Ward)
Kingston-on-Thames, Surrey. HERITAGE MUSEUM (Tim Everson)
Liverpool. WALKER ART GALLERY, NATIONAL MUSEUM/GALLERY, Merseyside (Joseph Sharples)
London. BRITISH LIBRARY, Newspaper Room
Print Room
LEIGHTON HOUSE MUSEUM (Joanna Banham, Curator)
NATIONAL GALLERY
NATIONAL PORTRAIT GALLERY
PATENT OFFICE, Hazlitt House (N. Hamdani)
PRINT QUARTERLY (David Landau, editor)
ROYAL ACADEMY OF ARTS, Piccadilly, Library (G. Smee)
ROYAL COLLECTION, Windsor Castle (Hon. Mrs. Roberts)
ROYAL COMMISSION ON HISTORICAL MANUSCRIPTS, Quality House
TATE GALLERY, Millbank, Archives (Louise Ray)
VICTORIA & ALBERT MUSEUM, Prints & Drawings Department
WATERHOUSE & DODD (Ray Waterhouse)
FRANCE, Paris. MUSEE D'ORSAY
IRELAND, Dublin. NATIONAL GALLERY
ITALY, Venice. CA' Pesaro Galleria Int. D'Arte Moderne. Giandomenico Romanelli
JAMAICA, Kingston. NATIONAL ART GALLERY
NATIONAL LIBRARY (Mrs. Eppie D. Edwards)
SCOTLAND, NATIONAL GALLERY, Mound. (Lindsay M. Errington, Ph.D.)
NATIONAL LIBRARY, Manuscripts Division
Edinburgh. UNITED DISTILLERS (Jennifer Campbell, Asst. Archivist)
Falkirk. Library (J. M. Sanderson, Curator)
Fife. UNIVERSITY OF ST. ANDREWS, Art History Department (Miss Dawn Waddell)
Glasgow. ART GALLERY & MUSEUM, Kelvingrove
SCHOOL OF ART (Ian C. Monie)
MITCHELL LIBRARY, Local Studies Department (Erda Ryan)
STRATHCLYDE REGIONAL ARCHIVES, Mitchell Library
UNIVERSITY, Archives (Michael S. Moss)
UNIVERSITY LIBRARY, Whistler Papers, Special Collections
(Nigel Thorp, Ph.D.)

RESESOURCES

Comment. The Hamilton bibliography is arranged as thirteen blocks of scattered published references and unpublished original materials. Information is arranged chronologically within a block and numbered serially by date of authorship or publication where known.

1	Retrieved Images of Hamilton's art works	A000
2	Books citing Hamilton or his works	B000
3	Dictionaries/Encyclopedias citing Hamilton or his works	D000
4	Exhibition Catalogs listing Hamilton's works	E000
5	Journals citing Hamilton	J000
6	The Hamilton Letter Collection	L000
7	News Stories citing Hamilton	N000
8	Unpublished Hamilton Materials	U000
9	The Hamilton Art Catalog (all documented works)	F000
10	Memorabilia Inventory	C000
11	Biographical Documents	G000
12	Miscellaneous Images	M000
13	Owners Recorded to 1940	H000

ABBREVIATIONS OF SOURCE LOCATIONS

(Antwerp Academy), Belgium	AnA
Newspaper Dept., *Public Library*, Antwerp, Belgium	APLN
Thornton Oakley papers, Brandywine River Museum, Chadds Ford, PA	TOP
University Library, Glasgow, Scotland	GUL
Mitchell Library, Glasgow	GML
POSTAL DIRECTORY, Glasgow	GPD
C. Roberts Collection, Library, Haverford, PA	HCRC
Archives, Spanish Town, Jamaica	JAST

National Library, Kingston, Jamaica	JNL
Land Records Office, Mandeville, Jamaica	JLROM
Land Records Office, Spanish Town, Jamaica	JLROST
Real Estate Tax Evaluation Office, Kingston, Jamaica	JTOK
British Museum, London, England	BML
Public Records Office, Kew, England	PROKE
National Art Library, London, England	NALL
POSTAL DIRECTORY, London	LPD
St. Catherine's House, London	SCH
Somerset House, London	SH
Print Room, Victoria & Albert Museum, London	VAPR
Orphans' Court, Norristown, Montgomery co.,PA	OCNP
Recorder of Deeds, above	RDNP
Metropolitan Museum, NYC	MMN
Archives, National Academy of Design, NYC	NADN
Oak Grove Cemetery, Enfield, NH	OGCENH
Tax Office, Enfield, NH	TOENH
Register of Wills, Hanover, Grafton co., NH	RWHNH
Archives, Carnegie Museum of Art, Pittsburgh, PA	CMAP
All Saints P.E. Church, Torresdale, Phila., PA	ASCP
City Archives, Phila., PA	ACP
Art Alliance of Phila., PA	AAP
Art Museum, Phila., PA	AMP
Library, College of Physicians & Surgeons, Phila., PA	CPSLP
County Medical Society, Phila., PA	CMSP
Newspaper Room, Free Library, Parkway, Phila., PA	FLNP
Vertical File, Art Dept., above	FLAP
Manuscript Room, Historical Society of PA, Phila.	HSMP
Marriage Records, Orphans' Court, City Hall, Phila.	OCMP
Estate Records, above	OCEP
Recorder of Deeds, City Hall, Phila.	RDP
Recorder of Wills, above	RWP
Archives, PA Academy of Fine Arts, Phila.	PAFA
Vertical File, Library, PAFA	PAFAL
Historical Medical Library, PA Hospital, Phila.	HMLHP
Presbyterian Historical Society, Phila.	PHSP
Sketch Club, Phila.	SCP
Archives, Rosenbach Museum, Phila.	RMP
Van Pelt Library, University of PA	UPVPLP
St. Michael's/Zion (German) Lutheran Church, Phila.	SMZLCP
Urban Archives, Paley Library, Temple University, Phila.	TUUA
Watercolor Club, Phila.	WCCP
U.S. National Archives, Phila. Branch	USNABP
Archives of American Art, Washington, D. C.	AAA
Journal, above	AAAJ
Archives, Corcoran Gallery of Art, Washington, D. C.	CGA

(Edgar Degas)[Young girl in party dress]. Watercolor
and graphite 10 7/8" x 10 1/8." Formerly of collection
in Scotland.

RETRIEVED IMAGES OF HAMILTON'S ARTWORKS

PHOTOGRAPHS
1993

sitters		source	#
Mr. Asquith		B012	A001
Mrs. Asquith		B012	A002
Canon Armour		B012	A003
Lord Armistead		B012	A004
Arthur James Balfour		B012	A005
Paul Wayland Bartlett in his Paris Studio		W-1	A006
above, sketch for		WCMHM	A203
Mrs. P. W. Bartlett		C-1	A007
Bismarck		B012	A008
Bismarck, JMLH		C-2A	A009
same as A009 "Gladstone reading"		C-2B	A010
General Booth		B012	A011
Buckley, Mrs. Nora King/Flowers in lap		HB-36	A066
C. M. Burns, 270		HB-1	A012
C. M. Burns, oil		HB-2	A013
Charles Marquedant Burns		B012	A014
Prof. Lewis Campbell, 1885		SA-1	A015
Thomas Carlyle, 1924 # 1		C-3	A016
Thomas Caryle, 1924 # 2 January		C-4	A017
Edward H. Coates		CGN-1	A018
Mrs. E. H. Coates (Florence Earle)		X	A019
Edward Clifford		B012	A020
Mathew Ridley Corbet		NPGL-1	A021
Cyrus H. K. Curtis		B012	A022
Dana Painting in Park, 220		HB-3	A023
Charles E. Dana, portrait of		PMA-1	A024
Group Portrait (Dana, Hamilton, Pennell, Welsh)		PAFA-1	A025
Mrs. Myles Edwards/ Mrs. Strickland at the Piano (Maud/Muffin)		SWRZ-1	A027
George Hall Hamilton (age 2/3 years) with string to unseen toy		HB-4	A028
Edward Onslow Ford, 1893, see A137		NPGL-2	A029
above, graphite sketch		NPGL-7	A137
Master Wolfram Ford		J003-1	A030
Sir Archibald Geikie in his Library		B012	A031
Sir Alfred Gilbert, 1887 #135		NPGL-3	A032
GOD SAVE THE KING! 1911 VI 22		DC-1	A033
King George V		HB-5	A034
King George V, T. Way. Impt. (Litho) 1913-12-13-26		BM-1	A035
Mrs. Catherine Gladstone, 1898 Harper's Weekly	x	NYPL-1	A036

Mrs. Catherine Gladstone at Hawarden, c. 1893	B031	A037
Baron Henry Gladstone	B012	A038
Stephen Gladstone	B012	A039
Wm. E. Gladstone, Luxembourg in color	MP-1	A040
Wm. E. Gladstone, above engraved by Plat	J002	A041
Rt. Hon. Wm. E. Gladstone at Downing St., fac. left	PAFA-2	A042
above, Detroit Publishing Co. reproduction, 13265 sepia	PAFAL-3	A043
Wm. E. Gladstone, Luxembourg, B & W	MP-2	A044
Wm. E. Gladstone, litho, color added	YCBA-1	A045
Wm. E. Gladstone, auto-litho in red, original	J056-1	A046
Wm. E. Gladstone, litho, color, signed	PAFA-4	A047
Wm. E. Gladstone, oil	HB-6	A048
Gladstone editing works of Bishop Butler, wc	HB-7	A049
above, oil	TL-1	A066
Wm. E. Gladstone, clay bust see A010	B012	A050
Wm. C. G. Gladstone	B012	A051
Charles Carroll Glover, young man	NPGW-1	A052
above, older man	HB-8	A053
Lord Charles Halifax	B012	A054
Lords of Appeal (nine men) as Christmas card	C-5	A055
Lord Halsbury, Lord Esher, Lord Fry, Lord Lindley	B012	A056
Caroline Hamilton, head study, oil	HB-9	A057
above, My Mother, litho.	NYPL PR-2	A058
above, & son of artist, George Hall Hamilton on her lap squirming	AP-1	A059
above, My Mother, facing left, oil cf M024 profile	HB-10	A060
Mrs. (Clara) Hamilton, plumed hat	PMA-2	A061
George Hall Hamilton, age 3, Green Coat, Cap, on Plush Stool	HB-11	A063
cf A028, A059, A202, A203, A204, A207, M018		
above, The Hunters	HB-24	A138
above, Prof. at Observatory Desk, 1924	JP-3	A064
John McLure Hamilton, Ford's bronze bust of, Hamilton engraved drawing	Chc-1	A065
above, Cellar Type, Self-portrait, High Hat, Cape, detail of	HB-12	A067
above, c. 1918	HB-12	A068
above, portrait to shoulders Freeman catalog	X	A069
A. S. Hartrick, litho, 227-318, 36226/2/1 1927-2-12-86	BM-2	A070
Miss Helen Weston Henderson, 1911	JP-4	A071
George Hitchcock, wc/gouache, graphite on linen	PAFA-5	A072
Colonel Edward M. House, David Lloyd-George, &...(man), detail	HB-13	A073
Col. E. M. House, "Hotel Crillon/Paris, 1919 IX"	HB-14	A074
above,	JP-5	A075
above, hat, oil	B012	A076
Sir Henry Irving	B012	A077
Mrs. Nora King BucKley as young woman, millinery, 1889	HB-15	A078
Lord Frederick Leighton, oil	LH-1	A079
above, pastel	B012	A080
David Lloyd-George, detail of A073	HB-16	A081

Nathaniel Lindley, 1st Baron, litho	1928 3-10-66		BM-3	A082
Charles Ludington			B012	A083
Cardinal Edward Henry Manning, engraved			Chc-2	A084
above, pastel, 1890 Westminister			PAFA-6	A085
above, oil			B012	A086
Prof. Edgar Marburg, C.E., D. Sc.			UP-1	A087
George Meredith, as christmas card			X	A088
above, Detroit Publishing Co., reproduction, sepia			VG-1	A089
above, oil			PAFA-7	A090
Mrs. Anna Lea Merritt, oil			PAFA-8	A091
Silas Weir Mitchell, M.D., oil			UP-2	A092
Wm. Cosmo Monkhouse, oil			NPGL-4	A093
Mrs. Arthur Edmond Oakley (Imogen)			X	A094
Joseph Pennell, standing			B012	A095
above, seated			PMA-3	A096
Judge William W. Porter			B012	A097
Mrs. W. W. Porter, 1917	1918 PAFA WCM		X	A098
Jean Francois Raffaelli			X	A099
Wm. Trost Richards, pastel			PAFA-9	A100
above, with glasses, reading, #459			HB17	A101
above, Detroit Publishing Co., reproduction, M320			PAFA-10	A102
above, globe, chair, lead windows, oil			PAFA-11	A103
Dr. George Inman Riche, Central High School, 4th President			FSE-1	A104
Governor Robert Pyle Robinson, DE (cousin)			DE-1	A105
Dr. Henri Rochefort			B012	A106
American Catholic Bishop (Robert Cardinal Seton), 1912, litho			BM-4	A107
presented by Hamilton #36226/1/4 1913-11-16-1				
Judge/Mrs. Alexander Carson Simpson, Jr.			X	A108
Judge Simpson (tent. ID), 267			HB-18	A109
Herbert Spencer, oil			NPGL-5	A110
Very Rev. Principal, John Story, sepia/ink original for PP			GAGK-1	A111
Mrs. Strickland, Maud/ Muffin, detail, A027			SWRZ-1	A112
John M. Swan			B012	A113
(third man) Peace Conference, 1919 with House, Lloyd-George			HB-14	A026
David Croal Thomson			B012	A114
Henry Joseph Thouron, head study, oil			B012	A115
above, Professor seated in office, oil			J005-1	A116
above, painting Goddess of Victory			PAFA-11	A117
above, Professor in smock to chest, oil			HB-19	A118
Count Leo Tolstoy, 1910		9 PW	X	A119
Mrs. John E. D. Trask, 1929		27 WC	PAFA-12	A120
Walter Tyndale			B012	A121
(cleric) Canon Harry Drew, Rev. Bowen, Bishop Tuttle			HB-20	A122
Prof. John Tyndall, F.R.S., ink well, pen, papers, oil			RS-1	A123
above, reading, books			NPGL-6	A124
above, litho, # 4881			WAGML-1	A125

Thomas Fisher Unwin in his London Office, publisher	BO12	A126
Hon. Richard Vaux, Phila. Mayor, pastel	FGW-1	A127
above, oil	PAFA-13	A128
above, Detroit Publishing Co., reproduction, sepia, M322	PAFA-14	A129
George Frederick Watts, R.A., engraved after Hamilton	CHC-3	A130
above, pastel	BO12	A131
above, pastel	HB-21	A132
Professor Anton Alexander von Werner, Berlin (Art)	HB-22	A133
(gentleman, seated at desk), oil	HB-23	A134
(Woman with yellow fan), oil	JP-6	A135
(Woman, decollete, chair, reverie) oil	HB-25	A136
I Won't! (facial details)	JP-27	A137
The Empty Bed, 1913, pastel	C-6	A140
Le papillion captiv, Faites Divers, L'Academie...#320	PAFA-15	A141
Afternoon Repose, oil	Sthb-2	A142
above, color	Sthb-1	A654
The Syren, pastel	J003-2	A143
Dame! L' Academie ...#223 (Mercer Coll.)	PAFA-16	A144
The Heiress (John G. Johnson Coll.)	J003-3	A145
The Vegetable Woman, graphite, 1 of pr.	JP-7	A146
Garden in Seville, Spain, 1883, #236	HB-25	A147
Cerise (aka Le Rire), 1875, engraved, 1878 (Paris)	NYPL-3	A148
The Knitting Lesson	NYPL-4	A149
Old Welsh Woman	HB-26	A150
above, color	JP-	A231
Two (Dancing) Women, 1920, pastel	BJ-1	A151
Two (Seated) Women, Lead Windows Clara/niece	PAFA-17	A152
(Woman,porch, in spring) #227	HB27	A153
A Coquette of Seville, Spain	BJ-2	A154
The Wind, 1914, on illust. bd.	JP-8	A155
above, portr. of a Lady, #187	PMA-4	A156
Dancing Girl, (Italy), 1910	MUFL-1	A157
Woman in Brown, sketch, 1909	C-7	A158
Seated Female Nude, sketch # 5, 1911 (Cat. # 12 Senefelder) 36226/1/2	BM-8	A159
The Curtesy, 1913 (Senefelder Club)	VA-1	A160
(facial details, Clara) Brooklyn Museum, 1925 cat. pastel	NYPL-5	A161
(Seated Model, Head Bowed down) #821	JP-9	A162
(Elegant Lady), 1914, The Wind BO37	JP-10	A163
(Girl) Yawning, 1914	C-8	A164
Pensive, pastel	JP-11	A165
(pastel)	VG-2	A166
(Woman in long dress) pastel	SHWZ-2	A167
(Woman, portrait of) pastel	SHWZ-3	A168
L' Asperante, 1915	PMA-5	A169
Figure Study, Seated Woman, Head lowered on Arm	PAFA-18	A170
(facial details, Clara) pastel	VNTYFR-1	A171

(fashion model, Provostess-like dress) # 580	JP-12	A172
(Model dressing) # 582	JP-13	A173
Dancer	PMA-6	A174
Drawing # 11, 1924, pastel	X PAFA-12	A175
Qui Vive!	C-9	A176
(Female Figure Study, sketch # 2), 1911. (litho, 1913)	BM-5	A177
1913 cat. Senefelder Club p. 14 #11. 36226/2/2 1913-12-16-34		
Woman Looking in Mirror	DD-1	A178
Standing Woman, 1910, # 30	VF NMAA	A179
(Female Figure Study, sketch #3), litho, 191(3)		
1913 cat. Senefelder Club p. 13 #8. 36226/1/3 1913-12-16-35	BM-6	A180
Bondeuse, 1915	SHWRZ-4	A181
(Figure Study : Back)	PMA-7	A182
After the Ball, 1911	C-10	A183
Back of a Girl	C-11	A184
(Stressing Her Tresses, ballet costume) What's in a back?	DM-1	A185
Taffetta Changeant	C-12	A186
(Concentration, c.1884)	JP-14	A187
above, detail	JP-14	A188
Tears, 1879	PAFA-19	A189
Reverie in a Brown Chair	JP-15	A190
(Seated Beauty, side view 2/3rds, chalk, oval)	JP-16	A191
above, color	JP-	A653
The Coquette, 1914	C-13	A192
The Oriental (woman), 1915	X PAFA-20	A193
Black Evening Gown, Red Flower (woman's back)	JP-17	A194
above, color	JP-17	A195
Study # 1, # 583	JP-18	A196
Nude Study, # 589	JP-19	A197
Nude Model, # 588	JP-20	A198
Woman Dressed in Blue	HB-28	A199
Baby, sketch of	C-14	A200
Man's shoe with spat, on A200	C-15	A201
Baby (George) in bonnet, chickens, picket fence, grass, yard	HB-29	A202
(George) The Green Robe	GAM-1	A204
George at age 3 years, blue outfit, flowers	HB-30	A205
George at Breakfast	X J005-2	A207
The Sisters, pastel, # 585	JP-23	A208
Four Children on Beach	WMGP-2	A209
Young Britons coursing, litho, 6971	WAGML-2	A210
The Young Navigator, 1884	Stby-2	A211
Male Wine Seller, graphite, second of pr see A146	JP-26	A212
(Man Spading Garden) # 225	HB-31	A213
(above, in Greenhouse) # 232	HB-32	A214
Corn Husker	X CHS-1	A215
(Mr. Jones, Sketch # 4), litho	CMA-1	A216

Monk, wc, # 208			HB-33	A217
Monk, Standing, wc, # 340			HB-34	A218
Dove/Mouse (with F. Atkinson) 227-329	36226/2/3		BM-7	A219
McLure's Dog (Belle) & Space heater			C-16	A220
(Horse) Crown Prince, pastel			B012	A222
(Horse) Vanilla, pastel			B012	A223
Roses wc			PMA-7	A224
Rose Bouquet wc # 7686			JP-26	A225
Roses & Children		X	J005-	A221
(Theatre curtain, landscape) Fairmount Water Works, B & W			HB-35	A226
(above, memo of colors, detail of four additional scenes)			HB-35	A227
(above, two scenes, detail)			HB-35	A228
The Thames (landscape)			BJ-3	A229

PUBLISHED ENGRAVINGS

(A=E002; B=The BAILIE; C=1897 cover,E018; D=St. Marnock, 1898/99; ET=EVENING TIMES;H=Hamilton;
P=THE Phila.TIMES; T=B002.)

(title	date	p.	N	#)
L'Academie pour Rire. cover	78		A	A609
H after Wharton [P.F. 1840--1880] # 104	78		A	A610
H after Lea, [Mrs. Anna Merritt] # 272	78		A	A611
H after Fowler, [Frank] # 227	78		A	A612
H after Bates, [Dewey] # 213	78	1	A	A613
H after Wood, [James L.] # 234	78		A	A614
H after Blum, [Robert] # 90	78		A	A615
H after Lambdin, [George C. 1830--1896] #231	78		A	A616
H after Linford # 309	78		A	A617
H after Blum, [Robert] # 118	78		A	A618
H after Poore, [Henry Rankin] # 200	78		A	A619
H after Way, [A.J.H., 1826--] # 240	78	2	A	A620
H after Mac Dowell, [Susan] # 262	78		A	A621
H after Uhl(e), [S. Jerome] # 269	78		A	A622
H after Darrah, [Mrs. S. T., d.1881] #179	78		A	A623
H after De Cranno # 189	78		A	A624
H after Brennan # 313	78	3	A	A625
H after Shearer # 242	78		A	A626
H after Trotter, [Mary K.] # 296	78		A	A627
H after Wharton, [P. F., 1840--1880] #310	78		A	A628
H after Uhl(e), [S. Jerome] .	78		A	A629
H after Blum, [Robert] # 131	78		A	A630
H after Winner # 295	78		A	A631
H after Drinker # 235	78		A	A632
H after Winebush # 278	78		A	A633
H after Bates, [Dewey] .	78		A	A634
H after Brown, [Charles V., 1848--] #258	78		A	A635
H after Franklin, [Mary] # 178	78		A	A636
H after Cassat, [Mary] # 175	78		A	A637
H after Nehlig, [Victor, 1830--] # 321	78	5	A	A638
H after James # 202	78		A	A639
H after Lewis, [Edmonia] # 303	78		A	A640
H after Brennan # 102	78		A	A641
H after Eakins, [Thomas C.] # 186	78		A	A642
H after Richards, [W.T.] # 216	78		A	A643
H after Fussell,[Charles Lewis, 1840--1909] #314	78		A	A644
H after Hobbs # 264	78		A	A645
H after Mme. Schussele, [Christian] #117	78		A	A646
H after Reich, [Jacque] # 209	78		A	A647

Title	Year				Series	Ref
H after Harnett, [William M., 1848--1892] #273	78				A	A648
H after Senat	# 300	78			A	A649
H after Winner	# 266	78			A	A650
H after Brennan	# 98	78			A	A651
H after Parrish, [Stephen] # 290	78				A	A652
New Extra. Dev. in Photography	92	I 13	4/5	B		A261
Candidates Dream of the Past	95	VII 24	1	B		A282
Tale of an Empty Pocket/ Umbrella	95	IX 4	5	B		A559
Tragedian's Interrupted Soliloquy	96	I 1	3	B		A283
New Sezrvant Wanted	96	I 5	2A	B		A233
Li Hung Chang's Visit/ Bailie's pro...	96	VIII 19	1	B		A284
Bailie's Experience with Mixed Bathing in France	96	IX 2	1	B		A285
How the Boodle Brothers Spent Their Holiday	96	IX 30	3	B		A286
Preparation for the New Year	96	XII 30	5	B		A287
Gradual Effect of a Few B & Ss	97	IV 21	3	B		A288
Love's Labour's Lost	97	V 19	5	B		A289
Puss in Boots at the Royal	97	XII 8	1	B		A290
Whyte, Millar, Mitchell, Richmond, Russell, Kelvin, Arrol, Mc Leod (State Dinner)	98	I 26	7	B		A232
Chatrian's Dance. St. Andrews Hall	98	II 9	1	B		A291
Restrauranteur's Dance, Windsor Hotel	98	II 23	1	B		A292
Man's Ambition	98	III 2	3	B		A234
Fancy Dress Ball, sketches	98	III 2		B		A293
Orpheus Club Fancy Ball	98	III 23	1	B		A294
The International, sketches at	98	IV 6	1	B		A295
Primrose Day	98	IV 20	4	B		A235
Policy! Scotch Whiskey. (advertisement)				B		A236
24th May, Her Leddyship! GOD BLESS HER.	98	V 25	7	B		A237
Two Reasons Why Brown's not at the Sea Side	98	VI 29	3	B		A238
At the Celtic Sports	98	VIII 13	6	B		A239
The Mod Academy (3 cartoons)	98	XII 14	2A	B		A240
Got Out Of It	99	IV 5	2A	B		A241
Why?	99	IV 19	6	B		A242
Brown's Coast House Hunting Expedition	99	VI 28	6	B		A243
Up To Date	99	VII 19	2B	B		A244
St. Mungo Gets Into Harness Again	99	VIII 2	6	B		A245
He Didn't Look It	99	IX 27	4A	B		A246
Music Hath Charms, etc.	00	I 3	2	B		A247
Glasgow Dinner. Volunteers for Front	00	II 7	1	B		A248
The Morn's Ma Birthday...	00	IV 18	2A	B		A249
His normal Condition	00	IX 26	4A	B		A250
George Alexander Dramatic Club. Performance at...	00	XI 28	6	B		A251
The Three Graces	01	I 2	2	B		A251
Flowers & Feathers	01	IV 10	2B	B		A252
Perthshire Society, Windsor Hotel	01	XII 25		B		A296

St. Alban (as stained glass window image) book cover, frontis	01		T	A560
Two Roman Soldiers, sword, tract	01		T	A561
Two Bobbies, Roman Soldiers, kilt, hatchet	01		T	A562
Bobby, keyhole in door, bat in hand	01		T	A563
Roman Soldier, climbing brickwall	01	15	T	A564
Bobby drinking large stein of beer	01		T	A565
Roman Soldier sliding down bannister	01		T	A566
Fleeing Bobby with brick necklace	01		T	A567
Torso in well, Bobby with brick necklace	01		T	A568
Castle/Mountain	01		T	A569
Flu, seated man, foot tub, sprinkle box	01		T	A570
Masked Headsman, hatchet block on ground	01		T	A571
Horse drawn coach, passenger, driver	01		T	A572
"Adieu," man, inkwell, quill	01		T	A573
(terminal : squiggle)	01		T	A574
(Floral device) A. N. Wallace, Printers	-		D	A575
(Swirl device) A. N. Wallace	-		D	A576
(Floral device) "J" Cincinnati Museum of Art	97		C	A578
(bush device : vines in triangular array)	03		H	A579
(newspaper masthead or logo)	75 III 13		P	A580
(above)	75 XII 20		P	A581
Nine passenger cart, twin horses, cab, carriage	98		D	A582

INK/SEPIA COLOR LITHOGRAPHS
PHOTOGRAPHY

P. P. L.	Chisholm	03	7	A583
P. P. L.	Primrose	03	9	A584
P. P. L.	Gourley	03	11	A585
P. P. L.	Inverclyde	03	13	A586
P. P. L.	Marwick	03	15	A587
P. P. L.	Story	03	17	A588
P. P. L.	Shearer	03	19	A589
P. P. L.	Jack	03	21	A590
P. P. L.	Overton	03	23	A591
P. P. L.	Blythswood	03	25	A592
P. P. L.	Kelvin	03	27	A593
P. P. L.	King	03	29	A594
P. P. L.	Bell	03	31	A595
P. P. L.	Berry	03	33	A596
P. P. L.	Mac Leod	03	35	A597
P. P. L.	Reid	03	37	A598
P. P. L.	Thompson	03	38	A599
P. P. L.	Dickinson	03	41	A600
P. P. L.	Kirkwood	03	43	A601

P. P. L.	Menzies	03		45		A602
P. P. L.	Baird	03		47		A603
P. P. L.	Maxwell (Stirling)	03		49		A604
P. P. L.	Allan	03		51		A605
P. P. L.	Cross	03		53		A606
P. P. L.	Maclay	03		55		A607
P. P. L.	Renshaw	03		57		A608

PUBLISHED ENGRAVINGS

We Won't Go Home Til Morning	02	I	1	2A	B	A253
Silver Slipper at the Royalty	02	I	8	1	B	A297
Wine Merchant's Benevolent Association	02	II	19	1	B	A298
The Great Motto Improver	02	V	28	8	B	A280
Bailie: The King, GOD BLESS HIM!	02	VI	25	1	B	A281
Broke!	02	VII	23	2B	B	A254
Young Doctors...	02	X	1	2B	B	A255
Shades of Autumn	02	X	1	1	B	A277
Mac Lachlan Distillers (advertisement)	02	VII	22	6	B	A256
A Bit of Old Glasgow	02	IX	2		ET	A316
Children's Day in the Parks...	02	IX	10	1	B	A279
Our Latest Deputation, Sampling Continental...	02	IX	17	1	B	A278
A Once Genteel Thoroughfare of Glasgow	02	IX	18		ET	A319
Physical Training, group of sketches	02	IX	30		ET	A327
group of sketches	02				ET	A328
Highlander with a Sword	02				ET	A329
St. Hibernian & Dragon	02	X	4		ET	A330
###Text Announcement, PROMINENT PROFILES, dedicated space	p. 4 every Wednesday !!!					###
Infatuated	02					A332
Gladstone Statue	02	X	11		ET	A333
Unveiling of the Gladstone Statue, Georges Square	02	X	13		ET	A334
Gaelic League, Glasgow	02	X	15		ET	A335
A Outrance	02	X	20		ET	A317
(Smoking)	02	X	21		ET	A336
###Second Notice, PROMINENT PROFILES, dedicated space	p. 4 every Wednesday !!!					####
P.P. Art & Industry	W 02	X	22		ET	A343
Two cartoons	02	X	23		ET	A318
Glasgow Art Gallery & Museum, River Kelvin	02	X	24		ET	A338
Lord Provost Chisholm, portrait of	02	X	27		ET	A339
Mems. for Madame	02					A340
P.P. Mathematics : Professor Jack	W 02	X	29		ET	A344
(portrait)	W 02	X	29		ET	A345
(group sketches) before Christmas	02				ET	A346
Obvious (cartoon)	02				ET	A347
Golden Wedding Anniversary : Mr. & Mrs. John Campbell	02				ET	A348
Mr. Chamberlain's visit to South Africa	02	X	29		ET	A341

(four small portraits)		02	X	29	ET	A342
Ah Sam (cartoon)		02	X	31	ET	A349
P. P. Philanthropy	W	02	XI	5	ET	A351
A. S. G., Cheer Up Old Man, Come In & Have Something to Drink.		02	XI	6	3 ET	A350
New Skipper		02	XI	12	1 B	A299
P. P. Peer/Citizen	W	02	XI	12	4 ET	A352
P. P. Cable/Compas	W	02	XI	19	4 ET	A353
St. Andrews Roman Catholic Cathedral. New Archbishop		02	XI	22	5 ET	A320
Mems. for Madame		02	XI	22	ET	A321
Glasgow Archaeological Society, Roman Wall		02	XI	22	ET	A322
Accident Scene		02				A323
Rev. A. Chapman		02				A324
R. K. Walker		02				A325
Tucker		02				A326
P. P. Campsie/ Carstairs	W	02	XI	26	4 ET	A354
P. P. Baronet/ Ex-Provost	W	02	XI	31	4 ET	A355
Thirsty Man's Companion		02	XII	3	ET	A356
(group of sketches)		02	XII	3	ET	A357
Primrose (group of sketches)		02	XII	10	ET	A358
Beauty & The Beast at The Royal		02	XII	10	1 B	A300
Entertainment (group of sketches)		02	XII	16	ET	A359
Meant to have his say (cartoon)		02			ET	A360
Interrupted Eloquence (cartoon)		02	XII	19	ET	A364
Mems. for Madame		02			ET	A365
Hampden Park Alterations, 3rd Lanarks		02	XII	25	ET	A361
.... Photographic Jottings		02	XII	25	ET	...
Taking the height, Greenhouse. (cartoon cf Man in Greenhouse,oil)		02			ET	A363
(map)		02	XII	30	ET	A366
A Crusher (cartoon)		02				A367
P. P. The Caley	W	02	XII	31	4 ET	A368
Three Little Maids at Royalty		02	XII	31	3 B	A301
A Guid New Year (cartoon)		03	I	3	ET	A369
(group of sketches)		03			ET	A370
It's An Ill Wind & c.		03	I	10	ET	A371
Mac Greggor Party		03	I	13	ET	A372
Business of the hour, soop it up. (cartoon)		03	I	17	ET	A391
Curling by signs (group of sketches)		03	I	19	ET	A391
P. P. Citizen/Soldier	W	03	I	21	ET	A373
Country Girl at the Royalty		03	I	21	1 B	A302
P. P. Central Division	W	03	I	28	4 ET	A374
(group of sketches)		03	I	31	2 ET	A543
P. P. College/Pollok	W	03	II	4	ET	A375
P. P. Genial/Generous	W	03	II	11	ET	A376
Masonic Gathering at Paisley		03	II	16	2 ET	A544
P. P. Camlachie	W	03	II	18	ET	A377
Bridgegate Old Ship Bank		03	II	24	8 ET	A545

P. P. Chipping / Spadework	W	03	II	25		ET	A378
Lloyd's Register, Staff Dinner		03	II	25	1	B	A303
Athenaeum, Musical Comedy (group of sketches)		03	II	26		ET	A547
Glasgow Technical College		03	II	27	4	ET	A548
Lord Lovat, Scotsmen in Colonies, speech		03	II	28		ET	A549
Gay Gordons. King's medals. Georges Square		03	III	2		ET	A550
P. P. West Renfrewshire	W	03	III	4	4	ET	A379
P. P. Challenger	W	03	III	11		ET	A380
(group of sketches)		03	III	13	7	ET	A551
P. P. Sir David	W	03	III	18	4	ET	A381
Shamrock III, Launching, Lipton	W	03	III	18		ET	A552
Roman Catholicism, Dunbarton Church/ St. Patrick's Archbishop Maguire		03	III	21		ET	A553
Dr. Torrey, American Revivalist		03	III	24	2	ET	A554
P. P. Schools / Charities	W	03	III	25	4	ET	A382
Bransby Williams at Empire Palace Theatre		03	III	25	1	B	A304
Thonlie Bank, Dramatic Club		03	III	27	4	ET	A555
P. P. Preceptor	W	03	IV	1	4	ET	A383
Bailie : Welcome Back Again, Mr. Allen, Chair		03	IV	1	1	B	A305
P. P. Humanities	W	03	IV	8	4	ET	A384
P. P. Ships/Volunteers	W	03	IV	15	4	ET	A385
P. P. Iron/Literature	W	03	IV	22	4	ET	A386
Orpheus Club : Yeoman of the Guard, Royal Theatre		03	IV	27	1	B	A310
P. P. Law/Archaeology	W	03	IV	29	4	ET	A387
P. P. Clyde Trust	W	03	V	6	4	ET	A389
Entertainment (group of sketches)		03				ET	A390
King Edward VII/ Queen Alexandra, Arrival in Edinburgh		03	V	12		ET	A394
King Edward VII, portrait		03	V	12		ET	A395
building : Technical College		03	V	12		ET	A396
ER/AR, coat of arms		03	V	12		ET	A397
Queen Alexandra		03	V	12		ET	A398
The Bailie's Welcome		03	V	13	1	B	A257
P. P. Sheriff	W	03	V	13	4	ET	A401
Arrival/ Queen St., scene		03	V	13		ET	A402
A Glasgow Nocturne! Royal Route in Rain, round		03	V	15		ET	A399
Foundation Stone Laid. Technical College, scene		03	V	15		ET	A400
P. P. School Board	W	03	V	20	4	ET	A403
P. P. Collieries	W	03	V	27	4	ET	A404
Hampden Sports : Alan Glens		03	VI	2		B	A393
P. P. GEM LINE	W	03	VI	3	4	ET	A405
P. P. Technical Education	W	03	VI	10	4	ET	A406
Glasgow's Corporation Octopus		03	VIII	12	1	B	A306
P. P. G. & S. W. R.	W	03	VI	17	4	ET	A407
P. P. Ex-Cathedra	W	03	VI	24	4	ET	A408
P. P. Tramways	W	03	VII	1	4	ET	A409
Mems. for Madame bust		03	VII	6		ET	A410

P. P.	Aqua Pura	W	03	VII	8	4	ET	A411
P. P.	Deacon Convenor	W	03	VII	15	4	ET	A412
P. P.	Highland/Agriculture	W	03	VII	22	4	ET	A413
P. P.	Senior Magistrate	W	03	VII	29	4	ET	A415
Grand Theatre, construction of			03	VIII	5		ET	A416
P. P.	City Chamberlain	W	03	VIII	5	4	ET	A417
P. P.	Civil Military	W	03	VIII	12	4	ET	A418
Lord Roberts, Glasgow, Volunteers Inspection by			03	VIII	12		ET	A419
P. P.	Shamrock II (Lipton)	W	03	VIII	19	4	ET	A420
	(sketch of his career)		03				ET	A421
Sir Thomas Lipton & The Cup			03	VIII	19	1	B	A258
P. P.	G. L. W.	W	03	VIII	26	4	ET	A422
P. P.	Genial Sheriff	W	03	IX	2	4	ET	A423
P. P.	Father of The Council	W	03	IX	9	4	ET	A424
P. P.	Elgin Place	W	03	IX	16	4	ET	A425
P. P.	Tradestion	W	03	IX	23	4	ET	A426
P. P.	Ex-City Treasurer	W	03	IX	30	4	ET	A427
P. P.	Queen Street	W	03	X	7	4	ET	A428
Highland Light Infantry Memorial (group of sketches)			03	X			ET	A429
Mr. Chamberlain/Proposal/ St. Andrews Hall, Glasgow speech			03	X	7		ET	A430
Queen's Park, Mt. Florida, Football Ground			03	X	10		ET	A431
P. P.	Blackfriars	W	03	X	14	4	ET	A432
Sir Henry Fowler's Meeting, St. Andrews Hall, Glasgow			03	X			ET	A433
National Palace of Varieties			03	X	19		ET	A434
Mems. for Madame			03	X	19		ET	A435
P. P.	Parks	W	03	X	21	4	ET	A436
Mr. Quarrier's Funeral, Church Service	W	03	X	21			ET	A437
George Alexander : If I Were King At Royal Theatre			03	X	21	1	B	A307
P. P.	Clinical Surgery	W	03	X	28	4	ET	A438
	(group of sketches)		03				ET	A439
P. P.	Municipal Criticism	W	03	XI	4	4	ET	A440
Disastrous Conflaguration, Glasgow Warehouses			03	XI			ET	A441
Fancy Dress Ball			03	XI	4	1	B	A308
What We May Expect To See In A Day Or Two			03	XI	9		ET	A442
P. P.	Deacon Convenor		03	XI	11		ET	A443
Newly Elected Magistrates			03	XI	11	3	B	A259
Our Italian Visitors, *King Victor Emanuel et ux*			03	XI	17		ET	A444
P. P.	Caledonian Railway		03	XI	18		ET	A445
Princess Henry of Brattenberg, At. Andrews Hall, Glasgow			03	XI		5	ET	A446
Modern Prodigal's Return (cartoon)			03	XI			ET	A447
P. P.	School of Art	W	03	XI	26	4	ET	A448
P. P.	The N. B. R.	W	03	XII	2	4	ET	A449
P. P.	Police Clerk	W	03	XII	9	4	ET	A450
Lord Balfour, East End Exhibition, opening ceremony	W	03	XII	9			ET	A451
P. P.	Forensic Humour	W	03	XII	16	4	ET	A452
Jack & The Beanstalk at Royal			03	XII	16	3	B	A309

P. P.	Cars	W 03	XII	23	4	ET	A453
P. P.	Benburb	W 03	XII	30	4	ET	A454
P. P.	Municipal Music	W 04	I	6	4	ET	A455
P. P.	Scottish Orchestra	W 04	I	13	4	ET	A456
P. P.	Wit/ Wisdom	W 04	I	20	4	ET	A457
P. P.	Wellington Church	W 04	I	27	4	ET	A458
P. P.	Sheriff/ Squire	W 04	II	3		ET	A460
New Cathkin Football Park		04	II	6		ET	A459
P. P.	Libraries (Carnegie)	W 04	II	10	4	ET	A461
P. P.	Church History	W 04	II	17	4	ET	A462
P. P.	Hebrew	W 04	II	24	4	ET	A463
North British Hotel/Georges Square Changes		04	II	29		ET	A464
Royal Institute of Fine Arts, opening ceremony		04	III	1		ET	A465
P. P. Art Institute	(Primrose)	W 04	III	2	4	ET	A466
New East End Theatre		04	III			ET	A467
Launching of H.M.S. Argyll/ Cruiser at Greenock		04	III	4		ET	A468
P. P.	Docks/Quays	W 04	III	9	4	ET	A469
P. P.	Anchor Line	W 04	III	16	4	ET	A470
P. P.	Parliamentary Bills	W 04	III	23	4	ET	A471
P. P.	Unionism	W 04	III	30	4	ET	A472
P. P.	Systemic Medicine	W 04	IV	6	4	ET	A473
P. P.	Town Clerk	W 04	IV	13	4	ET	A474
P. P.	Exhibition, 1901	W 04	IV	20	4	ET	A475
P. P.	Chairman/Chairmaker	W 04	IV	27	4	ET	A476
P. P.	Shipping Law	W 04	V	4	4	ET	A477
P. P.	Senior Magistrate	W 04	V	11	4	ET	A478
P. P.	A Cycling Sheriff	W 04	V	18	4	ET	A479
P. P.	Corn/Council	W 04	V	25	4	ET	A480
P. P.	The Bishop	W 04	VI	1	4	ET	A481
P. P.	Lawyer/Churchman	W 04	VI	8	4	ET	A482
P. P.	Artist/Raconteur	W 04	VI	15	4	ET	A483
P. P.	Chief	W 04	VI	22	4	ET	A484
P. P.	Sustentation Fund	W 04	VI	29	4	ET	A485
P. P.	Sanitation	W 04	VII	6	4	ET	A486
Sarah Bernhardt as Margarite Gauthier		04	VII	6	1	B	A260
P. P.	Law	W 04	VII	13	4	ET	A487
The Launch of the Caronia		04	VII	14		ET	A488
(Ceremonially Uniformed Man)		04	VII	14		ET	A489
A Fair Idyll	(cartoon)	04	VII	16		ET	A490
P. P.	Clerk of the Peace	W 04	VII	20		ET	A491
P. P.	City Engineer	W 04	VII	27		ET	A492
P. P.	Sheriff's Clerk	W 04	VIII	3	4	ET	A493
Election, N. E. Lanark (group of sketches)		04	VIII	5		ET	A494
N. E. Lanarkshire Unionist Campaign		04	VIII	9		ET	A495
P. P.	Lady Provostess	W 04	VIII	10	4	ET	A496
P. P.	Procurator Fiscal	W 04	VIII	17	4	ET	A497

P. P. Civic Cleansing	W 04	VIII	24	4 ET	A498
Welcome	04	VIII	29	ET	A499
P. P. Health	W 04	VIII	31	4 ET	A500
P. P. Gas	W 04	IX	7	4 ET	A501
P. P. Shipowner/critic	W 04	IX	14	4 ET	A502
P. P. Electricity	W 04	IX	21	4 ET	A503
P. P. Parks	W 04	IX	28	4 ET	A504
P. P. Master of Works	W 04	X	5	4 ET	A507
Glasgow Socialist Demonstration/Countess Warwick	04	X	6	ET	A508
All In (cartoon)	04	X	7	ET	A505*
P. P. Seascapes	W 04	X	12	ET	A509
P. P. Whaitevale/Central	W 04	X	19	4 ET	A510
P. P. United Free	W 04	X	26	4 ET	A511
P. P. Biblical Criticism	W 04	XI	2	4 ET	A512
P. P. Physiology	W 04	XI	9	4 ET	A513
Mr. Churchill at St. Andrews Hall, Glasgow·	04	XI	11	ET	A514
P. P. Moral Philosophy	W 04	XI	16	4 ET	A515
P. P. Greek	W 04	XI	23	4 ET	A516*
Chancellor of Glasgow University, Installed	04	XI	30	ET	A315
Chancellor, Glasgow University, Installation	04	XI	30	ET	A517
Children/Charity (group of sketches)	04	XII	2	ET	A518
Lord Rosenberry/ St. Andrews Hall	04	XII	6	ET	A519
P. P. Black Lands	W 04	XII	7	4 ET	A520
P. P. Red Cross	W 04	XII	14	4 ET	A521
Colonial Secretary Lyttlton/St. Andrews Hall, Glasgow	04	XII	20	ET	A522
P. P. Thread	W 04	XII	21	4 ET	A523
Christmas Time (cartoon)	04	XII	24	ET	A524
Entertainment (group of sketches)	04	XII	26	6 ET	A525
P. P. City Treasurer	W 04	XII	28	4 ET	A526
P. P. Fire Brigade	W 05	I	4	4 ET	A527
P. P. Depute/ Interim	W 05	I	11	4 ET	A528
Prime Minister Balfour's Visit	05	I	13	ET	A529
P. P. Boy's Brigade	W 05	I	18	4 ET	A530
P. P. Fire Master	W 05	I	25	4 ET	A531
P. P. Tramways	W 05	II	1	4 ET	A532
P. P. Lord Advocate	W 05	II	8	4 ET	A533
P. P. Patrick's Privy Councilor	W 05	II	15	4 ET	A534
P. P. Voice of Argyll Street	W 05	II	22	4 ET	A535
P. P. Trinity	W 05	III	1	ET	A536
P. P. Woodside	W 05	III	8	ET	A537
P. P. Glasgow/Aberdeen	W 05	III	15	4 ET	A538
P. P. Clan Line	W 05	III	22	4 ET	A539
P. P. St. Rollox	W 05	III	29	4 ET	A540
P. P. Labour	W 05	IV	5	4 ET	A541
P. P. South Lanarkshire	W 05	IV	12	4 ET	A542
#### non-Hamilton, P. P. Painter/ Poet	W 06	IV	19	4 ET	###

Our Premier (Balfour) Ventriloquist : Army & Navy	05	I 18	1	B	A311
The Weary Glasgow Deputationist	05	III 29		B	A275
"Falka" Grand Theatre	05	III 8		B	A276
Glasgow Distillers (advertisement)	05	IV 26	6	B	A269
What to do with Our Boys : Problem Solved	05	V 24	7	B	A312
The Weekend Weather 'Its an Ill Win' That Blaws naebody quid.	05	VI 21	6	B	A274
Glasgow's Sensible Sunday : Alien's Panic	05	VII 14	1	B	A314
Home From Camp	05	VIII 2	1	B	A313
Everything In The Garden is Lovely	05	XI 1	3	B	A273
Andrew's Pet Dog & Some Victims	05	XI 22		B	A272
Thompson's Flower Perfume (advertisement)	05	XII 13	6	B	A268
Nervtonine (advertisement)	06	IX 26	3	B	A267
perfume (advertisement)	07	VII 17	4	B	A264
perfume (advertisement)	07	XII 18	4	B	A266
Who Pays The Piper?	08	II 5	3	B	A270
Cooling His Vigilance	08	II 5	2	B	A271
Premier Scotch (advertisement)	08	VII 22	6	B	A263
Our Premier (Balfour) Ventriloquist : Army & Navy	05	I 18	1	B	A311
The Weary Glasgow Deputationist	05	III 29		B	A275
"Falka" Grand Theatre	05	III 8		B	A276
Glasgow Distillers (advertisement)	05	IV 26	6	B	A269
What to do with Our Boys : Problem Solved	05	V 24	7	B	A312
The Weekend Weather 'Its an Ill Win' That Blaws naebody quid.	05	VI 21	6	B	A274
Homeward's Trek (cartoon)	05	VII 2		ET	A414
Glasgow's Sensible Sunday : Alien's Panic	05	VII 14	1	B	A314
Home From Camp	05	VIII 2	1	B	A313
Everything In The Garden is Lovely	05	XI 1	3	B	A273
Andrew's Pet Dog & Some Victims	05	XI 22		B	A272
Thompson's Flower Perfume (advertisement)	05	XII 13	6	B	A268
Nervtonine (advertisement)	06	IX 26	3	B	A267
perfume (advertisement)	07	VII 17	4	B	A264
perfume (advertisement)	07	XII 18	4	B	A266
Who Pays The Piper?	08	II 5	3	B	A270
Cooling His Vigilance	08	II 5	2	B	A271
Premier Scotch (advertisement)	08	VII 22	6	B	A263

MATHEMATICS [=Professor William Jack, Glasgow
University] 1902 X 29 PROMINENT PROFILES, color
lithograph. Courtesy of Mitchell Library, Glasgow
Collection.

James Abbott McNeill Whistler lived at 21 Cheyne Walk,
Chelsea, London on March 28, 1890. [WINDOW SHOPPING] is
inscribed (verso, u.l.) Rosetti Mansions, Cheyne
Gardens, Chelsea. 10.75" x 8 5/8" ink and blue crayon
heightened with white on board. Formerly of collection
in London.

1898 Pennell, J. *LITHOGRAPHY & LITHOGRAPHERS*. T. Fisher Unwin, London. (Hamilton's
    lithograph, "*Gladstone*," included.   B001

1901 Hennell, T. B. *THE LAY OF ST. ALBAN*. A. N. Wallace, Kilmarnock. (Hamilton
    illustrated the text.)   B002

(1903) Hamilton, J. M. *PROMINENT PROFILES*. Artist, Glasgow. (Hamilton reproduced
    his first 26 caricatures previously published in *THE EVENING TIMES* [Sept.,
    1902] about May, 1903 from his original ink & sepia drawings.   B003

1905 Lambert, J. H. *THE STORY OF PA AT THE WORLD'S FAIR, ST. LOUIS, 1904*. PA
    Commission, Harrisburgh. II : 59 (Hamilton's name omitted from p. 335)   B004

    Isham, S. THE HISTORY OF AMERICAN PAINTING. MacMillan & Co., NY. p. 428
    "Richard Vaux"   B005

1907 Muther, R. *THE HISTORY OF MODERN PAINTING*. rev. ed. J. M. Dent & Co.,
    London / E. P. Dutton & Co., NY p.319   B006

1908 Pennell, E. R. / J. *THE LIFE OF J. McNEIL WHISTLER*. 5th ed. Lippincott,
    Phila. pgs. 285--288   B007

1911 Henderson, H. W. *THE PA ACADEMY OF THE FINE ARTS & OTHER COLLECTIONS OF
    PHILA.* L. C. Page & Co., Boston. pgs. 128/9 "*Gladstone at Downing St.*"   B008

1915 Pennell, E. R. / J. *OUR PHILADELPHIA* ^^^
    p. 393 Pennell met Hamilton in 187(6) after the latter's return from Antwerp   B009

1916 Pennell, E. R. *NIGHTS : ROME, VENICE IN AESTHETIC 1880s*. ^^^^
    frontis : "J(oseph Pennell)"   B010

1919 Drew, M. *CATHERINE GLADSTONE BY HER DAUGHTER*. ^^^
    "Mrs. Gladstone at Hawarden"   B031

1921 Hamilton, J. M. *MEN I HAVE PAINTED*. T. Fisher Unwin, Ltd., London. (Foreword :
    Mary Drew; 2 Ford bronzes; 47 Hamilton works reproduced.)   B012

    Lucas, E. V. *EDWIN AUSTIN ABBEY, R. A. : THE RECORD OF HIS LIFE & WORK*. NY &
    London. volume I : last page   B035

    Pennell, E. R. / J. *THE WHISTLER JOURNAL*. J. B. Lippincott, Phila. pgs. 82,
    143, 156, 214/5, 217--219, 277, 296   B013

THE EMPTY BED, 1913. Pastel, charcoal, and stump 21 15/16" x 28 5/16." In collection Corcoran Gallery of Art, gift of Mrs. E. H. Harriman.

251

Salaman, M. C. *WHITMAN'S PRINT COLLECTOR'S HANDBOOK.* rev. ed. G. Bell
  & Sons, Ltd., London. p.202   B011

1924 Fournier d' Albe, E. E. *THE LIFE OF SIR WILLIAM CROOKES, O.M., F.R.S.*
  Appleton, NY. (Written at THE HERMITAGE, Hamilton's home in Surrey.) B014

1925 Pennell, J. *THE ADVENTURES OF AN ILLUSTRATOR, MOSTLY FOLLOWING HIS AUTHORS IN*
  AMERICA & EUROPE. Little, Brown & Co., Boston. pgs 36,168   B015

1926 Morgan, G. *THE CITY OF FIRSTS : A COMPLETE HISTORICAL STUDY OF THE CITY OF*
  PHILA. ^^^   p. 227   B016

1929 Pennell, E. R. *THE LIFE & LETTERS OF JOSEPH PENNELL.* Little, Brown & Co.,
  Boston. II : 3--6, 11, 59, 78, 93--95, 98, 147, 149, 154--156, 201, 220,
  301/2   B017

  Weitenkampf, F. *HOW TO APPRECIATE PRINTS.* 4th rev. ed. C. Schribner's, NY.
  p. 235 lithography   B018

1930 Craig, G. *HENRY IRVING* ^^^
  p. 21 pastel : "Sir Henry Irving"   B019

  Masterman, L. (ed.) *MARY GLADSTONE (Mrs. DREW) HER DIARIES & LETTERS.*
  E. P. Dutton, NY. ^^^   B033

1933 Hamilton, G. *A HISTORY OF THE HOUSE OF HAMILTON.* J. Skinner, Edinburgh
  p. 1063 (Genealogy author was Solicitor, Supreme Court, England.)   B030

1936 Burroughs, A.   *LIMNERS & LIKENESSES : THREE CENTURIES OF AMERICAN PAINTING.*
  Harvard University Press, ^^^ . p.205   B020

1943 Isham, S. *THE HISTORY OF AMERICAN PAINTING.* MacMillan & Co., NY. p.429
  fig. 92 "Hon. Richard Vaux"   B021

1945 Eve, A. S. *THE LIFE & WORK OF JOHN TYNDALL.* C. H. Creasey, London. (Preface
  : Granville Proby, Tyndall's nephew. pgs xvii, 289 "John Tyndall"   B034

1956 Richardson, E. P. *PAINTERS IN AMERICA : THE STORY OF 450 YEARS.* Crowell,
  NY. p. 276   B022

1972 Warmington, C. M. et al *THE JAMAICAN LIBRARY SERVICE : 21 YEARS OF PROGRESS*
  IN PICTURES, 1948--1969. ^^^   p. 240--242, 244*, 247, 253, 258, 259 B023

1974 (annon.) *SCULPTURE OF A CITY : PHILA.'S TREASURES IN BRONZE & STONE.* Fairmount
  Park Association, Phila. p. 281 (Civil War Soldiers & Sailors Memorial, 1921;
  Hamilton served as chair of committee commissioning this memorial.)   B024

1977 Brown, M. W. *AMERICAN ART TO 1900 : PAINTING, SCULPTURE & ARCHITECTURE.* H. N.
     Abrams, Inc., NY.   Eakins' "Hamilton, 1895"   B032

1982 Goodrich, L. *THOMAS EAKINS.* National Gallery of Art, Washington, D. C.
     II : 275   Eakins' "Hamilton, 1895"   B026

1983 Johns, E. *THOMAS EAKINS : THE HEROISM OF MODERN LIFE.* Princeton University
     Press, N. J.   p. 154   B025

1986 Dorment, R. et al *ALFRED GILBERT : SCULPTOR & GOLDSMITH, ROYAL ACADEMY, LONDON.*
     Weidenfeld & Nicholson. ^^^   p. 130   B027

1989 Castagno, J. *AMERICAN ARTISTS : SIGNATURES & MONOGRAMS, 1800 to 1989.*
     Scarecrow, Metuchin, N. J.   p. 292   B028

1992 Homer, W. I. *THOMAS EAKINS : HIS LIFE & ART.* Abbeville Press, NY p.218
     Eakins' "Hamilton, 1895" color   B029

AFTERNOON REPOSE, 1878. Oil 40.5" x 60.75." Courtesy of Sotheby's, Inc., New York. This painting received top auction price for Hamilton's work.

1879 Clement, C. E. / Hutton, L. *ARTISTS OF THE 19th CENTURY*. Houghton / Mifflin, Boston.
    pgs. 327/8   D001

1885 Clement, C. E. / Hutton, L. op cit, 2nd ed.   D052

1887 Wilson, J. G. / Fiske, J. *CYCLOPEDIA OF AMERICAN BIOGRAPHY*. NY. II (G--L) : 64   D002

1887 Chaplin, J. D. / Perkins, C. C. *CYCLOPEDIA OF PAINTERS/PAINTINGS* C. Schribner's,
    NY. II : 384/5   D013

1889 Wilson, J. G. / Fiske, J. op cit, 2nd ed.   D054

1895 Graves, A. *DICTIONARY OF (LONDON) ARTISTS, 1760--1893*.   D003

1898 Levy, L. N. *AMERICAN ART ANNUAL*. I : ...   D004

1900 Levy, L. N. op cit   : 105/6   D005

1904 (^^^) *TWENTIETH CENTURY BIOGRAPHICAL DICTIONARY OF NOTABLE AMERICANS*   D010

1905 (^^^) *(LONDON) ROYAL ACADEMY OF ART EXHIBITORS : A COMPLETE DICTIONARY OF ARTISTS
        & THEIR WORKS*. Greves & Co., London. III   D011

1907 Clement, C. E. / Hutton, L. op cit, 3rd ed.   D053

1909 Levy, L. N. op cit   D006

1913 Champlin, J. D. / Perkins, C. C. op cit, 2nd ed. II : 205   D055

1920 Marquis. *WHO'S WHO IN AMERICA* XI:1212   D014

1921 Levy, L. N. op cit   XVII : 440   D007

1922 Thieme,U./ Becker,F. *ALLGEMEINES LEXIKON DER BILDENDEN KUNSTLER*. E. A. Seeman,
    Leipzig. XV   Godwin   D012

1923 Levy, L. N. op cit   XX   : 543   D008

1924 (^^^) *THE YEAR'S ART (1923)*. A.C.R. Carter, London. Hutchinson & Co.
    (Directory of Artists & Art Workers) p. 459   D016

    Benezit, E. *DICTIONNAIRE DES PEINTRES*...IV : 573   D023

1926 Fielding, M. *DICTIONARY OF AMERICAN PAINTERS...*   D026

1927 Champlin, J. D. / Perkins, C. C. op cit, 3rd ed.   D056

1928 *(^^^) THE YEAR'S ART (1927) op cit*   D057

1929 *(^^^) THE YEAR'S ART (1928) op cit*   D058

   Marquis. *WHO'S WHO IN ART. XIII :*   D028

192. Shenk, .. *ENCYCLOPEDIA OF PA.*   pgs. 235/6   D022

1930 *(^^^) THE YEAR'S ART (1929)   op cit*   D059

   Marquis. *WHO'S WHO IN ART.   XIV :*   D029

   Smith, R. C. *A BIOGRAPHICAL INDEX OF AMERICAN ARTISTS.*   Williams & Wilkins,
      Baltimore.   D030

1931 *(^^^) THE YEAR'S ART (1930)   op cit*   D060

   Levy, L. N. op cit   D009

1932 *(^^^) THE YEAR'S ART (1931)   op cit*   D021

1936 American Federation of Arts.   *WHO'S WHO IN AMERICAN ART, 1936--1937.*
      Washington, D. C.   A. C. MC Glauflin, ed.   I : 184/5   D031

1939 *(^^^) WHO WAS WHO AMONG NORTH AMERICAN AUTHORS.*   D032

193. *(^^^) AMERICAN BIOGRAPHIES.*   D033

1940 *DICTIONARY OF BRITISH ARTISTS, 1880--1940.*   p.225   D034

1941 *WHO WAS WHO, 1929--1940.*   Adam & Charles Black, London. p. 584   D035

1943 Marquis. *WHO WAS WHO IN AMERICA, 1897--1942.*   I : 511 B   D015

1945 Suzzallo, H. *NATIONAL ENCYCLOPEDIA.* Collier & Son, NY. (Painter/lithographer)
         VII : 483   D036

1951 *DICTIONARY OF NORTH AMERICAN AUTHORS DECEASED BY 1950.*   D037

1955 Vollmer, H. *ALLGEMEINES LEXIKON DES BILDEN DEN KUNSTLER DES XX JAHRHUNDERTS.*
      Seemann, Leipzig. 2nd ed.   D038

1966 Benezit, E. *DICTIONNAIRE DES PEINTRES...*   D024

1967 *BIOGRAPHICAL INDEX OF AMERICAN ARTISTS*   D039

1968 Young, W.   *A DICTIONARY OF AMERICAN ARTISTS*. Cambridge, MA.   p. 208   D040

1970 *BROOKLYN ART ASSOCIATION*   D044

1972 Merriam-Webster. *WEBSTER'S BIOGRAPHICAL DICTIONARY*. Springfield, MA. p.618   D041

1975 Waters, G. M. *DICTIONARY OF BRITISH ARTISTS WORKING, 1900--1950*.   J. Johnson,
       Eastbourne Fine Arts. I : 11, 148   D042

1976 Benezit, E. op cit   D051

1977 Busse, J. *INT. HANDBUCH ALLER MALER UND BILDHAUER DES XIX JAHRHUNDRETS.*   D043

197. MALLETT'S *INDEX OF ARTISTS.*   D045

1981 *INDEX OF ARTISTIC BIOGRAPHY.*   D046

1985 *WHO WAS WHO IN AMERICAN ART.* Soundview Press. Madison, CT.   D047

1989 Castagno, J.   *ARTISTS AS ILLUSTRATORS : AN INTERNATIONAL DIRECTORY WITH
       SIGNATURES & MONOGRAMS, 1800 TO PRESENT.*   D048

1991 *DICTIONARY OF AMERICAN PAINTERS* (Project in-progress) Vose Archives   D049

1993 Meissner, G.   *ALLGEMEINES KUNSTLER-LEXICON. DIE BILDENEN KUNSTLER ALLER ZEITEN
       UND VOLKER.* E. A. Seemann Verlag.   D050

ROSE BOUQUET, c. 1933. Watercolor 20" x 16." Formerly
W. Andrews Newman Collection.

ROSES, c. 1933. Watercolor 26 1/8" x 18 7/8."
Philadelphia Museum of Art : given by Philadelphia
Watercolor Club.

1876 PHILA. SKETCH CLUB (April) at P.A F.A. opening see: U005

1877 PENNSYLVANIA ACADEMY OF FINE ARTS, Phila. Catalogue of Pictures on Deposit.
    (October) p. 3   E001

1878 49me EXPOSITION DES BEAUX ARTS. Philadelphie. L' Academie pour Rire. (Hamilton
    authored and drew this satirical catalog of the 49th Annual Exhibition,
    P.A.F.A.) p.11 Hamilton's *"Une jeu de dames;"* p.14 Hamilton's *"Le papillion
    captif"*   E002

    NATIONAL ACADEMY OF DESIGN, 1861--1900, Exhibitions of, NY. p.389   E003

    BROOKLYN ART ASSOCIATION (April) *"My Janitor* #308 $ 60.00"   E093

    EXPOSITION UNIVERSELLE, Paris. (Hamilton's *"Cerise"* appeared as an engraving
      in the cat.) Gravure de Smeeton et Tilly   E111   E004

1879 SOCIETY OF ARTISTS, Phila. (Nov.1/Dec.1) First Ann. Exhib., Illus. Cat.,
    Mc Calla & Stavely.   L185/L186   E005

1880 SOCIETY OF AMERICAN ARTISTS, Phila. (Nov.1/Dec.6) Second Ann. Exhib., Illus.
    Cat.   *"A Friendly Pass"*   E006

1887 D002

    Murray, p. 290

1890 SALON SOC. ART. FRANCE, Paris. Ausst.--Kat.   E007

    NEW ENGLISH ART CLUB   E008

    LIVERPOOL AUTUMN EXHIBITION, ILLUST. CATALOGUE   E116

1891 GOUPIL GALLERY, London   E009

    ROYAL SOCIETY OF PORTRAIT PAINTERS, London.   E010

1892 Paris SALON,   J001 p. 456

    E092 *"Gladstone (gentleman) reading"*   L007

1893 L' ART, LIV : 12 ff   E011

WORLD'S COLUMBIAN EXPOSITION, Chicago. Official Cat. of Exhibits,
W. B. Gonkey Co., Chicago. (Gold medal to Hamilton)   E012

1895 SALON SOC. ART. FRANCE, Paris.   E013

1896 GOUPIL GALLERY, London (Oct./Nov.) "Portraits & Other Works by Hamilton"
J. Virtue, London (William Cosmo Monkhouse, an important critic, wrote
a four page introduction. The one man show presented 47 Hamilton works;
the P.A.F.A. copy has prices added by an unknown hand)   E014

SALON SOC. ART. FRANCE, Paris   E015

J003 (Important early works reproduced/commented on by H. S. Morris)

EXPOSITION, St. Louis   E016

1897 P.A.F.A., Phila. (March 15) "Four Groups of Paintings by American Artists :
Hamilton; Hobbs, G. T.; Smith, J. L.; & Stokes, F. W."   E017

Chicago, N003 through N010 inclusive

Cincinnati MUSEUM ASSOCIATION, Eden Park Art Museum, Exhib. (April 18/May 5)
"Pictures by Hamilton" (24 works by Hamilton; Ford bronze of Hamilton) E018

CARNEGIE INSTITUTION, Pittsburgh, Ann. Exposition   E019

1898 P. P. C. 3. Ann. Exhib. *H.J. Thouron*   E020

PASTEL SOCIETY, London   E021

SOC. NAT. FRANCE, Paris.   E022

1899 SOC. NAT. FRANCE, Paris.   E023

SOUTH KENSINGTON MUSEUM, London. Cat. Lithographs, 1898/9, 2nd ed.
(Avery Collection, NY PL)   E024

P.A.F.A., Phila. 68 Ann. Exhib. *J. F. Raffelli*   E025

INTERNATIONAL SOCIETY OF SCULPTORS, PAINTERS, & ENGRAVERS. London. Cat. 2nd
Exhib., Pictures/Drawings. W. H. Ward, London. (May/July) p. 136 #39
Henri Rochefort   E026

Munchen, GLASPAL. 1890/1. Sczess, 1899   E027

1900 J005 (An analysis of Hamilton's work, many reproduced)

P.A.F.A., Phila. GILPIN FUND purchase (April 9), *"Cardinal Manning 1900.2"*
pastel.   E028

1901 P.A.F.A., Phila. 70 Ann. Exhib. *"Old Welsh Woman"*   E029

FINE ARTS, Buffalo, NY. PAN-AMERICAN EXPOSITION, Exhib. Cat., W. A. Coffin,
Director; D. Gray. Buffalo. (Hamilton received gold medal for two works,
"Gladstone at Downing St." / *"H. J. Thouron"*   E030

1902 SOC. NAT. FRANCE, Paris.   E031

Cust, L. (ed., London) NATIONAL PORTRAIT GALLERY II : 254 *"J. Kelvin"*   E032

P.A.F.A., Phila. FELLOWSHIP purchase, *"George Hitchcock,1944.20"*   E033

1903 CORCORAN GALLERY OF ART, Washington, D. C. catalog p. 328/9 *"R. Vaux"* E034

SOC. NAT. FRANCE, Paris   E035

WATERCOLOR CLUB, Phila., Cat. 2nd Ann. Exhib. at P.A.F.A. (March 19/April 1) E036

U001 *"Prof. Lewis Campbell, St. Andrews University, Scotland"*

1904 UNIVERSAL EXPOSITION, St. Louis. (Gold medal to Hamilton, oils)   E037

1905 ROYAL ACADEMY OF ARTS, Exhibitors, London.   D011

1906 Lane, W. C./ Browne, N. E., eds., A. L. A. PORTRAIT INDEX IN BOOKS & PERIODICALS,
Library of Congress, G. P. O., Washington, D. C. II (F--M) : 646 A   E038

1907 CARNEGIE INSTITUTION, Pittsburgh, Ann. Exhib.   E039

(1908) D023 *"Le nuage qui passe"*

1909 EXPOS. INTERN. D'ARTE, Venedig.   E040

1910 CARNEGIE INSTITUTION, Pittsburgh, Ann. Exhib.   E041

J007 EXPOS., Romane LXXX

AUSST. AMER. KST., Berlin.   E042

Hake, H. M. (ed.) BRITISH MUSEUM CAT. OF ENGRAVED BRITISH PORTRAITS, London.
II : 428; VII : 492   E117

1911 GR. KST. AUSST., Dusseldorf   E043

1912 P.A.F.A., Phila., 107 Ann. Exhib.   E044

    Graves, A. (ed.,1970) A CENTURY OF ROYAL ACADEMY EXHIBITIONS, 1813--1912. p. 484   E045

1913 CARNEGIE INSTITUTION, Pittsburgh, Ann. Exhib.   E046

    P.A.F.A., Phila., 108 Ann. Exhib. (Feb/March 30, p.12/3) "Coates"   E047

    Sezess, Rom, 1913/4   E048

    Benedite, LUXEMBOURG MUSEUM, Paris.   E049

    NATIONAL PORTRAIT SOCIETY   E050

    SENEFELDER CLUB, London, Exhib. pgs. 13/4, 19/20   E051

(1914) *"Prof. E. Marburg, University of Pennsylvania, Phila."* E088

    INVENTORY OF AMERICAN PAINTINGS EXECUTED BEFORE 1914, N.M.A.A., Washington, D. C. E052

    CATALOG OF AMERICAN PORTRAITS, N. P. G., Washington, D. C.   E053

    INVENTORY OF AMERICAN SCULPTURE, Washington, D. C.   E054

1915 P.A.F.A., Phila., FELLOWSHIP, *"H.J. Thouron"*   U008

    PANAMA-PACIFIC INTERN. EXPOS., San Francisco, Official Illus. Cat. with awards
       Dept. of Fine Arts, Wahlgreen Co. p. 143/4 (39 Hamilton works)   E055

    Cat. de luxe, II : 329   E056

1916 Cincinnati MUSEUM, "Cat. of Paintings by Hamilton"   E057

    CARNEGIE INST., Pittsburgh, Dept. of Fine Arts (Nov.1/3, four pgs. notes, 64
       Hamilton works in oils, pastels, & sculpture.)   E058

    Leigh, W. R. (commentary, p.3) MEMORIAL ART GALLERY, Rochester, NY. (Oct. 30
       30 pastels by Hamilton)   E059

    San Francisco ART ASSOCIATION, "ILLUS. CAT. OF THE POST-EXPOSITION EXHIBITION"
       Department of Fine Arts (Jan./May)   E117

1917 Rinder, F. (compiler) ROYAL SCOTISH ACADEMY, 1826--1916. Kingsmead. (Index of
       lenderes/donors, p.447)   E060

    J021 Chicago

J022 METROPOLITAN MUSEUM, NY : Eakins Memorial Exhib.

J023

J024

INSTITUTE OF FINE ARTS, Minneapolis   E063

P.A.F.A., Phila., 112 Ann. Exhib.   *Mother*   E064

1918 ROSENBACH & CO., Phila. (Nov. 25/Dec. 7, 33 Hamilton oils & pastels)   E065

ART ALLIANCE OF Phila. (April 19, Mrs. Mary Harriman's collection of
    Hamilton's pastels)   E066

HACKLEY ART GALLERY, Muskegon, MI (Oct. 5/31) pastels   E067

J026

CORCORAN GALLERY OF ART, Washington, D. C. (March 5/31) pastels   E068

1919 Gregg, F. J., (Foreword) M. KNOEDLER GALLERY, NYC, Cat. of American Artists
    (March 15/29, 17 Hamilton works)   E069

P.A.F.A., Phila., 114 Ann. Exhib. *Judge Alexander & Mrs. Simpson*   E070

J028

1920 MUSEUM OF HISTORY/SCIENCE/ART, Los Angeles, Print Makers Society, First
    Ann.Exhib. (March)   E071

1921 J036

B012 pgs.13--15 (47 Hamilton works)

NATIONAL ACADEMY OF DESIGN, NYC, *WAYMAN ADAMS*   U005

1922 J040

J043

J044

1923 MUSEUM EXPOS. PARK, Los Angeles, 4th International Printmakers Exhib.,
    Printmakers of CA. (March)   E072

1924 P.A.F.A., Phila., Illus. Cat. Watercolor & Minature Exhib. (Nov. 9/Dec. 14)   E073

1925 THE ENGLISH CAT. OF BOOKS, 1921--25. p. 676 "Nov.,'21 : MEN I HAVE PAINTED,
     30 shillings."   E074

     MUSEUM,INSTITUTE OF THE ARTS & SCIENCES, Brooklyn, Exhib. Cat., frontis :
     pastel by Hamilton (April 14/May 10)   copy at NY PL AD   E075

1927 J047 "Flagellation of Madame Paluchin & other pastels"

1930 WORLD'S FAIR, Chicago   E076

1931 BARBIZON HOUSE, London, "Gladstone portraits & other Hamilton works, April 10".   E078

     ART INDEX   E079

     J049

     (^^^^) #30, Standing Woman, 1910, L. P.   at N. M. A. A., VF   E080

193(8) GEORGE McMANUS CO., Phila.   "Joseph Pennell"   E081

1934 SPINKS GALLERY, London. "Bismarck"   J051

     P.A.F.A., Phila., General Fund purchase (Feb. 5) "W. T. Richards, 1934.7" U007

1935 J052

     McCLEES GALLERY, Phila., HAMILTON RETROSPECTIVE EXHIB.   E083

     P.A.F.A.,Phila., U007

     ART INDEX   E084

1936 D035

1937 Singer, H. W. NEUER BILDNIS KATALOG. Verlag K. W. Hiersemann, Leipzig.
     "Corbet, Ford, Gladstone, Monkhouse, & Tyndall"   E085

     MUSEUM OF ART, Phila., 61 Ann Report   E086

     op cit, U009

     P.A.F.A., Phila., FELLOWSHIP, U009

     D038

1938 MUSEUM OF ART, Phila., U009

SAMUEL T. FREEMAN & CO., Phila., Auction Cat. (March 28, Hamilton's oils, pastels,
& watercolors were sold by his Phila. estate administrator in 165 lots including
lithographs & ephemera.)   E087

1940 Addison, A. UNIVERSITY OF PA PORTRAITS. Univ. of PA Press, Phila. p. 48 *Marburg,
Mitchell*   E088

1941 MUSEUM OF ART, Phila., four pastels, U009

1944 ARTHUR U. NEWTON GALLERIES, NYC. (April 24/May 6) *Col. E. M. House*   E089

1957 COLEMAN GALLERY, NYC (Spring)   E118

PARKE-BERNET GALLERIES, INC. (May 17/18, Sale # 1761   E119

1964 Chew, P. A., TWO HUNDRED FIFTY YEARS IN ART, Greensburgh, PA. *P. W. Bartlett
in his Paris Studio.*   E090

1968 Lee, C. PORTRAIT REGISTER. Biltmore Press. I : 511   E091

1970 Beall, K. F. AMERICAN PRINTS, LIBRARY OF CONGRESS COLLECTION, A CAT. BY ARTIST'S
NAME. Johns-Hopkins Press, p. 187 (foreword : C. Zigrosser)   E092

Marlor, C. S. BROOKLYN ART ASSOCIATION. A HISTORY OF THE & INDEX OF EXHIBITIONS.
J. F. Carr, NY.   E093

1973 Naylor, M. (ed.) NATIONAL ACADEMY OF DESIGN EXHIBITION RECORDS, 1861--1900.
NYC, I : 389/90 Kennedy Gallery, NY.   E094

1976 A CHECKLIST OF PAINTERS, c. 1200--1976 REPRESENTED IN THE WITT LIBRARY,
Courtauld Institute of Art, University of London. (47 Hamilton works)   E095

1980 Hislop, .. AUCTION CATALOGS, 1970--1980.   *Donkey Picture*   E096

1981 Yung, K. K. (ed.) COMPREHENSIVE CAT., (LONDON) NATIONAL PORTRAIT GALLERY,
1856--1979. St. Martin's Press, NY. p.725 (2 portraits added)   E097

THE (LONDON) ROYAL SOCIETY CAT. OF PORTRAITS. *p.308, illus.:John Tyndall* E077

1983 CORCORAN GALLERY OF ART, ILLUSTR. CAT., Washington, D. C. pgs. 99/100
(16 pastels remain of the Harriman Collection)   E098

1984 KEY, Nov.p.6.illus. *Turn-of-the-Century Woman Idealized at Dixon.*   E119

1985 P.A.F.A., Phila., CAT. OF PERMANENT COLLECTION. Hamilton's 574--581.   E099

    F. S. Schwarz & Son Galleries, Phila.   E100

1986 LEONARD'S ANN. PRICE INDEX OF ART AUCTIONS, 1986-87.   p.227   E101

    F. S. Schwarz & Son Galleries, Phila.   E102

1987 LEONARD'S ANN. PRICE INDEX OF ART AUCTIONS, 1987-88   p.261   E103

    Wilson, R. L. INDEX OF AMERICAN PRINT EXHIB., 1882--1940. Scarecrow Press,
      Metuchen, N. J. p. 203 (1920); p. 233 (1923)   E105

1988 SOTHEBY'S, INC., NY   *Afternoon Repose*   E117

1989 LEONARD'S ANN. PRICE INDEX OF ART AUCTIONS, 1988-89   p.288   E104

    Falk, P. H. (compiler) THE ANN. EXHIB. RECORD, P.A.F.A., 1876--1913.
      Soundview Press. (pgs. 8/9 Hamilton's work mentioned & illus. without
      credit to him; pgs 223, 230/1) Phila.   E106

    THE ANN. EXHIB. RECORD, P.A.F.A., 1884--1937. Phila.   E107

      1878 Ann Exhib Cat. #48
      1879   #49
                #55
                #56
                #61
                #63
                #68
                #70
                #71
                #72
                #73
                #100
                #101
                #102
                #105
                #107
                #108
                #110
                #112
                #113
                #114
                #119
                #121

192(4) P.A.F.A., Phila., Cat. Paintings in Oil pgs. 6,9; medal of Honor illus.   E115

       Watercolor & Minature Exhib. Cat., P.A.F.A. #8 1910
                                  #9 1911
                                #10 1912
                                #12 1914
                                #13 1915
                                #16 1918
                                #17 1919
                                #21 1923
                                #22 1924
                                #27 1929
                                #34 1936

19(90) Courtauld / Getty Art History Information Program, THE WITT COMPUTER INDEX
     The American School   E108

    SOTHEBY'S, INC. NYC. (Sept. 26) *Young Navigator*   E109

-   Billcliffe, R. (ed.) ROYAL GLASGOW INSTITUTE OF FINE ARTS, 1861--1989.
     Wooderd Press, Glasgow. II (G-K) : 182   E110

    Fink, L.M. AMER. ART AT THE 19th CENTURY PARIS SALONS, Smithsonian/
     Cambridge Univ.   pgs. 351;367   E111

    Havlice, P. P. WORLD PAINTING INDEX II Eakins' *Hamilton*   E112

    Munro,.. INDEX TO REPRODUCTIONS   E113

    Johnstone, M. / Hardie, W. THE GLASGOW BOYS, cat. exhib. (Oct. 10/ Nov. 3) E114

1993 SCHWARZ GALLERY Phila. "European & American Paintings" Phila. Coll. LIII Summer
     #29 Hamilton's *Young Woman Trimming Hat; #32* Young Woman Holding Flowers*
     Index page   E120

1884 THE ART AMATEUR (Feb.) 9/10 : 67. Wright, M. B. *The Photographic Display--*
Paintings shown by Henry Cook, W. T. Dannat & John Mc Lure Hamilton   J058

1892 GAZETTE DES BEAUX ARTS, June. pgs. 441--467. Pottier, E. "Les Salons de 1892.
Le Peintre" (Hamilton's *Gladstone,*" illus. received Honorable mention,
pgs.443,456   J001

1893 L' ART REVUE BI-MEUSUELLE ILLUSTREE 54 : 12/14. Dix-neuvieme Anne. Tome I.
LIV de La Collection, Paris Imprimerie de L' Art. E. Moreau & Cie.
41 Rue de La Victorie, 41 DCLXVI Notre Bibliotheque   J002

   INT. STUDIO (London) Feb. XIV : 135 *Gladstone*   J056
   (An international monthly, magazine of fine arts & applied arts edited by
   Charles Holme, published by John Lane, NY.

1896 ART JOURNAL 58 (N.S. 48) : 341--344. Morris, H. S. "John McLure Hamilton :
A Study," illus.   J003

1898 HARPER'S WEEKLY   "Mrs. Gladstone at Hawarden, engraving"   J004

1900 SCHRIBNER'S MAGAZINE, June. 27 : 733--738. Morris, H. S. "The Paintings of
John McLure Hamilton."   J005

(1906) n.d., n.s. :501 "Which is the best painting of a child? (an interview with noted
painter, Mrs. Anna Lea Merritt; she selected Hamilton's *Knitting Lesson*" at
NY PL, artist's file   J055

1907 THE SCRIP 2 : 363--366. Cary, E. L.   J006

   L' ART   J007

1910 INT. STUDIO (London) 40 : 159. In "Studio Talk," E. C. commented on P.A.F.A.
105th Ann. Exhib.   J008

   op cit 41 : 184. C. Lewis Hind : "American Paintings in Germany"
   Hamilton's *Gladstone*"   J009

1911 op cit 43 : 139. "Studio Talk" correspondent reported on Grafton Galleries
& National Portrait Society.   J010

   op cit 44 : ... "Studio Talk" on Pastel Society exhib. at Gallery of Royal
   Institute   J011

1912 op cit 46 : 240 "Studio Talk" F. G. on Phila.'s 107th Ann. P.A.F.A.
     Exhib. of "H. J. Thouron"   J012

     op cit 48 : 342 "Studio Talk" on "E. H. Coates"   J013

1913 op cit 49 : 250 "Studio Talk" on Phila.'s 108th Ann. P.A.F.A. Exhib.
     "E. H. Coates"   J014

     op cit 49 : 298 illus. : "Joseph Pennell etching"   J015

1914 op cit 52 (205,March #6) : 3--6. Pennell, Joseph on "The Senefelder Club"
     Hamilton a member.   J016

     op cit 53 : 298 "American Art at the Anglo-American Expos." illus. : oil
     "J. Pennell, seated etching,windows background"   J017

     op cit 53 : 301 Hamilton's lithographs, oils, pastels; "Gladstone"; "Pennell" J018

1915 op cit 56 : 128 "Studio Talk" on Royal Society of Portrait Painters exhib. at
     Grafton Galleries.   " Rev. Canon Armour"   J019

     ART & PROGRESS (August)   "Mother, an oil"   J057

     PANAMA-PACIFIC EXPOSITION, San Francisco, Prize for Hamilton.   J020

1917 BULLETIN, Art Institute of Chicago, Oct. 11 : 231--233 Hamilton pastels   J021

     BULLETIN, Minneapolis Institute of Arts VI (4):31, (Apr.4/May)   J059

     BULLETIN, Metropolitan Museum of Art, NYC. 12 (11, Nov.) : 218--220. Hamilton,
     J. M. & Morris, H. S. "An Appreciation of Eakins' work"   J022

     INT. STUDIO 62 : 63. Costello, E. on P.A.F.A. 112th Ann. Exhib. (Feb./March)
     "Mother, a portrait" pgs. 298, 301   J023

     op cit 63 : 262, 314   J024

     VOGUE Magazine, NY. Jan. 15th. pgs. 48,81 "ART" on exhib. of Harriman's purchase
     of the Hamilton pastels Collection   J028

1918 INT. STUDIO 64 : 142 "Studio Talk" E. C. on P.A.F.A. 113th Ann. Exhib.
     (Feb./March) "Judge Bregy;" & Wayman Adams' "Hamilton"   J025

     op cit 64 : xcviii " In The Galleries" on (Feb./ March) Exhib. at Phila.
     Sketch Club of P.A.F.A. Fellowship. "Henry Thouron #1"   J026

op cit 65 : 128   J027

1919 REVUE DE L' ART ANCIEN ET MODERNE (Nov.) 36 : 193--210 Moberg, Z. IN:
      Benedite, L. "L' Ecole Americaine an Musee du Luxembourg" *"Gladstone,illus."*   J029

    FELLOWSHIP, P.A.F.A., 23rd ANN. REPORT. (Hamilton, a member)   J030

    VANITY FAIR, NY. (Aug.) 12 (6) : 50 "An American Master of Pastel : John Mc Lure
      Hamilton" by the artist.   J031

1920 FELLOWSHIP, P.A.F.A., 24th ANN. REPORT. (Hamilton President & member) J032

    INT. STUDIO (March) 70 : Lxxx. Nelson, W. H. on "Hannevig Foundation" started
      Washington, D.C. NATIONAL PORTRAIT GALLERY. *"Col. E. M. House"* commissioned
      of *James* McLure Hamilton, an error in given name.   J035

    op cit 71 : 33 "Studio Talk" on Pittsburgh's 19th Ann. Exhib. The Wayman Adams'
      "Group portrait: The Conspiracy" included Hamilton   J036

    CORCORAN ANNUAL REPORT. Acquisition of works of art   J059

1921 THE CONNOISSEUR 61 : 174/5 "Current Art Notes" (Four additions to London National
      Portrait Gallery)   J037

    PA Magazine 45 : 394/5 Henderson, H. W. reviewed Hamilton's book, B012 J038

    BOOKMAN (London) 61 (Suppl. 6) Dec.   J039

    THE SPUR because the workers need a spur (to the Communist Republic),
      London, illus.   J040

    INT. STUDIO 82 : 40   *"Asquith"*   J041

    AMERICAN ART ANNUAL (Feder. of Arts) Who's Who in Art XVIII : 18 Corcoran
      Gallery of Art, Washington, D.C. to exhib. (Nov. 24th) former collection
      of Mrs. Harriman (Hamilton) pastels. She donated them to CGA on Feb. 11th. J034

1921/2 FELLOWSHIP, P.A.F.A.,25th ANN. REPORT. (Hamilton a resident member) J033

1922 THE CONNOISSEUR 62 : 64 Hamilton's book B012 reviewed   J042

    INT. STUDIO, London, "Art Year" on review of Hamilton's book & Tate Gallery J043

    op cit 83 : 289 *"Lord Leighton"*   J044

    op cit 84 : 54 *"Gladstone"* at Tate Gallery   J045

1923 FELLOWSHIP, P.A.F.A., 26th ANN. REPORT (Hamilton resident member)   J046

   INT. STUDIO (May) 77 : 89 Wayman Adams' "Hamilton" illus.   J047

   "WILLIAM EWART GLADSTONE by John McLure Hamilton" reprinted from B012 at
   West Indian Training College Press, Mandeville, Jamaica, 3 pgs.   J051

1927 THE CONNOISSEUR 77 : 253 The Pastel Society's 28th Ann. Exhib. at London's
   Royal Institute. *Flagellation of Madame Paluchin*   J048

1931 THE ART YEAR (Jan. 4) Hamilton's vitae   J049

   THE APOLLO, the magazine of the Arts for... June, 13 : 398 Furst, H. on
   Gladstone oil portraits & pastels by Hamilton at Barbizon House.   J050

1934 AMERICAN FOREIGN SERVICE JOURNAL (Oct.) 11 : 522--525, 647/8, 550 Corcoran,
   W. W.(provided an excellent career summary) "Last Wish of A Great American
   Artist"   J052

1935 THE APOLLO (Feb.) 21 : 116/7 illus. : "*Gladstone, M.P.*"   J053

1937 Phila, PA MUSEUM FINE ARTS, 61st ANN. REPORT, illus.   J054

HAMILTON LETTER COLLECTION
(Abbreviations for Sources)

ARCHIVES OF AMERICAN ART, Washington, D.C.	A
BRITISH MUSEUM, London, Manuscript Collection	B
Estate of Harry Burke	HB
CORCORAN GALLER OF ART, Washington, D.C., Archives	C
Drew, M., 1919 CATHERINE GLADSTONE BY HER DAUGHTER	B031
Simon Gratz Collection, Mss Room, HISTORICAL SOCIETY, PA, Phila.	SG
Whistler Collection, Library, GLASGOW UNIVERSITY, Scotland	GUL
Society Collection, Mss Room, HISTORICAL SOCIETY OF PA, Phila.	HS
Howe, Sydenham J. Microfiche, Artist's File: Hamilton, NYC PUBLIC LIBRARY	NYPL
Hamilton, John McLure	B003, B012
ART MUSEUM, KELVINGROVE, Glasgow, Scotland, Archives	K
Masterman, L., 1930 (ed.) MARY GLADSTONE (Mrs. DREW) HER DIARIES & LETTERS	B033
James Henry Moser Papers, A.L.S. (AAA)	M
NATIONAL MUSEUM OF AMERICAN ART, Washington, D. C.	NMAA
NEW YORK HISTORICAL SOCIETY	NY
PALL MALL GAZETTE, London newspaper B012	PMG
PA ACADEMY OF FINE ARTS, Phila., Archives	PAFA
Pennell, 1908. LIFE OF WHISTLER (1911,5th ed. pgs 285--295)	B007
Pennell, 1929. WHISTLER JOURNAL	B013
Pennell, E. R., 1929. LIFE/LETTERS J. PENNELL	B017
COUNTY MEDICAL SOCIETY, Phila.,PA U032	MS
Charles Roberts Autograph Collection of American Artists, Haverford, PA	CR
ROSENBACH MUSEUM, Phila., Archives	R
George W. Stevens Collection, "Autobiographies of American Artists" AAA	U030
MacLachlan, Howard. DATA ANALYSIS, New Canaan, CT.	U031
Microfilm, Newspaper Dept., UNIVERSITY OF LONDON	LUL
Thornton Oakley Papers, Brandywine River Museum, PA. AAA microfilm	TO
NATIONAL LIBRARY OF JAMAICA, Kingston	NLJ
Richard J. Alperin Collection, Hamilton Project correspondence	ARJ

HAMILTON LETTER COLLECTION

(YR,MO DY;	FROM/TO;	TOPICS;		SOURCE;	LETTER #)
1845	Kennedy, D.J.	16/17 Summer St., Phila.			
		K-III-58, Legend : wc		HS-1	U030
1881 VII 22	H to George Hamilton, M.D.			CR-1	L001
IX 12	H to Anna Lea Merritt			PAFA-1	L002
1889 Spring	H to E.R./J. Pennell			B007:101--103	L003
	J. Mc Neill Whistler to H			B007:287	L013
1890 III 28	op cit to H		H-51	GUL-1	L004
III 28	H to Whistler		H-52	GUL-2	L005
XI 17	H to Edward H. Coates re : "Corn Husker"			PAFA-2	L006
Sunday	H to Clara Hamilton re : "Spencer"			B012:101	L202
Sat.	H to ?			B012:102	L215
Tues.	H to ?			B012:102	L216
Sunday	H to ?			B012:104	L229
1892 VI 17	H to P. M. Wm. E. Gladstone re : "Bismarck"			B-1	L007
VII 17	(Sat.) H to Clara			B012:64	L197
n.d.	H to Nora (King)			B012:65-67	L199
(VII 18)	(Sun.) H to Clara			B012	L198
1893 X 5	Pe to H			B017 I :261	L008
1896 XI 23	H to Harrison S. Morris			PAFA-3	L009
1897 XII 29	H to Mo			PAFA-4	L010
1898 V 19	H (from Wolfscastle) to Mary G. Drew			B-2	L011
V 19	H to Catherine Gladstone			lost	L220
VI 7	Pe to H			B017 I :325/6	L012
X 22	H to Mo			PAFA-5	L014

n.d.	Pe		B007	L015
1899 III 15	H to Mo		PAFA-6	L016
1900 V 1	H to Mo		PAFA-7	L017
n.d.	H to Pe?		B013:156	L019
n.d.	H at Greaves studio		B013:143	L020
n.d.	Whistler arranged H's work for exhibition		B017 II:..	L021
(VII 29)	H to Pe ?		B017 II:..	L022
1901 II 21	H to Mo	"Old Welsh Woman" damaged; trip	PAFA-8	L023
III 18	H to Mo	proposed to pt U.S. Prexy Mc Kinley	PAFA-9	L024
V 4	H to Mo		PAFA-10	L025
X 6	H mentioned by Pe IN: Daily Chronicle		B013:217	L026
IX 16	H on Whistler's Enemies List		B013:214/5	L027
XI 2	H introduced to Whistler		B013:218	L028
n.d.	second meeting with Whistler post-GENTLE ART		B013:219	L029
XI 11	H snubbed by Whistler		B007:285	L030
1902 II 20	H to James Henry Moser	984/602-3 M-1		L031
1903 II 21	H to Pe; St. Louis Jury: Ives, Sargent, Whistler, (van Dyke), Hamilton, Pennell (photo)		B013:277	L032
II 26	H to Pe requested copy of Whistler obit		B013:296	L033
(VII 21)	H to Pe		B013:296	L034
IV 22	H to Principal, John Story		K-1	L035
VII 26	Pe to H Whistler's death		B017 II:5/6	L036
VIII 2	Pe to H		B017 II:6	L037
n.d.	Pe to H gold medal, St. Louis, text		B017 II:11	L038

1904 n.d.	H painted Pe in winter, text	B017 II:59	L039
1905 IV 28	H details, "GENTLE ART" incident; role of Sheridan Ford, etc.	B013:215	L040
XI 9	H to (J.E.D.) Trask	PAFA-11	L041
1909 III 5	H attended Whistler's Memorial Exhibition	B013:82	L042
VII 15	H interpreted Whistler's painting	B013:82	L043
1910 II 22	H to Editor, PALL MALL GAZETTE	B012:196/7	L203
III 9	H to M. Drew	B-3	L044
Autumn	Pe to H, send "*Gladstone*" to Berlin/Munich,text	B017 II:78	L045
VII 25	H to Editor, PALL MALL GAZETTE	B012:195	L204
XII 9	H to Editor, PALL MALL GAZETTE	B012:197/8	L205
1911 II 12	Pe to H, Venice Biennial Exposition	B017 II:98	L046
V 1	Pe to H Roman Exposition	B017 II:98	L047
n.d.	Pe to H King's portrait for DAILY CHRONICLE	B017 II:93	L048
V 5	Ives died, H contacted Embassy	B017	L050
V 11	Ives, friend of H	B017 II:94/5	L049
VI 1	Pe to H	B017	L051
VI 28	H to (J.E.D.) Trask (Coronation portrait,not)	PAFA-12	L052
X 15	H to ?	B012:34	L209
XI 9	H (Hotel Grand Central, London) to ?	B012:32	L206
XI 12	Pe to H	B017 II:98	L053
Friday	H to ?	B012:35	L210
XI 15	H to ?	B012:25	L018
Tuesday	H to ?	B012:33	L207

Thurs.	H (Buckingham Palace Hotel, London, S.W.) to ?	B012:33	L208
XI 20	H to ?	B012:36	L211
XI 22	H to ?	B012:37	L212
XI 23	H to ?	B012:58	L213
1912 II 14	H to ?	B012:39	L214
IV 7	H to Drew	B-4	L055
1913 VII 7	H to D	B-5	L056
1914 IX 16	Pe to H Anglo-American Exposition	B017 II:147	L057
IX 29	Pe to H *Gladstone* lithographic stone at Unwins	B017 II:147	L058
XII 24	Pe to H Panama-Pacific Exposition	B017 II:149	L059
XII 30	Drew to H world events, commentary	B033:480/1	L060
1915 I 20	Pe to H litho sold to Royal Academy of Arts	B017 II:154	L061
II 8	H to D Caroline D. Hamilton's death	B-6	L062
II 15	H to D	B-7	L063
II 23	J. Wm. White, Ph.D. to H	B-45	L064
II 26	Pe to H Panama-Pacific Exposition	B017 II:155	L065
III 9	H to (Henry Neville) Gladstone (Dr. White's)	B-8	L066
IV 2	H to D (Lord Armistead)	B-9	L067
IV 3	H sailed to NY bound for Phila.	B017	L068
IV 11	H to D (H alone) read books	B-10	L069
IV 19	Pe to H	B017 II:156	L070
IV 30	Pe to H Lt. Gladstone's death	B-46	L071
VI 25	D to H world events, commentary	B033:482/3	L072

n.d.	H (speech) to Phila. Art Club, Pe loyal American, text	B017 II:201/2	L196
1916 I 24	H (Century Club, NYC) to D	B-11	L073
III 21	H (Cogslea, Allens Lane, Phila.) to D	B-12	L074
1917 III 27	H to (Albert) Rosenthal P22/201-202	SG-1	L075
IV 11	H (Homestead,Hot Springs, VA) to D	B-13	L076
VI 3	H (Ritz-Carlton Hotel,Phila.) to D	B-14	L077
XII 27	H (Biltmore, NYC) to C. Powell Minnigerode	C-1	L078
XII 31	M to H	C-2	L222
1918 I 1	H to M	C-3	L079
I 7	M to H	C-4	L223
I 15	H (1904 Spruce St., Phila.) to M	C-5	L080
I 25	H to M	C-6	L081
II 10	H to D	B-15	L082
II 14	H to Charles Carroll Glover	C-7	L083
II 19	H to M	C-8	L084
III 12	H speech announcement,"Art A Necessity"	PAFA-..	U *
III 16	Secretary to M to H	C-9	L224
III 21	H to Miss Millard (Mrs. Rea's VOGUE activities)	C-10	L085
III 29	H to M	C-11	L086
IV 19	H to M	C-12	L087
IV 29	M to H	C-13	L225
V 8	H to (John Frederick) Lewis, Esq.	PAFA-13	L088

1919 II 12	H (Prexy PAFA Fellowship) to Hon. Simon Gratz, Esq., City Hall, Phila.		SG-2	L089
II 18	business ledger, first H entry		R-1	L090
XII 1	H (Hermitage, Surrey) to D		B-16	L091
XII 30	H to D		B-17	L092
n.d.	" *Mrs.Gladstone at Hawarden,c. 1893*"		B033	*
1920 I 24	H to M (Adams, Curtis, Ludington, Wood, Hoover, Sims, Palmer)		C-14	L093
II 12	H to D		B-18	L094
VII 18	H to D		B-19	L095
VIII 22	H to D	*"Col E.M. House" "P.M. H.H. Asquith"*	B-20	L096
IX 10	H to D		B-21	L097
IX 17	H (Wharf, Sutton Courtney, Berks) to D		B-22	L098
IX 19	H (Wharf, ink/pencil, illegible) to D		B-23	L099
IX 22	H to D		B-24	L100
IX 30	H to D		B-25	L101
XII 3	H to D	" *W.E.G. Gladstone*"	B-26	L102
XII 5	H to D		B-27	L103
XII 21	H to D		B-28	L104
XII 30	H to D	mentioned PA farm; Pe " NIGHTS"	B-29	L105
1921 II 11	H to M		C-15	L106
II 24	H to D	King George V, second sitting	B-30	L107
IV 17	H(Hotel Holie, Alassio, Italian Riviera; finished/unfinished art, Whistler's comment repeated) to D		B-31	L108

n.d.	D to H	B-41	L134
VIII 26	H to P. M., A. J. Balfour	BO12:87	L200
n.d.	H to Balfour #2	BO12:87/8	L201
X 20	H to D Clara comforted widow, Mrs Dorothy G. Parish	B-32	L109
X 25	H to Editor, LONDON TIMES :13E	LUL-1	L221
XII 30	H to D	B-33	L110
n.d.	H to M *Brittain*	C-16	L226
n.d.	H to M *Court of Appeals*·: christmas card	C-17	L227
n.d.	H to Mo *George Meredith* : christmas card	PAFA-14	L228
1922 I 24	H to D Cannes	B-34	L111
V 25	H to (Florence Earle) Coates	HB-1	L112
VII 8	H to D ceremony at NATIONAL LIBERAL CLUB	B-35	L113
VII 15	H to D	B-36	L114
VII 19	H (S.S. Majestic, White Star Lines) to D	B-37	L115
VII 24	H (S.S. Majestic, White Star Lines) to D	B-38	L116
1923 II 8	Pe to David Croal Thomson, H arriving Pe's racism	BO17 II:301/2	L117
III 24	H (Newleigh Cottage, Mandeville, Jamaica, B.W.I.) to D	B-39	L118
IX 24	H (Newton S. Brittain,Esq., Tobyhanna, Mt. Pocono, PA) to M	C-18	L119
X 25	H (Drexel & Co.,Phila.) to D	B-40	L120
XI 5	H (Brittain) to Miss Millard	C-19	L121
XI 5	H to M	C-20	L122

XII 2	H (Content Farms, Cambridge, Washington County, NY) to M	C-21	L123
XII 13	H (Ritz Carlton Hotel, Phila.) to M	C-22	L124
1924 n.d.	H to (Rosenbach & Co.)	R-2	L125
III 20	H to Percy E. Lawler	R-3	L126
IV 1	H to R	R-4	L127
VII 6	H to P. E. Lawler	R-5	L128
VII 14	H to R	R-6	L129
VIII 19	H to Lawler	R-7	L130
n.d.	H to Louis Griemard	R-8	L131
IX 19	H to Thornton Oakley	TO-1	L132
XI 24	H to O	TO-2	L133
1926 II 7	exhibition Pastel Society, London	*	*
II	H to M *"Lords of Appeal" "U.S. Senator,Stewart" "Peace on Earth"*	C-23	L135
X 15	H to D H's grandmother from Ulster	B-41	L136
1928 IX 14	H to M H returned from Jamaica	C-24	L137
IX 17	H to Sec., County Medical Society, Phila.	MS-1	L138
XI 22	H to M Mrs. Mary Harriman's Collection	C-25	L139
1929 II 16	H to M *"General Booth"*	C-26	L140
(IV) 23	H to Philip/Dr. A.S.W. Rosenbach	R-9	L141
X 4	H to O	TO-3	L142
XI 18	H to R	R-10	L143
XI 22	H to (Henry N.) Gladstone	B-42	L144

XI 28	H to Lord (H. N.) Gladstone	B-43	L145
XII 3	R typescript to H	R-11	L146
XII 6	H to R	R-12	L147
XII 21	R to H	R-13	L148
1930 I 3	H to R	R-14	L149
I 4	H to Gladstone	B-44	L150
II 26	H to Dr. R Rare Book Inventory	R-15	L151
II 26	H to Dr. R	R-16	L152
III 13	R to H	R-17	L153
III 27	H to R	R-18	L154
IV 9	R to H	R-19	L155
IV 28	H to O	TO-4	L156
V 26	H to R	R-20	L157
VI 15	H to Minnigerode	C-27	L158
1931 II 11	H to Oakley	TO-5	L159
II 23	H to O	TO-6	L160
IV 26	Barbizon House, exhibition	*	*
XI 15	H typescript to M, London National Gallery, Tate	C-28	L161
XII n.d.	H (Iona, Jamaica) typescript to M	C-29	L162
XII 29	M to H	C-30	L227
1933 I 16	H to O	TO-7	L163
IV 15	H to O	TO-8	L164
V 16	H to O	TO-9	L165

XII 28	George Hall Hamilton for H to O	TO-10	L166
1934 I 1	G. H. to O	TO-11	L167
I 8	G. H. to O	TO-12	L168
I 21	G. H. to O	TO-13	L169
II 3	G. H. to O	TO-14	L170
II 10	G. H. to O	TO-15	L171
1935 X 31	Mary Curtis Bok to O	TO-16	L172
X 19	Emily Drayton Taylor to O	TO-17	L173
XI 18	Wm H. Pickering to (Frank Cundall) George, 52	NLJ-1	L217
XI n.d.	P typescript obit to Dinard Editor, French Soc. of Astronomy; George Hamilton's career summarized	NLJ-2	L218
1936 I 15	John Allen for H to O bronzes	TO-18	L174
I 2(1)	Allen to O	TO-19	L175
II 8 to III 26	Mc Clees Galleries Retrospective Exhib.	*	*
II 2	Allen to O Two parcels for Phila. H's unfinished portraits	TO-20	L176
II 8	O (Watercolor Club) to (John Andrew) Myers	PAFA-15	L177
III 5	H's agreement authorizing Relief Committee to act in sale of his art (Mo, O, Taylor)	TO-21	L178
III 5	George Alexander Armstrong (U.S. Consul, Jamaica to O	TO-22	L179
III 5	Armstrong to H:send no more goods to ART ALLIANCE	TO-23	L180
III 6	H to O:Last shipment was five small pet pictures of H's intended as gifts for Mrs. Alexander C. Simpson & others (marked) for distribution.	TO-24	L181

III 27	H to O : Thanks for your positive words; O's letter arrived same day as Colin Campbell Cooper's.	TO-25	L182
III 30	Louis C. Grieumard to O: Acknowledged note of thanks for work done for H.	TO-26	L183
IV 20	Emily D. Taylor to O: Missed meeting; ill.	TO-27	L184
VII 4	Clara & Mc Lure to Myers	PAFA-16	L185
VIII 26	Clara to Myers re: "Tears"	PAFA-17	L186
IX 11	Hyacinth Rebhan for Clara to O; H died 20:30 hours, 1936 IX 10	TO-28	L187
IX 11	Taylor to O; sad news received, H died	TO-29	L188
X 20	Clara to O; H on O, "I like(d) that man!"	TO-30	L189
XI 2	Rebhan to O; Clara's death	TO-31	L190
	Sarah Allen first person there (1992 report)	*	*
XI 10	Taylor to O Clara's burial	TO-32	L191
1938 IV 26	W(m) Hobart Porter to Dr. R	R-21	L192
V 4	Porter to (James B.) Sword	R-22	L193
V 11	H painting sold	R-23	L194
1940 VII 11	Sydenham J. Howe to NY dealer,etc re:Hamilton Art Memorial Museum	NYPL-1	L195
1993 I 1	Howard Mac Lauchlan to Alperin (H's handwriting)	ARJ-1	U031

1877 IV 8	NY TIMES			N001
1878 IV .	PHILA. JOURNAL			N002
1897 V 15 124	CHICAGO POST "Art & Artists" on small exhibition at Art Institute (CAI)			N003
V 16 125	CHICAGO TRIBUNE watercolors, minatures, pastels at CAI			N004
V 16 126	CHICAGO INTEROCEAN 30 Hamilton works at CAI			N005
V 22 128	CHICAGO POST	CAI		N006
V 23 129/30	CHICAGO TIMES HERALD	CAI		N007
V 23 131	CHICAGO INTEROCEAN	CAI		N008
V 30 136/37	CHICAGO CHRONICLE	CAI		N009
V 30	CHICAGO TRIBUNE	CAI		N010
1909 IX 25 10	PHILA. PRESS "Want Mercer Fund Divided"			N099
1911 II 24	LONDON DAILY GRAPHIC "New Portrait of General Booth"			N091
VI 16	LONDON DAILY CHRONICLE "Coronation Portrait"			N011
VI 17 7	op cit "Commissioned to draw Coronation portrait;" photo of Hamilton			N012
VI 17	PHILA. EVEN. BULLETIN			N013
VI 18 1	NY TIMES (Sunday Front Page!)			N014
VI 22 3	LONDON DAILY CHRONICLE "God Save The King!" portrait by Hamilton			N092
1916 XII 11	PHILA. (INQUIRER) re: P. M. David Lloyd-George			N015
XII 11	PHILA. EVEN. BULLETIN			N016
... ..	PITTSBURGH (...) "Lent by Mrs. E. H. Harriman for a special exhibition of Mr. Hamilton's works, *Carnegie Institution*			N101
1918 I 20	WASHINGTON,D.C. SUNDAY STAR *"Glover portrait"*			N096

I 25	PHILA (...) Wayman Adams oil "HAMILTON"	N093
II 9	PHILA. EVEN. BULL.	N019
II 10	PHILA. PUBLIC LEDGER P.A.F.A. gold medal	N018
II 10 6	NY TIMES *Judge Bregy;* gold medal	N020
II 10	PHILA. (INQ.)	N021
II 11	op cit re: war in France	N022
II 19	PHILA. PUBL. LED.	N023
III 20	PHILA. (INQ.) Hamilton heads P.A.F.A. Fellowship	N024
III 21	op cit Hamilton addresses P.A.F.A. Fellowship	N100
III 29	op cit Hamilton receives honors	N025
1919 III 14	PHILA. EVEN. BULL. Dinner to plan Phila.'s War Memorial	N026
VIII 10	op cit Parkway proposal	N027
VIII 11	PHILA. (INQ.) moving statue	N028
1920 I 28:153	LONDON ILLUS. NEWS (The Sketch) "The Vogue for Backs : The Pastelists of Fashion"	N102
IV 23	PHILA. (PUBL. LED.) Hamilton heads P.A.F.A. Fellowship	N094
IX (10)	LONDON SPUR *Col. E. M. House,* *illus.*	N017
1921 I ..Sat.	LONDON DAILY TELEGRAPH "Pastel Society"	N103
IX .	T. FISHER UNWIN, LTD. (Publisher's 4 pg. book notice, B012	N030
X 25 135	LONDON TIMES "Letter to Editor" re: Furse/Swan exhibition, L221	
1922 VIII 6 (8,14)	NY TIMES, illustrated" Book Review:The World of Art:Recent Books"	N031
1924 II 14	PHILA. BULLETIN Hamilton pleads for Parkway plan	N029
III 3	PHILA. (INQ.) Mayor Kendrick's plan	N032

1925	V 13:281	LONDON ... Royal Institute Galleries *Silk Dress*	N104
1926	I (25)	LONDON DAILY TELEGRAPH	N097
	II 7 16a	PHILA. EVEN. BULL. Henderson:Jan.19th London pastels exhib. & critics	N034
(1926)		PHILA. (INQ.) Heads P.A.F.A. Fellowship again	N035
1927	XI 7	op cit *Gov. Robinson;* on Cubist art	N036
1929	I 2	LONDON MORNING (POST) Pastel Society, Potential Quality of a delicate medium	N105
1931	I 4	LONDON DAILY MAIL	N037
	IV 10 10	LONDON TIMES Barbizon House exhibition	N038
	IV 18 11	SURREY COMET interviewed at The Hermitage	N039
		LONDON MORNING POST	N040
	IV 26	PHILA. PUBL. LED. repeated London critic's praises for portraits	N041
1934	III 25 (9:7)	NY TIMES critic said Hamilton pastels equaled Degas/Renoir	N042
	IX 13	PHILA. EVEN. BULL. Hamilton requested *Dr. Riche* fee	N043
	IX 13	PHILA. RECORD "Forgotten Man in Oil"	N044
	IX 22	KINGSTON, JAMAICA DAILY GLEANER Long report of "Last Wish."	N045
	XI 11	PHILA. RECORD *Dr. Riche* fee unpaid	N046
	XII 16	PHILA. INQ. " Last Wish"	N047
1935	VIII ..	NY TIMES George Hall Hamilton's obit	N090
	VIII 7	KING.,JAM. DAIL. GLEAN. Death of George H. Hamilton	N086
	VIII 8	op cit Funeral of G. H. Hamilton	N087
	VIII 14	op cit G. H. Hamilton was Astronomer/Chess player; on children	N088
1936	II 29	PHILA. EVEN. BULL. Hamilton's Retrospective Exhibition	N048
	III 1	PHILA. (INQ.) exhibition	N049

III 2	PHILA. EVEN. BULL. H. S. Morris : on Hamilton's illness/need	N050
III 26 (20A ac) (NY TIMES) C. H. Bronte : on McClees Gallery exhib.; "Lion"		N051
IV 12	PHILA. INQ. H. W. Henderson : on Hamilton	N052
IX 11	PHILA. EVEN. BULL. "Hamilton dead at 83"	N053
IX 11	LONDON (EVEN. POST) Obit	N056
IX 11	PHILA. PUBL. LED. Obit	N057
IX 11	op cit long obit	N058
IX 12 (17:5) NY TIMES long obit		N059
IX 12	PHILA. EVEN. BULL. Hamilton obit	N054
IX 12	PHILA. INQ. Obit of Noted Painter	N055
IX 12	KING.,JAM. DAIL. GLEAN. long obit; photo : Clara, George, & Hamilton	N060
IX 26 14E LONDON TIMES Hamilton's obit : Victorian Era Portraits		N061
1937 V 26 16	PHILA. EVEN. BULL. Hamilton's art sold at auction brought $56.50	N062
V 27	PHILA. INQ. Hamilton's estate = paintings; sold	N063
X 27	PHILA. EVEN. BULL. Estate = pictures	N064
X 28	PHILA. INQ. Ancillary letters of Administration on estate/heirs	N065
1938 IV 3	PHILA. RECORD D. G. gave warning re: results of Hamilton art sale	N066
IV 16 4 (met.)a (NY TIMES) Phila.'s Freeman auction of Hamilton's art		N067
VI 16	PHILA. EVEN. BULL. Sale of estate brought $2,082.00	N068
VI 17	PHILA. INQ. Claim on estate paid	N069
XI 25	LONDON TIMES Hamilton's estate notice	N033
1939 X 24	PHILA. EVEN. BULL. (Post) Hamilton Real Estate awarded to minors	N070
1940 V 24	op cit (as typescript) Hamilton's career summarized	N071

1948 VIII 26	KING.,JAM. DAIL. GLEAN. Lady Asquith visited Mandeville/pastels there	N072
1949 V 5	op cit Manchester Free Library	N073
1950 VI 26	PHILA. EVEN BULL. W. E. Baum : "Hamilton's portraits brilliant; Sketch Club unique in art, observes 90th Anniv.	N095
1955 X 16	KING.,JAM. DAIL. GLEAN. Rev. W. Lewis pioneered Jamaican Free Library	N074
1961 I 13	op cit G. H. Hamilton : Mandeville Astronomy; Moon, Mars	N089
1981 IV 3 384	LONDON TIMES, Literary Suppl. Book Review:ROYAL SOCIETY, ILLUS. CAT. "John Tyndall"	N075
1990 IX/X 45	GENEALOGIST'S HELPER request information on art/letters of Hamilton	N076
XI 2 8d	USA TODAY want ad	N077
1991 I 17	KING.,JAM. DAIL. GLEAN. "Letter to Editor" on Project Hamilton	N078
VII 104	THE CONNECTOR (Hamilton National Genealogical Society) XIII # 7 ad	N079
	AUTOGRAPH QUARTERLY ad	N080
X 98	ART & ANTIQUES ad	N081
1992 VII/VIII	KING.,JAM. DAIL. GLEAN. seven week ad campaign	N083
VIII 118/9	THE CONNECTOR op cit Hamilton's genealogy published	N082
(Fall)	NEWSLETTER (A.H.A.A.) op cit 11 (4) : 9 ad	N085
IX	PRINT QUARTERLY IX (3) : 291 A (Notes) "Project Hamilton"	N106

[George Hall Hamilton pulling unseen toy = THE CHILD PLAYING], c. 1888. Oil 50.25" x 40." Formerly collection of Harry Burke.

[George Hall Hamilton, Astronomer], c. 1923. Oil 60" x 36." Formerly collection of Harry Burke.

1845   KENNEDY, D. J. authored legend for his watercolor drawing : "16/17 Summer
            St.,Phila." K-III-58, (Hist.Soc.PA.)   U026

1875   ACADEMIE ROYALE DES BEAUX ARTS A ANVERS, Registre D'Inscriptions Annes, 1870/
            71 A 1874/75   pgs. 132, 146, 175 (Antwerp, Belgium)   U024

1880   op cit 1875/76 A 1879/80   p. 1   U025

1885   COUNTY MEDICAL SOCIETY, Phila. index card (membership data); vitae   U032

1900   P.A.F.A..Phila., Acquisition record (index card) 1900.2; 1934.7; 1935.16 E. R.
            Pennell gift 1935 XI 8 "Study of Seated Woman;" 1937.12 P.A.F.A.
            Fellowship gift 1937 III 10 "Two Women reading : figure Studies;"
            1944.20; 1981.X.84   U007

(1903) UNIVERSITY OF ST. ANDREWS,(Fife, Scotland) Dept. of Art History. Acquisition
            record (index card) "Prof. Lewis Campbell"   U001

1915   P.A.F.A. Fellowship, Phila.,"Henry J. Thouron" presented by Hamilton, I 15   U008

1918   P.A.F.A., Phila., Printed Announcement "Art A Necessity" Hamilton's lecture,
            III 12   U027

1919   ROSENBACH & COMPANY, Phila., now a Museum, business ledger   U002

192(.) ARCHIVES OF AMERICAN ART, George Washington Stevens Collection D34/733, "Auto-
            biographies of Modern Artists" pgs.120/1   (Hamilton typescript)   U003

1921   CORCORAN GALLERY OF ART, Washington, D.C., Acquistion records   U004
            21.10 (650); 21.11 (648); 21.12 (651); 21-13 (652); 21-14 (653);
            21.15 (654); 21-16 (649); 21-40 (647); 64.42.1 (655); 64.42.2 (656);
            64.42.3 (657); 64.42.4 (658); 64.42.5 (646).

        NATIONAL ACADEMY OF DESIGN, NYC, "Wayman Adams"   U005

192(.) THE EMMA, COUNTESS OF OXFORD & ASQUITH COLLECTION   U020

192(.) THE EARL OF HALIFAX COLLECTION. "Charles Viscount Halifax"   U019

193(5) Lomas, S. HISTORY OF THE PHILA SKETCH CLUB,1860--1935. p. 84 Hamilton exhibited
            at 1876 IV 22 opening of P.A.F.A.'s new building (AAA film 3664)   U006

1936   P.A.F.A.,Phila., Receipt for 20+ paintings, B. H. Burgis (Fidelity 20th
        Century Storage Co.) to P.A.F.A. for delivery to Mc Clees Gallery,
        Phila.   U028

1937   MUSEUM OF ART, Phila., Acquisition record (index card) 1937.18.1 oil;
        1938.14.1 pastel; 1941.99.19 pastel; 1941.99.31 pastel; 1941.99.41
        pastel; 1941.99.46 pastel; 1941.99.116; 1971.173.1.   U009

1950   P.A.F.A., Phila., Deaccession record, oil *Corn Husker*   U031

1959   LEIGHTON HOUSE MUSEUM, London, Acquisition record (index card) *Lord Frederick
        Leighton* 000391, gift of Mrs. Joan Penny/Miss M. Conaghan   U010

1964   CORCORAN GALLERY OF ART, op cit, *Mrs. P. W. Bartlett* gift of
        Mrs. Armistead Peter,III (Artist's & Their Circles Exhib.,p.3)   U011

1981   Luik, K. E. FLEETING EXPRESSIONS OF CHARM & GRACE : THE PASTEL DRAWINGS OF
        HAMILTON,1853--1936. (V 1)   U012

1989   MUSEUM & ART GALLERY, Stoke-on-Trent, April 29/May 28, The Etruscan Painters
        of the Italian Landscape, 1850--1900. *M. R. Corbet*   U021

        ART GALLERY, York, Feb. 4/March 5, *M. R. Corbet*   U022

        LEIGHTON HOUSE MUSEUM, op cit, March 20/April 22, *M.R. Corbet*   U023

1990   Burke, H. to Hammer, Armin re: Hamiltoniana for sale   U013

        TELEPRAISAL, INC., NYC,   Hamilton Auction Sale Prices   U014

        CENTROX,INC., NYC,   Auction Alert : Hamilton art   U015

        Levy, S. (CIGNA MUSEUM/ART COLLECTION, Phila.) to Alperin, *E. H. Coates*
        VII 2   U016

1991   Rawlinson, T. D. (SEARCH UK, Ltd.) report: THE HERMITAGE, Kingston-on-Thames   U029

1992   Chew, P. A.(WESTMORELAND MUSEUM,PA) *P. W. Bartlett in his Studio, Paris* &
        Four Children on the Beach, VIII 4   U017

1993   MacLauchlan, H. (DATA ANALYSIS, New Canaan, CT) Hamilton's handwriting
        analyzed after Ciasa, Berkley, CA methods   U018

        Cumming, S. (THE ROYAL SOCIETY, London) *John Tyndall* acquired 1976, X 7
        gift of Mr. Jocelyn Proby, descendant of sitter, II 3   U030

CHAPTER NOTES

FOREWORD

1   The years 1880--1920 inclusive are sometimes referred to as the *TRANSITIONAL AGE IN BRITISH LITERATURE* since publication of Lauterbach, E. S. & Davis, W. E., 1973 (book), Whitston, Troy, NY.

2   N051

I : INTRODUCTION

(All data in this chapter relates to events and places in Philadelphia unless otherwise noted.)

1   Hamilton's critics included the *PHILA. JOURNAL* (1877), the *NY TIMES* (1878), William Cosmo Monkhouse (1896), Harrison S. Morris (1896, 1900, 1936), Helen W. Henderson (1911), Mary G. Drew (1921), and Howard Devree (1934).

2   *BUSINESS WEEK*, 1990 VIII 13:110. *Agony & Ecstasy in the Art Market : Dr. Gachet's portrait by van Gogh"* (J.H. Dobrzynski).

3   Hamilton appeared in a group photo, M029.

4   Eakins' portrait, *"HAMILTON,"* is inscribed and signed at the lower left, "To my friend, Hamilton, / Eakins, "95."

5   B007 : 100.

6   The birth order and names of Dr. George Hamilton's children : an unidentified son, who died in infancy, John Mc Lure Hamilton, Lillie Hall Hamilton (Mrs. John Alsop King), and Jennie Mercer Hamilton, who perished in the fire, 1885.

7   Janson, H. W., 1971. HISTORY OF ART. Prentice Hall / Abrams, NY. p. 749. *"ARRANGEMENT IN BLACK & GRAY : WHISTLER'S MOTHER."*

8   PUBLIC LEDGER, 1849 X 23. Rev. Thomas Love of Lower Brandywine M. E. Church, DE married Hamilton's parents. (Jones, G.E., 1876. CHURCH & ITS PASTORS FOR 156 YEARS, 1720--1876.)
Fosdick, L. J. 1906 : 316. THE FRENCH BLOOD IN AMERICA. Revell.

9   Frazier, M. M. 1987. DELAWARE ADVERTISER, 1827--1831. GENEALOGICAL EXTRACTS.

10   G002, Q. S. Court
        B030

11   G012, I.W. 9: 162--163.

12   G003, M.R. 2 : 22--25.

13   G008, I.W. 9 : 193--195.
        G013, G.W.R. 7 : 320--321. Investment paying ground rent.

14   N036
        Sobel/Raimo, 1978. BIOGRAPHICAL DIRECTORY OF GOVERNORS OF THE U.S., 1789--1978. I : 239.
                Delaware's Governor, Robert Pyle Robinson, the son of Frances Delaplaine, a
                younger sister of Hamilton's mother, was artist's first cousin.

15   Hamilton's uncle through marriage, Charles A. Yeager, Jr., a dry goods merchant at #7
                Strawberry St.(1893), and #40 North 7th St. (1909), was the father of Mrs. Ethel
                Hamilton Lucas.
        The artist, Yeager, lived 1792--1859. He was an engraver, 1816--1845 for various
                local publishers. His recorded works include an aquatint, 1821 & a line
                engraving, 1815.

16   B012 : 17

17   above note 12
        Architect, Kenneth Guscotte Rea, d. 1941, was the husband of Claire Hamilton Raiguel,
                a cousin of Mrs. Clara Hamilton. Rea was the father of Eleanor Adele Rea, John
                Kenneth Rea, and Mary Claire Rea, minor children mentionedin 1940 Montgomery
                county, PA records, G136.

18   Among them, the Canadian railroad builder/magnet,"*James Ross*," a benefactor
                of the Lennox School, Ottawa, Canada, 1916; and the "*Rev. John Campbell Bowen*,"
                Lt. Governor of Alberta province, Canada.

19   Among them : Seville, Paris, Rome, Venice, Berlin, Dusseldorf, Munich, Antwerp, Glasgow,
                Liverpool, London, Kingston-on-Thames, Buffalo, Cincinnati, Dover (DE), NYC,
                Phila., Pittsburgh, Washington, D. C., St. Louis, San Francisco, Los Angeles,
                Mandeville (Jamaica), & an unidentified South American city. (Tab. J.)

20   B016 : 227, The stellar Phila. artists were B. WEST, T. SULLY, R. PEALE, C. W. PEALE, G.
                STUART, J. SARTAIN, JOHN McLURE HAMILTON, T. C. EAKINS, T. ANSCHUTZ, & C.
                GRAFLY.

21   Ashhurst, John, Jr., M.D., 1886 VI 2, BIOGRAPHICAL NOTICE OF GEORGE HAMILTON, M.D. 11
                pages based on a memo by his son, the artist. It first appeared in TRANSACTIONS
                OF THE COLLEGE OF PHYSICIANS. 3rd series, 8 : xiv--liii. Dornan. and was
                reprinted.

22   L152 Hamilton to Raosenbach, A. S. W. included a list of old & rare books from the
               estate of Dr. Hamilton.
     L195 Howe, Sydenham J. to an unknown NYC recepient included the inventory of Hamilton's
               most treasured art works and memorabilia.

II : CRITICS

1   They were Wayman Adams, Paul W. Bartlett, Charles M. Burns, Mathew Corbet, Charles E.
               Dana, Edward Onslow Ford, Sir Alfred Gilbert, Archibald Standish Hartrick, Helen
               Weston Henderson, George Hitchcock, Rudolf Lehmann, Lord Frederick Leighton,
               George Meredith, Anna Lea Merritt, William Cosmo Monkhouse, Imogene Oakley,
               Joseph Pennell, Elizabeth Robins Pennell, Jean Francois Raffelli, William Trost
               Richards, Joseph Macallan Swan, Emily Drayton Taylor, John Madison Taylor, David
               Croal Thomson, Henry Joseph Thouron, Walter Tyndale, George Frederick Watts,
               Herbert Welsh, and Anton Alexander von Werner.

2   N001

3   N002

4   E014 included a note by William Cosmo Monkhouse introducing 45 works for the show.

5   N007 The authoress may have been Isabell Mc Dougall.

6   J005

7   N012

8   N016

9   N019

10   N034 The Phila. critic quoted an earlier London expert.

11   N041 The Phila. critic quoted the LONDON MORNING POST's critic.

12   N048

13   N049

III : GRANDFATHER

(All data relates to Phila. unless otherwise noted)

1   B030, Grandfather born in Ramelton, Ballymena county Antrim, Ireland.
     B012 : 100
     B024
     G002
     L127
     G022 : 254 Chestnut Ward, line...George St. below Chestnut St. / Schuylkill 6th Sts.

     Wolf, E.,II. 1975. PHILA., PORTRAIT OF AN AMERICAN CITY. Stackpole Books.

2   G001, Second Presbyterian Church, Records of, 1745--1833. Baptisms, Marriages, &
           Burials.
     G162
     G163 1799, I 10
     Biddle's CITY DIRECTORY, 1799 : 5

3   Hamilton, Catherine. 1800--1886
     G047 : 949, Tenth Ward. C (atherine) Hamilton, age 50 (+ 10)
     G088 #1003, 1888

     Hamilton, David. 1803--1864
     G047 : 949, op cit   D (avid) Hamilton, age 50 (+7)
     G083 Orphan's Court, 1886 V 22

     Hamilton, Elizabeth B(aird). 1805--184(8)
     later Mrs. David W. Gemmill, DE

     Hamilton, Jannette. 1807--...., a twin
     Hamilton, Euphenia. 1807--...., a twin
     see: Exam, Tenth Presby. Ch., 183..

     Hamilton, (M.D.) George. 1808--1885
     G080 born 1808 XI 15 [All Saint's P. E. Church Cemetery, Torresdale, PA tombstone
          inscription

     Hamilton, Margaret. 1818--19..
     G047 : 949 op cit M(argaret) Hamilton, age 42
     N099 alive in 1909

     Hamilton, Sarah Mc Clellan. 1813--19..
     born 1813 VII 19; baptized 1813 XII 23 at First Presby. Ch.

     Hamilton, William Newell. 1814--19..
     born 1814 XII 24; baptized 1815 IX 18

Hamilton, Ann Jane. 1817--1886
born 1817 X 2; baptized 1818 I 3 at First Presby. Ch.
later Mrs. John C. Mercer, Germantown, PA

Hamilton, Mary Frances. 1818--186.
member, Tenth Presby. Ch. 1832 III 18 (Register of Membership)
exam, op cit
later Mrs. William Walton, DE

Three minor Baird children were adopted. They were related to Hamilton's recently
        deceased partner, John Mercer, Sr. Their names were Margaret, William
        & Sarah.
G005, 1819 XII 11, I.W. 7 : 331--333
see: Harris, Robert, account as guardian of Children by John Hamilton, Sr. (HSP, Mss
    Room)

Hamilton, John, Jr. 1820--191(5), an attorney, gentleman farmer, land speculator.
born 1820 III 29; baptized 1820 VIII 5 at First Presby. Ch. (record at HSP)
authored numerous family documents, wills, Mercer Fund suit.
1837, A. M. Mc ELROY'S CITY DIRECTORY at 24 S. Second St.
1844, op cit at 20 S. SSecond St.
1845 I 16, MARTIN'S BENCH & BAR admitted to practice
1852 XI 20. deed. G040

(Member's Letter, showing causes of the decline/ fall of the First Presby. Ch. of
        City's Fairmount district. aka 13th Presby. Ch., 1840. On 1839 IX 3
        Joe Chapman, President, & W. Garrett was the Secretary.)

Hamilton, Lydia Isabella. 182(4)--1906
exam, 1832 III 18 at Tenth Presby. Ch. (Register of Membership)
later Mrs. Marks John Biddle

Hamilton, Jane. 1824 --....

3   Wilson's CITY DIRECTORY, 1825

4   First Presby. Ch., Baptism Records, 1813, 1814, 1817, 1820.

5   Tenth Presby. Ch. 1830 IX 30, exam recorded (Register of Membership)
                    1830 XII 19, op cit
                    1832 III 18, op cit

        13th Presby. Ch., Constitution, 1836
                            1842--46, attendance (Records of)

6   G016, South Ward
     attended Dr. Robert Cathcart's Church at Hopewell, PA after 1832 VII 10 (Register of
             Membership, Tenth Presby. Ch.)
     Nevin, A. (ed.) ENCYCLOPEDIA OF THE PRESBY. CH. IN USA.,Phila. p. 131

7   A. M. Mc ELROY'S CITY DIRECTORY,1846 : 144 at Summer St./Schuylkill 7th (John,Sr.)
     G032, Tenth Ward
     Business affairs : files at Mss Room, HSP under HAMILTON & HOOD (John. Sr. was senoir
             partner)

             records, letters 1798--1859
             account book, 1803--1863
             cash accounts : grocery
             charge book
             day books
             invoices
             ledger
             letter book
             memo day book
             merchandise receipts
             merchandise receipt book
             receipt book
             tax bills

     Wholesale grocers/ wine merchants

             succesor to LENTZ & HOOD, 1803--1806
                          HAMILTON & DREW, 1805--1810
             some papers HAMILTON & HOOD, 1813--1835 under Collection of Simon Gratz,
                          Commercial Records, XIII
             John Hamilton, Sr., extensive file original documents, 1809--1833

     A chronology of documents re: John, Sr.'s activity

             1814 III 17. Committee of Grocers. *STATUTE OF TARE (weights) ACCEPTABLE IN
                     PUBLIC/PRIVATE SALES* of coffee, sugar, green tea, bohea tea, souchong,
                     Indigo, soap, signed by John Hamilton, Sr.   HSP G004

                     M.R.2 : 22--25. Armstrong at Quebec, Lower Canada, wife, Margaret at
                     Elizabeth, NJ.   G003

             1817 VIII 1. *Bond* to John Hamilton, Sr. on Benjamin Whitecar. *F.J. DREER
                     Autograph Collection* Vol. Misc. III : 160   HSP G168

             1821 VI 6. *Agreement* (Deed) I.W. 9 : 645--648. Hasadiah P. Sampson, John M.
                     Hood, & John Hamilton, Sr. (three grocers) re: S. W. Cor. Sassafrass
                     St. & Delaware Front St. property.   G007

1822 XII 24. *cancelled bank check*. #532 FARMER'S & MECHANICS BANK to William
    Newell, $2,000.00 on Hamilton & Hood acct.   HSP G009

1820--1823. Hamilton & Hood bills. *Society Misc.* Box 1-A, pt. 1 & 2   HSP

1823 V 15. *deed*. J. H.^^^590--592. John Hamilton, Elizabeth h/wife to John
    Mc Clellan Hood, Elizabeth h/wife to John Newell (three grocers) re:
    W. side Schuylkill 5th/ N. side High St.   G010

    VIII 27. *deed*. I. H.^^^:185--187. James Newell (mariner) h/wife, Ann to
    John Hamilton & William Newell (merchant)   G011

    tax bill. Chestnut Ward (resident) John Hamilton,Sr. *Society Coll*. HSP
                                                                G169

1824 VII 26. *church membership*. First Presby. Ch., Northern Liberties. John
    Hood also Eliza Hood (1819--1848)   HSP

1825 II 26. *deed*. G.W.R. 7 : 230--231. Trustees, University of Pennsylvania to
    John Hamilton, $1,333.33 re: Front / 2nd Sassafrass St. property's
    ground rent.   G013

    WILSON'S CITY DIRECTORY. Hamilton & Leghorn, dry goods merchants. HSP

1828--29. *offer* John Hamilton,Sr., merchant. Francis D. Brinton papers,1789--
    1874. A-20   HSP G170

    John Hamilton,Sr. *knew Thomas Fanning Watson*, ANNALS OF PHILA.   HSP

1829 X 12. John Hamilton,Sr. (under Mc Grath) *Drew Coll*. Misc.,Mss. HSP G171

1830 South Ward, resident   G016

    IV 26. *promissory note*. FARMER'S & MECHANICS BANK, $484.49, on Hamilton
    & Hood acct.;   HSP G015

    XI 26 *inscription*. reverse of above, pd 3813. Hamilton & Hood   HSP

1837 *County poor tax*. Chestnut Ward resident, 13 : 49 #7. John Hamilton Sr.'s
    assessed value $ 6,000.00; tax due $ 24.50, sons David & W. N. paid
    a far lower sum from same address.   G017

1838 op cit, 14 : 30. John assessed at $ 5,500.00, taxed $ 27.50, sons John
    Jr. & W. N. paid far lower sums.   G018

1839 op cit, ^^ : 100 #50. John Hamilton,Sr. $ 5,500.00; taxed $ 25.05, sons
    not mentioned.   G019

1840 op cit, 26 : 124 #32. John Hamilton,Sr. $ 5,500.00; taxed $ 50.00, son
    William taxed $ 15.50.   G022

1845 *legend to Kennedy's watercolor.* K-III-58 at HSP   U026

    County poor tax. op cit.^^^:2 #43 John Hamilton,Sr. assessed $ 10,000.00
    paid $ 20.00 tax. No sons mentioned   G025

1846 *A.M. Mc ELROY'S CITY DIRECTORY* : 144. John Hamilton at Summer St./
    Schuylkill 7th Sts.   G026

1850 North Mulberry (Tenth) Ward 51 : 342 John Hamilton, Sr. resident   G032

8   1858 IX 19. *obituary.* John Hamilton, Sr. may have been 84 years old. Notice appeared
        EVEN. BULL. (Sat.) 1858 IX 25   HSP G172

9   1852 XI 20. *deed.* T. H. 74 : 308--309. Robert P. King et ux to John
        Hamilton, Jr.   G040

10   Tenth Ward. Mrs. Elizabeth Hamilton's servants were Martha van Horn (1872--1885)
        and Ms. M'Cune (Mc Ewen)   G061

11   op cit
    burial records, 1818. First Presby. Ch.
    op cit   1820
    op cit   again, 1820
    op cit   1827
    op cit   1828

HAMILTON GENEALOGY

John, Sr.   b. c. 1780   d. 1858 IX 19 Phila., PA obit/ will 1886
              m. 1799 I 10 Phila. Hall, Elizabeth
                 b. c. 1785   d. c. 1879
              children of John, Sr.
                 Catherine   b. 1800 Phila.   d. 1888 VI 21 Phila. will
                           not married, no issue
                 David   b. 1803 Phila.   d. 1864
                           not married, no issue
               Elizabeth B.   b. 1805 Phila.
                       m David W. Gemmill, DE 1836 VI 7
                           House of Representatives, 1862, New Castle county, DE
              Jannette, a twin b. 1807 alive 1830

Euphenia, a twin b. 1807 alive 1830
George (M.D.) b. 1808 XI 15 Phila. d. 1885 X 30 Phila. will
            educated 1831 Univerity of PA, Medical School
            m. Caroline Delaplaine, 1849 X 18
                    b. 1827   d. 1915
            children : son d. infancy
                    John Mc Lure Hamilton b. 1853 I 31 Phila.
                        m. Clara Augusta Raiguel, 1880 Phila.
                        child : George Hall Hamilton b. 1884 I
                            31 London
                                    m. Elizabeth Langdon
                                        Williams, 1922
                                        VI 22
                                        Flagstaff,AZ
                                    no issue
                    Lillie Hall Hamilton b. 1856 Phila. bapt.,1870
                            d. 1933 Phila. will
                        m. John Alsop King, 1877 III 22
                            b. 1847 d. 1885 II 26 fire
                        child : Nora H. King
                            m. Daniel Buckley
                            child : Mathew Brooke Buckley
                            b. 1908 artist's court appointed
                                    heir along with Clara &
                                    former Gov. Robinson.
                        child : Charles Ray King. Jr., b. 1878
                            d. 1885 II 26 fire
                        child : daughter
                            m.   Lennig
                            children: Charles K. Lennig
                                    Fred K. Lennig
                                    Rufus K. Lennig
                    Jennie Mercer Hamilton b. 1859 baptized 1870
                            d. 1885 fire

Margaret   b. 1812   d. post 1909   Phila.
            not married, no issue
Sarah Mc Clellan b. 1813   alive with John Jr. 1900
William Newell b. 1814   d. 1885 V 31 Phila. will
            m. Sarah
            children : Sarah   b ?   d. 1901 I 22 Phila.
                                                    will
                                    m. Charles A. Yeager, Jr. Phila.
                                        b. 1857   alive 1901
                                    child : Ethel Hamilton Yeager
                                        b. 1882 I 8 alive 1909
                                        m.   Lucas
                    Mary   b. c. 1870
                                m. 1891 X 14 Edward Ward, NJ

```
Ann Jane      b. 1817 Phila           d. 1886 IV 5 Phila. will
              m. John C. Mercer, Phila. 1843 XI 9
                        merchant
              no children
                  bequests to J. C. M. Boyd, Lillie Mercer Boyd (both
                  children of Mrs. Maria Boyd, niece of John C. Mercer)
Mary Frances b. 1818 Phila.           d. 1862 Phila.
              m. William Walton,DE 1830 IV 2
                        Coroner, Sussex county, DE, 1846--48
John, Jr. attorney,etc. b. 1820 Phila.  alive 1909
Jane         b. 1824
              m. James L. Biddle
                  b. 1817     railroad agent
              children
 Lydia Isabella  b. c. 1831       d. 1905
              m. Marks John Biddle, 1850 III 12 Reading, PA
                        railroad agent, 1860
                        shoemaker, 1862
                        b. 1825        d. 1887
                  deed Phila 1886 XII 20
                son: J. C. M. Biddle    b. 1857    d. 1941
```

(All data refers to Phila. unless otherwise stated)

1   Ashhurst, 1886. op cit

2   B012 : 17--22 "My Father."

3   cemetery records/tombstone, ALL SAINTS CHURCH, Torresdale, PA. op cit

4   op cit. note 1

5   L138 H to secretary, County Medical Society, Spruce St., re : request from Dr. Hinesdale
        (Hot Springs, VA) for image of George Hamilton, M.D. Artist sent "fresh" drawing
        to the *Society* with comment on E. Onslow Ford's bronze bust of late Dr.
        Hamilton.
    John F. X. Trevi (County Medical Society) to Alperin, 1990 VI 27

6   memo of artist to Ashhurst, note 1 (unlocated)

7   MEDICAL OBITUARY : 194a

8   E161. Dr. Hamilton was the 17th President, 1868ff.

9   The St. Andrews Society included many members later painted by artist including
        "Silas Weir Mitchell, M.D."

10   Documented chronology for George Hamilton, M.D.
        1828 Student at University of Pennsylvania, Medical School
            Clinical training under Dr. Hewson, Pennsylvania Hospital. (Historical
                Medical Library, PA Hospital, Mrs. Caroline Morris, Archivist.)
        1831 autograph. George Hamilton, M.D. College of Physicians, Library.
        1847 A. M. MC ELROY'S CITY DIRECTORY : 141, Summer & Schuylkill 7th Sts.
        1848 op cit, 13th above Wallace Sts.
        1849 op cit : 152
            X 18 *married* Caroline, daughter of James Delaplaine, an attorney, of New
                Castle county, DE
        1850 G032 with father & two brothers at same address
        1855 MC ELROY'S :220, 16th & Summer Sts.
        1860 G047 with mother & eleven others, same location.
        1861 MC ELROY'S, op cit.   near Vine St.
        1862 G054 U.S. Excise Law. PA Income Tax : 71 George, M.D. & John, Jr.
        1864 G056 op cit : 159 only George, M.D.
        1865 G057 op cit : 22 George, M.D. & John, Jr.
        1866 G058 op cit : 319 only George, M.D.

1876 daguerreotype."George Hamilton,M.D." in: MEDICAL CENTENNIAL ALBUM 230 :
        73. University of Pennsylvania, original a gift to College of Physicians
        by John Madison Taylor, M.D. in 1936 (unlocated).
1885 E079 #1303 Bond & Inventory. Artist executor of father's estate.
        X 30 G164
        obit Phila. DISPATCH (Sunday) 36 :..
        XI . burial E080
1886 MED. BULL. MED. & SURG. 8 : 23
1893 Ford's bronze bust of Dr. Hamilton
1933 B030

11   U026 see Abodes ch. notes

12   G047

13   G061

14   G072 : 362 with five others including one servant
      Atkinson, BIOGRAPHICAL DICTIONARY OF PHYSICIANS & SURGEONS I : 160
      MEDICAL & SURGICAL REPORTER
      PHILA. MEDICAL TIMES

15   Biographical publications of Dr. Hamilton:
            "Beck, Theodore Romneys. Eulogy on the Life & Character of...." Med. Soc. of NY.
                    Albany, 1856. 8
            "Gebhard, Lewis P. Obituary Notice of...1874. 8
            "Meigs, James Aitken. Biogra. Sketch of...late President of Co. Med. Soc."
                    extract, TRANS. OF MED. SOC. PA, Phila., 1880 II 25. Collins. 22 pgs.

      Scholarly publications of Dr. Hamilton:
            1869 II 24. "County Med. Soc., close of term address delivered before ...as
                    President." 24 pgs.
            1879. "On the relation between sewer gas and typhoid fever."
            1881. "Thoughts upon vivisection, with reference to its restriction by
                    legislative action." extract, TRANS. COLL. OF PHYSICIANS. 3rd ser.
            n.d. "The question of vivisection. Was the act of the British Parliament in
                    restricting vivisection inconsiderate and unnecessary?"
            1883. "Sewer gas & its alleged causation of typhoid fever."
                    "Status of professional opinion & popular sentiment re: sewer gas &
                    control-- as cause of typhoid fever with attention to paper by Dr. A. L.
                    Carrol.

16   tombstone inscriptions. ALL SAINTS CHURCH cemetery

17   Ashhurst, 1886. op cit

18   various index cards. Library, Reading Room, Coll. of Physicians & Surgeons.
                                            Library Company
      several books with Dr. Hamilton's signatures.Historical Society of PA

19   personal communication

DELAPLAINE GENEALOGY

Nicholas Delaplaine. arrived America, 1663
        son: James Delaplaine, Quaker, Germantown, PA active,1691   d. 1750
            grandsons: John
                      Joseph of Maryland

        four daughters: Mrs. Hoodt
                        Mrs. Griffith
                        Mrs. Cassel
                        Mrs. Belangee   all settled in Phila.

James Delaplaine, Esq. b. 1795 Christiana Hundred, New Castle county, DE
                        1850 DE census, lawyer
                        1860 op cit
                        1870 op cit
                        m. Mary Kirk c. 1817
                            b. 1801
                        m. Mary Henderson, 1817 X 29
                        1827, House of Representatives, New Castle county, DE
                        1851--1859, Treasurer, New Castle county,
                        1852, House of Representatives, second term
                        member, Board of Directors, bank, with E. I. du Pont
                        children: Peter   b. 1817
                                  Hester A.   b. 1821
                                  Elizabeth G. b. 1824
                                  Caroline   b. 182(6) d. 1915 I 7   [Artist's Mother]
                                      m. George Hamilton, M.D., 1849 X 18 . Rev Thomas Love
                                              Lower Brandywine Church, Red Clay Congregation,
                                              DE
                                  Mary J.   b. 1827
                                  James L.   b. 1830 farmer
                                      m. Rebecca c. 1859
                                      child: Josephine
                                  Frances E.   b. 1840
                                      m. Robert L. Robinson
                                      child: Robert Pyle Robinson, DE Governor, 1925--1929

        V : EARLY DAYS

        (All data refers to Phila. unless otherwise stated)

1   Wolf, E. II, 1975. op cit

2   Esler, L. A., 1935. PRESIDENTS OF OUR USA. Rand Mc Nally & Co., Chicago.

3   D031

4   1850 VIII 1, E032 : 342 Tenth Ward

5   Hamilton, Jennie Mercer b. 1858 IX 26; bap. 1870 III 19 on same day as the artist
            Tenth Presby. Ch., records of   HSP
     1860 VII 10, G047 : 949

6   B012 : 17; 131
     for Holmes, George W.(1812--1895) see : 1840, CITY DIRECTORY, 134 N. Eleventh St.
                                                1874, op cit   1926 Mt. Vernon St.
     Hamilton met T. C. Eakins about 1877 & the future Mrs. Eakins, Susan Mac Dowell.

7   Jackson, J. 1931.^^^^^^^^^^^^^^^^^^^^^^^^^Harrisburgh, National Histor. Association.
            Telegraph Bldg. II : 429--433. (William D. Gemmill, p.431)

8   op cit p.432. But Phila. was on its way to becoming a *Republican* town!

9   Edmonds, F. S., 1902. HISTORY OF CENTRAL HIGH SCHOOL. p.301
     N044 "School Board gets memory jogged by demand for payment for old portrait ("*Dr.
            Riche*"), artist wrote to protest 32 year delay over work 63rd Class gave.

10   1870, III 19. Tenth Presby. Ch. located at 17th & west Spruce Sts.   HSP

11   Thompson, Rev. J. C., 1886 V. "IN MEMORIAM : Mrs. ANN JANE MERCER." Grant & Faires.
            420 Library St. p. 10/11 mentions her poems/hymns   PHS

12   1870,CITY DIRECTORY. P.A.F.A.'s temporary location on 16th St. where Hamilton met
            E.A. Abbey, fellow student, J003.
     By 1874, Hamilton's early drawing teacher, Mr. Holmes, moved to 1926 Mt. Vernon St., a
            site two blocks from the residence/studio of Thomas C. Eakins (at 1729). Eakins,
            a fellow Irishmen, taught Hamilton at P.A.F.A. Eakins was Professor
            Schuessele's replacement in 1878.

13   E001, Hamilton exhibited in South corridor, Gallery "I."   HSP

14   E094

15   E106. Unfortunately, in a recent "official" P.A.F.A. catalog on p.8/9, Hamilton was not
            given credit for the work; instead it was attributed to an "anonymous group" of

students of P.A.F.A. in the 1989 report.

16   E004. An engraving of Hamilton's "*Cerise*" sometimes called "*Le Rire*" was included.

17   Valentry, D. 1992 XII, p.29, THE ARTIST'S MAGAZINE. "The Artist's Life : Insights On
        Being An Artist" OF BRUSH * BIBLE.

18   B012 :137--139. Mayor Richard Vaux had also been U.S. Attache to London.

19   for Sketch Club, Records of..see: Thornton Oakley papers. Hamilton joined 1876 XII but
        resigned 1878 I 24 with plans to migrate permanently to London.

1   B012

2   In 1873, the art school was called *Academie Royale des Beaux Arts d' Anvers* but
           currently its name is *Nationaal Hoger Instituut en Koninklijke voor Schone*
           Kunsten and continues at its original location of Mutsaertstraat 31, 2000
           Antwerpen. It deserves support given in memory of the alumnus, Hamilton.

3   D001
       D013 II :384/5
       D012 : 238/40
       * (dutch encyclopedia), 198..: 865/68 Fisher Fine Arts Library
       * DICTIONNAIRE BIOGRAPHIQUE DES SCIENCES DES LETTERS ET ARTS EN BELGIE I :... Van
            Pelt Library
       Ensor, R. C. K., 1915. BELGIUM, ch X : 222ff. "Art & Literature," Butterworth. London

4   D001
       BIBLIOGRAPHIE NATIONALE L'ACADEMIE ROYALE DE BELGIE XI : 894/96. Max Rooses, 1890/1.
       D013 III : 67
       D012 ...:112

5   D012 ..:116
       Wilenski, R. H., FLEMISH PAINTERS, 1430--1830. pt II :491. A DICTIONARY OF FLEMISH
            PAINTERS. Reynal. Viking Press. NY.
       Flippo, W. G., 1981. LEXICON OF THE BELGIAN ROMANTIC PAINTERS. Int. Art Press., Antwerp.

6   Valerio, E., 1923 XII/1924 X. ART IN AMERICA 12 (1) : 215--222. "Emile Claus, His Art &
            His Country."
       Weinberg, H. B., 1977. ARCHIVES OF AMERICAN ART JOURNAL 17 (1) : 2--18. " The Career of
            F. D. Millet."
       DICT. BIOGR. D SCI. D LETTERS ET D ART EN BELGIE I : 140/1 "Claus."
       B012
       KONINKLIJKE MUSEA VOOR SCHONE KUNSTEN VAN BELGIE. DEPARTMENT MODERNE KUNST. INVENTARIS,
            CATALOGUS VAN DE MODERNE SCHILDER KUNST, Brussel, 1984. p. 197--201. "Ensor."

7   L195, Courtesy of Shelley Mead, NMAA.

8   U024, student records from Hamilton's Flemish alma mater.
       U025, the last record of Hamilton's attendance in Antwerp.
       Jef van Gool, Research Librarian, at Hamilton's school during my expedition in 1992 was
            a mine of valuable information, insights, and leads.
       Jenny Martin, Ph. D., residing in Brussels, advised and counseled me prior to the
            expedition. She provided sage words.

9   ACADEMIE ROYALE DES BEAUX ARTS, A' ANVERS, RAPPORT. ANNEE ACADEMIQUE, 1871/2, 1872/3,
                1874/5, 1875/6.

10   D010 Historical volume : 398.
        D010   I : 38
        * D010 . : 5.
        D023   I : 256, 456
        D023 III : 573
        D023 IV : 103
        de Graet, G., 1898. p. 71. NOS ARTISTES ANVERSOIS. NOTICES BIOGRAPHIQUES. Anvers. "Boom,
                C."
        D023 I : 119 "Alma-Tadema"

11   POLITIE VREEMDELINGEN, 1840--1874. (City Archives, Antwerp)
         op cit, 1875--1885   above
        HISTORIEK (pamphlet) 1663. EEUWFEST. 1885--1985. Nationaal Hoger Instituut en
                Koninklijke Academie voor Schone Kunsten. Antwerp. p. 38 figure 43.
        de Graet, G., 1898 op cit "Boom, C. "

12   U024, U025 These records provided Hamilton's various addresses.
        A Census of tenants taken during Hamilton's years in Antwerp was recorded in many large
                volumes. A visit to the City Archives (Stadsarchief, Venus Straat 11) and the
                help of Mrs. Jeannine Schools and her colleague identified the names of the
                art students with whom Hamilton probably lived at #77 Morteus and later # 4
                Kaasrui.
        A site visit to each address followed, where a sketch could be made of the facade, G159.

13   Witthoft, B., 1992 Summer, AMERICAN ART REVIEW. p. 120--145. "George Smillie : The Life
                of an Artist." p. 134, "crash"

14   DE VLAAMSCHE SCHOOL TIJDSCHRIFT VOOR KUNSTEN, LETTEREN, WETENSCHAPPEN, OUDHEIDKUNDE EN
                KUNSTNIJVERHEID UITGEGEVEN DOOR DESIRE VAN SPILBEECK." 1873ff located bound at
                the Newspaper Dept., Public Library on Minderbroeder Straat.
        GUIDE COMMERCIAL, 1874, Antwerp yielded Prof. Beaufaux' residence as Marche aux oeufs
                3-10.
        Here again, Mr. Jef van Gool's helpful advice yielded a profit.

15   An interview with Mr. van Dam, Curator during Kathedraal restoration then under way
                yielded a copy of a rare pamplet, CATHAEDRALE D' ANVERS. Notes explicatives des
                Vitraux et Restaurations executes par Stains & Janssens peintres Verriers.
                Ateliers de peinture sur verre. Maison Fondee en 1863. Rempart du Lombard 38,
                Anvers. (Bellemans Feres. Marche aux Oeufs, 12) situated on the same street as
                the residence of Hamilton's Prof. P-C Beaufaux.

16   DE VLAAMSCHE SCHOOL op cit, 1875 I 16, p. 8.

17 DIAMOND MUSEUM, Antwerp. Exhibition, 1992.

18 N061
Hamilton fit side trips into his Flemish schooling days, B012 :243/4, to Malines,
    Brussels, Rotterdam, the Hague, Haarlem, and Amsterdam. Some of Hamilton's small
    wooden panels of cabinet size format, 5" x 8," may date from his Flemish period.

19 GUIDE COMMERCIAL, 1874, Antwerp

20 At the *Toegangskaart Leeszaal*, Dr. Mark Somers of *Archief en Museum voor het Vlaamse
    Culturleven Antwerpen* allowed me to search *Algemene Briefwisselin*. And among
    the *Societe Royale pour l'encouragement des Beaux-Arts a' Anvers*, 1873--1875,
    two letters indexed as their B126 were retrieved.

21 op cit

22 D013 : 128/9

23 Foster, K. A. & Leibold, C., 1989. WRITING ABOUT EAKINS : THE MANUSCRIPTS IN C.
    BREGLER'S T. E. COLLECTION. University of PA Press, Phila. pgs. 54--60.
    "Learning in Paris, 1866--1869."

24 B009 : 393

25 TIME, 1992 X 12 pgs. 82/3. "Art's Baroque Futurist (Ribera)," R. Hughes.

26 No Hamilton authored letters, diary, journal, sketchbook, scrapbook, original art or
    Hamilton copied art by the *old masters* survived. The engraving published
    of "*Cerise*" was ascribed by Morris (J003) to this Hamilton period.
Weinberg op cit provided valuable details from another young artist's life and training
    in Antwerp about this time.
Simpson, M. 199. AMERICAN ART JOURNAL 22 (3) : 65 ff. "Windows on the Past : E. A.
    Abbey/ F. D. Millet in England."
Lerius, Theodore van, 1874. MUSEE D'ANVERS. CATALOGUE. 3rd ed. (Univ. of PA, Fisher
    Library).

27 N038
   N061

VII : Clara

(All data relates to Phila. unless otherwise stated)

1   Philbrick, (compiler) PASSENGER & IMMIGRATION LISTS, III (G--Z) : 1698.
     Fosdick, 1906. op cit.

2   Clara Augusta Raiguel born 1854 XII 9; baptized 1855 V 6 at St. Michael's & Zion
            (German) Luthern Church.(records of) Baptisms, Marriages, & Deaths. Church
                  formerly located at Brown & St. John Sts.   HSP

3   G104, will 1912 # 1909 p. 2
     G049, 1860 VI 5, census 20th ward, N. of Master St.) p.522
     G095, 1900 VI 5, census E.D. 823, sh 8, p.12 : 1832 24th St.
     G103, 1910 IV 24, census E.D. 768, sh 11, p. B700 : 12th ward.
     BOYD'S DIRECTORY, 1895. Washington, D. C. p. 601.
       op cit   1912   above   p. 815.
     G113, 1920   , census Washington, D. C. 1514 17th St. Mrs. Raiguel's
            son-in-law Leffler, Milton L.

4   G074, Marriage license. Registration. 1880 X 7 Hamilton/ Raiguel.   CA
     G075, op cit. 1880 III 7 partially illegible   HSP
     MARRIAGES BY MAYOR, 1880. Pennell/Robins   HSP
     B009. Pennell/ Hamilton introduction, post 1875.

5   G072, 1880   , census E.D. 211
      G041, 1854 V 16 by Rev. Charles Rudolf Demme of 5th & Cherry Sts. Marriage recorded.
                                                                               HSP

6   L165, Marriage, Second Presby. Ch. located 16th N. of Race St. by Rev. John A. Dales.
            Hamilton/ Raiguel   CA

7   L185, L186.Dated, signed & inscribed, "Tears, 1879,/ Hamilton" was the first work done
            in London Period by artist. His future wife was the sitter.

8   L001. *Charles Roberts Autograph Collection, American Artists*, Library, Haverford
            College, PA.

9   G078. London, Birth Certificate, 1884 III 17. George Hall Hamilton.

10   Listing of oils not necessarily in chronological order : *Tears,* 1879;
            Clara & Violets, n.d.; *A Coquette of Seville, n.d.;* Afternoon Repose," n.d.;
            Clara at the Piano, n.d.; Mrs. Hamilton, n.d.

11   L106

12   Ellis Family Documents :
         1816, VII 3. Ship "Dibby & Eliza" arrived from Dublin at NYC. Abstracted from
                "The Shamrock" in : Tepper, M.,(ed.) 1979. NEW WORLD IMMIGRANTS II : 354
         1830 G014, census New Market ward p. 227.
         1840 G021, above   p. 168.
         1850 G030, above   p. 411. a shoemaker, from Wales.
         1860 G046, above   p. 233. Joseph, Jr., Clara's uncle was the case
                maker.
         1866 X 6, G166, Naturalization.
         1870 VI 20, G060, census 2nd ward, 6th Dist., p.280. Joseph, Jr.

13   Raiguel Family Documents :
         1830 G017 census, Berks Co. Reading City, p.290.
         1847 II 2, G027 deed assignment, Bk # 69 : 292/3.
         1850 G036, North ward, p. 319. Wm. Raiguel born in Ireland.
         1851 III 29, G038, deed, Bk # 80 : 253/7.
         1870 G064, census, 9th ward, 27th Dist., p.127. Wm. Raiguel was a dry goods
                merchant.

14   Wm. Raiguel's death notice, PHILA. INQUIRER, 1874,IV 10 p. 5 (died on IV 9)
         G069, will 1874 #282.

15   Hamilton met Clara Raiguel before 1879, site unknown. They were married in multiple
         ceremonies in Phila during 1880. Their only son, George, was born in London,
         1884. They were a team until 1936.

16   Clara's career as an artist was considered speculative until publication of E111. In it,
         we find the following entries: "1890, Salon of Societe Nationale des Beaux-Arts,
         Paris, Paintings #594 (portrait) & #595 (Enfants et Roses)" were listed as Mme.
         John McLure Hamilton's works.

17   L109

18   L082, L101, L102, L105.

19   L109

20   N039

21   L095, L096, L103, B012 : 75.

22   B007 contains L003

23   *

24   L076

25   L077, B012 : 93/4.

26   L105

27   G119, 1934 VII 31, Jamaican L.N.S. 438 folio 447. #1272 Bill of sale. (1934/35 file
            18/91.)

28   L141

29   L143

30   L146

31   *

32   G005 deed, op cit, ch III Baird children. John Mercer, Sr.
        G077 will 1883 #193, John C. Mercer, son-in-law of John Hamilton, Sr.

33   G085 will 1886 # 4521, Mrs. Ann Mercer, widow of John C. Mercer.
        G083 will 1886   , John Hamilton,Sr. probate delayed from 1858.

34   G081 deed/ legacy release 1886, IV 5, p. 442ff Caroline D. Hamilton et al to THE JOHN
            C. MERCER HOME FOR DISABLED CLERGYMEN OF THE PRESBYTERIAN FAITH.

35   N099 "Want Mercer Fund to be Divided. Heirs Claim Management of Home Not Complied with
            Will. Held Under Advisement."
        1894 I # 202 (1894 II 1) Mercer Home v. S. Wilson Fisher. 34 : 557/8 119, 234.

36   1908 XII # 2058. Common Pleas Court # 2, Hamilton v. Mercer Home.
        PA. DISTRICT REPORTS 19 (1910) : 169--178. H. W. Page, Phila. Hamilton v. John C. Mercer
            Home 19 D 169.
        PA. REPORTS 228 : 410--424. W. I. Schaffer, 1911. Banks Law Publishing Co., NY. Supreme
            Court of PA; Jan.--May term, 1910. Hamilton v. Mercer Home.

                            RAIGUEL GENEALOGY

William Magee Raiguel   b. 1799, Ireland   d. 1874 IV 9 Phila obit, will
        1830 census PA Berks Co., Reading City
        1847 deed Norristown
        m. Elizabeth D.   b. 1814 MA
        children: Mary   b. 1831
                Emily Frances   b. N.J.?
                Eviline   b. 1832

Harriette Louisa
     m.   Bingham
Fannie   b. 1834
Helen D.
Matilda   b. 1843
Ida
Ellen   b. 1847
Lizzie D. b.
Charlotta b. 1837
J. Howard b. 1849
Edward H.
relative : William C. b. 1845
     son: Wm. C. b. 1876   d. 1941 (artist/ architect)
relative : W. H. Raiguel
relative : Joseph W. Raiguel b. 1831   d. 187(6)
     1850 census   clerk
     1860 census   clerk
     m. Sarah C. (Sally) Ellis, 1854 V 16, Phila. b. 1833 d. 1912 XI 13
          Phila. will [Artist's Mother-in-law]
     children : Clara Augusta Raiguel b. 1855 d. 1936 XI .
              m. 1880 John McLure Hamilton, Phila.
        Joseph Lloyd Raiguel b. 1858 XI . Phila.   alive 1912
           m. Catherine
           daughter : Claire Hamilton b. 1886 III . m.1916 VIII 1
                 Kenneth G. Rea, Montreal, Canada architect
                 b. 1978 d. 1941 F.R.I.B.A.
                 tie in to "James Ross" commission
          grandchildren : Ellendelle (=Eleanor Adele)
                   John Kenneth
                   Mary Claire
                     heirs of Clara R. Hamilton's
                     estate.
           daughter : Ethel M. b. 1888 IV .
                 m. Joseph W. Rice b. 1886
                 child : Joseph L. Rice b. 1908
        Valerie Raiguel b. 1871 IX .   alive 1912
        m. Milton L. Leffler b 1867 IX. resides Washington, D.C.
        children : Marion b. 1888 II .
              Adalade b. 1895 X .
              Ellwood L. b. 1898 X .

Joseph Ellis, Sr. b. 1797 Wales
        1816 VII 3, Arrived NY with Bartholomew Ellis (ship: "Dibby & Eliza")
        m. Lydia   b. 1796 PA
        1830 census
        1840 census
        1850 census shoemaker
        children: Edward b. 1823 PA shoemaker
                Joseph, Jr. b. 1829 Pa silver casemaker   d. c. 187(6)
                        naturalized 1866 X 6 Phila. Dist. Court.
                        m. Hannah, c. 1854   b. 1832
                        son: Joseph Ellis, III b 1855, Phila.
                        m. Anna, 1870 b. 1831
                Mary b. 1830 PA
                Sarah b. 1833 PA
                        m. Joseph W. Ellis, 1854 V 16, Phila.
                Margaret b. 1835 PA

VIII : GEORGE & LANGDON

(All data refers to Phila. unless otherwise reported.)

1   *Hall* was the surname of George's paternal, great grandmother, Mrs. Elizabeth Hall
         Hamilton, wife of John Hamilton, Sr.
     McLure & Clara's visit to Seville, Spain was tentatively identified as the Spring, 1883
         from a dated & signed oil, "*Garden in Seville*," which was reproduced.
     Passports were not required of international passengers during most of the 19th Century.

2   Several of these portraits were purchased in the lot at the *Custom House* auction in
         1937.
     "*Master Wolfram Ford*," a contemporary of George was painted by Hamilton about 1893.

3   G047, 1860 VII 10, census 10th ward : 949
     G061, 1870 VI 18, census above : 338. Lillie Hall Hamilton born 1856.
     1874, CITY DIRECTORY placed Mrs. John A. King's home at 1539 Pine St.
     G166, 1880 VI 15, census 22nd ward Norwood Avenue p.555. Nora's husband, Daniel Buckley
         was born 1879 II . He was the son of Edward Swift Buckley & Mary Vaux.
     G101, census Eastern district, Whitemarsh township. Montgomery county,PA E.D. 161, sh
         2, p.7156 (Bethlehem Pike). The former Nora King became the wife of Daniel
         Buckley and later the mother of Mathew Brooke Buckley, an heir of the artist.
     N012, 1911 VI 17. "American to Paint Coronation Picture."
     Mrs. King provided health care for Miss Elizabeth Delaplaine for many years.

4   The King family were members of ALL SAINTS P.E. CHURCH, Torresdale, PA along with the
         Biddles and van Rensselaers.
     1920, Mrs. King owned some works by her brother, Mc Lure.
     1930, CITY DIRECTORY placed Mrs. King's home at the ALDINE HOTEL.
     1933, G118 will, inventory, & codicil # 1320, Lillie H. King.

5   J055

6   J003

7   J005

8   E109

9   G094, 1900 VI 1, census Chester City, PA. E.D. 144 S. D., sh 16--19 p. 120 revealed
         that George was not present at the *PA Military College* located above Chestnut
         St. but by age 18 Mc Lure's letter to Moser (L031) placed him there in 1902,
         apparently for only a brief time as he received no degree.

10   George was granted a degree in 1907, years after the press interviewed Mrs. A. L.
         Merritt, J055. From 1908 to 1910, George was a volunteer at the OXFORD
         OBSERVATORY, England.

11   George was granted a second degree in 1911 from CAMBRIDGE UNIVERSITY. His professional
         biography appeared in *AMERICAN MEN OF SCIENCE* for 1933 and *WHO WAS WHO* in 1935.

12   The College was located in Sarpy county, Nebraska where he taught from 1910 to 1914.

13   L076

14   G111, 1918 XI 23, George's deed was registered at Norristown, PA (bk # 778 :478--481)
            The property was located in Zieglerville, Frederick township, Montgomery county,
            PA.

15   L077

16   G073, 1880 census Bensalem township, Bucks county, PA. revealed that Uncle John
            Hamilton, Jr., the attorney & gentleman farmer, had neighbors named Pickering.

17   L082

18   L104

19   1922 VI 2, George and Langdon were married (bk # 4 : 530) by Judge J. E. Jones, in
            chambers. Two attorneys were present as their witnesses, F. Harrison and Edward
            Smith. George had arrived in Arizona in 1916, and officially joined the
            OBSERVATORY staff in 1917. This information appeared in a local newspaper's
            clipping found at Enfield Public Library, NH courtesy of Mrs. Marjorie Carr, a
            local historian.
        George was involved with a silver mine in Yavepai county, AZ for a time.

20   BOSTON SUNDAY GLOBE, 1903 VI 10.

21   Williams, Abram, 1905. GENEALOGY OF THE WILLIAMS FAMILY (typescript at Enfield Public
            Library) p. 19--21. Langdon was one of six children of Louis M. and Ella E.
            (Brigham) Williams. Langdon was born in Putnam, CT, 1879 II 8, a twin to Robert
            Longfellow Williams. The family resided in Chelsea, MA later. Langdon's father
            was a pharmacist in Holyoke, MA; Putnam, CT; Winefield, KS; and Chelsea, MA. Her
            father died in Mexico City while a representative of *People's Slot Machine Co.*
            of Boston on 1900 IV 26. Family members were buried in a reservation at OAK
            GROVE CEMETERY, Enfield, NH.

22   see note 20, above.

23   Williams, A., 1905. op cit

24   L112

25   L113

26   L114

27   Langdon suffered from a progressive genetic disease that damaged her neuromuscular
      control of walking. Information from a NH neighbor interviewed in 1991. They
      had no children.

28   L115

29   L118

30   Publications of George and Langdon's research in astronomy:
      1924 I 19, POPULAR ASTRONOMY 32 : 237--240. "Lunar Changes (Eratosthenes
            Region)" Northfield, MN.
          IX 21, POP. ASTR. 32 : 519--521. "The Eye of Mars"
          IX.., POP. ASTR. 32 : 595--600. "The Seas of Mars"
          XI 17, LONDON TIMES : 10c " Eye and Oases on Mars"
      1925 II .., POP. ASTR. 33 : 287--289. "A Dark Entering Wedge at the Termination
            of Mars."
          X.. , POP. ASTR. 33 (8) : 499--502. "Colligation of the Martian Markings."
          n.d. ASTRONOMICAL SOCIETY OF THE PACIFIC, San Francisco, CA. "Mars : a
            Comparison of Drawings."
      1929 IV 24, LONDON TIMES : 12A "Changes on Mars."

31   1925, MARS AT ITS NEAREST. Dinard (Bretagne) Edite "A l'enseigne de l' Hermine."
      A copy of George's book, just listed, found in the FRANKLIN INSTITUTE, Phila.,
            had a dedication within reading, "to my mother and father from G. H. Hamilton,
            1927." This volume was presented to the Library (1933 III) by Thornton Oakley,
            who knew the family and served on the *Hamilton Relief Committee* charged with
            liquidating a portion of the artist's estate during his life.

32   L218

33   N099, L217

34   L120, L162
      Two current members of the *BRITISH ASTRONOMICAL ASSOCIATION*, London, kindly provided
written analyses of Hamilton's publications re: Mars and the Moon according to contemporary
thinking. These individuals were: Richard Baum (Chester,England) 1992 IX 18 and Richard Mc Kim
(Ph.D., Chemistry; Peterborough, England; Director, Mars Section, BAA) 1992 IX 19.

              DETAILS OF LANGDON'S LIFE DOCUMENTED

      Her paternal grandmother was Mrs. Samuel Williams (nee: Ursula Day), 1823--1904.

      Langdon was affiliated with the SEVENTH DAY ADVENTIST faith.

She was a research associate of her husband in Mandeville cited on p. 287 (1925 II article, : A Dark...")

George died 1935 VIII 4 according to the official record, G122.

Langdon obtained a decree, awarding her real estate as part of the $ 5,000.00 allowance (1937 III 30 p. 273/4) in Orphan's Court, Norristown, Montgomery county, PA, G129.

Langdon sold the farm land at Zieglerville formerly owned by her late husband, George, to J. Logan Steward (1937 III 30, bk # 1231 : 407--410) .

Then Langdon went to reside with her niece, Louise Williams Ring, 1886--1964) and the niece's late husband, Henry C. Ring, on Moose Mountain Road in Enfield, NH from about 1937.

Langdon continued to pay taxes in NH until 1953, at age 65.

Her grandniece, Mrs. Myrtle Williams Brown, the designated executer of her estate, like her parents, predeceased Langdon, when they resided at New London, CT.   Langdon was eligible for Social Security benefits.

Langdon died (1981 I 6) at the Hanover Terrace Health Care facility in Hanover, NH, E143.

Her obituary titled, " Former Enfield Resident Dies at 101" reported that she was survived by several nephews including Samuel Williams of Enfield. (1981 I 6)

Langdon's will dated 1973 IX 6 made Mrs. Brown (1910--1980, Norwich, CT) her executrix according to the Canaan, Grafton county, NH probate record. E154

IX : ABODES

(Unless otherwise mentioned, all data refers to Phila.)

1   An artist's (1992 I 10) reconstruction of facade.
         Chain-of-Title on 1600 Summer St. (HAMILTON HOUSE) :
                 built,   Isaac S, Lloyd,   c. 1843.
                 1st owner, David Marston & h/wife Abigail,   1844 III 19.
                 2nd   Richard Shields & h/wife Catherine, c. 1845
                 3rd   John Hamilton, Sr. & h/wife Elizabeth, 1846
                 4th   Miss Margaret Hamilton   , 1886 VII 3.
                 5th   John McLure Hamilton & h/wife Clara, 1895 I 4.
                 6th   Trustees of Alexander C. Simpson, Jr. 1936
                              deceased
                 7th   Clara Hamilton, Mathew B. Buckley &
                              Robert P. Robinson   1938
                 8th   Joseph Zeidelman & Ida h/wife   1946
                 9th   Franklin Town Corporation   c. 1972
                 10th   Wyndam Frankilin Hotel   c. 1979

2   U026   Kennedy, D.J. (1817--1898) drawing/legend.

3   Interview held in 1991, Mr. Sorger maintained an extensive file of letters and
                 photographs re : Lloyd's Row home that he had owned and about his efforts to
                 save the other properties on Summer St. from proposed demolition.
         In 1836, T. U. Walter submitted his plans for the houses. A book was published which
                 presented some of the famous architect's other work.
         Walter, T.U./ Smith, J. J., 1846. TWO HUNDRED DESIGNS FOR COTTAGES & VILLAS. Carey &
                 Hart, Phila.

4   "Resident Holdouts Fight Franklin Town Bulldozers." an article and photos appeared in
                 PHILA. INQUIRER 1973 IV 22 and the DAILY NEWS.

5   CITY DIRECTORY, 1871 listed Hamilton (artist) at "1123 Chestnut St.," perhaps he had
                 obtained room-and-board near the art school.

6   Edmonds, F. S., 1902. HISTORY OF CENTRAL HIGH SCHOOL.
                 While I much enjoy Hamilton's art, I must complain about the legibility of his
                 handwriting samples from 1881--1936. They were frequently a challenge to
                 interpret.

7   op cit "Dr. Riche" portrait by Hamilton was reproduced.

8   E001, N001

9   E003, N002

10   U005, Sketch Club. Secretary's Notes. Hamilton joined 1876 XII 1, present at meetings:
     1877 XII 28; 1878 I 4; 1877 XII 27;   resigned 1878 I 24. (see AAA microfilm #
     3365 : Thornton Oakley Papers, Smithsonian).

11   L001

12   E110

13   L185, L186

14   E058

15   Islington subdistrict

16   E089, 1891 London, England census, Marylebone, #14 Alpha Road. (RG 12-103 :76)

17   B012 : 63

18   London POSTAL DIRECTORY, 1881 : 953
     op cit   1883 : 2176 et seq
     op cit   1889 : 2297 et seq
     op cit   1899 : 272 et seq
     op cit   1903 : 2803 et seq
     op cit   1911 : 2109 et seq

19

20

21   Glasgow POSTAL DIRECTORY, 1897/98 : 255
       op cit   1903/04 : 819 (# 93 Hope St.)
       op cit   1904/05 : 826
       op cit   1906/07 : 351

     Glasgow, (Tax) VALUATION ROLL, 1902/03 (#57 Hope St.)

     Glasgow, VOTER'S ROLL, 1911

22   Surrey, England, 1911, N039

23   L114 : 2; L151; L161

24   L011

25   L092; L102

26   L113

27   L120

28   U029

      X : LONDON

1   N061; B012 : 41

2   B012 : 41--48

3   L007

4   L009; L095

5   B013 : 217

6

7   B013 : 214/5; B007 : 100--103

8   B013 : 214; 219
      IN: B007 (5th ed.,1911 : 287) "Dedicated to JOHN McLURE HAMILTON, A Great Painter & a
            Charming Comrade. In Memory of Many Pleasant Days.
                    THE GENTLE ART OF MAKING ENEMIES. J. MC NEILL WHISTLER AS THE UNATTACHED
                    WRITER. WITH SOME WHISTLER STORIES OLD AND NEW. Edited By SHERIDAN
                    FORD. Bretano's, London, Paris, NY, Washington,(D.C.), Chicago, 1890."

9   L004, L005

10   B007 : 221

11   B013 : 218/9

12   B013 : 296, B017 II : 5

13   Work commissioned c. 1912, purchased 1913.

14   L007 : 54

15   B012 : 63--71

16

17   B012 : 2(unnumbered frontis), 262;   J003

18   N061

19   B029

20   E014

21   L009

22   L010

23   L011

24   L220 not retrieved

25   L012, L008

26   L014, L016

27   L017
      B012 : 209/10 Cross Reference Service.   C.R.A. DIGEST OF PA DECISIONS. 1898--1906.
              Pepper, G. W./ Lewis, W. D./ Matlack, S. D. I : 1460. Rees Welsh & Co., Phila.

                    Corporations, XXI.
              "(191) Wildwood Pavilion Co. v. Hamilton, 15 Super. Ct. 389 (1900), W. W.
              Porter, J. see on rule for new trial 7 D. R. 7477, 22 PA. C. C. 68, 43 W. N. C.
              303, overruled in principle; Galena M. & S. Co. v Frazier, 20 Super. Ct. 394
              (1902), Orlady, J. (W.W. Porter, J. dissenting); Shepp v. Schuylkill Valley
              Tract 9, 17 Montgy. Co. 52 (1901), Weand, J."

              WEEKLY NOTES OF CASES 43 (1898--99) : 303/4. Common Pleas C. P. no.1. Sept.,'97,
              721. Wildwood Pavilion Co. v. Hamilton.

              PA DIST. REPORTS 7 (1898) : 747/8.

              PA CO. COURT 22 (1899) : 68--70.

              PA SUPERIOR REPORTS 15. Schaffer Allison (1900--1901) : 389--392.

1   E110
Hamilton was described as an *engraver* when he exhibited in 1890, 1892, 1893, 1896, 1899, 1925, and 1927. *Boussod, Valladon & Co.*, Regent St., London W. and later *Twenty-One Gallery*, Adelphi, London WC2 were his agents for sales in 1893 and 1899, respectively.

2   A "correct" job description for Hamilton at this phase in his career from 1895 through August, 1905 would have been "*graphic journalist*" in the foot steps of France's *Honore-Victorin Daumier*, 1808--1879.

3   Hamilton published 136 caricatures, and 84 cartoons between Oct., 1902 and 1905 which have been retrieved.

4   Sports, theatre, politics, Royal visits, society news, construction of important buildings, church news, and the great fires were all "meat" for Hamilton to "chew upon." They numbered 62 published drawings.

5   The newspaper was subtitled, "My Conscience!" and appeared Wednesdays.

6   Copies of more than fifty "Hamilton-*signed* pieces have been retrieved from *the BAILIE* survey.

7   However, five other artists, more frequently, contributed to its pages including, W. Y. Calder, Harvey Lambeth, Norman Mac Lean, J. A. Ross, and SKOT.

8   The Glasgow POSTAL DIRECTORY op cit listed Hamilton for several years and his business address was confirmed from his luxury volume (reprints called PROMINENT PROFILES) issued in 1903. It was # 93 Hope St., there, L035 was written by the artist on his employer's stationary (GLASGOW HERALD, WEEKLY HERALD, & EVENING TIMES, 65 Buchanan St.).

9   In addition, there are numerous examples without discernable signature, at the reduction printed, implying that my HAMILTON ART CATALOG (A O O O) may err by reporting *too few* works of the Glasgow Period. As all observations from the EVENING TIMES were limited to studies made upon microfilmed images, something as small as a signature could have been lost during "preservation" in the frequently inferior, filming quality.
It is undocumented whether Hamilton was ever a *commercial* artist generating advertisements but several published ads during his tenure appear intriquingly Hamilton-*like* often using his cartoon characters for sales promotions. Tom Browne's famous JOHN WALKER & SON, Kilmarnock, *trademarked caricature* dates from 1908.

10   They included W. Milne Black, W. A. Donnelly, John Duncan, Tom Maxwell, and Dure Whyte.

11   All were estimated from microfilm and a rare glimpse at the partial run of bound
        original papers available exclusively at the MITCHELL LIBRARY'S Glasgow Room.

12   *"Mems. for Madame"* may have been a Hamilton creation and *by-line*.

13   It should be noted that the Italian business influence still continued in Glasgow in
        1991 along with evidence of many other foreign investors.

14   These included institutional tradegies, fires, parties, investiture whether of the
        Cardinal or College President and the opening ceremony of the *Exposition*.

15   The *Royal Hibernian Art Association*.
        Several comic post cards retrieved during the expedition contain cartoon
        characters that appear Hamilton-*like*.

16   He generally avoided archaeology stories and those about birds.

17   Buffalo, Chicago. Cincinnati, Philadelphia, and St. Louis.

18   1901.   Three years later, in 1904, Hamilton won his *third* gold medal for his oil
                paintings which may have included portraits of Gladstone, Thouron, or Richards
                at the St Louis UNIVERSAL EXPOSITION commemorating the acquisition of the
                Louisana Territory from France. Hamilton served as a member of the "Advisory
                Committee for American art in Great Britain and Belgium." Additionally, he
                served on the "London section of the National Jury of Selection for Art."
                His photograph was taken on the steps of the *St. Louis Museum* where the
                Exposition was held, in the company of his peers.
        It was during this period that Hamilton began some experiments with pastels of female
                subjects as genre drawings which were to become a cornerstone of the next phase
                of his career. The first documented model in 1909 is his unidentified niece,
                shown in *"Woman in Brown"* [A158], and (Woman millinery, oil) [A078]. She is
                mentioned (J028 : 48). Two women fit the category. First, Mrs. Nora King
                Buckley; second, Clara's niece, simply identified as Miss Raiguel (B017 : 93)
                c. 1911 by Pennell.

19   The sixteen GLASGOW BOYS included Thomas Austen Brown, Joseph Crawhall, Thomas Millie
        Doe, David Gauld, Sir James Guthrie, George Henry, Edward Atkinson Hornel,
        William Kennedy, Sir John Lavery, William York Mac Gregor, Charles Rennie Mac
        kintosh, Arthur Melville, James Stuart Park, James Paterson, Alexander Roche,
        and Edward Arthur Walton.

20   They included "Artist", "Photographic Artist," and "Enlarger to the Photographic Trade."

21   Perhaps he created photographic studies for future paintings though none are documented.

22   N099

1 N011
  N012 "Coronation picture : Hamilton to whom *King George V* has graciously given a special
    sitting."
  N091 "The work and career of J. M. Hamilton, who has done a Coronation Portrait of *King
    George.*"
  N013 It was published as "*GOD SAVE THE KING*" from a "charcoal sketch made at *Buckingham
    Palace*, 1911 V 25. J. M' Lure Hamilton" copyright.
  N092 Six column, full-page publication seen by millions.
  L052

2 Gladstone, Bismarck, Ford, Campbell, Burns, Richards, Raffaelli, Watts, Thouron,
    Leighton, Spencer, Tyndall, Haggard, Mitchell, Taylor, Manning, *King Edward VII*,
    and his *Queen, Alexandra, King Victor Emanuel III*, and his *Queen, Helena.*

3 A pastel study for the portrait of *King George V* done in his yellow (colored) uniform
    was in a private collection (Phila.,1990). At the *Victoria & Albert Museum's*
    Print Room (its item E1072-1911), is a signed and dated lithograph, 22" x 14,"
    of it published earlier in the London DAILY CHRONICLE's Portfolio of Historical
    Scenes at Coronation of King George & Queen Mary, 1911. A lithographic *proof*,
    with the artist's signature in chalk, lettered, " *T. Way. Impt. London # 4*" is
    its item E1094-1911. A second lithographic *proof from the process block* made
    for publication in the DAILY CHRONICLE, 1911 VI of King George, donated by the
    Editor, is its item E1082-1911.

4 N091

5 They were Asquith, Balfour, Chamberlain, Churchill, Gladstone, Lloyd-George, Bismarck,
    Kings Edward VII, George V, and Victor Emanuel III. Queens Alexandra, Mary and
    Helena were also recorded.

6 L044 Sold to the Luxembourg Palace collection, Paris, for $ 5,000.00.

7 Certificate, 1915.

8 L055, L068

9 Mrs. George Hamilton, the physician's widow, was listed in the *Register of Deaths*,
    Kingston-on-Thames, county Surrey, 1915 I 11. The certificate was issued 1992
    IX 8 from the General Register Office, London, G105.
  She was listed as a resident in her son's home in the 1891 London census (op cit) as
    Catherine, age 63, at all other times she was called *Caroline*. Further, it was
    noted that she was living on her own means in the artist's East Marylebone
    (parish) home, in Regent's Park, within the Christ Church (Ecclesiastical)

parish. Also resident in the house were her son, Mc Lure, his wife, Clara, and her grandson, George. They were served by a butler, cook, and housemaid.
L063

10   Her sister, ("Miss E")lizabeth G. Delaplaine (1819--1921), survived to age 102 and was probably the sitter whose portrait Hamilton exhibited under that title in 1877 at P.A.F.A.[A026] The artist's sister, Mrs. Lillie Hall King, had provided health care for their aunt, Elizabeth, for years in Phila.
G105 Inventory/Administration. Estate of Caroline Hamilton, deceased. 1915 #911. Orphans' Court, Phila.
G106 Will. Caroline Hamilton, 1915 #1328, Phila.

11   1941 XI. ROYAL ARCHITECTURAL INSTITUTE OF CANADA, Journal. 18 : 192 (Rea, Kenneth Guscotte d. 1941.
L074 1916, Rea family of 29 Cote des Neiges, Montreal, Canada. Architect held commission for $ 1.5 Million project.
Clara was involved with War time charities.

12   L074 The art collection of Hamilton subject Jack Ross' father included works by Franz Hals, etc.
Clara was very ill.
Several Hamilton portraits date from this northern expedition including "Rev. (John Campbell) Bowen," Lt. Gov., Alberta province, and a baptist Minister, and one of "Jack Ross," the philanthropist, who built the School, (Ottawa).

13   N015 "Predicts Success for Lloyd-George."
N022 "France not bled white"

14   Hamilton's work published in 1896 VIII 19 BAILIE. Cartoon Supplement p.1. "Li Hung Chang's Visit."

15   Hamilton's editorial cartoon IN: EVENING TIMES, Glasgow 1903 XI 9 "What We May Expect To See In A Day Or Two."

16   L073, E055, E056, E071, E072
The Hamilton's made expeditions to California in 1914,(1915), 1916, and an early one about 1894. Exhibition catalogs list his art works in 1920 and 1923.

17   B012

18   Hamilton's lithographs, 1920 catalog, included "John Tyndall," "The Old (Welsh) Woman," and "Girl (weeping)." The latter available in monochrome or with several colors added.

19   L076 from Virginia trip.

20   N093 1918 I 25. The news photo legend read, "Portrait of Hamilton by Wayman Adams,"
            (1883--1959).
        D050
        J047

21   L084 Mrs. Mary Harriman purchased about thirty Hamilton pastels in 1915 for $ 5,000.00.

22   N023 "Highest honor America can bestow on an artist."
        N021, U027 (Hamilton's lecture), N025, L083, E115.

23   Forty-six as cartoons (known collectively as *L'Academie pour Rire*), eight brilliant
            oil portraits, four as great pastels, one lithograph, and one watercolor.
        Other recipients of this medal are listed chronologically : Knight, Harrison, Chase,
            Homer, Abbey (1898), Beaux, Grafly (1899), Thouron (1901), Whistler (1902),
            Sargent (1903), Alexander, *Richards* (1905 [A103]), Oakley, Redfield, Tarbell,
            Anschutz, Metcalf, Cassatt, Weir, and P.A.F.A. President *Coates* [A018].

24   N024, N094

25   L078, L086, L089

26   L087

27   L091

28   Clara, an energetic and diminutive model would join him on a later voyage.

29   Hamilton was at first supported by grants-in-aid from his parents then by several small
            legacies (Tab. O).

30   In Hamilton's manners, speech, appearance and values.

31   *Hamilton House* was still located at 1600 Summwer St., Phila. from 1895 through 1937,
            inclusive.

32   Various tenants occupied *Hamilton House* following Aunt Margaret Hamilton's tenure. In
            1900, Howard Curry, M.D. and his three person family,G092. In 1910, William
            W. Fritz,M.D. and two lodgers,G102. By 1917, the house was described as a three-
            story, brick structure valued at $ 7,500.00 (G109).

33   The *Drexel & Company* partners included *J. Pierpont Morgan*, Edward T. Stotesbury, Charles
            Steele, J. P. Morgan, Jr., Henry P. Davison, Temple Bowdoin, Arthur Newbold,
            William Pierson Hamilton, *William Hobart Porter*, Thomas W. La Mont, and *Horatio
            G. Lloyd*. (CITY DIRECTORY, Phila., 1919. p.560)

1   L093

2   A074, The inscription (obverse, lower right) on the pastel portrait of Colonel
            E. M. House reads,"Hotel Coillon, Paris, Sept.,1919."

3   J035 reads,"*James McClure* Hamilton," : with two published errors in his name.

4   L095, L096

5   L098 written on "The Wharf's" stationery, L099, L100.

6   William Ewart Gladstone (1892), Mary Gladstone Drew (1898--1926), and Henry Neville
            Gladstone (1915--1929), the date range for the letters is in brackets after the
            addressee's name.

7   The binding for B012 was made in Italy, L108, L110.

8   The publisher for B012 and B001 was Thomas Fisher Unwin.

9   B001 contained Hamilton's lithograph, "*W. E. Gladstone reading*," executed in red.

10   E067, E068

11   J056, L106, L139, L140

12   L107

13   L108 and BM #135 n.d.

14   L112
        Meanwhile, Hamilton's son, George, now thirty-eight, married Elizabeth Langdon Williams,
            five years his elder, while both were working in Flagstaff, AZ on 1922 VI 22.
            They were associated with Prof. Pickering at his LOWELL OBSERVATORY, there.
            Miss Williams had been assistant to Prof. Percival Lowell for fifteen years and
            was considered a brilliant computer/mathematician. The parents of the groom
            learned of the marriage after the fact.

15   L113, B014

16   B012 Fournier d'Albe (1868--194(.), L120

17   L221 "Deceased artists' works ought to be shown at the Royal Academy." (Furse/Swan)
        L114 Hamilton presumably had first visited London in 1872 XII, as a student.

18   Though Pennell was clearly anti-semitic (L117), Hamilton was tolerant and at times
        friendly toward Jews (B012).

19   until late March, 1923.

20   L119 From the residence of "*Newton S. Brittain, Esq*"., Tobyhanna, Mt. Pocono, PA

21   L121

22   L122

23   L123 From Content Farms, Cambridge, Washington county, NY.
        Hamilton's oil, "*Corn Husker*" was painted in 1886. It was first mentioned in L006 to
        Coates then in letters of the 1920s. The painting might have been based on the
        famous poem of *Carl Sandburg* who, while working as a film critic/motion picture
        reviewer, CHICAGO DAILY NEWS, received one-half of the coveted POETRY SOCIETY
        prize for *the* poem in 1919.

24   N029

25   N032

26   N073 1924 IV 14 Exhibition. Mc Clees Galleries, 1507 Walnut St., Phila.

27   ROSENBACH CO. of Phila. & NYC
        While Hamilton spent the year 1925 in England, few details are available.

28   J048, N034

29   L135

30   N036
        Sobel/Raimo, 1978. op cit.

31   N036   Hamilton, a U.S. citizen 1927 XI 7

32   L137

33   L137

34   L140, L144, N051
        Household goods, paintings, and lithographs. E119 bill of sale.

XIV : FINANCE

1   Hamilton documents numbering more than 166 are listed in the Appendix (**GOOO**).
     They include deeds, wills, letters of Administration, relevant census data from
     Europe, and the Americas.

2   editorial, 1992 I 1. PHILA. INQUIRER
     radio interview, 1992 I 8. *Donald Eckert*, TEMPLE UNIVERSITY, Phila., Sociology Dept.,
          "Sociology of Art" aired on "Marty Moscoane Show, WXTU."

3   L120

4   B012 : 247

5   L016   A NYC dealer charged Mrs. A. L. Merritt a 32 1/2 % commission to sell a picture.
             Hamilton felt that the fee was outrageous.

6   As no passport was required in the 19th Century and records of passenger arrivals were
          not indexed, details to documented trips of Hamilton can only rest upon
          available letters and published reports in books.
     Reconstruction, 1993, of Hamilton's Itinerary from all sources :
             London/Antwerp 1872
             USA   1875
             London   1878
             USA   1880
                             1884
                             1889
                             1891
                             1892
                             1900
                             1901
                             1902
                             1904
                             1905
                             1907
                             1912
                             1914
                             1915
                             1916
                             1917
                             1918
                             1919
                             1920
                             1922
                             1923

```
                  1924
                  1926
                  1927
                  1929
                  1930
                  1931
       Jamaica    1922
                  1928
                  1930
                  1931
                  1934 (Mr. Jackson & the Treasure)
      Scotland    1881
                  1890
                  1892
                  1893
                  1894
                  1895
                  1896
                  1897
                  1899
                  1900
                  1902
                  1904
                  1907
                  1914
                  1925
                  1927
         Italy    1899
                  1910
                  1911
                  1921
       Germany    1910
       Austria    189(2)
        France    1875
                  1878
                  1892
                  1893
                  1896
                  1897
                  1898
                  1913
                  1919
    California    1894 ?
                  1914
                  1915
                  1925 ?
                  1927 ?
```

7   *Sefer Koheleth* (Ecclesiastes) ch 5 v. 14. "A baby enters the world with hands clenched,
          as if to say, 'the world is mine; I shall grab it.' A man leaves with hands
          open, as if to say, 'I can not take anything with me.'"
     Tosafot on the Pentateuch, 13th Century. "What you give to charity in health is gold; in
          sickness, is silver, and after death, is copper."

8   Zieglerville, Montgomery county, PA; Phila. county, PA; Kingston-on-Thames, Surrey,
          England; Pembrokeshire, Wales; and Mandeville, Manchester parish, Jamaica.

9   L179

10   Tables **M , O , Q**.

1   B002 contained Hamilton's cartoon, *"Adieu,"* reproduced here.

2   L151 contained an appended, three paged, "List of old books" owned by the artist from the rare book collection of his father, George Hamilton, M.D. Three are of particular interest, first, 1890, GENTLE ART OF MAKING ENEMIES; second, 1550, TUTTE LE OPERE DI NICOLO MACHIAVELLI. Appresso Pierro Alberto; and third, 1811, James Mease, M.D. THE PICTURE OF PHILADELPHIA. B. & T. Kite (Publisher), sold at Joseph Delaplaine's, Phila.

3   In 1993's autograph collector's market, Hamilton's *"Genereal George Washington"* letter would sell for more than half a million dollars.

4   L154

5   L161

6   L161

7   E097 listed the artist's 1920 donation of five oils : *"Corbet, Ford, Gilbert, Monkhouse and Tyndall."* In 1959, Messrs. *James, Bourlet* presented the oil, *"Spencer."* A graphite sketch of *"Ford (4391)"* was added in 1980.

8   Mrs. Catherine Gladstone, Rev. Stephen Gladstone, Baron Henry N. Gladstone, Lt. William G. C. Gladstone, Mrs. Mary G. Drew, Mrs. Dorothy D. Parish, and several of the Prime Minister, William E. Gladstone.

9   N039 "Famous Exponent of Drawing in Pastel," N038 "Gladstone," N041,   J050.

10   List of museums where Hamilton's work had been exhibited or owned.(*= currently owned)
     Buffalo, NY
     Brooklyn Museum, NY
     National Academy of Design, NYC
     *Research Libraries, NY Public Library, Print Room, NYC**
     Chicago Art Institute, IL
     Cincinnati Museum of Art, OH
     *Delaware State Museum, Dover**
     *Georgia Museum of Art, Athens**
     Los Angeles, CA
     *Philadelphia Art Museum, PA**
     Art Alliance of Phila., PA
     *Pennsylvania Academy of Fine Arts, Phila.**
     *Central High School, Phila.**
     *John G. Johnson Collection, Phila. Museum of Art, PA**
     *University of PA, Phila.**

CIGNA Museum/Art Collection, Phila.*
Carnegie Institution Art Museum, Pittsburgh, PA*
Westmoreland Museum of Art, Greensburg, PA*
Allentown Museum of Art, PA*
St. Louis Museum, MO
San Francisco, CA
Corcoran Gallery of Art, Washington, D.C.*
National Portrait Gallery, Washington, D.C.*
Yale Center for British Art, New Haven, CT*
Walker Art Gallery, Merseyside, Liverpool, England*
Barbizon House, London, England
British Museum, Print Room, London*
Burlington House, London
Leighton House Museum, London*
National Portrait Gallery, London*
Royal Academy of Arts, London
Royal Society, London*
Tate Gallery, Millbank, London
Victoria & Albert Museum, Print Room, London*
Art Gallery/Museum, Kelvingrove, Glasgow Scotland*
Mitchell Library, Glasgow*
Royal Institute Gallery, Glasgow
St. Andrews University, Fife*
Luxembourg Palace, Paris, France*
Salon, Paris
Berlin, Germany
Dusseldorf
Kunsthaus Museum, Koln
Munich
Rome, Italy
Venice

Hamilton is represented in more than twelve private collections in Europe and the Americas.

11   1931 VII 2, Mr. Silvera Victor Emanuel, by name a Sephardi, Jewish planter of Oracabessa
       in the parish of St. Mary (Jamaica) sold to former resident of
       Kingston-on-Thames, Hamilton, London artist, a parcel of land. (Conveyance 2047
       : 1931/32) G116

12   Conversion rate : one pound sterling equaled $ 5.00.

13   Jamaican L.N.S. 389, folio 303.

14   The size of Hamilton's handwriting in his later letters was larger and less legible.

15   *Butterfield's Auction House*, San Francisco, CA. *"Still Life with Poppies,"* 1933, oil. 1984 I 19.

16   L156
      Frederick E. Church, another American flower painter, had made an expedition to Jamaica in 1865. As the result of Church's months there many native flowers were illustrated in his watercolors. His tropical landscapes together with his still life works were exhibited in 1992 at the Ross Gallery, Fisher Art Library, University of Pennsylvania in the Furness Building.

17   N042 *The ROSENBACH CO.* of NYC gallery held an exhibition from late March to April 1st, 1934.

18   N042 "Seen in the Galleries" column by *Howard Devree*, "Pastels by Octogenarian."

19   U028 *MC CLEES GALLERIES*, Phila. address : 1615 Walnut St., N051.
      Over three hundred Hamilton pictures had been delivered to the Gallery to be sold to pay Hamilton's outstanding bills in Phila. and Jamaica.

20   The contract's term was to run from 1934 VII 25 through 1937 VI 13, inclusive. The agent was known locally as *"Masta Harry"* and still later as the *"King of Horse Racing."* A Jamaican racing trophy was named in his honor.

21   op cit L.N.S. 438 folio 447; Conveyance 1272 : 1934/35

22   op cit

23   L.N.S. 291 folio 442; Conveyance 1699 : 1934/35

24   N043, N044, N046.

25   N045, N047, N052.

26   1937 III 30. Deed bk # 1231 : 407, Montgomery co.,PA Langdon Hamilton, G131.
      L177, N048, N049, N050, N052.

27   L179

28   The cumulative effects of chronic exposure to Radon gas can not be ruled out as a contributing cause of George's death from lung cancer.

29   Langdon seems to have abandoned her in-laws in Jamaica for whatever, unknown reason.
      L185

1   L217, L218, N086, N087, N088, N089.
        Death certificate. Mandeville, Manchester parish, Jamaica, B.W.I. 1935 VIII 4,
                Hamilton, George.   I A 8061

2   Rector, Anglican Parish Church, Mandeville

3   Anglican Church section.

4   L187   Artist died at Hamilton Hall, Mandeville, 1936 IX 10 at 20:30 hours
                (AAA microfilm 4394)
        Death certificate. 1936, Hamilton, John Mc Lure. I A 8278

5   Mrs. Taylor of Bar Harbor, ME, was a family friend and Relief Committee member.

6   D031, D051, N053, N054, N055, N057, N058, N059, N060, N061, N071.

7   L189

8   L187   Mrs. Clara Hamilton died at Hamilton Hall, 1936 XI 1 at 03:30 AM.
        Death certificate. 1936 XI 3. Hamilton, Clara. I A 8300

9   County (parish) records are located at City Hall, Mandeville.

10   From the published obituaries.

11   The graves of John Mc Lure Hamilton (plot # 18), Clara Augusta Hamilton nee: Raiguel
                (plot # 19) and George Hall Hamilton (plot # 11) are all located in row one of
                the Anglican section, Mandeville Public Cemetery situated *beneath* Grove Road
                (1992 VII).

12   *"Our Artist,"* the title given to Hamilton in his days on the Glasgow EVENING TIMES.

13   "H. & C. H., London."

14   George Hall Hamilton's estate:
                Decree awarding Real Estate. Orphan's Court, Montgomery co.,PA. 1936 XII 23
                        et seq to 1937 III 30.
                Deed. Montgomery co., PA bk # 1231 : 407--410. Elizabeth L. Hamilton, widow to
                        J. Logan Steward. 1937 III 30, G131.

        John McLure Hamilton's estate:
                Letters of Administration (Jamaican). Intestate. 1937 III 1 to 1938 XII 14
                        High Court of Justice, Principal Probate Registry, Somerset House,
                        London WC2, G157.

Colonial Probates # 2. 91-2-0854, 1938 XI 30. Sealing of Letters of
        Administration,G156.
N033. Estate Notice. 1938 XI 25.
Whitaker's ALMANACK, 1936 p.380. Intestates' Estates, England & Wales.

15   Clara Hamilton's estate:
        Decree. Estate John Mc Lure Hamilton, deceased. Phila., PA Orphans' Court
            #1466 1938 p.188 Clara Raiguel Hamilton, deceased. 1940 VIII 10.
        Revised Statement. Tax on Transfer of Real Estate in name of non-resident.
            Guardian of Estate of Clara Raiguel Hamilton (Montgomery Trust Co.,
            Norristown, PA) 34 acres, Zieglerville, Frederick township, 1941 II 7,
            G137.

    By this date, George's widow had apparently abandoned (or waived) her financial
        responsibilities together with any future interests in the estates of
        her in-laws.

16   T. Oakley papers. Brandywine River Museum, Chadds Ford, PA. AAA Microfilms #4394 through
        #4397, inclusive and reel #4409 Free Library of Phila. collection.

17   L177

18   N062, N063

19   Phila. interview, 1990 V., Mr. Harry Burke.

20   N066, N067

21   Ancillary letters of Administration/Inventory. Phila. Orphans' Court. 1937 X 28,
        ADM # 2205. Estate of John Mc Lure Hamilton, deceased, G130.

22   L108 "H.N. Gladstone, letters of." *British Museum* (not in Hamilton's handwriting)

23   Clifford, D. 1970. COLLECTING ENGLISH WATERCOLORS. J. Baker, London. ch 6 "Mind of
        the Collector." p. 51.

24   N068, N069

25   L195 "text"

26   N070

27   NMAA, Shelley Mead to Alperin, 1991 I 30.
    NMAA, above   to Institute of Jamaica, 1990 IX 11.
    NMAA, above   to Alperin, 1991 II 5.

28   Deed. Montgomery co.,PA. 1940 VIII 3. p.399--402 Montgomery Trust Co., Guardian of
         Estate of Rea, Eleanor Adele; Rea, Mary Claire; & Rea, John Kenneth (minors) to
         Williams, John K. (buyer of land) pet. # 45224, G136.

29   N072

30   N089

31   Will. Mrs. Elizabeth L. Hamilton, deceased. 1981 I 6, Hanover, Grafton co., NH,G154.

32   N076, N077, N080, N081, N083, U030.

33   L195 "Inventory"

XVII : HUNTING

1   Coconut palms, banana trees, bread fruit, grapefruit, orange and evergreen trees, "sweet sup," coffee bushes, guava, cassava, and pineapple grow. Sugar cane, bamboo, papaya, mango, pecans, and peanuts grow also.

2   The DAILY GLEANER, Kingston, Jamaica.

3   Jamaica Bauxite, Ltd.

4   One Jamaican dollar equaled one/twenty-second of an American dollar in the summer of 1992.

5   Tax evaluation records.

6   Interview, 1992. Mrs. Hyacinth Rebhan.
see : Whitacker's ALMANACK, 1936, op cit

7   It included "Hamilton Hall," the 47 acres of land surrounding it, personal property and the 200 pieces of art. An inventory follows the notes of this chapter.

8   Interview, 1992. Mrs. Betty Moss.

9   Letters of Administration, Jamaican.

10   Interview, 1992. Mrs. Mary Hughes.

11   An Island attorney and his family live there currently.

12   These values quoted in American dollars, 1992.

13   Interview, 1992. Miss Sarah Allen, sister of the late John Allen.

14   Interview, 1992. *Brother* Martin Luther Campbell.

15   A Seventh Day Adventist Church-affiliated institution where Hamilton had had a chapter ("Gladstone") of B012 reprinted as a pamplet while visiting Jamaica, perhaps on his first expedition, 1922.

16   Interview, 1992. Mr. Keith Swaby

17   Interview, 1992. Mr. Godfrey Townsend

18   N037. A 1931 news photo and legend, "What's in a back?" reporting on the *Royal Institute Gallery's Pastel Society* exhibition.

19   N087. One of her kinsmen, *H. Vaughan Iver* had attended George H. Hamilton's funeral, 1935.

20   From a private collection.

21   B023. Hamilton had donated part of his book collection there; after two vists officials could not locate the books, however.

22   N076, N077, N079, N080, N081, N082, N083.
A survey was made by directing letters to the Rights/Reproductions Department of hundreds of U. S. museums and dozens of foreigr museums in Europe and the Americas.

23   From L195, 1940 VII 11 of Mr. Sydenham J. Howe :

LIST OF PICTURES, etc

NOW IN MY POSSESSION
from The ESTATE of

JOHN McLURE HAMILTON

Catalogue No.
No.	Description	Mark
51	OIL PAINTING said to be by LAWRENCE.	
2	do. gilt frl	
3	MEDALLION "The Smiling Sage" by R.T.M. 1919	
4	OIL "Del Sarto" on fr.	
8	Landsc. in OILS	
9	3 Engr. blk.fr.	
60	1 do. gilt	
1	Lge. LITHOgraph "The Crucifixion." abt 6ft in heavy fr. (val.?)	
105	2 Fr. Landsc. Engr. gilt	
6	Engr. Blk.	
8	OIL	
9	2 Pastels	
10	Japanese Pict.	
262	Pair Pastels	J.M.H.
3	One do.	J.M.H.
4	One do. Man	J.M.H.
5	ROSES by BUCCHI	
6	Landsc.	J.M.H.
7	2 Pastels	J.M.H.
8	do.	J.M.H.
9	Lge Pastel	J.M.H.
70	Port. of Lady	J.M.H.
1	do.	J.M.H.

```
  2  Unf. Picture    J.M.H.
  3  4  Pastels      J.M.H.
  4  2  Pictures
319  Lge Picture of George as a child. Life size in heavy frl
 26  Lge Picture  gilt fr.
  7     do         Blk.
  8  OIL  Game and Fruit
  9  OIL
 31    do       unfr
  2  Lord Astor     J.M.H.
  4  Pastel    unfr  J.M.H.
  5  3 OILS     unfr
  6  2 OILS
  7  2 P  on wood
  8  OILS by Cooper
465  OILS "Samson & Delilah" 3/4 life, GUIDO RENI on heavy fr.
  6  2  unfin       J.M.H.
  7  2        unfr.
  8  2  Pastels
  9  Picture in gilt
635  Pastel
  6  Picture of Voltaire
  7  2 P. on wood   J.M.H.
  8  do            J.M.H.
 40  2 Pictures
 41  4 Colored Engr. "The CRIES OF LONDON." An old "CONNOISSOIR" in
         my possession gives these 4 as being worth  L 320. in 1914.
         These may be the actual ones mentioned. S. J. H.
  2  1 Col Engr
  3  Small OILS
  4  2 Watercolors
  5  Sketch of Mrs. Drew by J.M.H.
  6  H RM. KING GEORGE      J.M.H.
  7     do   different   J.M.H.
  8  Pastel
  9  A CHRITUS in OILS
650  Lge Pastel   gilt
```

S. J. HOWE .2.   LIST OF PICTURES, concluded

```
651  OIL Painting
  2  Calves
  3  Scene
  4  Unf  Picture     J.M.H.
  5  GENERAL BOOTH     J.M.H.
  6  OILS UNF          J.M.H.
```

```
 7  OILS                J.M.H.
 8  2 Scenes in Spain    J.M.H.
 9  to 70  small P.      J.M.H.
72  Lord OXFORD
 6  6 Col. Prints
 7  19 sm. Engr. elgt. mounted; a set biblical subj.
 8  Pastel
 9  OILS, man with flute
80  Seascape
 1  Madonna and Child
 2  OILS in heavy fr.
 3   do  on wood         J.M.H.
 4   do                  J.M.H.
 5  Col. Engr  "Venus and Cupid"
 6   do          "Spring Morn"
 7   do
 8  Engr GENERAL WASHINGTON, after Stewart
 9  to 93 Pict.
94  Small  Engr.
 5  Pair   do
 6  do
 7  do
 8  Lge Engr
 9  3   small
700 Pair Engr
 1   do
 2  2 small Engr
 3  2 small OILS
 4  Pair OILS
 5  Pair Portraits in OILS
 6  OILS, Negro          J.M.H.
10  MOTHER               J.M.H.
 4  4 OILS in gilt fr
11  small Engr
 1  lge do
```

There is a BUST of GEORGE as a Child.
An unf canvas of Lady on ground playing with child
   (George) FACE of lady not painted

Several tincases contain LETTERS, Sketch books, and
              other things of interest

The damage to pictures is not so great as expected
Three cases are not yet opened.

S. J. Howe

Some REMARKS about a few of the PICTURES.
A few of the PASTELS by J.M.H.

LADY'S BACK   "SPRING"
"PENSIVE MOOD"   "ALARMED"
"THREADING THE NEEDLE"   "THE COQUETTE"
"WRITING THE NOTE"   "THE BLUE VEST"
"A MOMENT TO READ"   "CORONATION COACH"
"SEE MY SKIRT?"   "ESQUISSE"
"GEORGE MEREDITH"   "SISTER SEWING"
"GEORGE & GIRL UNDER TREE"   "SHE STRESSES HER TRESSES"
"SISTER WITH BEAUTIFUL HANDS"   "A NUDE"
"CLARA & VIOLETS"

All are framed, most are glazed. They range in size from
22" x 16" to 32" x 26."   All I think are signed.

OIL PAINTINGS by J.M.H.

"CLARA AT THE PIANO"   "MOTHER" (About Whistler complained)
"MOTHER & GEORGE"   "GEORGE IN THE LANE"   "CLARA" (later life)
"DANCING GIRL OF SEVILLE 60" x 24"   There is also the very large
                                        one of GEORGE as a child, heavy fr.

A great many smaller ones, many on wood.

OIL PAINTING which I was told is by LAWRENCE

PICTURE OF A MAN 30" x 25" (37" x 31" fr.) Half fig. Life size

OIL PAINTING
    MAN IN RED DOUBLET 33" x 36" (45" x 36" fr.) Half fig. Life size.

    The Man bearded, doublet heavily braided, as is also jacket
        over right shoulder. R. Hand rests on swordhilt. This
        picture reminds me of REMBRANDT.

    I have had no opportunity of examining these. they are not
        open yet, and when packed were taken direct from
        the walls.

    "ECCE HOMO DEI" 12" x 16"   The HOLY CHILD and St. John kissing
        Frame is marked on back "Del Sarto."

    A landscape by RAFFAELLI sgd. fr 19" x 25"

"GUESS ME MY NAME" Witherington

There are two PEN STUDIES from the "REYNOLDS COLLECTION"
ONE IS BY GUIDO RENI, the other by CORREGGIO.

ENGRAVINGS include, among many others, DARLEY, LECREUX,
    WITHERINGTON, KAUFMANN, J. BROWNE, RIGAUD, several.

Possibly you can give me some information about several of
    these.

The FOUR "CRIES OF LONDON" I have mentioned in former list as
    having been worth L 320. in 1914. I have this from "the
    CONNOISSOIR" which I have in my possession FROM ONE OF
    THE TINCASES. It is quite possible they are the ones
    referred to.

I am hoping an EXPERT will turn up here some day, and settle
    some of these matters. There are two LANDSCAPES that may
    very likely to turn out to be valuable.

I do not wish to sell any, but if compelled, would prefer
    to sell one so as to provide a HOME for the others.

XVIII : IMAGE, ETC.

1   L001. Photo courtesy, *Charles Roberts Autograph Collection of American Artists.*
            Library, Haverford College,PA.

2   E116. Photo courtesy, *Wadsworth Atheneum*, Hartford, CT.   B032

3   Hamilton's drawings IN: The Glasgow BAILIE. Cartoon Supplement, 1895 IX 4." *The
            Tale of an Empty Pocket and an Umbrella.*" re: Hamilton's experience.

4   B002 drawing reproduced at start of "Decline/Adieu" chapter.

5   B020 in B & W.   B029 in color.

6   B012 : 49, 50, 127.

7   quotation, Mencken, H. L., 1919. PREJUDICES : First series. Knopf. p. 77.

8   Table ⏋

9   B001, B002, B011, B015, B018.

10   B003, E051

11   ch IX, note 21.

12   L107. Second sitting granted by *King George V*, 1921 II 24.

13   N061. A picture, "*Madonna & Infant Christ*" by Hamilton was exhibited in Paris and Vienna
            and gained for him a gold medal at Chicago (1893) mysteriously disappeard. The
            sitters were Mrs. Myles Kennedy and her son.

14   N017, B012 : 99/100. Hamilton favored *Irish Home Rule* in the 1920s.

15   B012 : Foreword, N050. This observation reported by his forty-year long English
            pen pal, Mrs. Mary Drew, was confirmed by his last American critic, H. S. Morris
            (1936).

16   N091

17   N027

18   N036

19   Grandfathers : Delaplaine & Hamilton.

20   Uncle : John C. Mercer, the merchant residing in Germantown, PA. in 1883.

21   1934

22   N060   The 1934 photo was the last published in 1936.

23   B012

24   Hamilton's cartoon characters : *St. Alban,* * St. Hibernian* and *All In.*

25   L174 Ford's bronze bust sculpture of Hamilton's father.

26   U006 part of AAA reel #3664.

27   Lomas reported that on 1876 IV 22 an Exhibition included works by Chase, Shirlaw,
        Duveneck, Deilman, Tractman, Muhrman, Courier, & Carl Meer.

28   Hamilton may have been employed [A187] after that date by the firm of *W. Curtis Taylor*
        or *Samuel W. & Robert C. Broadbent* at the address mentioned. PHILA. CITY
        DIRECTORY, 1883, p.233.

29   The dinner was arranged by members of the *DIVISION OF PICTORIAL PUBLICITY*, 1918 XI 7.

30   Other artists so designated included : Abbey, Cecilia Beaux, C. C. Cooper, Florence
        Este, Harrison, Margaret Lippincott, Pennell, and Sargent. AAA microfilm
        # 3654 : "Phila. Watercolor Club, records/papers."

31   op. cit. 1918 IV 29.
        Wayman Adams (1883--1959) was an active member who painted Hamilton's second, third and
        fourth portraits in oil starting in 1918. [M009, M035, M013]

32   op cit 1924 I 24. This time Hamilton served with *Felicie Waldo Howell.*

33   op cit 1930 VI 5. Mrs. J. M. Taylor, Mrs. J. E. D. Trask, & Mr. C. M. Burns were
        Club members and friends of the Hamiltons.

34   op cit 1936 VI 4.

35   op cit 1934 IV 27.

36   op cit   Was it a portrait of Carl Sandburg, the poet?

37   op cit Dana, Dr. Dawson, Pennell, and Sargent.
        Walter Yeager had joined the Phila. Sketch Club in 1874, but Hamilton resigned his Club
        membership on 1878 I 24 to go abraod permanently. Joseph Pennell became a member
        in 1880. And another long term pal of Hamilton," *Dr. John Madison Taylor*" joined

in 1887. The later was associated with the scholar" *Silas Weir Mitchell, M.D.*"
It is uncertain whether Hamilton was a member of still a third organization which
flourished in the area. The *Pennsylvania Society of Miniature Painters*. Its
President was Mrs. Emily Drayton Taylor, Dr. John Madison's wife, a special
friend of the Hamiltons and a Relief Committee member.

38   L098.   1920 IX 17

39   Interviewed by phone, 1991. She reported on a meeting with Hamilton in 1924 when she was
            a child in the Simpson family.

40   L136

41   1931 III 14. Archives, *Corcoran Gallery of Art.*

42   Director, C. G. A.

43   Cohen, S., 1988. THE ADVENTURE GUIDE TO JAMAICA. Hunter Publishing Co., Edison, N. J.
            p.156 (Bath);   p.163/4 (Milk River Spa).

44   1934, U. S. *Consul* at Kingston, Jamaica.

45   L161

46   L176, 1936 II 2, by Mr. Allen

47   Trevi, F. X. op cit, ch IV note 5.
        Re: David Hamilton (1803--1864), the artist's uncle, see : G083

48   N026. "Artists Talking Free but not as per program." Hamilton chaired session. The three
            speakers were a sculptor, architect, and an illustrious, lithographer,
            respectively.

49   These three were a sea painter, impressionist painter, and a Phila. architect,
            respectively.

50   B024
        Wayman Adams painted three portraits which included Hamilton between 1917 and 1921. The
            third was titled, *"The Conspirators."* In addition to Hamilton it depicted
            Burns, and Pennell plotting.
        WHO WAS WHO IN AMERICA, 1951--1960. p.16 (W. Adams)

XIX : PUBLIC

1   B012 : 1

2   1878

3   N091

4   N016

5   N022

6   N027

7   N027

8   N028

9   N029

10   N032

11   N036

12   N039

13   N045

XX : PRIVATE

1   1993 I 31

2   L001   H to father, 1881 VII 22

3   L003   H to Pennell, re : story of 1889, Spring.
        L004   H to J. Mc Neill Whistler, 1890 III 28.

4   L007

5   L009   H to H. S. Morris, Director, P.A.F.A., 1896 XI 23.

6   L010   1897 XII 29.

7   L011   H to M. Drew, recently bereaved daughter of late Prime Minister, after death of
             her father Hamilton's most important commission, 1898 V 19.

8   L014   1898 X 22.

9   L023   H to Morris, 1901 II 21.

10   L024   1901 III 18.

11   L025   1901 V 4.

12   L052   H to P.A.F.A. Director John E. D. Trask, 1911 VI 28.

13   L067   1915 IV 2.

14   L073   1916 I 24.

15   L069   1915 IV 11.

16   L076   1917 IV 11.

17   L080   1918 I 15.

18   L084   H to Mr. C. Powell Minnigerode (Corcoran Director), 1918 II 19.

19   L087   1918 II 19.

20   L092   H to Mrs. Mary Drew, 1919 XII 30.

21   L093   1920 I 24.

22   L094   1920 II 13.

23   L100   1920 IX 22.

24   L102   1920 XII 3.
             Was Clara, the matron-of-honor at Miss Dorothy Drew's wedding?
             Was Mrs. Dorothy D. Parish's son, John, named for Hamilton?

25   L106   H to Minnigerode, 1920 II 11.   29   L114   1922 VII 15.

26   L107   H to Drew, 1921 II 24.   30   L115   1922 VII 19.

27   L111   1922 I 24.   31   L116   1922 VII 24.   B012 :109--111.

28   op cit   32   L119   1923 III 24.

                                                  33   L120   H to Drew, 1923 X 25.

                                                  34   L136   1926 X 15.

                                                  35   L139   1928 XI 22.

1   Gathered in Europe and the Americas after much travel and correspondence.

2   L195

3   *National Museum of American Art*, Washington, D. C. (=NMAA)

4   op cit

5   The original pastel portrait, 9" x 11," published IN: HISTORY OF HAVERFORD COLLEGE,
     1832--1892. (pgs. 245/6, 271=illus.) of "*Joseph Gibbon Harlan*" (1825--1857),
     M. A., a mathematician/astronomer/ President, Haverford College,PA. His
     biography published IN : N.C.A.B. 33 : 252/3. The Phila. artist was Frederick
     GUTEKUNST (1831--1917) a pastelist better known for his photography. His
     biography published N.C.A.B. 16 : 437.

6   1921. NMAA, Vertical File.

7   J052

8   N034

9   B012 : 41 (House, 1919); p. 153ff (Booth)

10   N097

11   U012

12   B005

13   B006

14   B007 : 9 Foreword by Mrs. Drew.

15   J050

16   N059

17   B012 : 45

18   B012

19   "*Machivelli*" and possibly" Washington," and " Voltaire."

20   J016

21   E108 print dated 1883, two signatures (36-226/2/3)
      D023 I : 274

22   E078, 1931 *Barbizon House* exhibition, "*John Tyndall, F.R.S.*"

23   B012

24   J016

25   B011

26   B018

27   J056

28   B001

29   E024, E117 Hake, H. M., 1925 VI : 492 (event, 1893 II)

30   E110

31   Traced to *Mitchell Library*, Glasgow, five copies.
      Traced to *British Museum*, London, a copy.

32   E117

33   Ramsey, L. G. G., 1962. COMPLETE ENCYCLOPEDIA OF ANTIQUES (Connoisseur's). Hawthorn, NY.
            p.1129/30.

34   London DAILY GRAPHIC, 1895 III 14, p. 1044 #p.4 col 1

35   E117

36   J016, In the words of that plain talker, Pennell.

37   N012
      Hamilton made a post-mortem sculpture of Rev. General, William Booth, the founder of the
            SALVATION ARMY (1912), while his body was lying in state. The project took from
            midnight to dawn to produce the mask in clay without touching the subject. B012
            : 160/1.

38   Hamilton's watercolors are vibrant, detailed, and on paper or linen.

39   This author was not related to the artist. George Hamilton, M.D., Falkirk, Scotland.
         p.11 1846 ed. RUDIMENTS OF ANIMAL PHYSIOLOGY for use in schools and for private
         instruction. Sorin & Bull (at) 42 N. Fourth St., Phila. The text was a rev. ed.
         of the Edinburgh first edition, 1839 X 14.

40   The firm was located at 22 Ct. Queen St., W.C., London and later moved to Great Queen
         St.

41   Home address : 1525 N. 8th St., Phila. (CITY DIRECTORY, p.1599)

42   Adams to Millet, Boston, 1874 III 3. cited IN : FRANK MILLET : A VERSATILE AMERICAN,
         ch III p. 25, 1938, Millet papers, AAA, cited by Weinberg, H. B., 1977. THE
         CAREER OF F. D. MILLET. AAAJ 17 (1) : 2.

XXII : EPILOGUE

1   B012 : 7 Foreword

2   D012 XV :...

3   Newman Galleries, Phila. "WOMAN WITH FAN, 1916" Registry # 11105

4   B030

5   B006

6   After a search at the Public Records Office, Kew, England.

7   D047

8   J052

9   N013

10   E016 : 8/9

11   ch II, AS CRITICS SAW HIS PICTURES

12   U012 : 1/2
     N095 Baum, W. E., 1950.

13   Table **A** and **C.**

14   Table **B**

15   His works are too often mistaken for art done by Boldini, Corot, Degas, Eakins, Hals,
        Renoir, Rubens, Sargent, van Gogh, or Whistler.

16   Hamilton's audience included his family, sitters, museum goers, and readers of the daily
        newspapers.

17   Avery, Balfour, Bernhardt, Burns (C. M. & J.), Carnegie, Carson, Eakins, Ford, France,
        Furse, Gladstone, Halifax, Harriman, Harris, Ives, Leighton, Pierpont Morgan,
        Morris, Oakley, Pennell (J. & E. R.), Rodin, Sargent, Simpson, Spencer, Swan,
        Watts, and Whistler.

18   That includes critic, historian, family member, artist, and possiblely not even
        Hamilton, himself.

19   ch XVIII note 7

20   De Sola-Pool, D., 1983. BOOK OF PRAYERS (Daily/Sabbath) Union of Sephardi Congregations,
        NY. 2nd ed

21   Contrived *minyan* (a collection of ten Jewish men for prayer) : Emanual Furth, Hon. Simon
        Gratz, Sir Henry Irving, Lord Frederick Leighton, Albert Rosenthal, Dr. A. S. W.
        Rosenbach, Philip Rosenbach, Dr. Solomon Solis-Cohen, Judge Mayer Sulzberger,
        Harry Burke, and Dr. Richard J. Alperin.

[Swiftwater Cottage, Delaware Watergap, PA], 1885.
Watercolor 7" x 10.25" from Pennsylvania.

CATALOG

(All documented works, 1993)

(sitter	b/d	profession	dated	source	medium style	owner	#)
Adams, Wayman		painter	(1921)	NAD			F001
Allen, John (Jamaican pine							
bow on his head)		butler	(1933)	SJH	oil		F002
Armistead, Lord George	1821/1915	merchant	(1911)	B012	oil		F003
Edinburgh					oil		F004
Armour, Canon James	1842/1928	Trinity	(1920)	B012	oil		F005
Ballymoney, Ireland		Church					
Asquith, Herbert Henry	1852/1928	P.M.	(1916)	B012	oil		F006
(Lord Oxford & A.)							
Asquith, Mrs.Margot Tennant	1865/1945	writer	(1916)	B012	pas		F007
dau. Sir Charles T.;							
2nd Mrs. Asquith							
Balfour, Arthur James	1848/1930	P. M.	(1920)	B012	oil		F008
Bartlett, Paul Wayland	1865/1925	sculptor	(1913)	B012	pas	WMAG	F009
					sktch	WCMHM	F010
in his Paris studio					oil	NPGW	F011
					oil	Lux	F012
Bartlett, Mrs. P. W.					pas	CGA	F013
Bernhardt, Sarah		actress			lith		F014
Sarah of Letterstone		writer					
		sculptress					
Brittain, Newton		Ex-Auditor	1926	L226	oil		F015
Jamaica		General					
Bismarck-Schonhausen,Prince	1815/1904						
Otto Edward von,study of		Chancellor			pas	CGA	F016
				Spinks	oil		F017
Blaikie, John Arthur	1849/...	poet					F018
England							
Blaxland, Edward		newspaper					F019
		publisher					
Booth, Rev. General William	1829/1912	Salvation			oil		F020
founded		Army		B012	oil		F020
			1912		clay		F021
Bowen,(Col.Hon. John Campbell	1872/1956	Lt. Gov.	(1916)		oil		F022
LL.D,KG,StJ.,educator		Alberta					
Buckley, Mrs. Nora King	1873/19..	niece	(1893)		oil	HB	F023
at age 5 years					oil		F024
					pas		F025

above flowers in lap			(1900)		oil	HB	F505
Burns, Charles Marquedant	1838/1922	architect	(1919)		char		F026
Phila					oil		F027
in uniform				B012	oil		F028
portrait					pas		F029
					wc		F030
head, study of					oil	HB	F031
Bregy, Francis Amedee	1846/1922	judge	1918		oil		F032
Phila.Common Pleas Court							
#2; R; Episcopalian							
Campbell, Lewis,	1830/1908	prof.	(1880)		oil	SAF	F033
Greek; Acad. Admin.							
Carlyle, Thomas #1	1795/1881	essayist	(1879)		pas	CGA	F034
#2		historian			pas	CGA	F035
Coates, Edward Hornor	1846/1921	PAFA,prexy	(1916)		oil	CIGNA	F036
					oil		F037
					pas		F038
					wc		F039
Coates, Mrs. E.H.					pas		F040
Florence Earle							
Clark, Clarence (Munroe)	1859/1937	banker			oil		F041
Phila. Union League		founded					
financier, bibliophile							
art patron							
Clifford, Edward (C.)	..../1910	R. I.	(1909)		oil		F042
Artist's Society, Hon.							
Secretary; Langham							
Sketch Club							
Corbet, Mathew Ridley	1850/1902	A.R.A.			oil	NPGL	F043
Curtis, Cyrus H. K.	1850/1933	publisher			oil		F044
Phila.					oil		F045
Dana, Charles Edmund,study	1843/1914	art crtitic			oil		F045
group port. Thouron,							
Dana, Hamilton,Welsh					oil	PAFA	F046
park painter(plein air)					oil	HB	F047
(Drew-Parish), Mrs. Dorothy							F048
Draughm, Marion					oil		F049
at the dressing table							
du Maton, Jean (port. of							
a lady &)					pas		F050
Edmonds, Franklin Spencer	1874/1945	lawyer			oil		F051
Phila.State Senator;							
Central H. S.faculty;							
expert, Tax System;							
Edmonds, Obermayer,							
Rebman.							
Edwards, Mrs. Myles					oil	SHWRZ	F052
(Alice Rowley) &							
Mrs. Maud Strickland							
(Maud/Muffin) at piano,dau. of Joseph Rowley							

Name	Dates	Description	Col	Year	Medium	Loc	No.
Flammarion, Nicol Camille	1842/1925	astronomer			draw		F053
France					pas		F054
					pas		F055
					oil		F056
Ford, Edward Onslow	1852/1901	sculptor	B012	1897	pas		F057
		A.R.A.			graph	NPGL	F058
in his studio					oil		F059
Ford, (Master) Wolfram				(1890)	trad.oil		F060
Geikie, Sir Archibald	1835/1924	geology			oil		F061
Ph.D.							
King George V	1865/1936	England	B012	1911	pas	HB	F062
					lith	BM	F063
					engr	DC	F064
					char	BM	F065
Gifford, (S.R.)		artist					F066
Gilbert, Sir Alfred	1854/1934	sculptor	B012	(1920)	cryn	NPGL	F067
Gladstone, Mrs. Catherine				(1893)	pas		F068
(nee:Glynne) at Home		P. M.s			oil		F069
dau. Sir Stephen Gly.		wife					
Gladstone, Baron Henry N.	1852/1935	Gov.Gen.	B012	(1916)	pas		F070
Gladstone, Rev.Steven E.	1844/1920	Rector	B012	(1914)	pas		F071
Hawarden & Barrowby,					engr		F072
Lincs.							
Gladstone, Wm. Ewart	1809/1898	P. M.	B012	(1891)	oil	Lux	F073
					engr	Lux	F074
Rt. Hon.,M.P.at DowningSt.					oil	PAFA	F075
above sketch at Hawarden					oil		F076
above Editing Bishop					wc	HB	F077
Butler's works at H.					oil	TL-1	F078
In The Library, Hawarden					o/w	BW	F079
W.E. G. at his desk					wc		F080
Mr. W. E. G. writing w							
momentary head study,c.							F081
Gladstone,Temple of Peace					oil		F082
Gladstone, W. E., bust			B012	1917	clay		F083
Gladstone, Wm. G. C.	1885/1915	M. P.	B012	1914	pas		F124
Glover, Charles Carroll	1846/1936	banker			oil		F084
Glover, C. C., mature				1930	oil		F085
Glover, C.C., sm. prt.	Washington, D. C.			1901	oil		F086
Haggard, Sir Henry Rider	1856/1925	legal			pas		F087
		scholar					
Halifax, Lord Charles							
Lindley Wood	1839/1934	writer	B012		oil		F088
Halsbury, Lord Harding							
Edward Gifford;	1852/1930	judge					
Esher,Lord Reginald							
Baliol Brett;							
Fry, Lord William;							
Lindley, Lord.*	(1853/1939)	judge					

360

(=Court of Appeals)				card	oil		F089
			B012		oil		F090
Hamilton, Mrs. Clara	1855/1936	wife			oil	PMA	F091
plumed hat							
IN: Tears				1879	o/w	PAFA	F092
IN: Tears					pas	Iver	F093
IN: Lady (no facial							
details on ground,							
playing w child)					oil	L195	F094
IN: Lady weeping					pas		F096
Hamilton, Caroline D.	1826/1915	mother			pas		F097
above, head study			# 233		oil	HB	F098
above			#710 SJH		oil	HB	F099
above					oil		F100
above					litho	NYPL	F101
above					litho	NYPL	F102
above					pas		F103
(Mother & child=							
George)					oil	APA	F104
Hamilton, George, M.D.	1808/1885	father	B012	gone	oil		F105
sketch					grph	PCMS	F106
Hamilton, George Hall	1884/1935	astronomer		(1922)	oil	JP	F107
at desk,w two							
globes							
as child, dog (Belle)					oil	JP	F108
as child			SJH		brnz		F109
as 3 yr old child					oil	HB	F110
pulling unseen toy					oil	HB	F111
velvet suit							
with Nora King					oil		F112
with girl under tree					pas		F113
Hamilton, John McLure	1853/1936	artist			oil		F114
chest length							
as wood cut					engr		F115
Top hat, cape		self			oil	HB	F116
full length					oil		F117
self, mother, child					oil		F118
Harris, Brian (child on							
horse)		Vanity					
		Fair?			oil		F119
Hartrick, Archibald S.	1865/1950	artist			lith		F120
English watercolor							
Henderson, Helen Weston		critic		(1911)	pas		F121
Hilder, D.				(1898)			F122
Hitchcock, George	1850/1913	artist		(1890)	wc	PAFA	F123
American wc					oil		F125
House, Colonel Edward				1919	pas	HB	F126
Mandell(President	1858/1938	diplomat		1919	pas	HB	F127
Wilson's Peace representative,			B012	1919	oil		F128
Paris)				1919	oil		F129

Huxley, John (Aldous)   188./191.   oil   HB   F130
    son of Leonard H.,
    St. Andrews Univ.;
    former asst. to Prof.
    Lewis Campbell.
Irving, Sir Henry   1838/1905   actor   B012   1887   pas   F131
    first knighted
    actor; scholar;
    Jewish
Jack, William, MA,   1834/1924   Prof.   P. P.   1903   IS   F132
    LL.D., D. Sc.,Mathe-
    matics, Astronomy,
    Glasgow,Publisher,
    MacMillan & Co.
                                                               engr   F133
Johns(t)on, Edward Hine 1872/1944   artist   F134
    CBE, calligrapher,
    designer of letters
Kelvin, Lord William
    Thomson,FRS   1824/1907   scientist P. P.   1903   IS   F135
    Irish mathematician,
    physicist, inventor   engr   F136
Kennedy, Mrs. Ethel
    Campbell, wife of
    Myles,* with her son 1862/1928*
    in her arms as :
    "Madonna & child."
    She was dau. of
    Joseph Rowley. Her
    husband trained at School
    of Mines; chaired Iron &
    Steel co.; He was high
    Sheriff, They resided in
    Flintshire.   1892   oil   F137
Lehmann, Rudolf   1819/1905   painter   1902   oil   F138
                                   author
Leighton, Lord   B012   (1885)   pas   F139
    Frederick, P.R.A. 1830/1896   painter   1885   oil   F140
Leslie, either Mr. or
    Mrs. (Robert)   F141
Lindley, Nathaniel   judge   1925   lith   F142
    first Baron
Lloyd-George, David   1863/1945   P. M.   1919   pas   F143
    Welsh lawyer,
    statesman
Ludington, Charles   1866/1927   attorney   1919   oil   F144
    (Henry), VP, Curtis
    Publishing Co., Phila.
    Ardmore resident.
Ludington, Mrs. C. H.   oil   F145

Name	Dates	Occupation	Year	Medium	Location	No.
Machiavelli, Nicol	1550	author	(1920)	lith		F146
				draw		F147
Manning, Henry Edward		Cardinal	1890	pas		F148
Palace Westminster			1890	pas	PAFA	F149
XI 3.			1890	oil		F150
Marburg, Edgar, C.E.,	1864/1918	Prof.	(1916)	oil	UP	F151
D.Sc.		author				
Marwick, Sir James, M.D.				oil		F152
May, Phil	1864/1903	artist				F153
Punch, Graphic.						
Melvin, Sir John	1879/1952			oil		F154
metals industry,						
humanitarian,						
Catholic						
Meredith, George	1828/1909	novelist		oil	PAFA	F155
British poet				pas		F156
				card		F157
				lith		F158
Merritt, Anna Lea	1844/19..	painter		oil		F159
Mrs. Henry, Phila.				satire		F160
England						
Mitchell, Silas Weir,						
M.D.	1829/1914	scientist		oil	UP	F161
Monkhouse, Wm. Cosmo	1840/1901	critic		oil	NPGL	F162
poet				pas		F163
Oakley, Mrs. Arthur						
Edmond				oil		F164
Packard, Charles Stuart						
Wood, Phila.	1860/1937	capitalist		oil		F165
Episcopalian						
Paluchin, flagellation						
of Madame				pas		F166
Pennell, Joseph	1860/1926	illustrator	(1926)	pas	Welsh	F167
at etching press			1913	oil		F168
in studio			1913	oil		F169
Pennell, Mrs. Elizabeth						
Robins (Mrs. J.)			(1936)	oil		F170
Plomer, Colonel			1919			F171
Pollock, Sir Edward						
James, M.D.	1841/1930	lawyer		oil		F172
Porter, Wm. Wagener	1856/1928	judge		oil		F173
PA Superior Court,						
Phila., R.						
				oil		F174
				wc		F175
Raffaelli, Jean						
Francois, French	1850/1924	painter		oil		F176
inventor						

Richards, Wm. Trost	1833/1905	painter		oil	PAFA	F177
Phila.				pas	HB	F178
				lith		F179
Riche, George Inman	1833/191.	lawyer	1902	oil	CHS	F180
Ph.D., 4th Prexy						
Central H. S.,						
Phila., teacher,						
Army paymaster						
Robinson, Robert Pyle	1969/1939	Governor	1928	oil	DE	F181
R., Presbyterian		cousin				
Rochefort, Victor						
Henri, Ph.D.	1831/1913	editor		oil		F182
French journalist,						
politician						
Ross, James,	1848/1913	railway contractor				
philanthropist		capitalist	1916	oil		F183
Canadian Lennoxville School,		Montreal				
(Rowley, Joseph, et ux)			1881	oil		F184
						F185
(Sandburg, Carl)						F186
Seton, Robert	1839/1927	Archbishop	(1912)	lith		F187
Dean, U.S.						
Monsignori,						
chamberlain to						
Pope Pius IX				wc		F188
Shearer, Sir John	1843/1908	engineer	P.P.	1903	IS	F189
Glasgow				engr		F190
			P.P.	lith		F191
Simpson, Alexander						
Carson, Jr.	1855/1935	judge	1924	oil		F192
seated						
Simpson, Mr. & Mrs.		wife		oil		F193
tea service						
Spencer, Herbert	1820/1903	author	1890	oil		F194
English engineer,						
economist, biologist,						
psychologist,						
sociologist						
Stewart, Wm. Morris	1827/1905	Senator	(1901)	oil		F195
U.S. Senator, NV						
Stille, Alfred Owen,						
M.D., Phila.	1813/1900	scholar	(1890)	oil		F196
Story, John	1835/19..	Principal	(1903)	IS		F197
Glasgow University				engr		F198
			P.P.	lith		F199
Swan, John Macallan	1847/1910	sculptor		oil		F200
English water-						
colorist, feline						
painter						

```
Strickland, Mrs. Maud
    Rowley                                                      oil        F201
Taylor, John
    Madison, M.D.    1855/1931    artist                        oil        F202
    Phila. scholar,
    friend of President
    Theodore Roosevelt
    on range,1886
Taylor, Mrs. J. M.
    Emily Heyward
    Drayton, Phila.              curator                        oil        F203
    Museum of Art
Thomson, David Croal 1855/1930  critic            B012         oil        F204
    art expert, editor
    ART JOURNAL
Thouron, Henry Joseph 1851/1915  Prof.            B012         oil        F205
    in his studio                                              oil        F206
                                                               oil    HB  F207

Tolstoy, Count Leo   1828/1910   novelist                      pas        F208
Trask, Mrs. John
    Ellingwood
    Donnell, director
    Art Schools of San
    Francisco, San Diego,
    Milwaukee, Phila.
    (PAFA)Marion Booth                                         pas        F209
Tuttle, (Daniel
    Sylvester)       1837/1923   Bishop                        oil        F210
    MI, Protestant
    Episcopal
Tyndale, Walter      (Courtier)                                           F211
    Frederick Roofe  1856/1943   artist  in uniform  (1915)               F212
Tyndall, John, FRS   1820/1893   scientist         (1890)      oil    RS  F213
    Prof. of Chemistry                                         oil    ..  F214
    Natural Philosophy                                         pas        F215
                                                               lith       F216

Unwin, Thomas Fisher 1848/1935   publisher                     oil        F217
                                                               oil        F218
                                                               oil        F219

Vaux, Richard        1816/1895   Mayor             (1890)      oil        F220
    Phila. attorney,                                           pas        F221
    Congressman, U.S.                                          wc         F222
    attache to London,                                         lith       F223
    penologist, President                                      rprd       F224
    PAFA
Watts, George        1817/1904   artist            (1890)      pas        F225
    Frederick, R.A.,                                           oil        F226
    O.M., D.C.L.,
    LL.D.
```

```
Werner, Anton
   Alexander von    1843/1915    Prof.
   Court painter,
   Berlin; Antwerp
   Academy, member;
   Bismarck's portrait.                        (1891)         oil  HB   F227
```

GENRE

```
L'Academie pour Rire(cover)                               PAFA F349
          1                                                    F350
          2                                                    F351
          3                                                    F352
          4                                                    F353
          5                                                    F354
          6                                                    F355
          7                                                    F356
          8                                                    F357
          9                                                    F358
         10                                                    F359
         11                                                    F360
         12                                                    F361
         13                                                    F362
         14                                                    F363
         15                                                    F364
         16                                                    F365
         17                                                    F366
         18                                                    F367
         19                                                    F368
         20                                                    F369
         21                                                    F370
         22                                                    F371
         23                                                    F372
         24                                                    F373
         25                                                    F374
         26                                                    F375
         27                                                    F376
         28                                                    F377
         29                                                    F378
         30                                                    F379
         31                                                    F380
         32                                                    F381
         33                                                    F382
         34                                                    F383
         35                                                    F384
         36                                                    F385
         37                                                    F386
         38                                                    F387
```

Title	#	Year	Medium	Cat
Old Pioneer				F430
Resignation				F442
Sculptor's Studio, The			pas	F450
(ship) Old Ironsides	#32	1905		F443
Shoe, A man's...& spat		1890	pas	F444
Slipper, The			pas	F445
Sunshine & Shadow, The				F451
Passing Show, The			pas	F452
Passing Shadow, A			pas	F453
Shimmer			pas	F454
Slumber				F455
Snow Ball, The				F456
Spring, The			pas	F457
After Storm			pas	F458
Syren, The			pas	F459
Changable Taffeta			pas C.	F466
Taffeta Changeant				
Tea Party, The				F461
Terrace, Figures on			wc	F465
Happy Thought, A				F460
La Toilette			pas	F468
Tomb in Bath Abbey, The				F469
Tulle Bow, The				F462
Tulle Frock, The				F463
Tulle Sleeve, The				F464
Victory				F465
Vivisection		1880	oil	F466
above, copper engraving & mezzotint by Tomkins, Charles John after H		1883	engrv	F1149
Old Welsh Woman		1899	pas	F467
			lith	F468
			rprd	F469
Wind, the			pas Iver	F470
One Sport of Women			M	
Un jeu de Dames				
I won't!			sat PAFA	F471
Watercolors, study in				F472
Woman, sketch of... fac left 3/4 rear view				F473
Woman, portrait profile of a				F474
Miss E		1870		F475
Lady, portrait of a		1874	oil w	F476
above				F477
Lady, portrait of a		1912	pas	F478
Carol & a Lady			pas	F479
above				F480
Woman, head of #1				
#2				
Lady of Fashion, A		1879	oil	F481
Elegant Lady			pas JP	F482
Figure Study : Female seated, head lowered on arm (dancer series)			pas JP	F483
Model seated, clothed in white				F484

Two Women Reading, Murestead (cf W. T. Richards)		pas PAFA		F485
Three	1914	pas		F486
Little Red Cap				F487
Standing Woman	#30 L.P 1910	pas		F488
Lady with (yellow) Fan (yellow Gown, Blue Shawl, Broach, two rings)	1901	oil	JP	F492
Woman in Evening Dress	1915	pas	JP	F493
Woman in Long Dress		pas		F494
Portrait of a Woman		pas		F495
in a Green Dress		pas		F496
in a Green Robe		oil		F497
Woman in Brown		pas		F498
Lady in Yellow Hat, portrait of #1		pas		F499
#2		pas		F500
Study #1 (woman clothed to waist from left shoulder)				F501
(female) Model (dressing)		pas	JP	F502
Fashion Model		pas		F503
Lady Holding Dress Out		pas		F504
Academie pour Rire, L'	1878	engr PAFA		
				F509--F551
The Bailie/Evening Times	1898-1905	engr		
				F552-F873
Prominent Profiles #1-#26	1902-1903	engr		F874-F899
above #27-#136		engr		F900-F1010
above, originals #1-#26		ink		
		sepia		F1011-F1037
above, originals				F1038-F1148

APPENDIX

[Woodgatherer's donkeys, landscape in Spain, c. 1883]
Oil 24" x 36" from England.

TABLE **A**. HAMILTON'S UNTOLD STORY. A search of the current
literature of art history concluded that reports of the
artist's contributions were not cited under more than thirty
index categories.

AMERICAN/BRITISH : ART CRITICISM
BOOK ILLUSTRATORS
CARTOONISTS
CARICATURISTS
EDITORIAL CARTOONISTS
DOCUMENTARY ARTISTS
GRAPHIC JOURNALISTS
ILLUSTRATORS, 1880--1930
IMPRESSIONIST PAINTERS
REALIST PAINTERS

ANTWERP ARTISTS
EDWARDIAN ARTISTS
GEORGIAN ARTISTS
GLASGOW ARTISTS

HISTORY OF AMERICAN/BRITISH : CARTOONS
ENGRAVING
LITHOGRAPHY
MODERN PAINTERS
OIL PAINTERS
PASTELISTS
POSTAL CARDS
SCULPTURE
WATERCOLORISTS

PENNSYLVANIA PAINTERS
PHILADELPHIA ARTISTS
VICTORIAN ARTISTS

TABLE B. DOCUMENTED HAMILTON ART. His work was placed into CLASSES (Content or Technique). This study done in 1992 sampled 1,050 works. A review of the numbers vs class reveals how each class contributed significantly to his reputation as an artist. (N=52)

	class (code : pie)	0	<4	<9	<19	<99	<500
					frequency found		
1	Animals (A)					49	
2	Advertisements			?			
3	Book Illustrations (BI)				15		
4	Bond Vignettes/borders	0					
5	Sculpture(bronze/clay,SC)			4			
6	Calendars	0					
7	Cartoons (Ct)						102
8	Cyphers/monograms		?				
9	Chalks		2				
10	Charcoals (Ca)		1				
11	Cigarette Cards	0					
12	Children's Portraits (Ch)				16		
13	Greeting Cards (C)		2				
14	Crayons		+				
15	Currency (portraits for)	0					
16	Diplomas	0					
17	Drink(ers, D)				+		
18	Etchings (E)					52	
19	Ethnics				+		
20	Fans	0					
21	Mems. for Madame (Fashion)				+		
22	Floral devises		+				
23	Genre oils (Ge)						101
24	Graphites (Pe)		2				
25	Interiors (I)			+			
26	Landscape (oils/wc, L)					+	
27	Lithographs (Lit)						111+
28	Mastheads,Logos		?				
29	Marine (Ma)			5			
30	Minature oils [1870s]				+		
31	Monochromes [1921,Mo]					45	
32	Monotypes	0					
33	Murals	0					
34	Graphic Journalism (DA)						220+
35	Nudes,semi-nudes		+				
36	Pastels (PA)						400+

37	Ink/Sepia (IS)					132
38	Politicians/Statesman				+	
39	Men in oils (O)					80
40	Postage	0				
41	Postal Cards		?			
42	Posters	0				
43	Clerics/ Religious themes			15		
44	Royals				+	
45	Souvenior Cards (Sc)		4			
46	Satires					46
47	Smoking				+	
48	Still Life (SL)					+
49	Stock Certificates	0				
50	Theater Drapes (Te)		5			
51	Watercolors (wc)					+
52	Women (all techniques)					67

TABLE C. HAMILTON STUDY COLLECTION, 1990--1993.
Alphanumerics refer to inventories in the Appendix following
Art Catalog.

```
Hamilton's Works cataloged                         1,050
     B & W / Color photographs)                      153
     xerographic               )AOOO                 488
     Percentage of Images retrieved                   61
     Measurements of sizes (sample for)              336
     Prices realized (sample for)                    125


Hamilton Memorabilia            COOO                  22
     Documents                  GOOO                 105
     Photos/xeroxes(misc.)      MOOO                  34

Reference Materials assembled :
     Acknowledgements for book                       100
     Associations,Clubs,Galleries,Museums             64
     Dictionaries/Encyclopedias DOOO (biography)     171
     Books citing H             BOOO                  34
     Chapter Notes                                   581
     Cities for exhibitions                           22
     Critics' opinions                                13
     Diaries citing (Pennell/Whistler)                 2
     Direct observations on H art                     86
     Exhibition catalogs        EOOO                 117
     Friends                                          42
     Genealogies                                       3
     Genre themes                                    220
     Honors for H                                     19
     Interviewees for book                            19
     Journals/Magazines on H    JOOO                  59
     Letter Collection          LOOO                 229
     News stories               NOOO                 100
     Owners Cumulative List     HOOO                 119
     Publications of H                               438
     Expeditions for Hamiltoniana                     11
     Sitters to H                                    128
     Sources : documents/art                          55
                 letters                              30
     Speeches by Hamilton                              2
     Unpublished materials      UOOO                  32
     Unavailable: Journals/Diaries of H
                 Ledgers of H
                 Photographic studies by H
                 Sketch books of H
```

TABLE D. HAMILTON'S EDUCATION documented, 1858--1896.
         (N=9)

(1858--1864) There is fragmentary evidence [B012] that
George Hamilton, M. D., the artist's father, directed
McLure's home study in ART APPRECIATION and GREAT LITERATURE
in several languages.

(1866) Hamilton was placed in the after hours drawing school
of *George W. Holmes* where he met Henry Joseph Thouron,
another pupil.

1870 Hamilton attended the prestigious *Central High School*
when *Dr. George Inman Riche* was its fourth president.
There, Hamilton received a rigorous education equivalent to
a bachelor's degree by the time he graduated in February's
63rd Class. The schedule included classes in drawing &
penmanship each year.

      Hamilton was baptised (March 19th) at Tenth
Presbyterian Church located at 17th & Spruce Sts.

      Hamilton attended a six week course, starting in
October, at the temporary campus, P.A.F.A., located on
Chestnut St. His teacher was *Professor Christain Schuessele*
(1824--1879). P.A.F.A.'s catalog (1905) listed Hamilton as
a student there.

1873--1875 Hamilton attended the prestigious Antwerp Royal
Academy Art School in Belgium at night for two and one half
years. He was taught by *Professor J. H. F. van Lerius*
(1823--1876) of Holland, *Prof. P-C Beaufaux* and *Director N.
de Keyser.* There were generally less than six Americans out
of 1,500 students attending each year.

1896 Hamilton identified as a student of *Professor J. L.
Gerome* (1824--alive 1884) at the Ecole des Beaux Arts of
Paris. Hamilton's first brief period of instruction in the
Paris school was probably during 1875 on his way back to
the *American Centennial Exposition.*

TABLE E : HAMILTON'S FAMILY

```
---------------------------        ---------------------------
I   JOHN HAMILTON, SR.   I        I   JAMES DELAPLAINE  I
I      (Ireland)         I        I      (Delaware)     I
I     17(80)--1858       I        I     1795--187(1)    I
I   Grocer/Wine Merchant/I        I   Lawyer/Politician I
I   Real Estate Speculator        I   Bank Director     I
I   wife : Elizabeth Hall I        I   wife : Mary Kirk  I
I                        I        I      (Hendrickson)  I
---------------------------        ---------------------------
            I                                  I
            I                                  I
---------------------------        ---------------------------
I   GEORGE HAMILTON, M. D. I        I   CAROLINE DELAPLAINE I
I          (PA)          I        I          (DE)       I
I        1808--1885      I--------------I   182(7)--1915     I
I   Physician/Bibliophile I        I   House wife        I
I     Art Collector      I    I    I                     I
---------------------------    I    ---------------------------
                               I
                               I
                ---------------------------
                I   JOHN McLURE HAMILTON   I
                I          (PA)          I
                I        1853--1936      I
                I   Painter/Illustrator  I
                I   wife : Clara Raiguel  I
                ---------------------------
                               I
                               I
                ---------------------------
                I   GEORGE HALL HAMILTON   I
                I        (England)       I
                I        1884--1935      I
                I        Astronomer      I
                I   wife : Elizabeth L.   I
                I      Williams (N.H.)    I
                I      Mathematician     I
                I       1879--1981       I
                ---------------------------
```

TABLE F : IN-LAWS

```
-------------------------------------       -------------------------------------
|    WILLIAM MAGEE RAIGUEL      |       |         JOSEPH ELLIS          |
|         (IRELAND)            |       |          (WALES)              |
|         1799--1874           |       |         1797--185(6)          |
| Farmer/Dry Goods Merchant    |       |         Shoemaker             |
|    wife: Elizabeth D.        |       |       wife: Lydia             |
-------------------------------------       -------------------------------------
              |                                          |
              |                                          |
-------------------------------------       -------------------------------------
|      JOSEPH W. RAIGUEL        |       |      SARAH C. ELLIS           |
|           (PA)               |       |      aka=Sally,(PA)           |
|        1831--187(1)          |-------|        1831--1912             |
|          Clerk               |   |   |       House wife             |
-------------------------------------   |   -------------------------------------
                                    |
                                    |
                                    |
           -------------------------------------------
           |        CLARA AUGUSTA RAIGUEL            |
           |               (PA)                     |
           |            1854--1936                  |
           | Hamilton's wife/George's mother        |
           |          Artist & Model                |
           -------------------------------------------
```

TABLE G. THE HOUSES, 1853--1936. Hamilton lived in numerous residences, hotels, etc. during his career accompanied by his wife, various family members, and servants. (N=30) Data summarized here includes documented date, location, and commentary.

1853 1600 Summer St., Phila.   Family ownership, 1846/1938

1870 1123 Chestnut St., Phila.   Artist rented room near temporary PAFA facilities

1881 41A Cathcart Rd., London   Early in year

     6 William St., Albert Gate, London   Team rented apartment, July/September

1884 GREY HOUSE, 102 Hornton St., corner Abbey Mews Kensington, London   George Hall, son, born in rented house

1889 ALPHA HOUSE, Regent Park, London, N. W.   Sheridan Ford used part of home, *April 28*

1888/ STONE HALL, Wolfscastle,
1931   R.S.O., Pembrokeshire, Wales   Team owned summer home, sport shooting & fishing

1892   Sarah Bernhardt sublet ALPHA HOUSE

1898 MURESTEAD, 6 Groves End Rd., London, N. W.   Many important portraits painted here

1901 1927 "G" St., Washington, D. C.   Visited brother-in-law, other friends, *Feb. 21st*

1902 HOTEL STENTON, Phila.   Temporary residence

1903 (57 Hope St.) Glasgow   Newspaper artist
     93 Hope St.   Documented studio

190(6) St. John's Woods, London   Anna Lea Merritt visited McLure's studio

1908 3 Tudor Lodge Studios, Albert St., Regent Park, N. W., London

(NOTE: several John M. Hamiltons lived in Glasgow including
       an architect.)

1911	HERMITAGE, Kingston-on-Thames, Portsmouth Rd., Surrey	Real home for team at last!
1912	100 Hollywell, OXFORD UNIVERSITY	Mailing address c/o son George in *June*
	1832 N. 24th St., Phila.	Mother-in-law ill, team visited brother-in-law, *Joseph Lloyd Raiguel*
1912/ 1920	Warwickshire	Vacations
1917	RITZ CARLTON HOTEL, Phila.	June
	BILTMORE HOTEL, NYC	December 27th
1918	1904 Spruce St., Phila.	January 15/25
	RITZ CARLTON HOTEL	March 18th
1919	1700 Walnut St., Phila.	Studio
	England	August
1920	THE WHARF	Residence of the *Prime Minister* & Mrs. Asquith, September
1921	CAMP ELSINORE, Adirondak Mts., NY	Vacation, May
1922	London	Fifty years concluded D'Albe rented HERMITAGE
1923	Jamaica	First visit ended March 23rd
1924	Phila.	ART ALLIANCE OF
1925	England	

1927	GOVERNOR'S MANSION Delaware	November
1928	Jamaica	Second visit
1930	Jamaica	Third voyage, to be resident
1931	HAMILTON OBSERVATORY Mandeville, Jamaica IONA, Mandeville	Guests of son, George, & daughter-in-law, Langdon
1934	HAMILTON HALL, Mandeville	Team's last residence

TABLE H.   ART ASSOCIATIONS, CLUBS, GALLERIES,
                  MUSEUMS, ETC. 1876--1936. AMERICAN & EUROPEAN
                  Institutions where Hamilton's activity was
                  documented. (N=65)

AGNEW GALLERY, London.
AMERICAN FEDERATION OF ARTS, Washington, D.C. 1917
ANGLO-AMERICAN EXPOSITION, 1913
ACADEMIE d'ANVERS, Antwerp, Belgium. 1873--1875
ARDEN STUDIOS, INC., NYC. 1917
ART ALLIANCE OF PHILA., (honorary member) 1918, 1923/24
ART ASSOCIATION OF PHILA., Advisory Council member

BARBIZON HOUSE, London. 1927, 1931
BOUSSARD, VALLADON & CO., London, 1893
(BROADBENT & TAYLOR), Phila. 1884
BROOKLYN (NY) ART ASSOCIATION, Mr. Fix. 1877, 1910, 1925
BURLINGTON HOUSE, London. 1891
JAMES, BOURLET & SONS, LTD., London. 1912

CARNEGIE ART MUSEUM, Pittsburgh, PA 1897, 1907, 1910, 1913
CENTRAL HIGH SCHOOL, Phila. 1866--1870, 1902
CENTURY CLUB, NYC. 1916
CHICAGO (IL) ART INSTITUTE, 1896, 1897, 1917
CINCINNATI (OH) ART MUSEUM, 1897, 1916
CORCORAN GALLERY OF ART, Washington, D. C. 1917, 1921

EARLS COURT GALLERY, London. 1897
ECOLE DES BEAUX ARTS, Paris

HENRY GRAVES & CO., London. 1897
GLASGOW INSTITUTE OF FINE ARTS, Scotland. 1914
GRAFTON GALLERY, London. 1915, 1929

HACKLEY ART GALLERY, Muskegon, MI. 191(7)
CHRISTOFFER HANNEVIG FOUNDATION, 1913

KINGSTON ART CLUB, Surrey, England. 1918
KNIGHTSBRIDGE, England. 1899
M. KNOEDLER GALLERIES, NYC. 1917, 1919

LUXEMBOURG PALACE, Paris, France. 1892, 1913

MANCHESTER FREE LIBRARY, Mandeville, Jamaica. 1936
MINNEAPOLIS (MN) INSTITUTE OF ARTS. 1917

NATIONAL ACADEMY OF DESIGN, NYC. 1877, 1878, 1890, 1918,
                              1921
NATIONAL PORTRAIT GALLERY, London.
NATIONAL PORTRAIT GALLERY, Washington, D.C.
NEW ENGLISH ART CLUB, London. 1890, 1903

PAN-AMERICAN EXPOSITION, Buffalo, NY. 1901
PANAMA-PACIFIC EXPOSITION, San Francisco, CA. Advisory
      Committee; Jury of Awards. 1915
      Exclusive one-man-show in special gallery.
PARIS EXPOSITION, France. 1878
PARIS SALON, 1890, 1892, 1893, 1895, 1896, 1898, 1899,
                     1902, 1903
PASTEL SOCIETY, London. Honorary member, 1893, 1921, 1926
PENNSYLVANIA ACADEMY OF FINE ARTS, Phila., student shows
                              Permanent Collection
                              Fellowship of, member
                                  recepient 1909/10
                              Vice President 1901,1904
                              President, 1918--1921
PHILA. CLUB, 1915
PHILA. SKETCH CLUB, 1876--1878, 1901, 1918--1936
PHILA. SOCIETY OF ARTISTS, 1879
PHILA. WATERCOLOR CLUB, Honorary member, 1901--1936
PHILOBIBLON CLUB, 1324 Walnut St., Phila. 1903 ff
POST PANAMA-PACIFIC EXHIBITION. 1916
PRINT MAKERS SOCIETY OF CA, Los Angeles. 1915 ff

ROCHESTER MEMORIAL ART GALLERY, NY 1916
ROSENBACH & CO., NYC/Phila., 1934
ROYAL ACADEMY OF ARTS, London. 1884, 1890, 1891, 1893, 1899,
                     1900, 1908
ROYAL HIBERNIAN ACADEMY, Dublin, 1902, 1917
ROYAL INSTITUTE GALLERIES, London. 1926
ROYAL INSTITUTE OF OIL PAINTERS, London. 1901
ROYAL INSTITUTE OF PAINTERS IN WATERCOLOUR, London. 1901
ROYAL SCOTISH ACADEMY. 1901
ROYAL SOCIETY OF BRITISH ARTISTS. 1901
ROYAL SOCIETY OF PORTRAIT PAINTERS. 1891, 1906
                        The Council of,
                        Honorary member, 1933

ST. ANDREWS SOCIETY, Phila. 1920
ST. JUDE'S GALLERY, Whitechapel, London. 1891
ST. LOUIS (MO) UNIVERSAL EXPOSITION. Louisana Purchase. 1904
SENEFELDER CLUB, London. 1913

SOCIETY OF AMERICAN ARTISTS, Phila. 1880
SOUTHPORT EXPOSITION, England. 1912
SPINKS GALLERY, London. 1934

TATE GALLERY, Millbank
THAMES VALLEY ARTS CLUB, Surrey. 1917
ARTHUR TOOTH & SONS GALLERY. 1901
TWENTY-ONE GALLERY. Adelphi House, London. 1899

WALKER ART GALLERY, Liverpool. 1920
WORLD'S COLUMBIAN EXPOSITION, Chicago. 1893

TABLE J. HAMILTON'S EXHIBITION CITIES, 1876--1936. (N=29)

Canada, (Montreal)
        (Ottawa)

France, Paris   *Exposition*
                Luxembourg Palace, works purchased for
                        permanent collection
                Salon

Germany, Berlin   1910
         Dusseldorf 1911
         (Koln)
         Munich   1890, 1891

Italy,   Rome   1905, 1911, 1912, 1914
         Venice 1905, 1909

Jamaica, Kingston
         Mandeville 1924, 1931, 1934, 1936

United Kingdom, England, Kingston-on-Thames
                        Liverpool *Walker Art Gallery*
                        London   *Anglo-American Exposition,*
                                    1914
                                 Barbizon House
                                 Burlington House
                                 Knightsbridge Exposition,
                                    1899
                                 National Portrait Gallery
                                 Royal Academy of Arts
                                 Royal Institute Galleries
                                   Pastel Society
                                 Royal Society
                                 Southport Exposition
                                 Tate Gallery, Millbank

                Ireland, Dublin

                Scotland, Glasgow *Art Gallery/Museum*
                                   Kelvingrove St.
                                   Mitchell Library Glasgow
                                   Collection

                        Fife, *University of St. Andrews*
                              Art History Dept.

United States,   Brooklyn, NY   *Art Association
                                Museum*
                 Buffalo, NY   *Pan-American Exposition, 1901,*
                                    medal
                 Chicago, IL   *Art Institute
                                World's Columbian Exposition,*
                                    1893, medal
                 Cincinnati, OH *Art Museum*
                 Dover, DE   *State House,* 1928
                 Los Angeles, CA
                 Minneapolis, MN
                 Muskegon, MI
                 New York City *National Academy of Design*
                 Philadelphia, PA *Art Alliance of
                                Central High School*
                                   collection
                                *Pennsylvania Academy of
                                   Fine Arts* exhibitions
                                      medal
                                      permanent
                                         collection
                 Pittsburgh, PA *Carnegie Art Museum*
                 Rochester, NY
                 St. Louis, MO *Universal Exposition,* 1904
                                      medal
                 San Francisco, CA *Panama-Pacific Exposition,*
                                   1915 one man show
                                   Mrs. Mary Harriman's
                                   purchase
                 Washington, D. C. *Corcoran Gallery of Art
                                National Portrait Gallery*
                                   one of the first 25
                                   pioneering artists
                                   selected

TABLE K. PROFESSIONAL HONORS FOR HAMILTON, 1878--1934.
      (N=20)

1878 Paris, France   American's oil *"Le Rire"* aka : *"Cerise"*
                     reproduced as a full page engraving in
                     the official catalog for the *Universal
                     Exposition.*

1892 Paris, France   Oil portrait *"Gladstone"* received
                     Honorable Mention, Paris Salon.

                     French government purchased (above) work
                     for *Luxembourg Palace.*

                     Oil exhibited permanently beside
                     Whistler's and Sargent's.

1893 Chicago, IL   As London resident, awarded *gold medal*
                     at *World's Columbian Exposition.*

                     Hamilton served on *Jury of Awards* (Hors
                     concours).

1901 Buffalo, NY   As London resident, awarded his second
                     gold medal at *Pan-American Exposition.*

     Phila., PA   Unique *Sketch Club* elected him to
                     Honorary Membership.

1904 St. Louis, MO   As London resident, awarded his third
                     gold medal at *Universal Exposition.*

                     Hamilton served on *Jury* with Ives, (van
                     Dyke), Pennell, Sargent, and Whistler.

1913 Paris, France   French government commissioned Hamilton
                      to paint *"P. W. Bartlett."*

1914 San Francisco, CA   Appointed *Advisory Committee*
                          member, *Panama-Pacific Exposition.*

1915 San Francisco, CA   One-man-show.
                          Awarded prize.

1918 Phila., PA   P.A.F.A. awarded his fourth *gold medal*
                   for lifetime achievements.

                   Elected President, *The Fellowship,*
                   P.A.F.A.

1919 Washington, D. C.   *Hannevig Foundation* commissioned
                          portrait *"Col. E. M. House"* for
                          embryonal Smithsonian/National
                          Portrait Gallery.

1920 Phila., PA   Reelected President, *The Fellowship,*
                   P.A.F.A.

1933 London, U. K.   *Royal Society of Portrait Painters*
                      elected him to *Honorary Membership.*

1934 Phila., PA   *McClees Galleries* held Retrospective
                   Exhibition.

     New York City   *Rosenbach & Company* exhibited pastels.

TABLE **L**. HAMILTON'S PUBLICATIONS, 1878--193(1).
(N=451)

1878 Phila., PA	*"L'Academie pour Rire,"* a satire of P.A.F.A's annual exhibition.
1898--1905 Glasgow, Scotland	IN: THE BAILIE, cartoons, graphic journalism, & editorial cartoons. N=80
	IN: THE EVENING TIMES, news documentary art, *Prominent Profiles,* etc. N=320
1901 Kilmarnock, Scotland	IN: T. B. Hennel, THE LAY OF ST. ALBAN, A. N. Wallace, Printer. 15 illustrations by Hamilton.
190(3) 93 Hope St., Glasgow	Hamilton, PROMINENT PROFILES. The Artist reprinted & bound 26 luxury lithographs of his series IN: THE EVENING TIMES (Sept., 1902 et seq.). Biographies were added.
1910 London, U.K.	Hamilton pseudonymed *"The Constitutionalist."* Sent three letters to the editor, PALL MALL GAZETTE (Feb. 10 et seq.) on: Reforms proposed for the House of Lords, etc. some times signed with his pseudonym. Reprinted IN: B012.
1911 London	IN: Pennells, 5th ed., THE LIFE OF JAMES McNEILL WHISTLER, (Lippincott. ch 34 pgs. 285-288) Hamilton presented his actual role re: THE GENTLE ART OF MAKING ENEMIES.

1917 New York City	IN: BULLETIN, Metropolitan Museum, Hamilton wrote *"An appreciation of Eakins works."* Exhibition started *Nov. 5th*.
1918 Phila., PA	Hamilton delivered an invited lecture to *The Fellowhip, P.A.F.A.* titled, ART A NECESSITY (*March 12th*).
1919 NYC	IN: VANITY FAIR, the modest Hamilton wrote a full page item, *"AN AMERICAN MASTER OF PASTEL."*
1921 London	Hamilton's MEN I HAVE PAINTED (T. Fisher Unwin, Ltd.) provided forty-eight vignettes about most famous portrait subjects.
1923 London	Artist delivered invited lecture, titled *"THE STATE OF ARTISTS"* at St. Martin's Lane Theatre.
(1931) Mandeville, Jamaica, B.W.I.	Hamilton's *WILLIAM EWART GLADSTONE,* (chapter) from the artist's 1921 book, was reprinted as a pamphlet (West Indian Training College Press.).

TABLE **M** HAMILTON'S LIFETIME ESTIMATED INCOME, 1875--1936.
The facts about the artist's sales receipts, rents,
legacies, grants, interest income, dividend income, etc.
have been assembled from many sources.

SALES   (1 pound = $ 5.00, 1904)

```
    $   30,000.00 Pastels : 100 @ $ 300.00/each
    $    5,000.00 Pastels : Harriman collection, 1915
    $  100,000.00 Oils    : 100 @ $ 1,000.00/each
    $   10,000.00 Watercolors : 100 @ $ 100.00/each
    $    1,500.00 Bronzes : 1 @ $ 1,500.00
    $    1,000.00 Graphites : 100 @ $10.00/each
    $    1,000.00 Prominent Profiles luxury bound
                            lithographs in color
                            : 100 @ $10.00/each
    $      125.00 Postal Card Cartoons : 5 x 250 x
                            $0.10/each
    $  130,000.00 Lithographs : 130 x 100 x $ 10.00/each
    $   10,000.00 Etchings : 20 x 100 x $ 5.00/each
           *       Chalks & Crayons
    $    2,500.00 Souvenir Portrait Cards (Detroit
                            Publishing Company) : 5 x 1,000 x
                            $0.50
           *       Monochromes
    $    1,850.00 Book Illustrations (Wallace Printers) 13 x
                            30 shillings x 10% x 1,000
    $      400.00 Royalties (T. Fisher Unwin, Ltd.) 48 x
                            $ 4.00 x 10% x 1,000
    $    5,000.00 Real Estate, Wales
    $   10,000.00               Kingston-on-Thames
    $   10,000.00               Observatory, Jamaica
    $   10,000.00               Hamilton Hall, Mandeville
```

SERVICES

```
    $      500.00 Honoraria for speeches, gifts
```

SALARY

```
    $    1,000.00 Documentary artist & Photographic artist
    $   10,000.00 London to 1897
    $   10,000.00 Glasgow to 1906
    $   10,000.00 London to 1919
```

RENTAL INCOME

$	200.00	Sarah Bernhardt, 1892 (London month)
$	5,000.00	D'Albe, 1922/1923 (Surrey two years)
$	10,000.00	Doctor's Office/Home (Phila. 40 years)
$	1,500.00	Farm (Montgomery co. 34 years)
$	3,300.00	Seasonal Home (Wales 33 years)
$	5,000.00	Bye, Cheeseman, Smith (Surrey two years)

INVESTMENT INCOME

$	5,000.00	Interest on Legacies, Jackson contract
$	5,000.00	Dividends on Stock Portfolio
$	6,000.00	Interest on *Mercer Fund* Recovery

DIRECT GRANTS-IN-AID

$	1,000.00	From his parents, 1878--1885

LEGACIES

$	51,000.00	*Mercer Fund* Recovery
$	140,000.00	Hamilton family
	*	Raiguel family

CASH

$	2,080.00	Committee Bank Account, 1936, Phila.
$	2,160.00	S. T. Freeman, Auctioneers 1938, Phila.
$	400.00	Relief Fund Phila.
$	610.00	Jackson contract

----

* no data

TABLE N. LEGACIES TO HAMILTON & HIS WIFE, 1874--1921.


```
1874 WILLIAM M. RAIGUEL grandfather          $        **
1883 JOHN C. MERCER, uncle-in-law            $     5,000.00
1886 JOHN HAMILTON,Sr. grandfather           $     3,300.00
     ANN JANE MERCER aunt                     $    50,000.00
                       real estate    *      $    38,408.00
              Mercer Fund Recovery    *      $    68,000.00
                  annual interest on  *      $     3,000.00
     GEORGE HAMILTON, M.D. father            $     7,020.00
1888 CATHERINE HAMILTON  aunt                $     4,100.00
1895 MARGARET HAMILTON    aunt's house       $     7,500.00***
1912 SARAH RAIGUEL mother-in-law             $       200.00
1916 CAROLINE D. HAMILTON  mother            $    19,279.00
1921 ELIZABETH G. DELAPLAINE aunt            $     2,500.00
1936 CLARA A. HAMILTON wife Phila.house      $     3,633.00
                    Mandeville house         $    10,000.00
                    Montgomery co. farm      $     1,200.00
```

```
*    1910 estimate
**   no data
***  gift
```

TABLE O. HAMILTON'S NET WORTH ESTIMATED, 1936. A best case estimate was assembled from a listing of the artist's known assets, liabilities, and expenses.

ASSETS

Principal amount,Mr. Jackson's mortgage	$	1,750.00
Real Estate : *Hamilton Hall*	$	5,250.00
Furnishings @ above, 1931	$	4,000.00
Real Estate (Pembrokeshire, Wales)	$	5,000.00
: Phila., PA 1936 estimate	$	10,500.00
: Zieglerville, PA	$	1,200.00
Drexel & Company, portfolio/ account	$	*
Rare Books	$	500.00
Autographs, historical letters	$	1,000.00
Old Master paintings & drawings	$	3,000.00
Original Hamiltons/reprod.Hamiltons	$	5,000.00
Personal property	$	5,000.00
Three graves, Jamaica	$	1,000.00
Interest, Mr. Jackson's mtg.	$	*

LIABILITIES

Mortgage Interest : *Hermitage*	$	*
: *Hamilton Hall*	$	*
: 2nd mtg.	$	*
Taxes due, Phila. 1931--1936	$	*
Jamaica 1931--1936	$	100.00

EXPENSES

Housing	50 years	$	25,000.00
Meals, Heat, Light	50 years	$	25,000.00
Travel (4 million miles)		$	400,000.00
Education (son: George)		$	5,000.00
Research, Development, *Observatory*		$	20,000.00
Publications (Hamilton, 1921)		$	3,000.00
(George, 1925)		$	1,000.00

TABLE P. DONOR'S TO HAMILTON'S RELIEF FUND and related
matters. Information abstracted from *Thornton Oakley Papers*
(AAA microfiled letters).

1933 P.A.F.A. purchased *"Group Portrait"*	$ 500.00

1934 For placement of bronze busts (Ford's),
      organizing *Retrospective Exhibition*, etc.
      Hamilton offered one pastel to Oakley for
      services given

1935 Mrs. Mary Curtis Bok	$ 50.00
Mrs. Mary Butler	$ 100.00
Mrs. Emerson	$ 10.00
Mrs. Fleischer	$ 10.00
Mrs. Elizabeth R. Pennell	$ 100.00
Mrs. Thouron	$ 25.00
Mrs. J. E. D. Trask	$ 75.00

      (Mr. Oakley sent artist $ 200.00 of
              of the above funds *Nov. 12*)
1936 (Mr. Oakley sent additional $ 200.00
              via U. S. Consul, *Jan. 18*.
          40 pounds = $ 200.00, 1936)
      Hamiltons sought $ 3,000.00 to erect
              memorial library in Mandeville
              for father's rare books, *Jan. 21*
      Philadelphia's Committee Bank balance
              from art sales was $ 2,136.00,
              Mar. 5

Colin Campbell Cooper	$ *
Arthur H. Lea	$ 100.00

      Hamiltons presented *P.A.F.A.* with
              "Tears", the first genre oil done
              in London fifty-seven years
              earlier (1879), Aug.19
      (John McLure Hamilton died, 20:30 PM
              Sept. 10
      Clara Hamilton died, 03:30 AM *Nov.1*)

TABLE **Q**. ART PRICES REALIZED DURING HAMILTON'S CAREER,
1877--1936. Information secured from a survey of sales
results on lithographs, oils, and pastels. (N=63)

$	1,000.00	o	Le Rire	1877	E001, NAD
$	10.00			1878	
$	150.00	o	Gloom	1878	
$	60.00	o	My Janitor	1878	E093, NAD
$	5.00	o	Tears	1879	
$	75.75	p	That Strange Baby	1880	E006
$	75.75	p	The Coquette	1880	
$	2,050.00	o	The New Coat	1881	
$	1,500.00	o	portrait pair	1881	
$	155.00		Little Red Cap	1881	
$	75.75	p	Siesta	1882/3	
$	1,500.00	o	Corn Husker	1890	L006, NAD
$	1,050.00	o	Young Navigator	1890	
$	265.00		Chalk Cliffs	1890	
$	1,575.00	o	Children/Roses	1891	E009
$	525.00		Despair	1892	
$	1,000.00	o	Gladstone @ Down-ing Street	1894	
$	5,000.00	o	Gladstone	1896	Luxembourg
$	3,000.00	o	Nunnery Garden	1896	
$	1,500.00	o	Gladstone writing momentary sketch of head (corner)	1896	E014, Goupil
$	750.00	p	Children in White	1896	
$	1,000.00	p	Prof.John Tyndall	1896	
	60 guineas	p	The Embroiderer	1896	
$	750.00		Breakfast	1896	
$	1,250.00		Geo. F. Watts	1896	
$	1,500.00	p	Cardinal Manning	1896	
$	5,000.00	o	Mr. Gladstone edit-ing works of Bishop Butler	1896	
$	300.00	p	sketch		
$	750.00	p	Mrs. Catherine Glad-stone @ Home		
$	1,500.00	o	Lord F. Leighton		
$	150.00	p	After Storm		
$	200.00		Pugg		
$	300.00		Water Lily		
$	600.00		Despair		
$	500.00		Heiress		John G. Johnson

```
$         75.00 p Woodcock, study of
$        100.00 p Blue, study in
$        500.00 p Bismarck, study of
$      1,750.00 o Childhood
$        250.00 p Sisters
$      1,000.00   The Duet
$      1,750.00   The Nunnery Garden
$        375.00   The Young Master
$        300.00 p The Syren
$         50.00 o Tears
$      2,000.00   In The Library
$        200.00   Child, study of    1896              Goupil
$        300.00 p Cardinal Manning   1900         E028
$                o Dr. Riche          1902
$         27.50   Le nuage qui passe              D023
$                  (1881)             1908
$        155.10   The Listener        1913         E051,Senefelder
$         75.75   Girl Reading        1913
$         33.00   A Blot of Color     1913
$         16.50   framed lithograph   1913
$         11.00   unframed lith       1913
$        200.00   small works         1919         E065, Rosenbach
$         10.00 l A. S. Hartrick      1925
$         15.00 l Girl Weeping        1927
$      1,500.00 o W. T. Richards      1929
$      2,500.00 o Dr.S. W. Mitchell   1930
$        500.00 p                     1930
$        400.00 p C. M. Burns,sketch
$                p                     1933
$        250.00 p W.T. Richards
$         15.00 l
$         10.00 l
$        500.00 o Group Portrait      1936              P.A.F.A.
```

TABLE R. RECENT ART PRICES REALIZED, 1937--1993.
Information collected from published sources was
supplemented with unpublished data about sales prices at
auction for Hamilton's work in oils and pastels. (N=50)

$	65.00	o General Booth		<1> 1938
$	22.00	o Cyrus H. K. Curtis		<1> 1938
$	250.00	o Ludington		<1> 1938
$	5.00	o C. M. Burns, head		
		sketch, study		<1> 1938
$	3.50	Lady, 1874		<1> 1938
$	20.00	o Mother		<1> 1938
$	4.50	Rochefort		<1> 1938
$	60.00	o Joseph Pennell		<1> 1938
$	16.00	C. M. Burns in		
		uniform		<1> 1938
$	6.00	Artist's wife,		
		portrait		<1> 1938
$	25.00	George/Nora		<1> 1938
$	22.50	Geikie		<1> 1938
$	6.00	Man Reading,		
		sketch		<1> 1938
$	3.50	South Snow Ball		<1> 1938
$	3.50	w Roses/Children		<1> 1938
$	1,800.00	o figures		<2> 1940
		still life		<2> 1940
		illustrations		<2> 1940
$	200.00	p		<2> 1940
$	*	p		<3> 1948
$	1,760.00	o Donkey Picture, 1883,s,	14"x18"	<4> 1980
$	419.00	c.e.m Vivisection,1883,s,	24"x17"	<35> 1981
$	1,090.00	o Interior Scene	s, 17"x22"	<5> 1982
$	830.00	p Seminude	1914,s, 24"x18"	<34> 1982
$	140.00	o Still life/		
		Poppies	1933,s, 19"x14"	<6> 1984
$	1,500.00	p		<8> 1985
$	440.00	p Woman in Even-		
		ing Dress	1915,s, 23"x17"	<33>1985
$	870.00	o Lady of Fashion	1879,s, 25"x14"	<7> 1986
$	3,500.00	o Maud/Muffin		<8> 1986
$	440.00	p The Slipper	1915,s, 19"x15"	<9> 1987
$	550.00	o Canon Armour	62"x48"	<10>1987
$	3,910.00	o New Coat	1880,s, 19"x35"	<11>1987
$	44,000.00	o Afternoon		
		Repose	s, 40"x61"	<12>1988
$	1,760.00	p Seminude	1914,s,	<13>1989

```
$     6,000.00 o Woman/fan        1916,s, 42"x36"  <14>1990
$     1,500.00 p Seated Model             20"x16"  <14>1990
$       850.00 p Pensive                  21"x26"  <14>1990
$       850.00 p Sisters (2)              20"x20"  <14>1990
$       850.00 p Model dressing           20"x13"  <14>1990
$       750.00 p Nude Model               23"x11"  <14>1990
$       750.00 p Study #1                 21"x16"  <14>1990
$       750.00 p Nude study               23"x14"  <14>1990
$       750.00 p Fashion Model            25"x18"  <14>1990
$    39,600.00 o Young Navigator,1874,s,           <15>1990
$       450.00 w Rose Bouquet             20"x16"  <16>1990
$     1,200.00 o (George/Nora)                     <17>1990
$     4,500.00 p Helen W. Henderson                <18>1991
$     4,000.00 p Bondeuse                          <19>1991
$     4,000.00 p                                   <19>1991
$       250.00 w (Delaware Water Gap)              <20>1991
$       660.00 o Reverie in Brown Chair 9.8"x6.5"<21>1991
$     5,000.00 o Lord Leighton                     <22>1991
$       400.00 o Cat/Dog/Baby/Kitchen             <23>1991
$       325.00 g (Miss E)                  7"x9"  <24>1992
$     2,700.00 o Woodgatherer/donkey      24"x36"  <25>1992
$     1,250.00 p Lady,profile    1914,s,22"x17"   <26>1992
$     1,850.00 p Elegant Lady    1910,s,28"x21"   <27>1992
$       600.00 w (flowers)                         <28>1992
$     2,200.00 o George @ Observatory Desk 60"x36"
                                                   <29>1992
$       605.00 p Col. E.M. House, 1919,s,          <30>1992
$       495.00 p Evening Dress, 1915,s, 17"x23"    <31>1992
$     1,210.00 p Lady,profile,1914,s,(Wind)        <32>1992


----------------------------------------------------------
List of sources:
<0> 1937 auction  $ 56.50 < 13 = $ 4.35              N062
<1> 1938 S.T.Freeman & Co.; Auction Sale Catalog,
         annotated by Thornton Oakley
<2> AMERICAN ARTISTS AT AUCTION TO 1940
<3> 1948                                             N072
<4> 1980 Christie's.South Kensington,London,England  U014
<5> 1982 Kunsthaus Museum, Kuln, Germany             U014
<6> 1984 Butterfield's, San Francisco, CA            U014
     1985
<7> 1986 Sotheby's. Glasgow, Scotland                U014
<8> 1985 F. S. Schwarz & Son, Phila.                 E100
<19>1986        above                                E102
```

```
<9> 1987 Christie's East, NYC [Leonards 86/87]          U014
<10>1987 S.T.Freeman & Co. lot #432    [above 87/88]
<11>1978 Christie's. South Kensington
<12>1988 Sotheby's NYC [Leonards 87/88]                 U014
<13>1989 Weschler's.Washington,D.C.[Leonards 88/89]     U014
<14>1990 Newman Galleries,Phila.
<16>          above
<18>          above
<25>          above
<15> E019                                                U015
<17> 1990 private treaty, Phila.
<20>          above
<23>          above
<24>          above
<21>                                                     U015
<22> 1991 Leighton House Museum,London                  U010
<26>          C.G.Sloane & Co.,North Bethesda, MD        U015
<27>          above
<32>          above
<28> 1992 Freeman/Fine Arts, Phila.
<29>          above
<30>          above
<31>          above
<33> 1985 Fine Arts Co. of Phila.                        U014
<34> 1982 Christie's, NY
<35> 1982 Gordon's Print Sales, Sotheby's London
```

INHERITANCE DIAGRAM S. HEIRS OF HAMILTON & HIS WIFE, CLARA. Their one biological heir, their son George, had died 433 days before Clara. Their daughter-in-law had inherited her husband's estate. The parents died intestate within a month & a half of each other. Probate was a very slow procedure in Jamaica in the 1930s. The courts made bequests to three heirs from the artist's estate (doubled circles), and to three heirs of Clara's estate (dashed circle), but no bequests to others (shown with asterisks). Settlement of the three estates required numerous court actions in several cities under the prevailing American *and* English intestate laws through 1940.

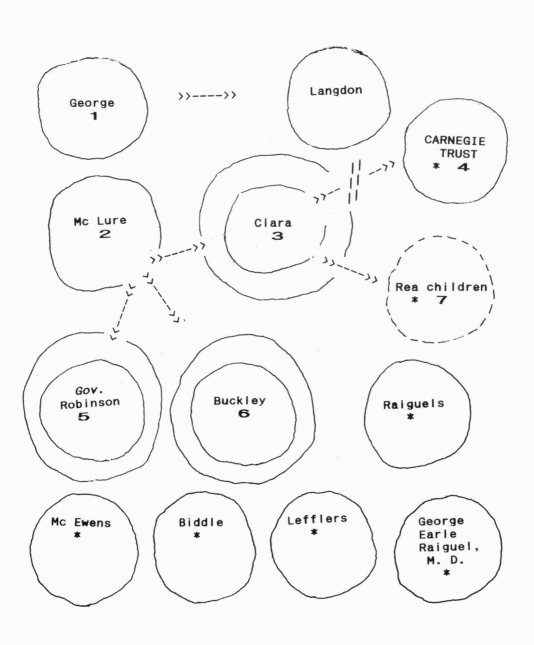

Legend:

1. son: George Hall Hamilton, d. 1935 VIII 7
   daughter-in-law & George's widow: Elizabeth Langdon
       Hamilton, d. 1981
2. artist: John McLure Hamilton, d. 1936 IX 10
3. artist's widow: Clara Raiguel Hamilton, d. 1936 XI 1. Her
       will was ruled invalid by the Montgomery county, PA
       court. Instead the Phila. Court ruled that her heirs
       were to receive one-third of the artist's estate.
4. CARNEGIE TRUST: Clara's estate's only designated heir.
5. Former Governor Robert Pyle Robinson, d. 1939, was the
       artist's maternal cousin as both their mother's were
       Delaplaines and sisters.
6. artist's grandnephew: Mathew Brooke Buckley was the
       grandson of the artist's deceased sister, *Mrs. Lillie
       Hall King.*
7. three minor Children of Canadian architect, Kenneth G.
       Rea, relatives and heirs of Clara designated by the
       Montgomery county, PA court to inherit the
       Zieglerville farm.
* McEwens : artist's cousins were kin through uncle,
       John Hamilton, Jr.
* artist's paternal cousin: John C. Mercer Biddle, d. 1942.
       His deceased mother was artist's aunt, *Mrs. Lydia I.
       Biddle.*
* Lefflers: Clara's nieces and nephews were descendants of
       her deceased sister, *Mrs. Valerie R. Leffler.*
* Raiguels: relatives of Clara's brother, *Joseph Lloyd
       Raiguel.*
* George Earle Raiguel, M. D. was alive in 1950.

TABLE **T**. HAMILTON'S ILLNESSES & RELATED MATTERS. From a survey of 26 relevant letters written by Hamilton, his illness episodes that affected appointments or works in progress, were recorded. This data is important in Hamilton's biography because artists trained in the 19th Century used toxic materials. Moreover, various other occupational hazards caused lung defense impairment, often increasing the probability of opportunistic, microbial infections, which triggered later auto-immune responses to the introduced allergens. In addition, studios could harbor insects whose bites initiated arthritis, an auto-immune disease, which Hamilton suffered from for years. For sources of these observations, refer to the Hamilton Letter Collection in appendix.

1881 VII 22   Illness undisclosed.

1890 ? 19   Hamilton plagued by "fleas" while working at Alpha House on "*Herbert Spencer.*" (B012 p.102) These parasites could have been very small (*Lyme Disease*-like) ticks ultimately responsible for his arthritis.

1912 I/II   "flu"

1915 II 8   sick in bed [after mother's death]

    XI 15   sick in bed

[Flu, man ill in a chair], 1901. 2.25" x 2" Engraving T. B. Hennell book (op. cit). Courtesy Mitchell Library, Poetry Collection.

1917	III	27	in bed, infectious cold

1917 III 27   in bed, infectious cold

1920 II 12   in bed with "cold"

      IX 10   in bed with "cold"

1922   V 25   illness

      VII 24   Recent illness [after George's marriage,
               artist age 70; artist 50 years in London]

1923   X 25   bronchitis

1926   X 15   Arthritic pains relieved by temporary
               prescription of morphine.

1928 XI 22   severe illness

1929 XI 28   illness

1930 II 26   Hamilton's previous plan to give up Hermitage
               unrealized; Team going to Jamaica.

      III 27   Artist in bed, gouty arthritis.

1931 VI .   in Jamaica for cure.

      XI .   Gout episode continued.

      XII 12   Crippling by arthritis, legibility of
               handwriting/painting skills effected.

               Artist alternated between chair-ridden and
               bed-ridden condition for subsequent five
               years of his life.

1932   address: *Iona,* Mandeville

1933   I 16   Illness episode for prior 18 months.

      III 14   Handwriting worsened.

      III 20   Handwriting far worse.

1934   Cataracts inferred as handwriting's height
              now doubled.

              [Financial distress caused artist to
              initiate collection of unpaid commission,
              "Dr. Riche."]

1936 I   21 [His butler, *John Allen,* wrote letters for
              Hamilton.]

              [Friend, *Hyacinth Rebhan* wrote letters for
              Clara.]

      II 2   Hamilton's math acuity slightly impaired.
              He said he was age 85 when only 83,
              reasoning ability sound. He stipulated that
              Relief Funds shall go directly to him *not*
              through intermediary, like *U. S. Consul to
              Jamaica,* who Hamilton said was *not* to be
              involved in *his* business activity!

TABLE **U**. HAMILTON'S ATTRIBUTES, 1878--1933. A study of all documents, letters, news stories, and interviews gathered during a 58 year interval of his career provided insights to his recipe for success. They included 80 personal factors, educational factors, career factors, and other attributes of Hamilton. Some may be personality traits.

PERSONAL FACTORS

    analytical
    early riser
    non-smoker
    never carried a watch
    deep family commitment
    clear religious identity
    church-goer
    keen observer for evidence of "faith" in others
    not intolerant of Jews
    diplomatic
    complaisance
    formed lasting friendships (personal/professional)
    compassionate
    openhanded with charity, etc.
    light drinker
    supported school/community projects
    loyal to/inseparable from wife
    valued solitude
    supported war effort
    man of values/opinions
    enjoyed company of women at social gatherings, as
        sitters, as friends
    sense of humor
    even tempered when provoked
    cheerful alacrity when frustrated
    zest for debate/discussion of politics
    knowledgeable about philosophy/religion/causes/issues
    curiosity
    could share good/bad experiences
    adopted European attitudes/views
    out of doors man (liked to hunt, fish, boat)
    American expatriate in Britain but "more English than
        the English"
    frequently went home to America in triumph
    assimilated French costume, etc.
    rarely ill/never hypochondriac
    prosperous, middle class lifestyle to 1934 (life of
        ease)

EDUCATIONAL FACTORS

    rigorous education equaled bacculaurate degree
    strong language skills (English, French, German, Scot)
    committed reader of *"good books"* (life-long)
    continuing self-education (facts, intellectual skills,
        trade skills)
    sympathetic/practical listener
    passionate recorder of people he knew
    ethologist (faded into *"blind,"* studied undisturbed
        sitter's actions/activity)

CAREER FACTORS

    always planned ahead
    self-taught new techniques
    modified existing styles
    broad repertoire of materials/media of expression
    always experimented
    prolific quality letter writer (228 found)
    industrious (1,050+ works documented)
    peripatetic artist/reporter/commentator
    frugal customer (bought used, repaired frames)
    comparative shopper
    accommodated to client's criticisms
    negotiated fees with galleries
    trusted but verified a gallery's statements
    excellent social mixer
    delegated responsibilities/functions
    publicity conscious
    non-litigious
    no *bona fide* enemies in a highly competitive field
    tenacious fee collector
    anti-German
    accountant's outlook
    worked rapidly
    valued wife's criticism of his work
    work always uppermost in his mind
    almost absent minded in other matters

"NEVER"

feared to be alone
regarded himself as a genius
critic of the Arts
violently amusing at dinner parties
a "talking" artist
engaged in "art showmanship"
improvident of his energy/money
had creditors
portrayed nude female breasts
portrayed male frontal nudity
a misanthrope
a misogynist

TABLE **V**. STYLES HAMILTON ADMIRED. A survey of B012, news stories, his art & his art collection revealed 58 styles of other artists that Hamilton assimilated. (N=58)

	Century					
Artist	15th	16th	17th	18th	19th	20th
Abbey,E.A.						C
Atkinson,F.						C
Audran					F	
Beardsley,A.						CIS
Beaufaux,P-C.					A	
Boldini,G.						C
Browne,J.						
Bucchi						
Cooper,S.			O			
Corot,C.					C	
Correggio,A.A.		OIS				
Dana,C.E.					C	C
Darley,M.				OE		
Daubigny					C	
Diaz					C	
Degas,H.G.E.						C
del Sarto, A.	OO					
Devret,C.			F			
Eakins,T.C.					A	
Edelinck					F	
Ford,E.O.					OS	
Furse,C.W.					C	
Gerome,J.L.					A	
Hals,F.			C			
Hartrick,A.S.					C	
Helleu,P.					C	
Hitchcock,G.						C
Holmes,G.W.					A	
Kauffmann,A.				OE		
Lamb,C.R.					C	
Lawrence,T.				OO(2)		
La Tour,M.Q.de				C		
Lecreux,N.				OE		
Millet,J.F.					C	
R.T.M.						OS
Monet,C.						C

412

Pennell,J.				C		OPA
Pyle,H.				C		
Raffaelli,J.F.				OE		
Reni,G.	OO OIS					
Renoir,P-A.					C	
Reynolds,J.			C OO			
Rigaud,H.			C OE			
Romney,G.			C			
Rubens,P.P.	C					
Sargent,J.S.					C	
Stevens,A.				C		
Swan,J.M.					C	
Thouron,H.J.				C	C	
Tyndale,W.				C	C	
van Gogh,V.				C		
van Lerius,J.H.F.				A		
Velasquez		C				
Watts, G.F.				C		
Way,T.R.				C	C	
Whistler,J.A.M.				C		
Wille				F		
Witherington,W.F.				OE		

Legend:
A	a student of
C	influenced by
O	owned
E	engraving
F	father collected
IS	pen study
OO	oil
PA	pastel
S	sculpture

TABLE **W**. THEMES IN HAMILTON'S RETRIEVED ART. This survey
documents 23 theme classes the artist produced from a study
of retrieved images in all techniques.   (N=640)

1	(Advertising attrib.)	9
2	Animals	43
3	Artists, Architects, Critics, Sculptors	30
4	Cartoon characters	69
5	Children	20
6	Drink(ers)	14
7	Editorial cartoons	6
8	Ethnics	17
9	Hamilton's family	39
10	Holiday greetings	10
11	House interiors	24
12	Judges, Lawyers, Law	56
13	Landscapes	25
14	Military	13
15	Politicians/Statesmen	44
16	Religion/Clerics	22
17	Royals	30
18	Science/Medicine/Engineering	29
19	Sculpture	6
20	Smoking	4
21	Still Life	12
22	Theatre/Actors/Entertainment, Sports	45
23	Women	65

TABLE X. HAMILTON'S ART TECHNIQUES IN RETRIEVED IMAGES.
     N=640

1	Bronze/Clay Sculptured Portraits	4
2	Chalks	3
3	Charcoals	1
4	Crayons	1
5	Engravings/Etchings	121
6	Graphites	3
7	Lithographs	13
*	Monochrome reproductions	46
8	Oil Genre & Portraits	123
9	Pastels	146
*	Photogravure reproductions & other types	99
*	Souvenir Portrait Cards; reproductions by	
	Detroit Publishing Co.	4
10	Watercolors	143
11	(Wood Cuts attrib.)	1

----

* Authorized commercial copies by others.

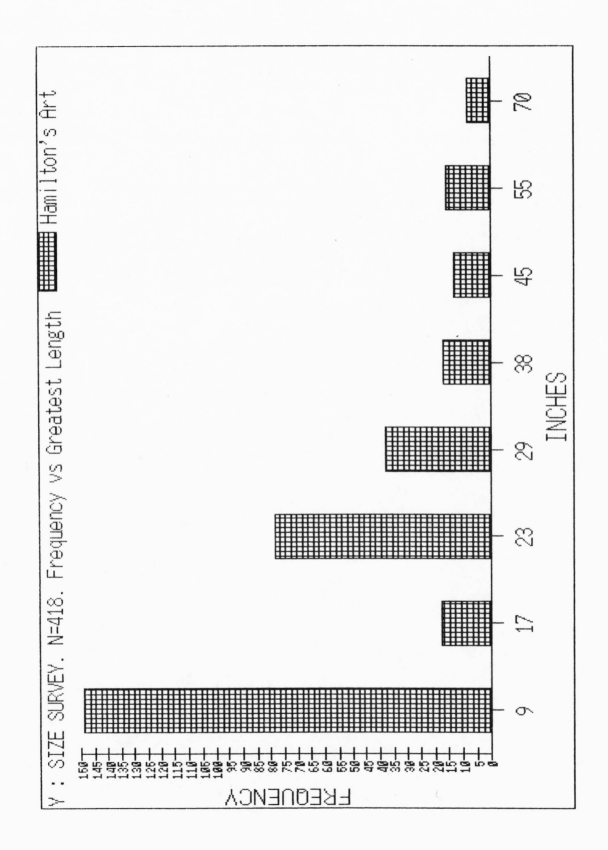

TABLE Z. HAMILTON'S SUPPORTS. Observations on more than 80 Hamilton works provided information about the various supports used in the form of papers, linen, canvas, and wood.
(N=1,050 documented)

	techniques		
	pastel	watercolors	oils
D=1,050	400+	197+	400+
O= 86	22	9	35

support:

Illustration Board	double thick brown 2		single thick cream 1
Paper:		136*	
kraft	few [1911]		
laid down	many		
rough 140 lbs.		5	
wove	modest [1890]		
colors			very thin paint layer

pale tones cream
buff
tan
gray
brown[1911]
brown flecked
[1890]

Linen		2	

canvas:

French twill	many, early works; 50 threads/inch
slick	72 threads/inch
stretcher stock	1 7/8" wide x 5/8" deep, flared away from canvas [1916]
	2 1/8" wide x 1/2" deep [n.d.]
keys/corner	2
wood panel	some

----

materials absent	silk
techniques absent	impasto, textured

----

* PROMINENT PROFILES

CHRONOLOGY

1831 Hamilton's father received his M. D. degree from *University of Pennsylvania* on Chestnut Street. Father practiced medicine in rural Delaware for more than ten years.

1846 Grandfather bought *Hamilton House* located in Northern Philadelphia's suburban Mulberry ward.

1849 Artist's parents married and returned to Philadelphia.

1850 (July), early death in office of Zachary Taylor made Millard Fillmore, the former V.P., the 13th U. S. President.

1853 (January), artist born, second child of Caroline Delaplaine Hamilton and George Hamilton, M. D.

   (March), Franklin Pierce was inaugurated the 14th U. S. President.

1856 Artist's sister, Lillie Hall Hamilton was born.

1858 Artist's younger sister, Jennie Mercer Hamilton born.

1859 Father became member of *Phila. Co. Medical Society*.

1860 Father practiced in City's busy Tenth Ward near his residence.

1861 Father listed in *City Directory* at mansion *(1600 Summer Street)*.

   American Civil War started. It would last four years.

1864 Artist, age eleven, painted landscape in oils as proposed curtain for *New Chestnut Street Theatre*.

1865 Artist attended private drawing school (George W. Holmes).

1866 Artist started bacculareate training (*Central High School*) at Penn Square campus.

1868 Father elected President, *Phila. Co. Medical Society*.

1870 Artist graduated from high school with college degree equivalent. He moved to 1123 Chestnut Street to attend

P.A.F.A. He may have met Thomas C. Eakins about this time.

Franco-German War started. It would last two years.

1873 Artist attended Antwerp Belgium's *Royal Academy of Fine Arts* for two and one half years. He studied under *Professors* de Keyser, van Lerius, and Beaufaux. He met Walter Tyndale, Emile Claus, and August Rodin while in Belgium.

(September) U. S. stock market crashed.

1875 Artist studied under *Professor* Gerome in the Paris France's *School of Fine Arts*.

Artist's professional career began in Phila. perhaps in a fashionable photographic studio or newspaper office.

1876 Artist first exhibited at *P.A.F.A.*'s opening under auspices of *Phila. Sketch Club* where he was a member.

Bell invented telephone.

Philadelphia held *American Centennial Exposition*.

1877 Artist's work debuted at *National Academy of Design* show in N.Y.C. The New York TIMES published the first complimentary review of his oil painting and his brochure satirizing P.A.F.A.'s art exhibition. The latter was a first in America. He would exhibit at the N.A.D. three more times (1878,1890,1920).

(March) Rutherford B. Hayes inaugurated 19th U. S. President.

1878 Artist immigrated permanently to London; he would stay until 1932. His first *Paris Salon* exhibition took place in 1878. An engraving of his oil occupied a full page in the official catalogue of the *Paris Universal Exposition* in 1878.

1879 Artist met Joseph Pennell about this time. They would form a fifty year professional and social association including their respective spouses.

Artist painted Clara, the future Mrs. Hamilton, in London.

His first professional biography was published.

Edison invented the light bulb.

1880 (October) Artist married Philadelphia's Miss Clara Augusta Raiguel. She was twenty(six) and the artist twenty-seven.

1881 Artist exhibited at *P.A.F.A.*

Hamiltons vacationed in Scotland after he debuted as commissioned, oil portrait painter.

1883 Artist and wife vacationed and painted in Spain.

1884 (January) Their only son, George Hall Hamilton, born at *Grey House* on Abbey Mews on artist's birthday. They moved to *Alpha House*.

1885 Philadelphia fire killed the artist's younger sister, Jennie Mercer Hamilton, nephew, brother-in-law, and a servant. The family mansion was severely damaged. Contents lost including art by Hamilton. Artist's father died months later.

1886 Artist's aunt, Mrs. Ann Jane Mercer, died leaving sizeable but complicated legacy to artist, his wife, his surviving sister and their mother. Immediately, they donated it to form a *Home for Disabled Ministers* named for artist's deceased millionaire uncle, John C. Mercer.

1888 Hertz discovered radio waves.

Eastman made the box camera.

1889 (Spring) *Alpha House*, in London, still home.

1892 Artist received *honorable mention* for his work at the *Paris Salon*.

French government purchased oil *"Gladstone"* for famous Luxembourg Palace.

Artist traveled to Austria to paint *"Prince Bismarck."*

1893 A friend, Edward Onslow Ford sculpted bronze busts of Hamilton and painter's father.

Hamilton awarded his first gold medal at Chicago's *World's Columbian Exposition.*

1895 Thomas C. Eakins, a friend and former teacher, painted full-length, commissioned, oil portrait of Hamilton.

Artist's aunt, Miss Margaret Hamilton, deeded *Hamilton House* to artist in exchange for life tenancy.

1896 Hamilton held major, one-man-show at London's Goupil and Company Gallery.

Hamiltons had beach vacation at *St. Moritz.*

(November 23rd) Artist exhibited in Paris.

(December) Artist studied under Gerome in Paris through March,'97.

1897 Hamilton exhibited works at *Carnegie Art Museum* in Pittsburgh, PA while in London.

1898 (May) Hamiltons vacationed in Wales.

Spanish-American War started.

1899 Hamiltons moved to finer London home, *Murestead,* Grove End Road., N. W.

1900 Artist exhibited at London's *National Portrait Gallery.*

1901 (January) Philadelphia.

(March) Washington, D. C.

(May) While in London, Hamilton informed of his second gold medal awarded at Buffalo, NY's *Pan-American Exposition.*

1902 Painter's son briefly attended *Pennsylvania Military Academy,* (Chester, PA) while artist resided at Philadelphia's *Hotel Stenton.*

(April) Artist in Washington, D. C.

(September) Hamilton appointed the first, principal
artist to Glasgow (Scotland)'s *EVENING TIMES*. It was
the largest newspaper in the world's English-speaking
community. There his important Prominent Profiles
caricature series was launched. This three year period
led to numerous oil portrait commissions and upward
career changes.

1903 Hamiltons bought thirty-four acres of farm land near
Zieglerville, PA as hunting retreat.

First powered aircraft flight.

1904 Artist awarded his third gold medal (St. Louis, MO)
at *Louisana Purchase Centennial Exposition*.

Painter's son began undergraduate training (Cambridge
University).

Hamilton served on art jury with his distinguished
peers [Abbey, Ives, Pennell, Sargent, (van Dyke),
and Whistler].

1905 (November) Hamiltons visited his work on exhibition in
Venice, Italy.

1906 Hamiltons resided at *Murestead* (St. John's Woods,
London) and painter maintained studio there. Mrs. Anna
Lea Merritt rated *Hamilton the finest painter of
children's portraits ever.* She had known his work since
1870s at *P.A.F.A.*

Hamilton exhibited at *Royal Academy of the Arts*,
London.

1907 Commissions brought painter $ 1,000.00 fee for each
work. Genre pieces sold from the equivalent of
$ 25.00 to $ 3,000.00.

1908 Henry Ford invented the Model T car.

1909 Hamilton awarded *a* fellowship by *P.A.F.A.*

Painter exhibited in Venice.

(May) Hamiltons in Paris.

Mother-in-law, *Mrs.* Sarah E. Raiguel, died in Phila.

1910 (March) Hamiltons in London.

Painter exhibited in Berlin.

1911 London's DAILY CHRONICLE arranged for sitting by King
George V (England's new monarch) prior to his
Coronation.

French National Gallery bought (*"Paul W. Bartlett"*) a
second portrait.

Painter exhibited in Dusseldorf and other German
cities.

Hamilton's son, was a volunteer scientist, at *Cambridge
University's Trinity College*. Subsequently, son
received M. A. degree.

1912 Hamiltons vacation in Warwickshire.

Philadelphia's Ripka sold Hamilton artist's materials.

Picasso begins Cubism.

1913 *Luxembourg Palace* placed *"Gladstone"* portrait in its
Permanent Collection on exhibition.

1914 Artist served on San Francisco's art jury with
distinguished peers *(Panama-Pacific Exposition)*.

Hamilton acquired new suburban home,
(Kingston-on-Thames, Surrey) called the Hermitage.

World War I started.

1915 Large, one-man-show at San Francisco's exposition.

Artist's mother, *Mrs.* Caroline Hamilton, died after a
long illness in England.

(April) Hamiltons voyaged to NY bound for San
Francisco.

Hamilton established Philadelphia studio.

(November) Hamiltons visited Wilmington, DE.

Mrs. Mary Harriman bought more than thirty Hamilton pastels for $ 5,000.00.

1916 Hamiltons in Pasadena, CA

(January) While in NYC, Hamilton sought to meet with Andrew Carnegie and Pierpont Morgan.

(March) Hamiltons in Philadelphia.

Painter exhibited in Cincinnati, OH.

Wife's family visited while commissions fulfilled in Montreal and Ottawa, Canada.

(December) Hamiltons in Wales.

1917 Hamiltons resided in Philadelphia's *Ritz Carlton Hotel.*

(April) Visited Burlingame, CA.

Russian Revolution.

(September 20th) N. E. Harbor, ME.

Eakins died. Hamilton wrote an appreciation of his masterpieces of American art for *Metropolitan Museum,* NYC's loan exhibition.

(December 27th) Hamiltons in NYC with friends, the Pennells.

1918 Philadelphia residence, *Ritz Carlton Hotel.*

Hamilton awarded fourth gold medal for life-time achievements by *P.A.F.A.*

Artist elected president, *P.A.F.A's Fellowship.*

1919 Philadelphia studio now at 1700 Walnut Street, a fashionable location.

(August) Hamiltons traveled to England after
"*Judge/Mrs. Simpson*" painted. Judge was a patron of
many artists in America.

1920 (February) Hamiltons in Paris.

Hamiltons entertained *Prime Ministers* Asquith and
Balfour in their Surrey home.

(July) Hamiltons in Wales.

American visit.

1921 Official publication date of painter's book about his
V.I.P. commissions published by Thomas Fisher Unwin.

Mrs. Mary Harriman donated her Hamilton pastels to the
Corcoran Gallery of Art, Washington, D. C.

1922 Painter's son, George, married Miss Elizabeth Langdon
Williams, a mathematician and astronomer like himself
(Flagstaff, AZ). Painter and wife learned of it by post
at the Hermitage.

(May 25th) Hamiltons vacationed at *Camp Elsinore,* in NY
state mountains.

Hamilton's biography appeared in *Thieme-Becker*'s
artists' encyclopedia.

1923 Painter listed in *American Art Annual.*

First visit to Jamaica.

1924 Mailing address c/o *Drexel & Company,* Phila. bankers.

1925 silence

1926 (to April) At the *Hermitage.*

Philadelphia thereafter.

1927 (late in year) Hamilton painted his maternal cousin
"*Governor Robert P. Robinson,*" at Wilmington, DE.

Hamiltons traveled to *Pocono Mountains, PA* to hunt grouse.

Connoisseur (The magazine) published item re: artist.

1928 Second Jamaican visit.

Hamiltons subsidized astronomer/son's research activity.

1929 Artist's pastels sold well at high prices in America and Canada.

Listed in *Who's Who in Art*.

U. S. stock market crashes.

1930 Hamilton exhibited at *Philadelphia's Art Alliance*.

1931 Third Jamaican visit.

Health problems.

(April) London's Barbizon House exhibition.

Painted last commissioned oil portrait.

Arthritis effected Hamilton's writing ability.

Painter invested in a fifty-four acre Mandeville, Jamaica home site.

1932 Silence

1933 Hamilton's handwriting much worse.

Artist's sister, *Mrs.* Lillie Hall King, died leaving a significant estate to her grandson, Mathew Brooke Buckley, who would be declared an heir of Hamilton's estate by the Philadelphia court, also.

Hitler became *Chancellor* of Germany.

1934 Artist's address: *Hamilton Hall*, Mandeville, the last home for the Hamiltons. Handwriting size doubled.

Rosenbach & Company exhibited ninety Hamilton pastels in NYC.

1935 Artist's only son and logical heir died of cancer in Jamaica. Son's estate included assets from parents. Lengthy probate created cash flow problems for aged parents. Daughter-in-law left Jamaica for New Hampshire.

McCLEES GALLERY (Philadelphia) held a Hamilton Retrospective Exhibition.

1936 (September 10th) Hamilton died having resided abroad for fifty-eight years.

(November 1) Artist's devoted wife and model, Mrs. Clara Hamilton, died at *Hamilton Hall,* Mandeville.

Last biography published in *Who's Who in American Art.*

1939 Artist's cousin and one of Court's designated heirs to his estate, former *Governor* Robert P. Robinson, died.

1942 Artist's paternal cousin, John C. Mercer Biddle, died.

1981 Artist's daughter-in-law, Elizabeth Langdon Hamilton, died at age 101 in New Hampshire.

[Mrs. Nora King Buckley = Young woman holding flowers]
Oil 42.25" x 35.5." Formerly of Harry Burke Collection;
Courtesy of Schwarz Gallery, Philadelphia.

1892 XII 13	certificate	WORLD'S COLUMBIAN EXPOSITION, Chicago, Hamilton an Advisory Committee member	HB-36	C001
1893	gold medal	op cit	unlocated	C002
(1898)	photo	Edwards,Fishgaard, YEAR'S ART. "Hamilton" 2/3rd left to chest level. NYPL AD microfiche file		C003
1900	inscription /signature	"MR.GLADSTONE EDITING BISHOP BUTLER'S WORK"	HB-7	A049
1901	gold medal	PAN-AMERICAN EXPOSITION, Buffalo	unlocated	C004
1903 IV 22	stationary /signature	THE EVENING TIMES, Glasgow	K-2	L035
1904	photo	JOSEPH PENNELL & ST. LOUIS ART JURY Abbey,Hamilton,Ives,Pe,Sargent,(van Dyke), Whistler.	HSP	B017:4
	gold medal	Louisana Purchase UNIVERSAL EXPOSITION, St. Louis B004 II : .. unlocated		C005
	certificate	Advisory Committee member, above	HB-37	C006
	certificate	gold medal for oils, above	HB-38	C007
1909	post card	Museum Royal Beaux Arts, Antwerp		C008
1914	inscription /signature	(legend on rev.) "Lithograph" ANGLO-AMERICAN EXPOSITION (label) #821 Jas. Bourlet & Sons, Ltd., 17 & 18 Nassau St. (near Mortimer St.), London HB-39		C009
	fascimile artist's signature	capitol letters, year of work B028:292		C010
1918	post card	Museum Royal Beaux Arts, Antwerp/ Belgian flag		C011
	post card	Musee Mayer van den Bergh, Antwerp (architecture)		C012
	oil /canvas	Wayman Adams,"HAMILTON"(wearing coat, hat, gloves) sepia photo VF PAFA-17		C013

	oil /canvas	Wayman Adams,"HAMILTON"(carrying hat, gloves) sepia photo M035	VF PAFA-18	C014
II 9	gold medal	P.A.F.A. Medal of Honor founded 1893 by John H. Converse. Hamilton 22nd recepient.	PAFA-19	C015
II 10	photo	"Hamilton" (!eft side to shoulder level)	TUUA-2	N019
III 11	announcement	Hamilton lecture at P.A.F.A. : "ART A NECESSITY"		N100
III 12	admission ticket	above	PAFA-20	C016
	photo	Richard Dooner, Phila., "Hamilton painting "Curtis" FLP PKWY PR-2		C017
1919	bronze plaque	(sculptor) R. T. M.,"SMILING SAGE" (=Hamilton) lot 53 L195 unlocated		C018
(1921)	inscription /signature photo	holiday greeting card "Happy New Year/from Mr. & Mrs. J. McLure Hamilton" VF PAFA-21 B012:"GEORGE MEREDITH"		C019
	above	printed holiday greeting card " With the/very Best Good Wishes/for/Your Health & Happiness/ in the Coming Year." (signed) J. McLure Hamilton CGA-31 B012:"LORDS OF APPEAL"		C020
1923	map	Europe		C021
1934 IX ..	photo	W. W. Corcoran, "HAMILTON"(oval) J052:523		C022
1935	oil /canvas	unknown author's handwriting, "McCLEES" on edge of Hamilton's painting from Retrospective Exhibition, Phila., HB-40 A213		
1936 IX 12	photo	1934, attributed to Elizabeth Langdon Hamilton, "HAMILTON, CLARA, GEORGE" N060		

DOCUMENTS
(The documents studied in Europe, North & South America numbered 171 and exceeded 447 pages)

Year	Type	Town	Individual Involved	Length	
1799	R	12	Hamilton,Sr., John / Hall, Elizabeth	1	G001
	P	12	above	1	G163
1800	E	12	Hamilton,Sr., John p.373	1	G162
1813	U	12	Hamilton,Sr., John	1	G002
1814	K	12	Armstrong, Wm./wife to Hamilton, Sr.,John	4	G003
	ZA	12	Hamilton,Sr.,John et al (Tares,bulk commodity sales)	1	G004
1817	ZN	12	to Hamilton,Sr.,John on Whitecar, Benjamin	1	G168
1819	S	12	Hamilton,Sr.,John (Baird children, wards of)	2	G005
1820	E	12	Ellis, Wm.	1	G006
1821	B	12	Samson, H.P. et al	4	G007
	K	12	Sargent, L.M. to Hamilton,Sr., John	3	G008
1822	F	12	Hamilton & Hood, Grocers	2	G009
1823	K	12	Hamilton,Sr.,John to Newell, John	2	G010
	K	12	Newell, James to Hamilton,Sr.,John	3	G011
	K	12	Newell,Jr.,John to Hamilton,Sr.,John	2	G012
	ZJ	12	Hamilton, Sr., John	1	G169
1825	K	12	University of PA to Hamilton,Sr.,John	2	G013
1828/29	.	12	Hamilton, Sr. John's offer (Brinton papers)	1	G170
1829	.	12	above (Drew Coll. under Mc Grath)	1	G171
1830	E	12	Ellis, Joseph	1	G014
	ZB	12	Hamilton,Sr., John	1	G015
	E	12	Hamilton,Sr.,John	1	G016

	E	13	Raiguel, Mw. M.	1	G017
1837	ZI	12	Hamilton,Sr.,John	1	G018
1838	ZI	12	above	1	G019
1839	ZI	12	above	1	G020
1840	E	12	Ellis, Joseph	1	G021
	ZI	12	Hamilton,Sr.,John	1	G022
	E	12	above	1	G023
	E	13	Raiguel, Augustus	1	G024
1845	ZI	12	Hamilton,Sr.,John	1	G025
1846	ZM	12	above	1	G026
1847	K	11	Putzel, Barnhart to Raiguel, Wm.M.	2	G027
1849	R	12	Delaplaine, Caroline to Hamilton,M.D., George (X 23) PUBLIC LEDGER	1	G028
1850	E	5	Delaplaine, James	1	G029
	E	12	Ellis, Joseph	1	G030
	E	5	Gemmill, David W.	1	G031
	E	12	Hamilton,Sr.,John	1	G032
	ZD	12	Hamilton,Sr.,John, estate of, #105	1	G033
	E	12	Raiguel, Augustus H.	1	G034
	E	12	Raiguel, Henry	1	G035
	E	12	Raiguel, Wm. (M.) Joseph (W.)	1	G036
	K	12	Shields, Richard to Hamilton,Sr.,John	3	G037
1851	K	11	Brooke, Elijah et al to Magee,James/Michael	5	G038

433

	(K	12	Flanagan, Wm. G. et al to Crozier, Andrew	5	G039)
1852	K	12	King, Robert P. to Hamilton,Jr.,John	2	G040
1854	R	12	Raiguel, Joseph W. to Ellis, Sarah (St. Michael/Zion Church)	1	G041
1855	C	12	Raiguel, Clara (St. Michael/Zion Church)	1	G042
1858	J*	12	Hamilton, Sr.,John	1	G172
1860	E	5	Delaplaine, James	2	G043
	E	5	Delaplaine,Jr., James	1	G044
	E	12	Ellis, Edward F.	1	G045
	E	12	Ellis, Joseph	1	G046
	E	12	Hamilton, Elizabeth	1	G047
	K	12	Gheen, John, R. et ux to Hamilton, John(Jr.)	5	G048
	E	12	Raiguel, Joseph	1	G049
	E	12	Raiguel, (Wm.)	1	G050
	K	12	Smith, Hiram to Hamilton,John.(Jr.)	3	G051
	E	5	Walton, Wm. (B.)	1	G052
	E	12	Yeager, Charles (A.)	1	G053
1862	ZG	12	Hamilton, M.D.,George John (Jr.)	1	G054
(2)	I	PA	Hamilton, David d. 1864	1	G055
1864	ZG	12	Hamilton, M.D., George	1	G056
1865	ZG	12	Hamilton, M.D., George John,Jr.	1	G057
1866	ZG	12	Hamilton, M.D., George	1	G058

1870	E	5	Delaplaine, James	1	G059
	E	12	Ellis, Joseph	1	G060
	E	12	Hamilton, Elizabeth (Hall)	1	G061
	E	2	Hamilton, John, Jr.	1	G062
	D	2	above	2	G063
	E	12	Raiguel, Wm.	1	G064
	E	5	Walton, Wm. (B.)	1	G065
1873	E	1	Bates, Dewey Tyndale, Walter	1	G066
1873/4	ZF	1	Hamilton, John Mc Lure	1	G067
1874	E	1	Arthur, Robert	1	G068
	ZK	12	Raiguel, Wm.	5	G069
1874/5	ZF	1	Hamilton, John Mc Lure	2	G070
1877	E	1	Frost, George Albertus	1	G071
1880	E	12	Buckley, Edward S.	1	G166
	E	12	Hamilton, M.D., George	1	G072
	E	2	Hamilton, John, Jr.	1	G073
	P	12	Hamilton, John Mc Lure/ Raiguel, Clara	1	G074
	P	12	above (2nd Presby. Church)	1	G165
(	P	12	Mc Clure, Johann (St. Michael/Zion Church)	1	G075)
1881 et seq	Z	9	Hamilton, John Mc Lure	21+	G076
1883	ZK	12	Mercer, John C.	10	G077
1884	C	9	Hamilton George (Hall)	1	G078

1885	N	12	Hamilton, M.D., George	5	G079
	H	12	above	1	G080
	J	12	above	1	G164
n.d.	M	12	above	1	U032
1886	ZE	11	Hamilton,Mrs.Caroline D. et al to Mercer Home	9	G081
	K	12	Hamilton,John,Jr. to Biddle, Mrs. Lydia I.	4	G082
	X	12	Hamilton, John,Sr., deceased 1858	6+	G083
	ZD	12	Hamilton, Margaret #105	1	G084
	ZK	12	Mercer, Mrs. Ann (Jane Hamilton)	17	G085
1887	K	20	Biddle, Mrs. Lydia I. (Hamilton)	*	G086
	K	12	Hamilton, John, Jr. to Mrs. Lydia I.	4	G087
1888	N	12	Hamilton, (Miss) Catherine	8	G088
1891	E	9	Hamilton, John Mc Lure	1	G089
1895	ZD	12	above # 105	1	G090
	K	12	Hamilton, (Miss) Margaret	3	G091
1900	E	12	Curry, M.D., Howard	1	G092
	E	15	Hamilton, John,(Jr.)/Hamilton, (Mrs.) Sarah (Mc Ewen)	1	G093
	E	4	PA Military College	4	G094
	E	12	Raiguel, (Mrs.) Sarah (E.)	1	G095
1901	ZK	12	Hamilton, (Mrs.) Sarah (Mc Ewen)	3	G096
1902 et seq	Z	19	Hamilton, John (Mc Lure)	9	G097
1902/3	ZG	19	above	1	G098

1902	K	11	Sites, Rosetta L. to Hamilton, John Mc Lure	4	G099
1906	ZK	12	Biddle, (Mrs.) Lydia I.	5	G100
1910	E	21	Buckley, Daniel	1	G101
	E	12	Fritz, M.D., Wm. W.	1	G102
	E	12	Raiguel, (Mrs.) Sarah E.	1	G103
	ZK	12	above	3	G104
1915	N	12	Hamilton, (Mrs.) Caroline (D.)	5	G105
	ZK	12	above	37	G106
	H	18	above	1	G107
	ZK	12	Hamilton, John, (Jr.)	4	G108
1917	ZJ	12	Hamilton, John Mc Lure	1	G109
1918	K	11	Grimley, Jacob G. et ux to Hamilton, John Mc Lure	*	G110
	K	11	Hamilton, John Mc Lure to Hamilton, George Hall	4	G111
1919	K	11	Bolton, Jacob et ux to Hamilton, John Mc Lure	*	G112
1920	E	16	Leffler, Milton L.	1	G113
	E	12	Raiguel, M.D., George	1	G114
	E	12	Rice, Joseph W.	1	G115
1931	K	14	Silvera, Victor Emanuel to Hamilton, John Mc Lure	4	G116
	K	14	Silvera, Victor Emanuel to Rebhan, Hyacinth S.	4	G117
1933	ZK	12	King, (Mrs.) Lillie Hall (Hamilton)	8	G118
1934	K	14	Hamilton, John Mc Lure to Jackson, Henry J.	12	G119
	K	14	above above	5	G120

	T	14	Rebhan, Roger E. to above	4	G121
1935	H	10	Hamilton, George Hall	1	G122
1935/7	ZJ	10	above, estate 2469	1	G123
	ZJ	10	Hamilton, John Mc Lure, estate 12877	1	G124
1936	H	10	Hamilton,(Mrs.) Clara (Raiguel)	1	G125
	H	10	Hamilton, John Mc Lure	1	G126
	V	12	above (BULLETIN ALMANAC)	1	G127
	K	12	Hamilton, John M. (cousin)	4	G128
1937	J	11	Hamilton, George Hall (estate of)/ Hamilton, (Mrs.) Elizabeth Langdon	2	G129
	N	12	Hamilton, John Mc Lure (estate of)	13	G130
	K	11	Hamilton, Elizabeth L. (Williams) to Steward, J. Logan	4	G131
1938	ZD	12	Robinson, (Gov.) Robert P. #105	1	G132
1940	J	12	Hamilton, John Mc Lure (estate of), 1938	1	G133
	J	11	above	1+	G134
	K	11	above to Williams, John K.	1+	G135
	K	11	Rea, Eleanor et al to Williams, John K.	4	G136
1941	ZH	11	Hamilton, (Mrs.) Clara (Raiguel) estate of	1	G137
	W	17	Robinson, Mrs. Robert P. (Margaret F.)	1	G138
(1944	ZH	11	Raiguel, (Mrs.) Ellen P. estate of	1	G139)
1946	ZD	12	Zeidelman, Joseph/ Mrs. Ida #105	1	G140
	ZD	12	Zeidelman, Ida #105	1	G141
1953	K	14	Alumina Jamaica, Ltd.	3	G142

	K	14	Nathan, (Major) Albert Alexander	4	G143
1961	K	14	Todd, John Utten	2	G144
1963	K	14	Lyn, Leslie Clifford	3	G145
1965	K	14	Todd, John Utten	3	G146
1965 et seq	R	10	WOODLAWN (tract=pen)	2	G147
197(3)	ZD	12	Franklin Towne Corporation #105	1+	G148
1981	ZK	6	Hamilton, Mrs. Elizabeth Langdon Williams	1	G149
1984	Q	10	COTTON TREE (Land valuation of homes)	4	G150
	K	14	Swaby, Leicester Keith (Hamilton Hall)	2	G151
1990	H	12	All Saints (P.E.) Church, Torresdale,PA Cemetery (Hamilton, M.D., George; Hamilton, Caroline D.; others)	6+	G152
1991	O	7	Hamilton, George Hall/ Williams, Elizabeth Langdon, 1922 VI 2	1	G153
	ZL	20	Hamilton, Mrs Elizabeth L. (deceased)	1	G154
	H	6	above Oak Grove Cemetery Association	1	G155
	ZC	8	Hamilton, John Mc Lure, estate of, 193(8)	2	G156
	ZC	9	above 1938	7	G157
1992	A	8	Dunn, Cox, & Orrett, interview	1	G158
	L	1	(house) #4 Kaasrui, Antwerp (architecture)	1	G159
	W	10	(Senior Librarian) to Alperin	1	G160

Legend:

Town:		Type:	
Code:		Code:	
1	Antwerp, Belgium	A	attorney interviewed
2	Bensalem township, Bucks county, PA	B	agreement (deed)
3	Canaan, Grafton county, New Hampshire	C	baptism/ birth certificate
4	Chester City, Delaware county, PA	D	census (agricultural schedule)
5	Christiana Hundred, New Castle county, DE	E	census
6	Enfield, Grafton county, N.H.	F	cancelled bank check
7	Flagstaff, Coconino county, AZ	G	court decree
8	Kingston, Jamaica, W. I.	H	cemetery records
9	London, England	I	Civil War soldier's record, PA
10	Mandeville, Jamaica, W. I.	J	death certificate
11	Norristown, Montgomery county, PA	K	deed to real estate
12	Phila., PA	L	house facade, sketch of
13	Reading City, Berks county, PA	M	index card (County Medical Society)
14	Spanish Town, Jamaica, W. I.		
15	Washington county, PA	N	letters of Administration
16	Washington, D. C.	O	marriage, affidavit of
17	Wilmington, DE	P	marriage announcement (newspaper/ civil record of)
18	Kingston-on-Thames, Surrey, England		
19	Glasgow, Scotland	Q	map, house plots
20	Springfield, Delaware county, PA	R	map, land tracts
21	Whitemarsh township, Montgomery county, PA	S	petition for adoption
		T	mortgage
		U	naturalization
		V	published necrology
		W	personal letter
		X	petition for partition
		Y	tax record : excise
		Z	Post Office Directory
		ZA	printed grocers' petition
		ZB	promissory note
		ZC	probate
		ZD	property description
		ZE	release of legacy
		ZF	student record
		ZG	tax record : income
		ZH	tax record : inheritance
		ZI	tax record : poor
		ZJ	tax record : real estate
		ZK	will
		ZL	Social Security record
		ZM	CITY DIRECTORY
		ZN	bond

(James Abbott McNeill Whistler, butterfly monogram,
l.r.),[Bonneted girl with gloves, fruit seated in
garden] Oil 18" x 12"

441

OWNERS
(Published & Recent)

Allen,John		H001
Allentown Art Museum,PA		H002
Archambauld, Mrs.		H003
Art Alliance of Phila.		H004
Biddle, Alexander; Cadwalader, John; Antelo, Anthony J.; Thomas, George C.; Elkins, William L.;		
Harrison, Charles C.; Mc Fadden, George H.; Converse, John H. & Coates, Edward H.		H005
British Museum,Print Room, London.		H006
Brooklyn Museum, NY.		H007
Butterfield's, San Francisco, CA.		H008
Carnegie Museum of Art, Pittsburgh, PA.	10	H009
Central High School, Phila.,PA	2	H010
Chicago Art Institute, IL.		H011
Christie's, South Kensinton, England		H012
Christie's NY.		H013
CIGNA Museum/Art Collection, Phila.,PA		H014
Cooke, Gustavus Wynne		H015
Corcoran Gallery of Art, Washington, D. C.	16	H016
Curtis, Cyrus H.K.		H017
David David, Inc.,Phila.,PA		H018
Dawson,(Dr.)...		H019
Delaware, Division of History & Culture, Dover.		H020
Detroit Publishing Company, MI	4	H021
Drew, Mary Gladstone		H022
Dublin National Gallery, Ireland		H023
EVENING TIMES, The Glasgow		H024
Fleisher, Mrs.		H025
Samuel T. Freeman & Company, Auctioneers, 1938		H026
197.		
1992		
1993		
Gladstone, Mrs. Catherine Glynne		H027
Glover, Charles Carroll	1	H028
Henry Graves & Company, London		H029
The Earl of Halifax Collection		H030
Hamilton, (M.D.) George		H031
George Hall		H032
John McLure		H033
Harriman, Mrs. Mary	31	H034
Henderson, Helen Weston		H035
Hilder, Miss D., Teviot House, Upper Tooting, 1898		H036
Hohenlohe, Mrs.		H037
Holme, Charles, Red House, Bexley Heath, Kent, 1898		H038
Howe, Sydenham J.	200	H039
Hutchinson, Charles L., Chicago, 1897		H040
James, Bourlet, 1959		H041
William Graves Johnson Collection, Phila.,PA		H042
Art Museum, Kelvingrove, Glasgow, Scotland		H043

Kunsthaus Museum, Koln, Germany		H044
Lea, Arthur H., 1936.23.1		H045
Lennox School, Montreal, Canada		H046
Lewis, Edmund D.		H047
Libby, Miss		H048
Ludington, C. H.	2	H049
Luxembourg Palace, Paris, France	2	H050
McClees Gallery, Phila.,PA	200	H051
McEwen, Clement, Phila.,PA		H052
George Mc Manus Company, Phila.,PA, 193(.)		H053
Mercer, Mrs. Ann Jane, Phila.,PA, 1878		H054
Mitchell Library, Glasgow, Scotland	5	H055
Morris, Harrison S.		H056
Myers, Andrew		H057
National Portrait Gallery, London	7	H058
National Portrait Gallery, Washington, D. C.		H059
Newman Galleries, Phila.,PA.		H060
Arthur U. Newton, NYC, 1944		H061
NY Public Library, Print Room, NYC	10	H062
Oakley, Thornton		H063
The Emma, Countess of Oxford & Asquith Collection	2	H064
Parish, Mrs. Dorothy Drew		H065
Pennsylvania Academy of Fine Arts, Phila.,PA	10+	H066
Peter, Mrs. Armistead (III)	3+	H067
County Medical Society, Phila.,PA	2	H068
Museum of Art, Phila.,PA	6	H069
Sketch Club, Phila.,PA	2+	H070
Watercolor Club, Phila.,PA	2+	H071
Photographische Gesellschaft, Berlin		H072
Proby, Jocelyn		H073
Raiguel,(M.D.) George Earle		H074
Rodale, J.I./Anna, 1961		H075
Rosenbach & Company, NYC/Phila.	90	H076
Royal Society, London		H077
Royal Society of Portrait Painters, London		H078
Salvation Army, London		H079
Simpson, (Judge) Alexander Carson, Jr.	+++	H080
R. W. Skinner, & Company, MA, Auctioneers		H081
C.G. Sloan & Company, Inc., Washington, D.C. later MD		H082
(South American museum)		H083
St. Andrews University, Scotland		H084
Sotheby's, NYC		H085
Sotheby's, Glasgow, Scotland		H086
Spinks Gallery, London		H087
Tashian, Mr. & Mrs. Haig		H088
Taylor, Mrs. Emily Drayton		H089

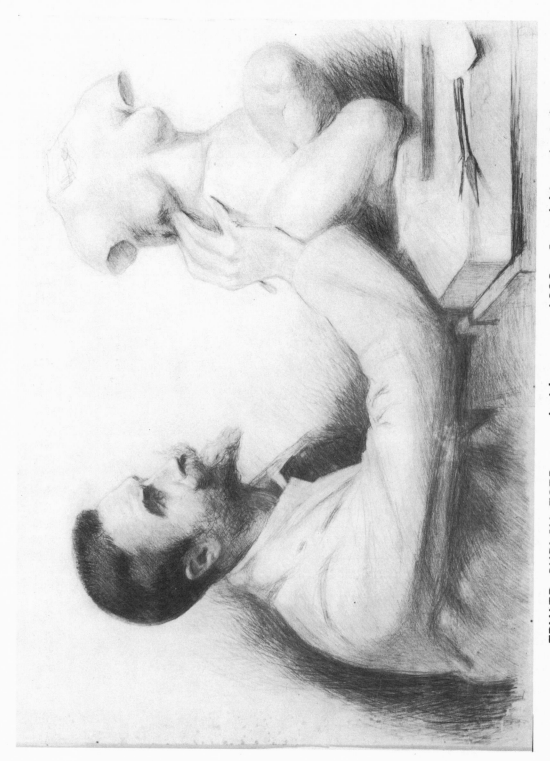

EDWARD ONSLOW FORD, sculpting. c. 1893. Graphite sketch
18" x 24." National Portrait Gallery, London.

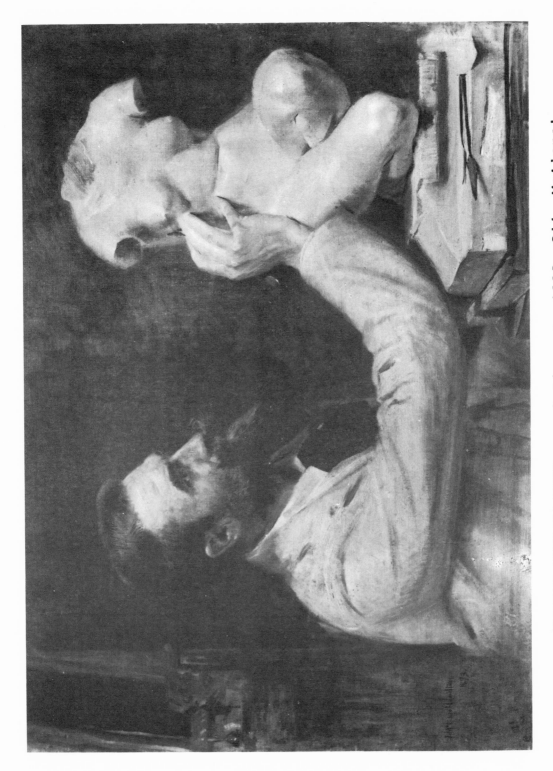

EDWARD ONSLOW FORD, sculpting. c. 1893. Oil. National
Portrait Gallery, London.

445

Taylor, (M.D.) John Madison   H090
Trask, Mrs. John E. D.   H091
University of Georgia/ Georgia Museum of Art, Athens   H092
University of Pennsylvania, Phila.   2   H093
Victoria & Albert Museum, Print Room, London   4   H094
T. R. Way, London   H095
Walker Art Gallery, Merseyside, Liverpool, England   H096
Weiner, L., 1878   H097
Weschler's Auctioneers, Washington, D. C.   H098
Westmoreland County Museum of Art, Greensburg, PA   H099
Young, Charles Morris, 1936.21   H100

Private Collections 1990--1993

                                                                     H101
                                                                     H102
                                                                     H103
                                                                     H104
                                                                     H105
                                                                     H106
                                                                     H107
                                                                     H108
                                                                     H109
                                                                     H110
                                                                     H111
                                                                     H112
                                                                     H113
                                                                     H114
                                                                     H115
                                                                     H116
                                                                     H117
                                                                     H118
                                                                     H119
                                                                     H120
                                                                     H121
                                                                     H122
                                                                     H123
                                                                     H124
                                                                     H125
                                                                     H126

Pie graph. HAMILTON'S REPUTATION   M001

Ink/sepia drawing. S.S. Bailey,1992. RECONSTRUCTION : 1600 SUMMER ST., PHILA.   M002

Line drawing. Atlas map detail, c.1900 : 10th WARD, PHILA.   M003

Xerox,B012. GEORGE HAMILTON, M.D.; Ford's bronze bust, c.1893.   M004

Antwerp post card, color. P.P.Rubens, self-portrait.   M005

HSP photo, Kennedy watercolor,1845. 16th/SUMMER ST.,PHILA.(during construction)   M006

Xerox,B012. McLURE HAMILTON; Ford's bronze bust, c. 1893.   M007

Photo."Walery,Photographer to the Queen, 164, Regent St., London": EDWARD ONSLOW FORD,
c. 1893. (waist length,full face, smoking); Ford's signature   M008

Xerox,photo. Wayman Adams, 1918 o/c: HAMILTON #1(hat on head, gloves on hands) C013   M009

Xerox, photo. Richard Dooner,1918 : HAMILTON (stickpin/tie) FLP PR   M010

Photo. Roberts Coll.,Haverford College,PA. HAMILTON, (no beard) 1881.   M011

Photo. Wadsworth Athenaeum. Eakins' o/c, inscribed "To Hamilton/my friend,
Eakins '95."   M012

Photo. PAFA. Wayman Adams, 1921 o/c : The CONSPIRACY (Burns, Hamilton, & Pennell)   M013
Hamilton #2

Dublin post card. Lawrence Publishing. NOW THEN PAT, c.1903. Hamilton attributed art   M014

Photo. Alperin, 1992. GLADSTONE STATUE in GEORGES SQ., GLASGOW.   M015

Xerox, pastel/paper. FREDERICK GUTEKUNST, 1857. JOHN GIBBON HARLAN, PHILA.   M016

Photo o/c BONNETTED GIRL with fruit/butterfly, c. 1876. Whistler attributed art   M017

Photo o/c BABY, DOG, CAT, KITCHEN STOVE, PARLOR CHAIR. Hamilton attributed art   M018

Photo Goupil & Co., NY/London o/c CHILDREN IN WHITE #2, c.1896. Hamilton attrib. art   M019

London post card.<c> H & C. H., c.1906. THE END OF THE WHOLE D...FAMILY. Hamilton attr.   M020

Photo woodcut engrav.,1895. British Museum, Print Room. MR. McLURE HAMILTON. Hamilton
   attributed art after photo attrib. to Eakins,1895 of Eakins,1895 o/c   M021

Photo watercolor, c. 1878, MacILVAINE'S STILLWATER COTTAGE, DELAWARE WATER GAP, PA
    Hamilton attributed art   M022

Photo o/c, c. 1883, WOODGATHERER'S DONKEYS/Landscape. Hamilton attributed art.   M023

Photo graphite/paper, c. 1875, PORTRAIT OF MISS E (profile in this drawing matches
    profile of lithograph, 1912 "MOTHER" (both women were Delaplaine sisters)
    Hamilton attributed art.   M024

Photo ink portrait, George Frederick Watts, 1880, later etched by P. Rijon.
    LORD LEIGHTON   M025

Xerox, Ink/paint on board, c. 1890. CHELSEA GARDENS. Couple window shopping with
    muzzled dog. Whistler attributed art.   M026

Certificate, The Historical Research Center, Family Name History : HAMILTON, 1992 M027

Certificate, op cit   : HALL, 1992   M028

Photo, ST. LOUIS EXPOSITION ART JURY, 1904 after Pennell B017:4 included Abbey,
    Hamilton, Ives, Pennell, Sargent, (van Dyke), & Whistler in front of Museum   M029

Photo, Alperin, 1992. Hamilton's Studio at 93 HOPE ST., GLASGOW.   M030

Xerox, Ink drawing, c. 1874. SAILBOAT. unattrib.   M031

Xerox, Ink drawing, c. 1874. BUTTERFLY COLLECTOR. unattrib.   M032

Photo, Degas, E. H. G.   Ink/paint/paper drawing. OLD WOMAN, REPAIRED TEAPOT   M033

Xerox, Degas, E. H. G.   Watercolor/graphite drawing/board. YOUNG GIRL (bust length,
    2/3 profile portrait)   M034

Xerox, Adams, W., 1918. o/c: HAMILTON #3 (no hat, no gloves   M035

BOOK REVIEW

This monograph traces the life and career of portrait artist John McLure Hamilton; it operates on the premise that Hamilton's life, until now, has been relatively ignored in view of his substantial contributions to the art world. Dr. Alperin's detailed and meticulous research provides a wealth of information not only about Hamilton's work but his unique experiences as well. In addition, the monograph is supplemented by a number of relevant tables, graphs, and abundant illustrations.

John McLure HAMILTON's story was a glaring omission from the literature about American painters and illustrators. Now the artist's *detailed career biography* has been published. The monograph is based upon a *documented chronology* of the artist's travel activities extending nearly four million miles. This monograph was organized to reveal his *development as a professional*. This monograph is set against a background of his times, 1853--1936, including four wars that impacted upon Imperial England and the United States.

This monograph, ART'S ANGLO-AMERICAN PAPER LION reveals how the critics of the *Transitional Age* viewed Hamilton's work. It traces *his family origins* from Ireland through *his early education* in Philadelphia with Holmes, Schuessele, and Eakins and relates Hamilton's Flemish experiences in the 1870s with fellow students like Claus, Millet, Rodin, and Tyndale. The monograph enables us to visit his many houses, meet *his favorite model,* Mrs. Clara Hamilton (his wife), and see *his son's growth* from childhood stages to his arrival as an expert in planetary Astronomy. This monograph gives samples of the illustrator's *adventures in Glasgow* at the turn of the Century and his finest fifty years in London's main arena for painters. This monograph records *his influential friends* (Prime Ministers and artists) in lithographs, paintings, and even in editorial cartoons. It enables the reader to snoop into *his finances* and inquire into *prices realized* for Hamilton's art at auctions. It introduces *his various style periods* and excerpts *from his writings*. In its pages, the reader discovers Hamilton's perceptions of his career experiences, his insights to the great men and women of his day, the painter's political opinions, his devotion to golf, and his insecurities as an aging professional.

This monograph contains an innovative and revolutionary biography and a *Hamilton art catalog*. This book is written for a wide audience including artists, auction houses, collectors, dealers, historians, librarians, museums, and anyone who enjoys learning about *Anglo-American portraiture* recorded in more than 1,050 paintings and drawings.

ABOUT THE AUTHOR

Richard J. Alperin, Ph.D., FIICS, LFIBA, DDG, IOM, is a *Professor of Biology* at Community College of Philadelphia with an avocation in *Art History*. This monograph is the product of his research expeditions to ten U.S. cities, Canada, Jamaica, Ireland, Scotland, England, France, and Belgium during four years. Dr. Alperin is a member of the *ASSOCIATION of HISTORIANS of AMERICAN ART* and he is listed in the *List of AUTHORITIES & EXPERTS in AMERICAN ART.* Professionally, he is a REGISTERED EMBRYOLOGIST (Utrecht, Netherlands), a DEVELOPMENTAL BIOLOGIST, and an ELECTRON MICROSCOPIST specializing in cytochemistry. He was elected to life membership in the *GENEALOGICAL SOCIETY of PENNSYLVANIA, AMERICAN SOCIETY of ZOOLOGISTS,* and the *AMERICAN MICROSCOPICAL SOCIETY*. Dr. Alperin has memberships in the *SOCIETY for the STUDY of DEVELOPMENT, PATTERN RECOGNITION SOCIETY, NEW YORK ACADEMY OF SCIENCES,* and the *AMERICAN SOCIETY of TESTING & MATERIALS* and has worked on fifty projects for publication. Dr. Alperin is listed in *AMERICAN MEN of SCIENCE, DICTIONARY of INTERNATIONAL BIOGRAPHY, WHO'S WHO in the EAST, WHO'S WHO in TECHNOLOGY, WHO'S WHO in SCIENCE & TECHNOLOGY,* and *WHO'S WHO in AMERICAN JEWRY.* He was awarded a gold medal for his five year post-doctoral studies on *Submicroscopic Distribution of Nucleic Acids* in vivo *during Determination & Metaplasia* at Labs of Anatomy, School of Veterinary Medicine, University of Pennsylvania with Research Professor of Anatomy, Isidore Gersh. The medal was awarded in Naples by the *ACCADEMIA INTERNAZIONALE di PONTZEN (ITALY) di Lettere, Scienze, ed Arti.* Dr. Alperin received a second medal for his twenty-seven years of excellence in college teaching and a third, the Medalha Pro Mundi Beneficio, was awarded by the *ACADEMIA BRASILEIRA de CIENCIAS HUMANAS* (Sao Paulo, Brazil).

WARNING - DISCLAIMER

This monograph is designed to provide information regarding the artist's career and his catalogued works. It is sold with the understanding that the publisher and the author are not engaged in rendering *legal, financial, appraisal, artistic, or other professional services*. If legal or other expert assistance is required, the services of a competent professional should be sought.

It is not the purpose of this monograph to reprint all the information that is otherwise available to the dealers and / or the collectors, but to complement, amplify, and supplement other texts. You are urged to read all the available material, learn as much as possible about Hamilton's artworks and to tailor the information to your individual needs. For more information, see the many references in the Appendix.

Every effort has been made to make this monograph as complete and as accurate as possible. However, there *may be mistakes* both typographical and in content. Therefore, this monograph should be used only as a historical guide and not as the ultimate source on Hamilton's artworks. Furthermore, this monograph contains information on Hamilton's artworks only up to the printing date.

The purpose of this monograph is to educate and entertain. The author and Junius, Inc. shall have neither liability nor responsibility to any person or entity with respect to any loss or damage caused, or alleged to be caused, directly or indirectly by the information contained in this monograph.

If you do not wish to be bound by the above, you may return this monograph to the publisher for a full refund.

REPORT AN ADDITION TO THIS PUBLISHED
HAMILTON ART CATALOG

Today's date : _____
Person filing report : _____
Address : _____
City :_____ State : _____ ZIP :_____

Please, help author update his files. Copy this Report Form
for multiple submissions. Send completed report(s) for use
in research project in progress. Privacy respected, reports
of private collections shall be held in strictest
confidence.

TITLE OF WORK : _____

DESCRIPTION (circle one) : portrait genre piece landscape
                   cartoon   PROMINENT PROFILES(=caricature)
    SIZE in inches : HEIGHT : _____ X WIDTH : _____
    MEDIUM : lithograph oil   pastel   chalk   crayon
      (circle one)
           charcoal   graphite (=pencil) watercolor
           clay ink/sepia   bronze copper engraving
           wood engraving   mezzotint souvenir card
           post card   sketchbook   diary   ledger
    SIGNATURE (How & Where Signed?)_____

    DATE of work (How & Where) _____
    CONDITION _____
PHOTOGRAPH enclosed is : B & W   color   slide
PROVENANCE (=name of past owner(s),if known)

_____
_____

PRESENT OWNER : _____
     address : _____
     city : _____ State: _____ ZIP :_____

Please send report to JUNIUS, INC.: 842 LOMBARD
ST.,PHILA.,PA 19147-1317, USA.

Leads to related materials are also desired :
    Hamilton's letters
    his book (MEN I HAVE PAINTED)
    L'Academie pour Rire, 1878 satire
    Hamilton memorabilia
    PROMINENT PROFILES (color lithographs), 1903
    Hennell, T.B. 1901 poem THE LAY OF ST. ALBAN
    THE BAILIE (original engravings by Hamilton)
    THE (Glasgow) EVENING TIMES (original engravings by
      Hamilton)
    photography of the artist and by his hand

```
                          ORDER FORM


    Postal Orders : JUNIUS, INC., 842 Lombard Street,
              Philadelphia, Pennsylvania 19147-1317,
              U.S.A.


    Please send a copy of ART'S ANGLO-AMERICAN PAPER LION,
    I understand that I may return the monograph for a
    full refund -- for any reason, no questions asked.


    Name : ---------------------------------------------

    Address:---------------------------------------------

    City : --------------- State --------ZIP : ---------



    Sales Tax : Please add 7% for books shipped to Phila-
              delphia addresses.
              Please add 6% for books shipped to Penn-
              sylvania addresses.


    Shipping : $ 8.00 for first book and $ 4.00 for each
              additional book. Surface shipping may require
              four weeks for delivery.

    Payment :  Please pay by check in U. S. Dollars.

          $ 95.00 per book

      +   $  8.00 shipping
          -------
          $ 103.00

      +   ------- applicable taxes

    Remit   $         Total enclosed,

      Thank you for your order!
```